PRAEGER SPECIAL STUDIES IN
U.S. ECONOMIC AND SOCIAL DEVELOPMENT

Racial and Social Class Isolation in the Schools

IMPLICATIONS FOR EDUCATIONAL POLICY AND PROGRAMS

Edited by

Robert P. O'Reilly

Published in cooperation with the
Office of Research and Evaluation,
New York State Education Department

PRAEGER PUBLISHERS
New York • Washington • London

The purpose of Praeger Special Studies is to make specialized research in U.S. and international economics and politics available to the academic, business, and government communities. For further information, write to the Special Projects Division, Praeger Publishers, Inc., 111 Fourth Avenue, New York, N.Y. 10003.

PRAEGER PUBLISHERS
111 Fourth Avenue, New York, N.Y. 10003, U.S.A.
5, Cromwell Place, London S.W.7, England

Published in the United States of America in 1970
by Praeger Publishers, Inc.

Library of Congress Catalog Card Number: 70-128105

Printed in the United States of America

PREFACE

This study of racial and social class isolation in the
schools was first published in December 1969, by the New
York State Education Department. It was initiated by the
Regents of the University of the State of New York and the
Commissioner of Education, Ewald B. Nyquist, who together
asked the Division of Research, New York State Education
Department, to gather and interpret the available facts relating to the topic of racial isolation in the schools--particu-
lary as they might clarify the problem in New York State.
This volume is a slightly revised version of the initial document published by the New York State Education Department:
the appendixes documenting policy or special Department
reports relating to integration have been deleted; the summary
section has not been included; and numerous, though minor,
revisions have been made in the original chapters.

ORGANIZATION OF THE STUDY

As now organized, this volume includes seven chapters
presenting the substance of the findings and interpretations
of them. Chapter 1 consitutes a brief review of the legal
background of racial isolation in the schools and a further review of official policy and programatic efforts relating to the
elimination of de facto segregation in the schools in New York
State.

The second chapter is an analysis of growth trends in the
white population and among the Negro and Puerto Rican minority populations in the State and Nation. The degree to
which Negro and Puerto Rican student populations are isolated in the public schools of the State is analyzed, as is the
degree to which such isolation has increased or decreased in
recent years. The results of the analyses delimit the problem
of ethnic isolation in the schools of the State and provide
some indications whether racial isolation in the schools may
be expected to increase in the near future.

The third chapter is a review of selected studies relating
to differences in intellectual, educational, and psychological
development associated with social class and ethnic group

membership. The purpose of the chapter is to define certain educational and psychological deficits that have implications for the design of educational environments for different groups of socially and economically disadvantaged children. The findings reviewed in the chapter also provide a background for the findings of subsequent chapters.

Chapter 4 is a critical examination of major studies of the relationship between racial and social class isolation in the schools and intellectual, educational, and attitudinal development in advantaged white student populations and disadvantaged minority group student populations. The studies examined in the chapter deal principally with probable causes of differential educational development in students in schools and classrooms characterized by different levels of racial and social class isolation. The contributions of school and non school factors to educational development in majority and minority group student populations are also considered. A number of implications emerge in relation to the possibility of manipulating conditions in the schools to increase the likelihood of equal educational opportunity for socially and economically disadvantaged children, and these implications for the development of positive interracial attitudes and contact are examined.

Chapter 5 presents a critical review of studies of integration initiated in local schools in response to the national and State commitment to school integration. These studies comprise a variety of integration techniques initiated principally in urban and metropolitan areas where de facto segregation was in existence. The studies are analyzed with a view to determining whether the relationship between integration and educational development varies as a function of such factors as duration of integration, social class composition, type of transfer program, elementary or secondary level, and proportion white students and whether students transferred to integrated schools compare favorably in educational development with students who remain in segregated schools. The final section of Chapter 5 examines the potential of the integrated school setting for promoting interracial acceptance and positive interracial attitudes.

Chapter 6 is a selective review of studies of compensatory education programs, from preschool through college. Through a critical examination of research on the effectiveness of various programs, an attempt is made to evaluate the validity of different approaches to compensatory education. The final section of Chapter 6 summarizes studies of the

Racial and Social Class Isolation in the Schools

relative effectiveness of compensatory education and school integration programs in affecting the educational development of disadvantaged children.

Chapter 7, the final section of the study, explores in further detail certain implications for research and practice suggested by the findings reviewed in the main body of the report. Generally, the nature of the evidence precludes making highly definitive recommendations. Nevertheless, certain stable findings do suggest a number of guidelines for school desegregation, as well as other ways in which the instructional and community context might be manipulated to increase the chances that Negro and other disadvantaged children may have improved educational opportunity. Chapter 7 includes, in addition, some material not covered in previous chapters: (1) a brief examination of data relating to the correspondence between racial and social class isolation in the schools in New York State and (2) a brief summary of recent evidence of increasing racial cleavage in the schools, as shown by surveys of the incidence of interracial conflict occurring at the secondary level in 1968-69. For obvious reasons this last topic has considerable consequence for planning school integration programs, and it has therefore been placed within the context of other recommendations.

A NOTE ON LIMITATIONS

Though the scope of this volume is broad, there are a number of important omissions that deserve recognition at this point. First, there is no extensive exploration of the literature on particular sources of educational failure of disadvantaged minority group students, as distinct from relatively gross contributing factors in the family and school contexts. Second treatment of the issue of racial separatism is far from comprehensive, though current evidence indicates that this issue is of great importance for contemporary planning of school integration programs (Sizemore, 1969). Third, the interdependent issues of interracial conflict in the schools and community factors that impinge on the process of integration are discussed only briefly in Chapter 7. These factors deserve more detailed treatment, because they appear to be highly important in planning school integration programs (Sullivan, (1969). Fourth, Chapter 2 lacks information on the ethnic composition of private schools in New York State (20.4 percent of the school age population in 1968-69) and does not differentiate between the elementary school population and the secondary school population, between which differential degrees of racial isolation are to be expected. Fifth, this work focuses on racial isolation in New York. Whenever possible, an attempt has been made to relate conclusions, based on restricted information, to the broadly based conclusions found in more representative reports. Still, the study focuses on research findings that apply at best, only to the North, or possibly only to the Northeast.

The reader is encouraged to keep two additional considerations in mind in examining the conclusions of the study. First, knowledge of the process of school integration and related factors is incomplete and subject to modification through more sophisticated research. Second, despite the avowed national commitment to eliminate segregation in the schools, a neutral stance has been adopted in the analysis and evaluation of the research findings reviewed in this study and in the discussion of their implications for contemporary educational policy and practice. This stance has been discarded however, in the attempt made to derive from the study guidelines for more systematic planning of school integration programs or for the development of new and more effective programs for the child in the disadvantaged school.

Robert P. O'Reilly

ACKNOWLEDGMENTS

Without the concerted help of many individuals, over a very short time considering the size of the effort, this study would not have come into being. Particularly, I thank the chapter authors, whose contributions far exceeded the call of duty; Peter Schriber, whose organizational abilities were a major factor in putting this report together; and Gregory Illenberg, Zelda Holcomb, Arreed F. Barabasz, and William Kavanagh who assisted in the preparation of parts of this report. John J. Stiglmeier, Director, Information Center on Education; Lee R. Wolfe, Chief, Bureau of Statistical Services of the Center; and Joan Peak, statistician, graciously strained the resources of the Center in obtaining much of the data that provided the basis for Chapter 2. I am further indebted to those who reviewed the study in draft form, offered their criticisms, and further contributed to the substance of Chapter 7: John Ether, specialist in teacher training (urban education), State University of New York at Albany; Vernon Hall, psychologist, Syracuse University; John Harding, psychologist, Cornell University; Mauritz Johnson, curriculum specialist, State University of New York at Albany; and Robin Williams, sociologist, Cornell University. A special note of thanks is due to Carl E. Wedekind, Director, Division of Research, Office of Research and Evaluation, New York State Education Department, who patiently read the many drafts of the study, offered encouragement, and ministered to the many secretaries who graciously faced the demands made by the production of the study; also particularly to H. Woollatt, Associate Commissioner, Office of Research and Evaluation, who carefully reviewed the study and patiently endured the many delays in production. A final note of thanks is due to the secretaries who made the major contribution to typing the study, Mrs. Darlene Messina, Miss Peggy DeLuke, Miss Edith Palmer, and Mrs. Donna Acker; and to the staff of the Bureau of Publications, New York State Education Department, under the direction of Bruce Meservy, who produced the initial printing for the Education Department.

CONTENTS

LIST OF TABLES

LIST OF FIGURES

Racial and Social Class Isolation in the Schools

CHAPTER **1** SCHOOL DESEGREGATION
IN NEW YORK STATE:
A REVIEW OF POLICY,
PROGRAMS, AND
DECISIONS

Esther Smith Patti,
William A. Shapiro, and
Robert P. O'Reilly

The purpose of this chapter is to provide an up-to-date
review of the major factors that have influenced the progress
of desegregation in the schools in New York State. The account
begins with a brief history of legal landmarks relating to desegregation of the schools in the nation and State, up to the
1954 United States Supreme Court decision in Brown v. Board
of Education. Policy statements of the Commissioner of Education and the State Board of Regents relating to racial integration in the schools are documented and so are the administrative and programatic resources devoted to the elimination
of racial imbalance in the schools in New York State. Concluding sections present a brief analysis of leadership factors affecting the progress of school desegregation and a selective
review of recent legal decisions relating to actions designed to
eliminate de facto segregation in the schools of New York and
other states.

EARLY LEGAL DECISIONS

The early history of the United States discloses no formal
procedures to educate the American Negro. Proceeding from
a massive and unreasoning prejudice, laws were even passed
to prevent the fearful prospect of educating slaves, presumably
based on the notion that such education would eventually destroy
a slave-based economy. South Carolina, for example, im-
posed a fine upon anyone caught teaching slaves to write. In

1831, the General Assembly of Virginia prohibited the teaching of reading and writing to slaves. Similar legislation was
passed from 1832 to 1866 in Alabama, Washington, D.C.,.
Missouri, and Texas.

Shortly after the Civil War, however, liberal crusaders
from the North had become convinced that lack of education
prevented the Negro from attaining equality--though they assumed, of course, that he would retain a separate place in
American society. According to Lomax (1962), the federally
supported Freedmen's Bureau, established in 1865 with representatives throughout the South, concentrated on aiding education of Negroes. By 1896, the separation of educational facilities for Negroes from those for Whites was sanctioned by law
in the rendering of the Plessey v. Ferguson decision, which
ruled that laws segregating people by race did not violate the
United States Constitution. This decision by the United States
Supreme Court legalized segregation--"separate but equal facilities"--throughout the country and stood as the law of the
land until 1954.

By 1900, certain areas in the South had allocated small
amounts of money to support separate educational facilities
for Negroes. Such unequally supported schools as existed
were controlled by whites and were used primarily for elementary or vocational education. Two years after the Civil War,
for example, the Peabody Fund was established to support
Negro education in the South, and although a Northern-based
organization, it adhered to the same separatist philosophy as
did the South, as explained by Frazier (1957):

> The trustees of the [Peabody] Fund opposed the
> mixed schools for whites and Negroes and opposed
> the Civil Rights Bill before the United States Con-
> gress which was designed to guarantee equal edu-
> cational facilities and other civil rights for Negroes.
> Negro teachers who were beneficiaries of the fund
> were expected to conform to the racial policy of this
> foundation. From the time when this philanthropic
> foundation was created until the present, the Negro
> intellectual has been forced to shape not only his
> philosophy according to the social philosophy of
> racial adjustment but his general social philosophy
> according to the social philosophy of the northern
> philanthropic foundations (p. 96).

Similarly, the Rosenwald Fund, backed by Booker T. Washington, subsidized the study of art, literature, the sciences, and teaching for Negroes who did not display independent thought regarding racial and economic problems (Franklin, 1969).

After the _Plessey_ v. _Ferguson_ decision, differences between the North and South in relation to segregation in the schools were often merely a matter of degree of enforcement. With the Negro migration to the North in the twentieth century, Negro children were frequently forced, or at least urged, to attend predominantly Negro schools--and strong enforcement measures were unnecessary because Negroes lived in restricted areas. Few states followed the early lead of New York, which, in 1900, passed Section 3201 of the Education Law, prohibiting discrimination in education because of race, color, or creed.

In New York City, steps were taken to bring about better integration in the city schools after studies had shown the extent of de facto segregation in the city. Actually, Negroes began their fight against discrimination and segregation in public schools in New York State and New York City in 1857. As a result, Grover Cleveland, Governor of New York in 1884, abolished Negro schools and opened all the schools to all children regardless of race or color.

In other Northern states efforts were varied. Franklin (1969) reports that--

> most of the Northern states were inclined to provide separate schools for Negroes, especially where white patrons brought pressure upon school officials. The practices varied greatly from place to place. In several Northern states there were separate schools where all races could attend, such as New Jersey, Ohio, Illinois, and Indiana. In two states, Kansas and Arizona, only on the elementary level was separate education mandatory; but in both cases several communities had separate schools on the secondary level (p. 549).

In the 1800's, at least one attempt at desegregation failed, in the case of Benjamin Roberts, a Negro from Boston, who, in 1849, attempted to enroll his five-year-old daughter in a white elementary school closer to his home than the nearest Negro school. In the case that followed the rejection of the child by the white school, the Massachusetts court ruled that the school board did have the power to enforce segregation (Stoff, 1967).

In 1923, an Oklahoma court ruled that inequality in education existed in a particular school district in which the Negro
school was of poorer quality than the white school. In 1936,
a Negro's admission to the University of Maryland Law School
was ordered by a court of appeals. In 1938, the United States
Supreme Court ruled in Gaines v. University of Missouri that
Missouri must admit a Negro applicant to the university. In
1946, refusal to admit a Negro to the University of Texas led
to the Sweatt v. Painter case. Westley (1953) recorded certain
events related to the case as follows:

> On March 26, 1947, the Court of Civil Appeals re-
> manded the case to the county court of Travis. This
> gave the State of Texas opportunity to improvise a
> law school in Austin for . . . Sweatt. This consisted
> of a three-room basement, several desks and chairs
> . . . In February, 1948, the Texas Court of Civil
> Appeals declared that the basement law school was
> equal to the law school of the University of Texas
> and that Sweatt could not attend the latter institution
> (p. 420).

The Sweatt v. Painter case was carried to the Supreme
Court, where the question was presented whether the Four-
teenth Amendment permitted the establishment of separate
schools by race. Along with McLaurin v. Oklahoma State
Regents and Johnson v. University of Kentucky, the resultant
decision left little ground for maintaining the "separate but
equal" doctrine in relation to graduate and professional schools
(Westley, 1953; Saye, Pound, and Allums, 1964).

The long series of legal attacks against segregated schooling culminated in 1954 with the Brown case. Brown v. Board
of Education dealt with the constitutionality of statutes in Kansas,
South Carolina, Virginia, and Delaware requiring the maintenance of separate elementary and high schools for Negro and
white students (W. L. Katz, 1967). The unanimous decision
of the United States Supreme Court, supported by social science
research, attacked the very center of the segregation issue
by impeaching the validity of the "separate but equal" principle.
The majority opinion, written by Chief Justice Earl Warren,
contained the following:

> To separate them [minority group children] from
> others of similar age and qualifications solely be-
> cause of their race generates a feeling of inferiority

as to their status in the community that may effect
their hearts and minds in a way unlikely ever to be
undone . . . . We concluded that in the field of public education the doctrine of "separate but equal"
has no place. Separate education facilities are in-
herently unequal.

This 1954 decision and other Supreme Court rulings following the Brown case indicated that the goal of public school
desegregation was at least a legal reality. The principal problem since then has been to carry out an orderly and nonviolent
desegregation process in the schools. Progress in school desegregation has been inordinately slow, however. According
to the New York Times (January 16, 1964), on the tenth anni-
versary of the Supreme Court's Brown decision, 98.9 percent
of the Negro students in the eleven southern states were still
in all-Negro schools.

Concerning desegregation in the North, Young (1966) notes
that, until 1959-60, the North reacted with "moral indignation
to the South's various shameful techniques of resistance and
to the miserably slow pace of desegregation after the Brown
decision" (p. 103).

Young further notes:

This self-righteous attitude continued until, in many
Northern communities, civil rights groups and Negro
citizens became aware that, because of housing segregation and some rather odd school district lines, education in the elementary schools of the North was as
rigidly segregated as in the South.

Probably the most celebrated example of this
was the New Rochelle school case, which clearly
revealed that the school board had some time earlier
drawn district lines purposely to keep Lincoln an all-
Negro school. In this case, Judge Irving Kaufman
of the Southern District of New York held on January
24, 1961, that the local board of education had maintained racial segregation through a policy of gerry-
mandering school boundary lines and permissive
transfers.

At any rate, this case did not touch the fundamental question: that an all-Negro school, regardless of
how the district lines are drawn, is innately inferior.
But the case did lead to dialogue between civil rights
groups and local boards in Northern communities and

brought the term "de facto segregation" into current
usage (p. 103).

The Brown v. Board of Education decision provided the
legal basis for federal action in those cases in which state law
compelled or permitted segregated educational facilities. Eventually, the Brown decision was applied in those cases in which
segregation resulted from administrative action by state or
local public officials, irrespective of legal sanction or dictate
(U.S. Commission on Civil Rights, 1967). The Supreme Court,
however, has yet to act formally on the issue of de facto school
segregation, which results largely from segregated housing
patterns. Even so, when state and local officials have moved
to reassign students on the basis of race to eliminate de facto
segregation, they have been upheld by the courts (U.S. Commission on Civil Rights, 1967).

The responsibility for the elimination of de facto school
segregation is now squarely in the hands of State and local
officials. The impetus for such action has a more rational
basis now than at any other time in history, especially since
the publication of two extensive empirical reports: Equality
of Educational Opportunity (Coleman et al., 1966) and Racial
Isolation in the Public Schools (U.S. Commission on Civil Rights,
1967). Coleman et al. document the fact that, on a national
scale, equality of educational opportunity does not yet exist in
terms of school facilities, school programs, and quality of
teaching staff. Of much greater significance, both Coleman
et al. and the report of the Commission on Civil Rights clearly
show that segregated educational facilities, whether segregated
de jure or de facto, negatively affect the educational and occupational opportunities available to certain ethnic minorities and
the poor of the nation. The net effect is to perpetuate an educational system in which educational quality is unequally available to individuals on ethnic and socio-economic grounds.

POLITICAL AND EDUCATIONAL POLICY RELATING
TO THE ELIMINATION OF DE FACTO SEGREGATION

After 1900, the political and educational leadership in
New York State made positive attempts to eliminate the inequalities resulting from de facto segregation. Moreover,
gubernatorial and legislative policies in recent years have
generally evidenced strong support of the import of the Brown

decision. Former State Commissioner of Education James E.
Allen, Jr., the Regents of the University of the State of New
York, and the State Education Department staff have acted in
concert in issuing guidelines and policy statements directed
toward creating the conditions favoring equality of educational
opportunity.

In response to the recommendations of the Regents, the
Legislature has appropriated funds to assist school districts
in eliminating de facto segregation. Funds have also been
appropriated to assist urban schools in upgrading their educational programs in response to the educational problems of
the urban minorities and the urban poor. The result of all
these efforts is that New York State, along with Massachusetts,
has been recognized as possessing the most advanced legal
basis for the elimination of segregated educational facilities
(U.S. Commission on Civil Rights, 1967).

Governor Nelson A. Rockefeller and the New York State
Legislature have voiced a commitment to pass laws against
discrimination in the area of educational opportunity. This
policy has been stated in the Governor's speeches, messages,
and memoranda and in legislative resolutions (Poling, 1960;
Rockefeller, 1960; Desmond, 1964; New York State Assembly,
1964; New York State Senate, 1965a, 1965b).

In 1969, however, the Legislature passed and the Governor
signed into law Chapter 342 of the Laws of 1969, which became
effective September 1, 1969--an act to amend the Education of
Law of the State in relation to prohibiting discrimination on
account of race, creed, color, or national origin. This legislation effectively prohibits appointed school boards and the
Commissioner of Education from directing assignment of pupils
and altering school boundaries or attendance zones for the purpose of reducing racial imbalance in the schools. At the same
time, the Legislature appropriated $3 million to the State Edu-
cation Department to assist school districts in paying costs
involved in solving problems of racial imbalance in the schools.

The existence or establishment of legal and other machinery
designed to eliminate either de jure or de facto segregation in
the schools has generally appeared to make relatively little
difference in achieving progress in school desegregation (Sullivan and Stewart, 1969), as has proved true in Massachusetts,
where the Commissioner of Education is empowered to with-
hold state aid when local boards fail to comply with the order
to correct racial imbalance in the public schools. Sullivan
and Stewart list a number of other states in which legal provisions that expressly recognize the rationale of Brown have

failed to show any real effect on the existence of de facto segregation in the schools in the North. Similarly, the Civil Rights Act of 1964 has been generally circumvented in a variety of ways in the South. And slowness of the progress in school desegregation achieved through State and federal laws and programs suggests that essentially the same human factors that created extreme inequality among the races in America in earlier years are still in operation today. Given this situation, the educational leadership at all levels becomes a potentially potent factor in initiating noticeable progress in the elimination of racial segregation in the schools of the Nation.

Major policy statements of the State Board of Regents and the efforts of the State Education Department in implementing policy have demonstrated the commitment of the educational leadership in New York State to the principle of equality of educational opportunity. Former Commissioner of Education James E. Allen, Jr., at a hearing before the U.S. Commission on Civil Rights (1966), spoke of the goal of education in New York State as follows:

> Within the basic goal of education in New York State, there are two overriding objectives:
> 1. Ensuring that the young people of the State are provided with opportunities for the highest possible quality of education.
> 2. Ensuring that these opportunities are made equally available to every individual wherever he may live in the State and without regard to creed, color, handicap, social or economic circumstances.
>
> We believe that the existence of racial isolation anywhere in the schools of our State is a barrier to the achievement of these objectives. Hence, it is the accepted responsibility and duty of the State Board of Regents, which coordinates and supervises all of education in New York State, of myself, as Commissioner of Education, and of the State Education Department to do everything within our power to remove this barrier. We believe the elimination of racial isolation and the achievement of quality education on an integrated basis to be the major challenge to education of our times (p. 305).

In an earlier statement to the teachers of New York State, Commissioner Allen had described the challenge represented

by the existence of de facto segregation in the schools in this
way (New York State Education Department, 1963; hereafter
referred to as NYSED):

> The meeting of this challenge will not be easy. The
> situations which have created segregation have been
> long in the making--and their correction will not be
> quickly achieved. The emotional involvement is in-
> tense and turmoil and uncertainty, uneasiness and
> unrest are inevitable. That these are difficult, and
> at times discouraging days, is undeniable. Yet it
> is stimulating and heartening to realize that the
> struggle to eradicate segregation, while pointing
> up the weakness of our imperfections also empha-
> sizes the strength of a society that honors the prin-
> ciple of equality and is sound enough and vigorous
> enough to endure this time of trial.
>
> A special responsibility rests upon educators
> in this period. Not only must we act firmly and
> with all possible speed to eliminate segregation,
> de jure or de facto, but we must also give renewed
> emphasis to the teaching of the principles of equal
> rights and freedom that motivates our actions (p. 1).

Policy Statement, 1960

In an effort to cope with the de facto segregation of schools
in the State and to lend support to school communities, the
Advisory Council on Intercultural Relations in Education recommended that the Board of Regents issue a statement of policy
and principle, and the Regents issued such a statement in 1960,
calling for the elimination of racially isolated schools as follows (NYSED, 1960):

> The State of New York has long held the principle
> that equal educational opportunity for all children,
> without regard to differences in economic, national,
> religious or racial background, is a manifestation
> of the vitality of our American democratic society
> and is essential to its continuation. This fundamental
> educational principal has long since been written into
> Education Law and policy. Subsequent events have
> repeatedly given it moral reaffirmation. Neverthe-
> less, all citizens have the responsibility to reexamine

the schools within their local systems in order to
determine whether they conform to this standard so
clearly seen to be the right of every child.

Modern psychological knowledge indicates that
schools enrolling students largely of homogeneous,
ethnic origin, may damage the personality of minority
group children. Such schools decrease their motivation and thus impair the ability to learn. Public
education in such a setting is socially unrealistic,
blocks the attainment of the goals of democratic
education, and is wasteful of manpower and talent,
whether this situation occurs by law or by fact.

In seeking to provide effective education for all
the children of this State, boards of education are
faced with many obstacles in the form of complex
social and community problems. Among them is
the existence of residential segregation which leads
to schools with students predominantly of one race
on the elementary and high school levels.

In spite of these and other difficulties, the
Regents are determined to accept this challenge facing our schools today. We charge the Regents Advisory Council on Intercultural Relations in Education,
working in close cooperation with the State Education
Department, to assist in seeking solutions to the educational aspects of the problem . . . .

We recognize that we who have been given the
responsibility for the education of the children and
youth in our State can deal directly with only these
educational aspects . . . . So long as these larger
social problems remain unsolved, it will be difficult
to solve some of the basic and related educational
situations. For this reason, therefore, we call upon
all our citizens and their agencies of government and
their civic organizations to take concrete steps to
provide the social climate which will make it possible for us to increase the effectiveness of education. Only with this cooperation, will we be able to
provide that type of democratic education which will
enable all children to contribute their understanding,
knowledge and skills to increase the greatness of
our State and our Nation (pp. 2-4).

Policy Statement, 1967

In keeping with the Governor's publicly announced twenty-point program for dealing with the urban crisis in New York State, the State Board of Regents in November 1967 released a position paper on Urban Education (NYSED, 1967). In this paper, the Regents "direct the State Education Department to develop a strategy for the revitalization of urban school systems" (p. 6). The statement discusses quality incentive grants for urban education, urban teacher recruitment, and training and planning grant demonstration projects and evaluation.

The first proposal contained in this position paper is for the establishment of a program for quality incentive grants for urban education, providing coordinated and concentrated educational services to youth and adults in those parts of the State in which there are high concentrations of children with low educational attainment. The second proposal is for the establishment of a new program to recruit, train, and place teachers and auxiliary personnel in disadvantaged urban areas. This program was intended to modify current teacher training practices, giving high priority to the use of personnel indigenous to disadvantaged areas for teaching and related tasks. The third proposal deals with the development of a master plan for education in each of the major metropolitan areas of the State, to be developed cooperatively by the officials of the school districts and the State, with the help of qualified private or public planning agencies.

Policy Statement, 1968

In January 1968, the State Board of Regents issued a position paper, Integration and the Schools (NYSED, 1968c), reaffirming their determination to see that segregation in education was eliminated. This policy statement cites the need for stronger action:

Current conditions of unrest, frustration, and violence show all too clearly that not only is the struggle against racial prejudice and injustice far from over, but that a perilous weakening has taken place in the foundation of understanding and mutual respect upon which true social justice and human progress can be built.

These conditions also dramatically point up the importance of education as the strength of this

foundation--education that brings children together to
grow up in natural, genuine understanding, and mutual respect, that produces responsible citizenship,
that fosters behavior based on moral and spiritual
values, that prepares for jobs, that creates the competence and instills the confidence for managing
one's own life--education that does not mirror society's ills but provides a demonstration of the practi-
cality, the workability of the principles of democracy,
thus leading the way and setting the pattern for society to follow (pp. 7-8).

The statement discusses the growing problem as follows:

Despite the determination and significant accomplishments of many in education, the growth of the problem has outstripped the efforts to deal with it.
        Racial imbalance within school districts is in-
creasing in both suburban and urban communities:
racial census reports show that between 1961 and
1966, in the 41 school districts with the highest percentage of Negro pupils (exclusive of New York City),
the number of elementary schools with more than 50
percent Negro pupils increased from 60 to 72; the
number with more than 90 percent Negro pupils increased from 25 to 33.
        Racial isolation among school districts is also
increasing. In this same period, the percentage of
Negro pupils in one suburban district rose to 82 and
in another, to 71. In three other districts, the percentage surpassed 50 (p. 9).

The paper clarifies five guiding principles and offers
thirteen recommendations or proposed applications of the
guiding principles.

ADMINISTRATIVE AND PROGRAMMATIC RESPONSES
TO DE FACTO SEGREGATION

The primary function of the Board of Regents is to formu-
late educational policy for the State. The Commissioner of
Education is responsible for administering the policies established by the Regents. Following is a brief account of the

efforts of the State Education Department in establishing administrative units and carrying out certain programs to eliminate segregation in the schools of New York State.

Fair Educational Practices Act

In 1948, the Regents appointed an administrator of the Fair Educational Practices Act, a law enacted by the State Legislature, to promote the elimination of discriminatory practices in any of the State's institutions of higher education. In 1954, the State Board of Regents established the Advisory Council on Intercultural Relations in Education to study discrimination in admission to colleges and universities and to offer possible solutions. Later, the purview of the Council was extended to include the elementary and secondary schools, and the Council pinpointed the disparity in the quality of education in segregated and nonsegregated schools in the State and the resultant educational damage to school children.

Division of Intercultural Relations in Education

In January 1957, the responsibilities of the school administrator were broadened when the Board of Regents created the Division of Intercultural Relations in Education, for the purpose of devoting intensive attention to problems of discrimination and segregation in education at the elementary and secondary school levels. The Division administers antidiscrimination legislation, assists in the development of programs designed to achieve integration, and provides consultative services to local school officials. The Division has worked closely with the Advisory Council and has carried out an ethnic census in the public schools.

Specifically, the Division of Intercultural Relations in Education--

1. Provides advisory and consultative services to local school officials on courses of action designed to eliminate racial imbalance.

2. Administers funds appropriated by the State Legislature to assist school districts in defraying excess costs in solving problems of racial imbalance.

3. Provides consultative services to school personnel on developing curricula that incorporate material on the contributions of minority groups to American life and history.

4.   Publishes handbooks on intergroup relations for teachers.   Prepares and distributes bibliographies of books, pamphlets, and visual-aid materials and lends films dealing with intergroup understanding.

5.   Provides consultative services on in-service training for school personnel.   Conducts workshops for the development of materials and methods for teaching all children respect for the inherent worth of other human beings and an understanding and appreciation of racial and cultural diversity.

6.   Provides assistance for surveys and studies to determine the extent to which equal educational opportunities are available to school children of different racial and cultural backgrounds.

7.   Cooperates with other public and private agencies concerned with the improvement of intergroup relations in a community.

8.   Provides consultation and assistance to school districts in developing programs for school-community cooperation.

During the 1960's, the Division was heavily involved in efforts to accelerate the progress of integration in the schools. In recent years, in cooperation with the New World Foundation, the Education Department has made available publications designed for integrating information about the Negro into daily teaching.   Attempts are also being made to prepare materials for use in teacher education, classroom instruction, and community enlightenment.

Guiding Principles

In 1962, the State Education Commissioner's Advisory Committee on Human Relations and Community Tensions was created.   This Committee was asked to advise and assist the Commissioner of Education and local school officials in dealing with the growing problems of de facto segregated schools. In June 1963, the committee published Guiding Principles for Dealing with De Facto Segregation in Public Schools, (NYSED, 1963b), which received wide circulation throughout the State, enunciating as primary the principle that all schools should have a balanced distribution of the various ethnic and cultural groups in the municipality of the school district.

Center on Innovation

In July 1964, the Center on Innovation was established in the Office of the Commissioner to encourage and guide constructive change in the educational system. This Center was requested to give priority to innovations and changes that would speed the achievement of integrated education of high quality. Largely funded by The Elementary and Secondary Education Act (ESEA), Title III, the Center's primary concern has been the promotion of changes that will overcome the most crucial and persistent educational problems: the elimination of those educational inequalities associated with race or economic class. Projects funded throughout the State have attempted to reflect the urgent needs of Negroes and Puerto Ricans.

The development of increased sensitivity to, and awareness of, the multiethnic and multiracial impact of minorities on all segments of the community is being promoted. Programs are operating that focus on sensitivity training for teachers, preparation of new teachers for teaching in urban systems, and promotion of community-school-parent communications. Examples of such programs are A School-Community Approach to Improve Ethnic-Racial Relations: in Nassau County; Induction and Follow-up of Beginning Teachers, Teacher Self-Help, and Project Outreach of the New York School Community Interaction Program.

In January 1969, the Center on Innovation became the Center for Planning and Innovation, and its function was expanded to include provision of planning service to all units in elementary, secondary, and continuing education. The new mission of the Center was to facilitate the State Education Department's organizational capacity for change, through participating with other units of the Department in the determination of critical educational needs, the assignment of priorities for solution, and the development of educational programs to solve the problems.

As the Education Department develops its own capacity, it is more and more challenged to develop ways to facilitate, with increasing effectiveness, meaningful change at the local level through broadly based community planning.

Urban Education Office

The Office of Urban Education was created by the State Board of Regents on August 1, 1968, to administer the funds

allotted by the Legislature and to carry out the Regents' direc-
tive to develop a strategy to revitalize urban school systems.
The Legislature appropriated $52 million for the school year
1968-69 to carry out the proposals of the Board of Regents.
The same amount ($52 million) was appropriated for 1969-70.
These funds are being used in part to create racial harmony in
urban areas through community education centers.

The Urban Education Program provides for a wide range
of local, State, and federal programs and services for the
participating school districts. The following factors are taken
into consideration in planning the programs: (1) integration,
(2) community and student participation and planning, (3) utilization of community facilities, (4) realistic program design,
(5) flexibility of projects, (6) economic use of resources, and
(7) provisions for coordination with other community services
and related programs. The following program priorities are
considered to be most important for meeting pressing educational problems in urban school districts, and approval of
projects submitted by school districts is related to the degree
to which these priorities have been recognized:

1. Early childhood education and appropriate follow-up
2. Education in basic skills
3. Guidance and counseling
4. Innovative programs for disaffected youth
5. Model demonstration schools
6. Adult basic education.

Since 1960, the movement to provide compensatory education has taken form because education of the disadvantaged in
the inner cities has been recognized as inadequate. And the
Urban Education Program in New York State is a major effort
to alleviate the educational problems of urban school districts
through compensatory education.

School Census

In 1961, the Division of Intercultural Relations conducted
a special census of the school population to determine the areas
of concentration of Negro pupils in the elementary schools of
the State. A questionnaire form was mailed to each district
that had at least one elementary school building. The census
showed that forty-one school districts had de facto segregated
schools and that a large proportion of these schools were in the
"big six" cities, which enroll 40 percent of the public school population that has concentrations of Negro students. The census

served as an impetus to the Department to solve the problem of racial imbalance in several areas, for example, Mount Vernon, Albany, Nyack, and Schenectady.

Racial Imbalance in the Schools

In June 1963, the Commissioner of Education circulated a special message to all chief local school administrators and presidents of boards of education requesting all school districts in the State to submit by September of that year certain information as follows (NYSED, 1963c):

1. A statement indicating the situation in your district with regard to any problem of racial imbalance, regardless of the number of Negro children enrolled, or to the actual existence of or trend toward racial imbalance.

2. A statement of policy by your board of education with respect to the maintenance of racial balance in your schools.

3. In districts where racial imbalance exists, or is a problem, a report of progress made toward eliminating it.

4. In such districts, your plan for future action, including estimates of the additional cost, if any, and of the time required for carrying out your plan (p. 3).

The purpose of this request was to survey plans for desegregation at the local level, since the principle of local control makes it the responsibility of local school authorities to develop and implement the necessary plans for correcting racial imbalance.

Pupil Evaluation Program

In the fall of 1965, the State Education Department instituted the Pupil Evaluation Program involving the administration of achievement tests in reading and arithmetic to beginning first, third, sixth, and ninth grade pupils in public, parochial, and private schools throughout the State. The tests were administered to 1.3 million school children that first year, and results of these and subsequent tests have since provided teachers, schools, and the State Education Department with an annual inventory of areas of academic weakness and pupil achievement. The pupil evaluation data provide a comparison of school districts of similar size and afford a look at the inner city and its contiguous districts, thus throwing considerable light on the need for integration and other approaches in certain areas of the State.

Funds for Correcting Racial Imbalance

For several years, with the support of Governor Rockefeller, the State Education Department requested special funds from the Legislature for use in stimulating and assisting school districts in developing plans and programs for correcting racial isolation in the schools and for improving the quality of integrated education. The Legislature approved an initial sum of $1 million in 1966. This was increased to $3 million in 1967 and remained the same in 1968 and 1969. These funds are administered by the Division of Intercultural Relations in Education.

A report (NYSED, 1968b) on the projects funded under State Aid for Correcting Racial Imbalance was prepared for the years 1966-67 and 1967-68 by the Bureau of Department Programs Evaluation in cooperation with the Division of Intercultural Relations in Education and is now in the process of being updated. In 1966-67, twenty-five school districts were aided; in 1968-69, the number was twenty-nine. The study divided the projects funded into two categories: (1) desegregation projects involving the abolition of racial imbalance and (2) integration projects involving the unlearning of prejudices and establishment of new democratic values through interaction in a nonsegregated environment.

The desegregation projects involved (1) rental of relocatable classrooms, (2) transportation, (3) minor alterations of school buildings, (4) demographic studies, and (5) integration planning. The integration projects involved (1) improvement of school-community relations; (2) development of in-service training programs and integrated curriculum materials; (3) reduction in class size; (4) the use of special services to support integration; and (5) the use of teacher aids, special instructional materials, tutorial programs, and pupil personnel services.

In 1966-67, the State's share of the actual expenditures amounted to nearly $0.8 million; in 1967-68 this figure was increased to almost $2.5 million. In the first year, about 17 percent of the state aid was spent on transportation of pupils,

83 percent being spent on all the other types of projects. In the second year, 11 percent of the state aid was spent on transportation, 89 percent or approximately $2.2 million being spent on all other types of projects for correcting racial imbalance. The racial and ethnic census data for 1966-67 and 1967-68 indicated that in more than 30 percent of the districts receiving state aid, or sixteen districts, the number of schools having a large percentage of Negroes tended to decrease.

The report concludes that State Aid for Correcting Racial Imbalance has proved to be an incentive to districts to proceed at a more rapid rate in effecting racial balance. The program has also given the districts in which racial imbalance is not a problem an opportunity for greater understanding of minority groups and has inspired suburban districts to accept Negro children from the inner city into their schools.

Other Activities

The State Education Department, at the request of local school authorities, has also conducted comprehensive studies of public school needs and presented such authorities with detailed findings and recommendations for correcting racial isolation and for raising generally the quality of the school systems. Studies of this nature were made in New York City and Buffalo (NYSED, 1964, 1966). Moreover, numerous seminars and conferences have been conducted throughout the State in an effort to widen and deepen understanding of the problem and of how best to deal with it, and several teaching guides on integration have been prepared and distributed to the schools of the State.

In-service training programs for teachers on the special problems of teaching in integrated schools have been sponsored and supported. Tuition grants have been made available to recent college graduates to encourage them to prepare to teach disadvantaged children in New York City. Integration has been encouraged in projects submitted by school districts under the provisions of Title I of ESEA. And the enactment of State bills that would be a handicap to State and local officials in correcting racial imbalance in the schools has been resolutely opposed.

LEADERSHIP FACTORS

A study published as Citizen Response to School Desegregation was undertaken by the Division of Intercultural Relations in Education in 1968 to examine the broad spectrum of variables found in the school systems of the State in dealing with de facto segregation (Dodson, 1968). Ten communities in New York State were examined and an attempt was made to analyze various approaches to dealing with racial imbalance in the schools and to educe some generalizations about citizen involvement. The foreword refers to the great loss to the social sciences through the failure to research the social engineering that has gone into school desegregation during the years following the United States Supreme Court decision in the Brown case in 1954. Leadership factors were examined in an effort to determine why some school districts have been able to integrate without much trouble while others are apparently unable to reach a workable plan without great pressure--specifically the leadership roles of the Commissioner of Education, the Superintendent of Schools, the Board of Education, and the State Board of Regents.

Commissioner of Education

In New York State, several of the integration cases requiring corrective action to eliminate racial imbalance involved legal action, based in large measure on the power given to the Commissioner of Education under Sections 305 and 310 of the Education Law.

Section 305 outlines the general powers and duties of the Commissioner of Education, and Section 310 provides for appeals to him. The Commissioner's duties are both executive and judicial. In his executive capacity, he directs the work of the State University of New York and the State Education Department. He is responsible for administering the policies established by the Regents and for the general supervision of the schools of the State. With the approval of the Regents, he promulgates regulations for putting into effect the Education Law and the Regents Rules. As a judicial officer, the Commissioner serves as a court of appeals for the public school system, adjudicating all controversies that may be brought before him under the provisions of the Education Law.

A number of appeals concerning racial imbalance have been brought to the Commissioner of Education under Section

310 of the Education Law; indeed, actions have been brought
against the school boards of Amityville, Buffalo, Malverne,
Mount Vernon, Westbury, Glen Cove, and Roosevelt.

In Amityville, the Section 310 proceedings were brought
about because of racial imbalance in the elementary schools.
Of the three elementary schools, one was 96.8 percent Negro,
one was 4 percent Negro, and the third was 36.4 percent Negro.
On December 21, 1965, the Commissioner of Education ordered
the School Board to prepare and deliver to him on or before
March 15, 1966, a plan for the elimination of racial imbalance,
to be effective for the school year 1966-67. As a result, the
local Board approved a plan to reorganize its schools so that
one building would house grades K-1, another grades 2-4, and
the other grades 5-6.

In Glen Cove, Section 310 proceedings were brought in
1963 as a result of a complaint that the South School, an elementary school, was segregated. In November 1965, the
Board of Education met with representatives of the National
Association for the Advancement of Colored People (NAACP).
The Commissioner's Advisory Committee on Human Relations
and Community Tensions was present at the meeting. An agreement was reached to operate the schools on a 4-4-4 plan, * and
both parties agreed to terminate the proceedings. The agreed-
upon action was made official on December 15, 1965.

In Westbury, Section 310 proceedings were filed in September 1963 on the ground that the New Cassel School was more
than 90 percent Negro. In April 1965, the Board of Education
voted to desegregate the school, and the Section 310 proceedings were withdrawn.

The 1961 school census, made to secure facts about the
racial pattern in the public elementary schools of the State,
was instrumental in pinpointing the areas in which it was necessary to attack the problem of racial imbalance--and Mount
Vernon was one of these. Given impetus by the census results,
the Board of Education of Mount Vernon on July 5, 1963, approved a model statement of policy declaring its intention to
correct racial imbalance within the city.

Dodson (1968) supports the view that a strong State Education Department can contribute significantly to integration. In
his report, he states:

_____

*That is, all children in grades one through four, five
through eight, and nine through twelve, respectively, were to
meet in separate school buildings.

Most important of all, perhaps, is the leadership of
the Commissioner of Education of the State. It would
be hard to overestimate his leadership through these
years, as he has with patience, but firmness provided the most forward leadership of men of his position
throughout the country. The census he required and
the subsequent pressure he has exerted have gone far
toward eradicating this matter as an educational issue
in the State. But equally important, he has set the
tone of the remainder of the nation. His skill in inducing the State Legislature to provide supplementary
funds to assist communities facing this problem has
been of inestimable value. Above all has been the
diplomacy of his office as it has helped forge answers
in the fields in which no answers or any adequate answer hitherto existed (p. 146).

Board of Education and Superintendent of Schools

In his summation Dodson spells out one of the major generalizations to be drawn from his study: "The impetus for change
must come from the outside, thereby providing the school de-
cision-makers the rationale that they have no choice but to
move" (p. 140). He further reports: "There is no record of a
board of education or a superintendent of schools who, on his
own initiative, challenged the community to act on the desegregation problem without some prodding" (p. 140).

Another major generalization made by Dodson is that
"successful desegregation is dependent upon the leadership of
the power arrangement of the community" (p. 142). He continues:

The most brilliant desegregation efforts have been
those where the power arrangement was cohesive
and reasonable to the entire community. It was the
greatest failure at those points where community
power was fragmented and the leadership used its
leverage to oppose desegregation. The leadership
role of the superintendent appeared to be, perhaps,
the most significant factor of all those considered
in the study. Some data suggest that in larger
school systems the principal is, perhaps, the most
important single factor at a local level, but that the
attitudes of the principal and the faculty, in no

small measure, are a reflection of the leadership
at the top (p. 142).

Dodson's data show that the appointive or elective status
of a school board is not a determinant of correction of racial
imbalance.   But he asserts that "when separate interests are
polarized, the elected board as in Mount Vernon and Malverne
tends to be a tyrannical majority (p. 142). "

Dentler (1966) believes that the factors that make integration possible are of particular nature:*

From participation in several school desegregation
programs in smaller Northern communities, I would
speculate that there are some rather uniform conditions under which desegregation becomes possible
politically and educationally. Negroes must protest
in a visible, unequivocal manner. This must reso-
nate positively with some segment of the white population which already commands the attention of local
schoolmen or board members.
Of equal importance is a clear, sufficiently intense stimulus from state or other extra-local
authorities. Little change has occurred in Pennsylvania and Illinois, where many smaller cities
maintain segregated schools because of weak state
educational agencies. It also seems plain from case
experiences that a community must be free from a
very highly statified class structure grounded substantially in religious or racial groupings. The
prospect of too severe a change in the foundations
of the local structure of social rewards is relatively certain to present school desegregation (pp.
48-49).

Dentler concludes:

Northern school desegregation is not difficult to accomplish in smaller cities and suburbs. Where the
school superintendents of such communities have
allied themselves with state authority and have responded to the protest from their Negro clientele,

---

*From Dentler, R. A. "Barriers to Northern School De-
segregation. " Daedalus 95: 45-63 (1966). Copyright by
Daedalus, 1966. Reprinted by permission.

desegregation has been proven politically safe as
well as technically feasible. Moreover, the educational outcomes of most of the efforts to date
have been highly encouraging to professionals . . . .

The major part of the problem centers in a
dozen of the largest central cities. The ability to
advance desegregation depends mainly on state authority and on board and community politics (pp.
59-62).

Crain (1969), on the other hand, states:

It is commonly assumed that school superintendents exert much more influence over the policy
of the school system than does the school board.
Our data show the precise opposite: the school
board sets the tone of the integration decision and
the superintendent plays a less important role
(p. 378).

The views presented appear to be contradictory. However,
when the types of districts that were examined are considered,
analysis tends to bring the statements into better perspective.
Crain's study deals with a number of cities in various parts
of the country; Dodson investigated ten districts in New York
State that included several cities, but, were, for the most
part, suburban. Dentler reports that "no Northern big city
superintendent has committed himself emphatically to the pur-
suit of school desegregation" (p. 57). And so it appears that
the superintendent may play the leading role at the local level
in certain types of districts while the board of education may
play the leading role in other districts, namely big cities.

The city in New York State that has had the least trouble
in desegregating is White Plains, and Dodson (1968) offers a
number of reasons for the general lack of friction experienced
in the White Plains integration program:

In White Plains, it is difficult to separate the role
of the Board from that of the Superintendent. In
many communities the impression is given that a
board dominates the superintendent or else that the
superintendent dominates the board. One does not
get this impression of White Plains. It appears to
be a bringing together of the policy-making body
and the expertise of the educator in the most creative way.

One is tremendously impressed in White
Plains with the role of the superintendent. The
skill he has brought to resolving differences,
allaying fears and securing forward movement
without disruption is scarcely short of phenom-
enal. One, of course, must be reminded that
White Plains is probably an easy place in which
to be superintendent; but undoubtedly, his leadership has contributed to making it that kind
of community (p. 85).

Board of Regents

The primary function of the Board of Regents is to formu-
late the educational policy of the State and to promote and encourage the extension and improvement of education throughout
the State. The Regents are firmly dedicated to the provision
of opportunities for each student to develop his unique abilities,
talents, and interests to the fullest--and a broad range of efforts,
discussed earlier in this chapter, is under way to overcome
the conditions that limit the attainment of equal opportunity.
The 1960's was a decade of renewed and constant effort to eliminate racial imbalance in New York State school districts, to
ensure the young people of New York State the highest possible
quality of education, and to ensure that opportunities were
made equally available to every individual regardless of color,
creed, or social or economic status.
On January 28, 1960, the Regents issued a statement on
intercultural relations in education. They pointed to their
determination to accept the challenge of de facto segregation,
which results in unequal educational opportunity. In this statement the Regents charged the Advisory Council on Intercultural
Relations in Education, in cooperation with the State Education
Department, to assist in seeking solutions to the educational
aspects of the problem. The efforts of the State Education
Department that followed this statement included the following:
the school census beginning in 1961; a statement of "Guiding
Principles for Dealing with De Facto Segregation in Public
Schools" in 1963; the Commissioner's survey of integration
plans in 1963; and the establishment of the Center on Innovation in 1964 and the Office of Urban Education in 1968--all of
which culminated in the Regents' "Policy Statement on Integration and the Schools" in January 1968.

Progress Assessed

The progress made in reducing racially imbalanced schools in New York State has been the result of a number of factors, including the leadership of the Board of Regents and the State Commissioner of Education; the pressure of groups seeking aid in the Commissioner's office, in the courts, or in the local school districts; leadership from the office of the Superintendent and the Board of Education; and the initiative of local school districts. Dodson (1968) reports that the greatest impetus for change was the Commissioner's leadership, beginning with the census request. In any case, the evaluation of State-funded projects for correcting racial imbalance (NYSED, 1968b) reported that the number of schools having a high proportion of Negroes was decreasing in more than half the school districts receiving State aid for this purpose. In some school districts in New York State the problem of racial imbalance has been completely solved; in other districts considerable progress has been made; in a number of school districts, however, particularly the large cities, the situation has grown more acute. Chapter 2 of the present volume shows that the number and proportion of minority group children in schools with more than 49 percent minority group pupils has grown substantially since the 1967-68 and 1968-69 school years. Racial isolation in New York State schools has increased and has been most severely intensified in those schools that already had large proportions of Negroes and Puerto Ricans.

RECENT LEGAL HISTORY IN THE
STATE AND NATION

Since the United States Supreme Court decided Brown v. Board of Education in 1954, the problem of school desegregation has come before various forums in a variety of guises. Being highly controversial in terms of its political sociology, the Brown decision has become the subject of conflicting interpretations with respect to its legal import, and so it seems appropriate here to present a brief review of the various ways in which the problem has been treated, analyzed in terms of the position of the litigant involved.

In terms of the facts of the case, Brown prohibits only positive governmental action directly achieving separate school systems for Negroes--but the rationale of this unanimous decision of the Supreme Court is much broader. It is concerned with the injury caused by separation of the races in the educational process. The opinion specifically states that the "impact is greater when it has the sanction of the law"--and the opinion thus clearly shows that the rationale of Brown includes de facto segregation.

At the same time, however, it is a fact that the United States Supreme Court has not yet directly ruled on the question of de facto segregation. It may be presumed that the reason is the extreme difficulty, if not impossibility, at this point, of formulating any kind of a workable general rule that will fit all situations. Although some partial answers have emerged, there remains the problem of what to do, for instance, in areas in which the concentration of Negroes is so heavy that any solution that would be suitable for small, heterogenous communities is simply impractical. Granting this lacuna, the fact remains that both State and Federal courts have consistently sustained any reasonable action taken by State and local agencies for the purpose of reducing racial imbalance (U.S. Commission on Civil Rights, 1967).

In a 1963 decision in the Matter of Mitchell, the Commissioner of Education, ordered that attendance zones in a school district be redrawn to eliminate racial imbalance growing out of residence patterns. The Commissioner's order was upheld in the State and Federal courts, and the United States Supreme Court declined to review the decision in the Matter of Vetere v. Allen (sub. nom. Olsen v. Allen). A challenge to the implementation of a plan ordered by the Commissioner for the alleviation of racial imbalance was similarly rejected by the Federal courts in the case of Offerman v. Nitkowski. Since then, the Commissioner has ordered numerous school districts in the State to take appropriate action for alleviating racial imbalance, and though his decisions have been met with some local opposition, they have been well received on the whole.

Thus, at least prior to the enactment of Chapter 342 of the Laws of 1969, the Commissioner's position was that, upon an appeal brought by school children of the affected district, under the appropriate circumstances the local board of education would be ordered to take positive steps to alleviate or, if possible, eliminate racial imbalance. Usually the Commissioner found that an imbalance existed and ordered a plan, or alternative plans, to be submitted to him for approval before being implemented. In evaluating the proposals submitted, and in formulating his own alternatives, the Commissioner drew

heavily upon the expertise of the State Education Department
in the areas of educational finance, intercultural relations,
and educational policy. And it was largely in recognition of
the Regents' powers in the area of educational policy and
the Department's expertise in the field that the courts sustained his determinations. Thus, in Matter of Vetere v. Allen,
the Court of Appeals said:

> The issue posed by the petitioner in terms of racial
> balance, which balance the Commissioner now avers
> is essential to a sound education, is not reviewable
> by this court . . . .
>   Here the Board of Regents under authority of
> Section 207 of the Education Law has declared ra-
> cially imbalanced schools to be educationally inade-
> quate. The Commissioner under sections 301 and
> 305 of the Education Law has implemented this po-
> licy by directing local boards to take steps to elim-
> inate racial imbalance. These decisions are final
> absent a showing of pure arbitrariness.
>   The Commissioner's decision in this case rests
> squarely on his findings of the inadequacy of such
> schools from the viewpoint of educational sound-
> ness. . . .
>   Disagreement with the sociological, psycho-
> logical and educational assumptions relied on by
> the Commissioner cannot be evaluated by this court.
> Such arguments can only be heard in the Legislature
> which has endowed the Commissioner with an all but
> absolute power, or by the Board of Regents, who are
> elected by the Legislature and make public policy
> in the field of education.

Of course, some boards of education have taken positive
steps to improve racial balance without being prodded by the
Commissioner. And such actions have been upheld in the State
courts with reference to a variety of plans, including the designation of attendance zones in New York City in the Matter
of Balahan v. Rubin and an arrangement whereby inner city
pupils were transferred to suburban schools in the case of
Etter v. Littwitz.
    Thus, the State courts have uniformly upheld orders of
the Commissioner as well as action taken in the first instance
by local boards of education. On the other hand, there appear
to be no cases in which a local board of education was sued

in the first instance in a State court to compel desegregation.
Although Chapter 342 of the Laws of 1969 was clearly aimed at
diminishing the powers of the Commissioner of Education, it
appears that a side effect will be to take the matter of racial
imbalance out of the State courts, because de novo actions are
not, as a matter of practice, brought there.

It should be noted, however, that the courts of other states
have not found it difficult to arrive at the same conclusions as
did the New York State Board of Regents, with respect to the
effects of racial isolation in the public schools. In the case of
Jackson v. Pasadena City School District, for instance, the
California Supreme Court declared:

> So long as large numbers of Negroes live in segre-
> gated areas, school authorities will be confronted
> with difficult problems in providing Negro children
> with the kind of education they are entitled to have.
> Residential segregation is in itself one evil which
> tends to frustrate the youths in the area and to cause
> antisocial attitudes and behavior. Where such seg-
> regation exists, it is not enough for a school board
> to refrain from affirmative discriminatory conduct.
> The harmful influence on the children will be re-
> flected and intensified in the classroom if alone
> attendance is determined on a geographic basis
> without corrective measures. The right to an
> equal opportunity for education and the harmful
> consequences of segregation, require that school
> boards take steps, insofar as reasonably feasible,
> to alleviate racial imbalance in schools regardless
> of its cause.

As mentioned above, the Federal courts have likewise upheld the Commissioner's power to order the alleviation of
racial imbalance when school desegregation suits have reached
the United States courts either by means of litigation instituted
by private parties against the local school district or by means
of suits brought by the United States Government. Regardless
of the particular nature of the suit, the courts have been enunciating broad principles that, like the statement quoted above,
are fully consistent with the position taken by the Board of Regents and the Commissioner of Education in New York State.

In a few instances, the courts have been reluctant to intervene in the absence of a showing of bad faith on the part of
school authorities, particularly where the factual circumstances

were highly complicated, as in the cases of Bell v. School City of Gary, Indiana and Henry v. Godsell. Nevertheless, most courts have had no trouble in construing long standing policy or official inaction as an illegal maintenance of separate or unconstitutionally imbalanced schools.

Thus, as stated previously, one court found that the New Rochelle School District in New York State was acting unlawfully when it gerrymandered attendance zone lines so as to perpetuate a high degree of racial imbalance and then refused to alter those lines so as to alleviate the situation: the perpetuation of separate schools was held to be as great a constitutional evil as the establishment of separate schools. In discussing the Brown case in Taylor v. Board of Education, the court said: "Necessarily implied in its proscription of segregation was the positive obligation of eliminating it."

Likewise, dealing with a New York State school district in Branch v. Board of Education, a United States district court found that--

> the central constitutional fact is the inadequacy of
> segregated education . . . that the public schools
> must deal with the inadequacy arising from adventi-
> tious segregation . . . [and] . . . can not accept and
> indurate segregation on the ground that it is not co-
> erced or planned but accepted.

The court further stated:

> Failure to deal with a condition, as really inflicts it,
> as does any grosser imposition of it . . . How far
> that duty extends is not answerable perhaps in terms
> of an unqualified obligation to integrate public educa-
> tion without regard to circumstances and it is cer-
> tainly primarily the responsibility of the educational
> authorities and not the courts to form the educational
> system.

School pairing plans have been upheld consistently; as in the cases of Abado v. Donovan, Schnepp v. Donovan, and Van Blerkom v. Board of Education. Likewise, transfers between schools for the purpose of correcting racial imbalance in Rochester and Syracuse were upheld by the state courts against claims of unconstitutional interference with the rights of white children involved: Katalinic v. Syracuse Board of Education, Di Sano v. Storandt, Strippoli v. Bickal.

Similar actions have also been upheld in New Jersey in the cases of Morean v. Montclair Board of Education and Fuller v. Volk et al. and in Massachusetts in the case of Barksdale v. Springfield School Committee.

Another Federal court decision involving a school district in New York State similarly held that a failure to rezone, which resulted in almost total racial isolation, was unconstitutional. In Blocker v. Board of Education, the Court expressed this view of the function of the public schools:

> The denial of the right not to be segregated cannot be
> assuaged or supported by evidence indicating that
> underachievement in the three R's may be due in whole
> or in part to low socioeconomic level, home influence
> or measured intelligence quotient. The role of public
> education in our democracy is not limited to these
> academic subjects. It encompasses a broader pre-
> paration for participation in the mainstream of our
> society. Public education is the very foundation of
> good citizenship.

Another well-known case involved the school system in Washington, D.C. There the judge reviewed many aspects of the operation of the system and found that the schools were failing in their task. In Hobson v. Hansen, the particular function of the schools in our society was commented on in the following words:

> If the situation were one involving racial isolation
> but in some facility other than the public schools,
> or unequal educational opportunity but without any
> Negro or poverty aspects (e.g., unequal schools
> all within an economically homogeneous white sub-
> urb), it might be pardonable to uphold the practice
> on a minimal showing of rational basis. But the
> fusion of these two elements in de facto segregation
> in public schools irresistibly calls for additional
> justification. What supports this call is our horror
> at inflicting any further injury on the Negro, the
> degree to which the poor and the Negro must rely
> on the public schools in rescuing themselves from
> their depressed cultural and economic condition,
> and also our common need for the schools to serve
> as the public agency for neutrality and normalizing
> race relations in this country. With these interests

at stake, the courts must ask whether the virtues
stemming from the Board of Education's pupil
assignment policy (here the neighborhood policy)
are compelling or adequate justification for the
considerable evils of de facto segregation which
adherence to this policy breeds.

Thus, it is clear, in principle, that law suits aimed at
ending racial imbalance will probably succeed in the courts,
although each new decision, particularly in the North, is still
greeted with considerable interest. Nonetheless, the burden
of pursuing litigation in the Federal courts is a heavy one,
and about five years ago, many began to feel that the Federal
government should assume the task of enforcing desegregation.
Title IV of the Civil Rights Act of 1964 gives the Federal government the power to bring court actions to compel desegregation. And this power has been used, but with varying degrees of effectiveness.

In United States v. School District 151 of Cook County,
Illinois, the judge spoke in ringing terms of the promises of
the Constitution and the realities of denial of equal educational
opportunity. He said:

It is more than fourteen years since the Supreme
Court ruled that "in the field of public education the
doctrine of separate but equal has no place." It is
more than thirteen years since the Court said that
desegregation should proceed "with all deliberate
speed". Too often there has been deliberation but
no speed. There has not even been a beginning in
some cases, despite increasing and well documented
evidence showing that racial segregation in the
schools has been detrimental to the Negro child, the
white child, and to the United States.

School segregation, however the cause, has the
effect of stigmatizing Negro pupils and retarding
their educational development. The mere fact of
separation encourages invidious comparison; and
the false conclusion that the Negro pupil is inferior
to the white pupil is tragically forced on the black
child himself through constant elaboration and repe-
tition . . . .

The white opponents of pupil and faculty integration, on the other hand, are doing a disservice to
their own children when they deprive them of the

opportunity to know members of another race and
to be saved from the ignorant, arrogant belief that
a white skin is proof of preeminence. The white
child's education is woefully inadequate if it does
not illuminate those dark corners of the mind in
which prejudice lurks. Both white and black children are being misled when they are told, directly
or by implication, that it is best for them to be
taught only by members of their own race. They
are being cheated when they are deprived of the
experience of working together and learning about
one another in school as preparation for life in an
interracial world of adults.

Barriers to understanding not only cripple the
individual but also endanger the nation. Clearly,
the future of the United States depends in no small
part on education--not the education of white
children but the education of all children. We do
not need another fact-finding commissioner to tell
us that something must be done to prevent a school
situation which produces apathy and hopelessness
that cause a life to be wasted, or frustration and
anger that cause it to be risked in public disorders.
It is not rational to maintain a situation which is
conducive to the kind of behavior that we must prevent or to expect schools to produce law abiding
citizens in a school system that flouts the law.
School boards and school administrators have a
moral and civic duty as well as a legal duty to end
segregation. To fail the Negro child would be to
fail the nation (United States v. School District 151
of Cook County, Illinois, 286 F. Supp. 786, 788-789).

SUMMARY

In the early history of the United States there were no formal provisions for educating Negroes, and in fact, many states
passed laws prohibiting their education. Following the Civil
War, efforts were made to make education available to the
Negro in both the North and South. By 1900, the South was
providing limited financial support for Negro education, mainly in the areas of elementary and vocational education.
Though the North generally provided greater support for Negro

education, most of its facilities were segregated, as were those in the South. New York State, however, recognized the inequality inherent in separate educational facilities and in 1900 passed Section 3201 of the Education Law, which prohibited discrimination in education because of race, color, or creed. New York thus anticipated the results of many court battles that reached their climax in 1954 in <u>Brown</u> v. <u>Board of Education</u>.

Though New York moved relatively early to eliminate de jure segregation, the <u>Brown</u> decision drew attention to the extensive de facto segregation in the State, resulting largely from housing patterns. As in the case of de jure segregation, the State has made a positive and consistent attempt to eliminate de facto segregation.

The New York State Commissioner of Education, in carrying out the policies of the Board of Regents, began taking steps in the late 1940's to provide administrative and programmatic resources for the elimination of segregation. These include the following:

1. The establishment of an office for the administration of the Fair Educational Practices Act of 1948

2. A formal inquiry into discrimination in admission to institutions of higher education through a study made in 1954 by the Advisory Council on Intercultural Relations in Education, whose responsibilities were later expanded to the area of elementary and secondary education

3. The creation of a Division of Intercultural Relations in Education in 1957, which administers funds provided by the State Legislature to assist school districts in solving problems of racial imbalance, assists in the development of programs designed to achieve integration, provides consultative services to local school officials, and administers antidiscrimination legislation

4. The creation of the State Education Commissioner's Advisory Committee on Human Relations and Community Tensions in 1962 to advise and assist the Commissioner and local school officials in dealing with the growing problem of de facto segregation in the schools

5. A statement of <u>Guiding Principles for Dealing with De Facto Segregation in Public Schools</u> in 1963

6. The establishment of a Center on Innovation in 1964, to encourage and guide constructive change in the educational system

7.   The creation of the Office of Urban Education in
1968 to administer funds and carry out the Regents' direc-
tive of developing a strategy to revitalize urban school systems

8.   The conduct of an ethnic census to indicate how
the Department could be better prepared to attack the problem of racial imbalance

9.   The institution of the Pupil Evaluation Program,
which affords a look at the inner-city and its contiguous
districts in regard to integration and compensatory education in certain areas of the State.

In support of the Board of Regents' and Commissioner's
efforts to provide equal educational opportunity to all school
children, Governor Rockefeller and the New York State Legislature have voiced a commitment to legislate against discrimination and to work to equal educational opportunity for all.
This policy has been stated in the Governor's speeches, messages, and memoranda and in legislative resolutions. The
Legislature has appropriated funds designed to assist school
districts in eliminating de facto segregation, and funds have
been appropriated to assist urban schools in upgrading their
educational programs in response to the educational problems
of urban ethnic and racial minorities and the urban poor.

Despite this effort, which has placed New York State at
the forefront nationally in efforts to eliminate segregated
schools, the Legislature passed and the Governor signed
Chapter 342 of the Laws of 1969, which became effective September 1, 1969.   Chapter 342 is an act to amend the Education
Law in relation to prohibiting discrimination on account of
race, creed, color, or national origin in connection with the
education of the children of the State; the legislation effectively prohibits appointed school boards and the Commissioner
of Education from directing assignment of pupils and altering
school boundaries or attendance zones for the purpose of reducing racial imbalance in the schools.   At the same time,
the Legislature appropriated $3 million to the State Education
Department for assisting school districts in paying the costs
involved in solving problems of racial imbalance in the schools.

The inconsistency in recent legislative action relating to
school desegregation in New York State reflects the influences
of a number of factors, including the current politically con-
servative climate of the State and Nation, continuing irrational
fears among large segments of the population, and a splinter-
ing of the Negro movement into a variety of separatist groups.
The situation is now indeed complicated, as some Negro

groups demand the continuation of segregated schooling, with control in the hands of the Negro community (Sizemore, 1969; Wilcox, 1969). The majority of whites and Negroes, however, still favor school integration as a prime solution to the problems resulting from separation of the races in most major facets of life in the United States (Pettigrew and Pajonas, 1964; Pettigrew, 1968; Newsweek, 1969).

As this report shows, racial isolation in public schools of the State has increased substantially in the past few years, and all indicators suggest that this increase will continue unless strong, positive action is taken. Current administrative and programmatic efforts toward the advancement of school desegregation have stemmed only a small part of the tide of increase in racial isolation in the schools, a trend recognized by former Commissioner Allen as early as 1966, (U.S. Commission on Civil Rights, 1966): ". . . despite the depth of our commitment and the strong efforts that have been made, only a beginning has been achieved" (p. 307). At present, it appears that initial efforts to prevent racial isolation in the schools have been outrun.

CHAPTER **2** POPULATION
PATTERNS AND
SEGREGATION IN
THE SCHOOLS

Ruth Salter

The purpose of this chapter is to review nationwide population trends and their effects on school integration and to
examine population trends in New York State and the current
status of integration in the public schools of the State.   The
examination of integration in the schools identifies school districts that have concentrations of minorities, analyzes enrollment trends within these districts, and measures the extent to
which pupils of various racial and ethnic backgrounds are min-
gled in the schools.

The demographic facts and figures provide a clear definition of the magnitude of the problem to be confronted in the
continuing quest for equality of educational opportunity.

THE NEGRO IN THE NATION

In 1950, there were 15 million Negroes in the United
States; in 1966, 21.5 million.   In 1950, 10 percent of the American population was Negro; in 1966, 11 percent (U.S. National
Advisory Commission on Civil Disorders, 1968; hereafter referred to as NACCD).

In 1910, 91 percent of the Negro population lived in the
South; 73 percent of all Negroes lived in rural areas and cities
of less than 2,500 persons.   By 1966, only 55 percent of the
Negro population lived in the South; 69 percent of all Negroes
lived in metropolitan areas--and nearly half of these, or one-
third of all Negroes in the country, lived in twelve major
cities (NACCD, 1968).

These figures establish two facts: (1) the increase in
the number and proportion of Negroes in the total population
and (2) the concentration of Negroes in urban areas.

Population Increases

The growth of the Negro population is part of an over-all
increase. The entire population of the United States has moved
upward from 133 million in 1940 to 152 million in 1950 to 197
million in 1966 (U.S. Bureau of the Census, 1967). The Negro
population is increasing at a faster rate than is the white population, however. Between 1940 and 1960, following the de-
pression of the 1930's, the number of whites increased by 34
percent while the number of Negroes increased by 46.6 percent. Since 1960, the white population has increased 7.4 percent while the Negro population has increased 14.4 percent.
The more recent figures reflect the decline in the nation's
birth rate that began in 1958 and has been more marked for
whites than for Negroes. In 1965, the fertility rate for white
women was 91.4 per 1,000; for nonwhite women, it was 133.9
(NACCD, 1968). Thus, a higher Negro birth rate forecasts
an ever-increasing proportion of Negroes in the total population. In 1950, at least one of every ten Americans was Negro;
in 1966, one of nine was Negro--and the trend appears to be
continuing (NACCD, 1968).

Because of the higher Negro birth rate, there is a greater
proportion of Negroes in the lower age groups than in the total
population. In 1968, the median age for Negroes was 21.1,
whereas that of whites was 29.1. One out of every six children
under the age of five was Negro.

Concentration in Urban Centers

The movement of Negroes from the South to the big cities
of the North began before the Civil War. This migration--the
Negro's effort to find a better life away from slavery and its
aftermath--was given periodic impetus by the decline of agri-
culture in the South and the industrial needs of the North and
West in times of national crisis. World War II brought an especially heavy influx of Negroes to urban centers, an influx
that continued into the late 1950's.

Once in the city, the Negro has remained a city dweller.
Economic limitations and residential restrictions have barred
further movement, while there has been a trend among the
rest of the population, since the mid-1940's, to move from the
city to the suburbs. The combination of in-migration of Negroe
and out-migration of white city residents has resulted in a
disproportionate concentration of Negroes in the cities, which
will increase as the disparity between the Negro and white

birth rates becomes more pronounced. It is predicted that
more than 50 percent of the population of thirteen major central cities will be Negro in 1985 (NACCD, 1968).

Moreover, over-all statistics on urban centers do not reflect the segregation of Negroes within the cities. Like other
immigrants, Negroes, as newcomers to the city, have lived
in the oldest sections. Economic disadvantage and discriminatory practices have kept them from moving elsewhere.
When breakthroughs have been made, white flight--the rush
of homeowners to dispose of their property and move away--
has often brought about resegregation.

Consequences for the Schools

The growth, comparative youth, and higher birth rate of
the Negro population are having a predictable effect on public
school populations. Negro school enrollments are rising
throughout the country. Moreover, because of their concentration in urban centers, Negroes already dominate many
large city school systems, or soon will. In 1965-66, for example, seventeen large city school systems in the country,
including seven of the ten biggest, had Negro majorities in
the elementary schools. In only two of these cities--Washing-
ton, D.C., and Newark, New Jersey--did Negroes exceed 50
percent of the general population (NACCD, 1968).

Within a school system, the proportion of Negroes in individual schools is apt to be far greater than in the total enrollment. In 1965, in seventy-five major central cities, 75
percent of the Negro elementary school pupils attended schools
that were 90 percent or more Negro, while 83 percent of the
white elementary school children were in schools that were
91 percent or more white. These figures represent both the
North and the South and show educational isolation regardless
of the proportion of Negroes in the total system (U.S. Commission on Civil Rights, 1967).

POPULATION TRENDS IN NEW YORK STATE

As a major Northern industrial state, New York has
shared with the Nation the effects of Negro migration and
population growth. It has also experienced the development
of a second minority group, the Puerto Ricans. Following

are some facts that highlight the population picture in New
York State:

    1.   Nonwhites--Negroes, Orientals, and Indians--
increased from less than 600,000 in 1940 to an estimated 2
million in 1967. Negroes make up 95 percent of the nonwhite
population (New York State Commission for Human Rights,
1967).

    2.   The proportion of nonwhites in the total State pop-
ulation jumped from 4.4 percent in 1940 to an estimated 10.1
percent in 1967 (New York State Commission for Human
Rights, 1967).

    3.   In 1967, 97 percent of the nonwhites in New York
State lived in six metropolitan areas; 86 percent lived in the
New York City Metropolitan Area; 75 percent of the total
lived in New York City itself (New York State Division of the
Budget, 1969).

    4.   The vast majority of nonwhites live in urban centers
within the metropolitan areas, with the result that the proportions of nonwhites are much greater in the cities than in surrounding communities. In two urban communities, nonwhites
exceed 25 percent of the total population (New York State
Commission for Human Rights, 1967).

    5.   Nonwhites outside the cities are concentrated in
color pockets in otherwise white suburban communities.

    6.   The Puerto Rican population, the second largest
minority group in New York State, has increased an estimated
59 percent since 1960. Of all Puerto Ricans in the State, 95
percent live in New York City (New York State Division of
Human Rights, 1969).

Population Increases

As in the Nation, the increase in the Negro population
in New York State is part of an over-all increase. In 1940,
the population of New York State was 13.5 million; in 1967,
an estimated 18 million, a 33 percent increase. During the
same period, the nonwhite population increased from less
than 600,000 to nearly 2 million, more than trebling (New
York State Commission for Human Rights, 1967).

FIGURE 1

Total Population in New York State: 1940-67[1]
(in millions)

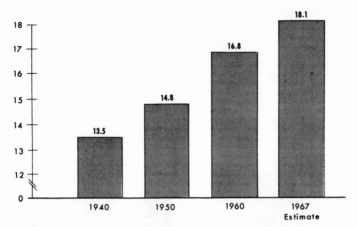

[1]Based on data from the New York State Commission for
Human Rights (1967).

FIGURE 2

Nonwhite Population in New York State: 1940-67[1]
(in thousands)

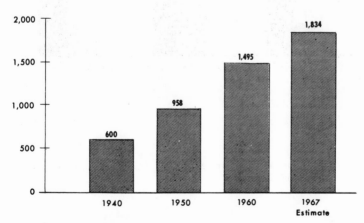

[1]Based on data from the New York State Commission for
Human Rights (1967).

43

FIGURE 3

Increases in Total, White and Nonwhite Populations
in New York State: 1940-67[1]

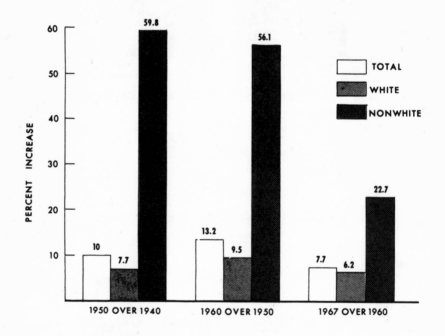

[1]Based on data from the New York State Commission for
Human Rights (1967).

FIGURE 4

Nonwhite Population as Percent of Total
Population in New York State: 1940-67[1]

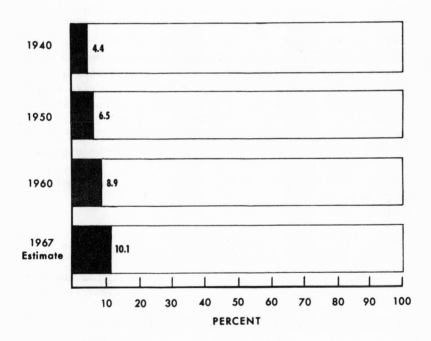

[1]Based on data from the New York State Commission for
Human Rights (1967).

Figures 1 and 2 show the upward progression of the total population and the nonwhite population in New York State from 1940 to 1967; Figure 3 shows the percentage increases for the total population, whites and nonwhites; and Figure 4 shows the proportion of nonwhites in the total population from 1940 to 1967. Tabular data for Figures 1 through 4 are given in Table 41 in the Appendix.

The radical decline in the rate of nonwhite increase reflects the drop in Negro migration from the South. However, in absolute numbers, the average annual increase for nonwhites remained nearly as high in the 1960's as in the 1950's when it was 54,000 per year (New York State Commission for Human Rights, 1967).

During these years of population growth, the percentage increases for nonwhites have far outstripped those for whites as, shown in Figure 3. In the 1940's, when nonwhites increased by nearly 60 percent, whites increased by 7.7 percent; in the 1950's, when nonwhites increased by 56 percent, whites increased by 9.5 percent. In the first seven years of the 1960's nonwhites increased by 23 percent, whites by only 6 percent. As a result of the greater rate of increase of nonwhites, the proportion on nonwhites in the total population has more than doubled: as shown in Figure 4, it has gone up from 4.4 percent in 1940 to over 10 percent in 1967. Given the difference in white and nonwhite birth rates, it can be expected that the proportion of nonwhites in the State will be even greater in the years ahead (New York State Commission for Human Rights, 1967).

Concentration of Nonwhites in Metropolitan Areas

The concentration of Negroes in metropolitan areas and in major cities in the United States is well demonstrated in New York State.

Nearly 1.5 million nonwhites, 75 percent of the State's total nonwhite population, live in New York City alone. Although nonwhites make up a smaller proportion of the total population in New York City than do nonwhites in other major cities in the United States--17 percent as compared to 28 percent in Chicago, 34 percent in Detroit, 38 percent in Baltimore, and 66 percent in Washington (NACCD, 1968)--the Negroes in the City constitute about 6 percent of the 21.5 million Negroes in the entire country.

An additional 200,000 nonwhites, 11.1 percent, live in

FIGURE 5

Distribution of Nonwhite Population in New York State
by Standard Metropolitan Statistical Areas: 1967[1]

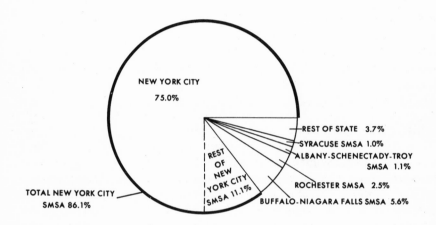

[1]Based on data from the New York State Division of
the Budget (1969).

the four counties adjoining New York City--Nassau, Suffolk,
Westchester, and Rockland; thus, more than 86 percent of the
State's nonwhite population lives in the New York City Metropolitan Area. An additional 11 percent is found in the six
upstate metropolitan areas. The next greatest concentrations
of nonwhites outside the New York City Metropolitan area are
in the Buffalo area, 5.6 percent, and the Rochester area, 2.5
percent. Figure 5 shows the distribution of nonwhites by
Standard Metropolitan Statistical Areas (SMSA's).

To provide another perspective on the State, the distribution of nonwhites in the counties outside New York City is
shown in Figure 6. Erie County dominates with 20.0 percent
of the total outside New York City. Westchester, Nassau, and
Suffolk counties follow with 17.4, 13.3, and 11.3 percent,
respectively. These three counties combined account for 42
percent of the nonwhites outside New York City. Monroe,
ranking fifth with 8/7 percent of its population being nonwhite,
has more than twice the proportion of nonwhites as any of the
remaining counties in the State.

The total and nonwhite populations of each of the SMSA's
and their component counties, as reported in the 1960 census
and as estimated in 1967, are given in Table 1 along with the
proportion of nonwhites in both years and the extent of nonwhite increases between the two years. All seven metropolitan areas show increases in total population, in nonwhite population, and in the proportion of nonwhites in the total
population. Similarly, there is an increase in the nonwhite
population in each county and, with three minor exceptions,
there is an increase in the proportion of nonwhite residents.
The increases in the nonwhite SMSA populations range from
15 percent in the Buffalo area to 58 percent in the Rochester
area (New York State Commission for Human Rights, 1967).

The county increases in nonwhite population shown in
Table 1 range even more widely than the SMSA increases,
from 3 to 65 percent, twelve out of twenty-two exceeding the
23 percent increase in nonwhite population for the State. The
most striking changes in terms of percentage increase are
those for Nassau, Suffolk, and Monroe counties. In Nassau
County, an additional 18,000 nonwhites raised the nonwhite
population by 44 percent; in Suffolk, 17,000 increased it by
50 percent; and in Monroe, 15,000 increased the nonwhite
population by a sizeable 61 percent. Increases of 17,000 and
13,000 in Westchester and Erie counties were similar in number, though smaller in proportion, being 27 and 16 percent,
respectively. The New York City numerical increase exceeds

FIGURE 6

Percent Distribution of Nonwhite Population in
New York State Counties Excluding New York City: 1967[1]

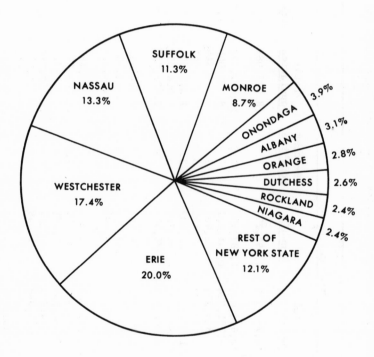

[1]Based on population estimates published by the New
York State Commission for Human Rights (1967).

TABLE 1

Total and Nonwhite Residents in Standard Metropolitan Statistical
Areas and Component Counties in New York State: 1960 and 1967[1]

Area	1960 Census Data			1967 Estimates			
	Total Population	Nonwhite	Percent Nonwhite	Total Population	Nonwhite	Percent Nonwhite	Percent Increase Nonwhite
Entire State	16,782,304	1,495,233	8.9	18,072,089	1,834,026	10.1	22.7
New York SMSA	10,694,633	1,287,878	12.0	11,591,723	1,578,367	13.6	22.6
New York City	7,781,984	1,141,322	14.7	8,096,000	1,374,903	17.0	20.5
Westchester	808,891	62,485	7.7	870,649	79,546	9.1	27.3
Rockland	136,803	7,152	5.2	202,044	10,933	5.4	52.9
Nassau	1,300,171	42,132	3.2	1,428,391	60,693	4.2	44.1
Suffolk	666,784	34,787	5.2	994,639	52,292	5.3	50.3
Long Island	1,966,955	76,919	3.9	2,423,030	112,985	4.7	46.9
Buffalo SMSA	1,306,957	89,237	6.8	1,324,432	102,712	7.8	15.1
Erie	1,064,688	79,245	7.4	1,089,955	92,195	8.5	16.3
Niagara	242,269	9,992	4.1	234,477	10,517	4.5	5.3
Rochester SMSA	732,588	29,025	4.0	829,187	45,973	5.5	58.4
Monroe	586,387	25,067	4.3	668,131	40,451	6.1	61.4
Orleans	34,159	1,491	4.4	37,728	1,975	5.2	32.5
Livingston	44,053	918	2.1	48,516	986	2.0	7.4
Wayne	67,989	1,549	2.3	74,812	2,561	3.4	65.3
Syracuse SMSA	563,781	14,732	2.6	620,989	18,564	3.0	26.0
Onondaga	423,028	14,094	3.3	468,879	17,815	3.8	26.4
Madison	54,635	389	0.7	59,353	460	0.8	18.3
Oswego	86,118	249	0.3	92,757	289	0.3	16.1

50

Albany-Schenectady-Troy SMSA	657,503	17,379	2.6	686,177	20,689	3.0	19.0
Albany	272,926	11,512	4.2	286,174	13,891	4.9	20.7
Schenectady	152,896	2,358	1.5	148,505	2,719	1.8	15.3
Rensselaer	142,585	2,623	1.8	148,111	3,167	2.1	20.7
Saratoga	89,096	886	1.0	103,387	912	0.9	2.9
Utica-Rome SMSA	330,771	5,232	1.6	348,679	6,637	1.9	26.9
Oneida	264,401	5,084	1.9	279,073	6,438	2.3	26.6
Herkimer	66,370	148	0.2	69,606	199	0.3	34.5
Binghamton SMSA	250,463	1,701	0.7	268,262	2,268	0.8	33.3
Broome	212,661	1,487	0.7	223,699	1,955	0.9	31.5
Tioga	37,802	214	0.6	44,563	313	0.7	46.3
Outside SMSA's	2,245,608	50,049	2.2	2,402,640	58,816	2.4	18.0

[1] Based on data from the New York State Commission for Human Rights (1967).

all others, being an estimated 230,000. Nevertheless, the
percentage increase for New York, 20.5, is below the statewide increase of 23 percent between 1960 and 1967 (New York
State Commission for Human Rights, 1967).

Concentration of Nonwhites in Urban Centers

The magnitude of the nonwhite population in New York
City has already been noted. Numerically, the New York City
situation is unique in all of the United States, not only New
York State. Most nonwhites outside New York City are also
concentrated in urban centers. The notable exceptions are
the 113,000 nonwhites on Long Island, where there are no big
cities, and the growing number of nonwhites in Rockland County, until recently a relatively rural area. Reference to Long
Island and Rockland County will be made in the following section on nonwhites in suburbia.

Recent population estimates are not as readily available
for urban centers as they are for counties, but special city
surveys made since 1960 reveal a continuation of the increases
in the number of nonwhites in the cities shown by the 1950 and
1960 federal censuses. These surveys also confirm and show
an extension of a trend away from the cities--an actual decline
in urban populations. That trend was well established by the
1960 census: in 1960, nine of the State's fifteen largest cities
showed population losses. Since then, population losses have
been reported for four others (New York State Commission
for Human Rights, 1967; New York State Division of the Budget, 1969).

The combination of population losses--which are white
losses--and the growth in the Negro segments of urban communities has resulted in marked changes in the proportions
of nonwhites in the cities. Table 2 shows the changes that
have occurred in New York State urban centers (cities of over
50,000) and in four smaller cities outside metropolitan areas,
where nonwhite concentrations also exist. In seven of the ten
cities surveyed since 1960, the proportion of nonwhites exceeded the 10.1 percentage for the State as a whole. The
highest proportions were in Mount Vernon, 27 percent nonwhite, and Newburgh, 26 percent. In Mount Vernon, a 32
percent increase in the nonwhite population in five years,
from 15,000 to nearly 20,000, was accompanied by a white
loss of 13 percent and an over-all population loss of 4 percent. In Newburgh, a city half the size of Mount Vernon, the

TABLE 2

Population Trends in New York State Cities of More
Than 50,000 (1960) and Selected Smaller Cities: 1950-67[1]

City	1950 Census		1960 Census				Special Census since 1960				
	Total Pop.	Percent Nonwhite	Total Pop.	Percent Nonwhite	Dir. of Change Total	Dir. of Change Nonwhite	Year	Total Pop.	Percent Nonwhite	Dir. of Change Total	Dir. of Change Nonwhite
New York City	7,891,957	9.8	7,781,984	14.7	-	+					
Buffalo	580,132	6.5	532,759	13.8	-	+	1966	481,453	17.4	-	+
Rochester	332,488	2.4	318,611	7.6	-	+	1964	305,849	10.6	-	+
Syracuse	220,583	2.3	216,038	5.7	-	+					
Yonkers	152,798	3.3	190,634	4.2	+	+	1965	201,573	5.5	+	+
Albany	134,995	4.4	129,726	8.5	-	+					
Utica	101,531	1.6	100,410	3.2	-	+					
Schenectady	91,785	1.6	81,682	2.7	-	+					
Niagara Falls	90,872	4.1	102,394	7.5	+	+	1967	88,286	8.9	-	+
Binghamton	80,674	1.0	75,941	1.7	-	+	1966	69,435	2.0	-	+
Troy	72,311	1.4	67,492	3.1	-	+					
Mount Vernon	71,899	11.0	76,010	19.9	+	+	1965	72,918	27.4	-	+
New Rochelle	59,725	12.6	76,812	13.6	+	+	1965	75,206	13.5	-	-

(Continued)

TABLE 2 (Continued)

City	1950 Census		1960 Census				Year	Special Census since 1960			
	Total Pop.	Percent Nonwhite	Total Pop.	Percent Nonwhite	Dir. of Change Total	Nonwhite		Total Pop.	Percent Nonwhite	Dir. of Change Total	Nonwhite
White Plains	43,466	10.0	50,485	11.9	+	+	1965	50,040	13.6	-	+
Rome	41,682	1.4	51,646	2.8	+	+					
Poughkeepsie	41,023	4.5	38,330	9.6	-	+					
Newburgh	31,956	6.4	30,979	16.6	-	+	1967	27,171	25.9	-	+
Peekskill	17,731	5.7	18,737	11.5	+	+	1965	18,504	15.2	-	+
Beacon	14,012	8.5	13,922	13.0	-	+					

[1]Based on data from the New York State Division of the Budget (1969) and the New York State Commission for Human Rights (1967).

nonwhite population increased by more than 36 percent, from
5,000 to 7,000, in seven years; the white population dropped
by 22 percent; and the total population declined 12 percent.
Yonkers, the big city with the smallest proportion of nonwhites
(5.5 percent), is the only one to show an increase in total population since 1960. Data reported here, plus that derived from
school census counts, indicate that the 1970 federal census
will continue to show declining total populations and increasing
nonwhite populations in most large cities (New York State
Commission for Human Rights, 1967).

Precise comparisons between city and county data are
not possible because of differences in years reported, but the
information in Tables 1 and 2 does suggest a disparity between nonwhite populations in urban centers and in surrounding
communities. In addition, for example, in 1967 the estimated
proportion of nonwhites in Erie County, including Buffalo, was
8.5; in 1966 the proportion in Buffalo itself was 17.4. In Monroe County, including the city of Rochester, the estimated
proportion was 6.1 in 1967; in Rochester itself, the proportion
was 10.6 as early as 1964.

The preceding tables and discussion demonstrate the
isolation of nonwhites in New York State. And this isolation
could be made even more evident by an exposition of the distribution of nonwhites by neighborhoods within cities.

The phenomenon of large and increasing numbers of nonwhites isolated in a small portion of a total community is demonstrated in Westchester County. With the exception of New
York City, Westchester County has the highest proportion of
nonwhites of any location in the State, 9.1 percent in 1967.
But, in 1965, 89 percent of all nonwhites in Westchester County lived in eleven of its forty-four communities. Moreover,
55 percent of the nonwhites in the county were found in its
three largest cities--Yonkers, Mount Vernon, and New Rochelle. Mount Vernon alone had 27 percent of the nonwhites,
but only 8.5 percent of the total population of the county.

Within Mount Vernon in 1965, the nonwhite population,
which was then 99 percent Negro, was concentrated in eight
of the city's twenty-one census tracts, in which 89 percent of
the nonwhite population lived. The proportions of nonwhites
in these tracts ranged from 35.6 percent to 84.4 percent. As
further evidence of the concentration of the nonwhite population of Mount Vernon, it can be noted that more than half the
increase of 5,000 nonwhite residents in Mount Vernon between
1960 and 1965 occurred in three of the eight census tracts and
that, in each of these, the increase was nearly equalled or

exceeded by white losses. In one tract alone, the nonwhite
population rose from 607 to 1,652--an increase of 1,045--
while the white population dropped from 4,070 to 2,982--a
loss of 1,088 (New York State Commission for Human Rights,
1965).

Nonwhites in Suburbia:
Nassau, Suffolk, and Rockland Counties

Nassau, Suffolk, and Rockland counties, along with Westchester County, comprise the suburbs of New York City.
Whereas Westchester County contains four urban centers, the
three other counties are made up of small cities, towns, vil-
lages, and unincorporated communities ranging in size from
a few hundred to several thousand.

Nassau County

The suburban boom that began at the end of World War II
produced great changes in Nassau County. The population grew
from just over 400,000 in 1940 to nearly 1,400,000 in 1965,
when a special census was made. During this period the nonwhite population, which was 94 percent Negro, increased from
13,500 to more than 55,000. The greatest growth occurred
in the 1950's, when the total population increased by nearly
100 percent and the nonwhite population went up by 137 percent (New York State Commission for Human Rights, 1965b).
With the filling up of available land, the rate of growth in
Nassau County has slackened for both whites and nonwhites.
Estimates for 1967 indicate that the nonwhite population had
increased by 44 percent since 1960 while the white population
had increased by only 9 percent. In 1967, nonwhites made up
an estimated 4.2 percent of the total population as opposed to
3.2 percent in 1960 and 2.6 percent in 1950 (New York State
Commission for Human Rights, 1967).
Nonwhites are not spread throughout Nassau County, but
concentrated in a few of its ninety-three local communities,
and most of.the communities having substantial numbers of
nonwhites are located in the western, more urban, section of
the county. Table 3 lists twelve communities that each had
more than 1,000 nonwhite residents in 1965 and together accounted for 75 percent of all nonwhites in the county, although
they contained only 20 percent of the total population of the
county. Nearly 55 percent of the nonwhites lived in five of

TABLE 3

Concentration of Nonwhites
in Nassau County Communities: 1965[1]

Community	Total Community Population	Nonwhite Population		
		Number	Percent of Total	Percent of Co. Nonwhites
Hempstead	37,192	11,904	32.0	21.5
New Cassel	9,277	4,924	53.1	8.9
Roosevelt	13,715	4,642	33.8	8.4
Freeport	38,429	4,423	11.5	8.0
West Hemstead-Lakeview	25,837	4,196	16.2	7.6
Inwood	8,833	2,221	25.1	4.0
Glen Cove	25,048	2,090	8.3	3.8
Uniondale-Garden City East	22,396	2,052	9.2	3.7
Long Beach	28,994	1,697	5.9	3.1
Manhasset	8,942	1,454	16.3	2.6
Elmont-South Floral Park	31,525	1,037	3.3	1.9
Rockville Centre	26,413	1,018	3.9	1.8
Subtotal, 12 Communities	276,601	41,658	15.1	75.2
91 Other Communities	1,121,120	13,732	1.2	24.8
County Total	1,397,721	55,390	4.0	100.0

[1]From the New York State Commission for Human Rights (1965b).

these communities. The proportion of nonwhites in the twelve
communities ranged from 3. 3 percent in Elmont-South Floral
Park to 53. 1 percent in New Cassel. In seven communities
it exceeded 10. 1 percent, the proportion of nonwhites in the
State as a whole in 1967. Four of the communities were more
than 25 percent nonwhite in 1965: Hempstead, a village of over
37, 000; Roosevelt and Inwood, unincorporated communities
of 14, 000 and 9, 000; and New Cassel, a section of Westbury,
itself having a population of 9, 000. Within these communities,
there was further concentration of the nonwhites by neighborhood. In Hempstead, for example, one census tract was 88
percent nonwhite and another only 2 percent. Of a total of
220 census tracts in all of Nassau County, 20 had a nonwhite
population of more than 10 percent in 1965 and 142 had a
nonwhite population of less than 1 percent.

      Hempstead, New Cassel, Roosevelt, Freeport, and West
Hempstead-Lakeview--the five communities with the largest
numbers of nonwhites--absorbed almost all the nonwhite increase in Nassau County between 1960 and 1965--12, 158 out
of 13, 258 residents, and in four of these, the white population
dropped as the nonwhite population increased. Nonwhites increased in forty-five other Nassau County communities though
they declined in forty-one. In three communities--East Mea-
dow, Inwood, and Rockville Centre--the loss of nonwhite residents exceeded 300 between 1960 and 1965.

      The figures for Nassau County show that while more non-
whites are living in this portion of suburbia than previously,
they are more and more concentrated in individual communities. In these communities, their proportions may be even
higher than in urban centers. Though community boundaries
are not co-terminous with school district boundaries, these
community population figures are good indicators of the ethnic
composition of some Nassau school districts (New York State
Commission for Human Rights, 1965b).

Suffolk County

      Further from New York City than Nassau County and hav-
ing some land still undeveloped, Suffolk County is currently
an area of rapid population growth. The total population nearly
quadrupled in less than twenty years, increasing from 276, 000
in 1950 to more than a million in 1968, according to estimates
in that year. During this period, the Negro population expanded at a similar rate, from 13, 000 to an estimated 52, 000,
Negroes making up about 95 percent of the total nonwhite

population of 55,000. An estimated 5 percent of the total
population was Negro in 1968.

Increases in the Negro and white populations of Suffolk
County were about the same between 1960 and 1968: 57.3 percent for whites and 58.7 percent for Negroes. When the county's high institutional population is excluded, however, the
rate of Negro increase exceeds that of white increase: 72 percent as against 60 percent.

Most of the Negro population growth has occurred in four
of Suffolk County's ten townships: Babylon, Islip, Huntington,
and Brookhaven. In Babylon between 1960 and 1968, the Negro
population increased by nearly 9,500. In Islip and Huntington,
the Negro population outside institutions increased by almost
4,000 and 2,000 respectively. In Brookhaven, the increase
was nearly 3,000.

The Town of Babylon, immediately adjacent to Nassau
County, had the largest proportion of Negroes in 1968, 10.6
percent of its total population, nearly 21,000. Riverhead and
Southampton, farther out on Long Island, had higher proportions, 16.0 and 11.2 percent, but lower numbers, 2,800 and
3,900. In Babylon, Negroes were most numerous in two
communities, Wyandanch and North Amityville, one census
tract in Wyandanch being 92 percent Negro. In this census
tract the Negro population increased by more than 4,000 between 1960 and 1968, and white losses accompanied large
Negro increases, as they did in some other neighborhoods.

Table 4 shows the distribution of the Negro population of
Suffolk County by town and by areas within towns, as estimated
in 1968, some of the subdivisions, such as North Amityville,
being intact communities and others being single census tracts.
These figures indicate the same pattern of racial pocketing in
Suffolk County that is found in more densely populated Nassau
County and in the cities (New York State Division of Human
Rights, 1968).

Rockland County

Rockland County, having a population in 1966 of 193,000,
is another relatively rural area that has recently felt the impact of suburban development. The population rose by more
than 47,000 between 1950 and 1960 and went up another 56,000
in the six years between 1960 and 1966. During these sixteen
years, the nonwhite population increased from 4,600 to 10,400,
making up 5.4 percent of the total population of the county in
1966.

TABLE 4

Distribution of Negroes in Townships of Suffolk County: 1968[1]

Town	Total Community Population	Negro	% Negro	% of County Negro Pop., Excluding Institutions
Babylon	196,975	20,838	10.6	44.7
North Amityville	11,351	8,400	74.0	18.0
Wyandanch: Census Tract BA-24	11,748	2,756	23.5	5.9
Census Tract BA-25	6,781	6,205	91.5	13.3
Huntington	183,406	4,183	2.3	9.0
Major Census Tracts in Huntington Station	18,834	2,547	13.5	5.5
Islip	248,118	6,343	2.6	13.6
One Census Tract of Brentwood	3,929	1,344	34.2	2.9
One Tract of Central Islip	9,807	1,476	15.1	3.2
Smithtown	95,752	233	0.2	0.5
Brookhaven	207,613	6,530	3.1	14.0
One Census Tract of Coram-Yaphank	2,217	1,668	75.2	3.6
One Tract North of Bellport	5,237	1,711	32.7	3.7
Riverhead	17,742	2,841	16.0	6.1
Riverhead (Village)	6,414	1,211	18.9	2.6
Southampton	35,096	3,932	11.2	8.4
One Census Tract South of Riverhead	7,269	1,237	17.0	2.7
Southampton (Village)	4,924	960	19.5	2.1
East Hampton	12,112	527	4.4	1.1
Southold	16,412	1,180	7.2	2.5
Shelter Island	1,620	16	1.0	--[a]
County Total (Excluding Institutions)	1,014,846	46,623	4.6	100
Institutions	34,129	5,795	17.0	
Total	1,048,975	52,418	5.0	

[1]Based on data from the New York Division of Human Rights (1968).
[a]Less than 0.1 percent.

Nonwhites, of whom 96 percent are Negro, are unevenly distributed in Rockland County, and the nonwhite growth, as shown in Table 5, has been uneven. The picture is complicated by the fact that Rockland County, like Suffolk, has a substantial institutional population--in 1966, for example, about 23 percent of all nonwhites in the county were inmates or staff members of State facilities. Of the nonwhites outside institutions, 37. 5 percent were found in two communities in 1966-- Spring Valley and Nyack. In Spring Valley, a fast-growing residential area, the nonwhite population increased from 675 to more than 2, 500 between 1960 and 1966; during the same period the white population grew by 4, 500. In Nyack, on the other hand, both the white and the nonwhite populations declined by about 300 persons. As a result of these changes and other shifts within the county, the proportion of nonwhites living in Spring Valley rose from less than 10 percent in 1960 to nearly 25 percent of the county total in 1966. Thus, in a six-year period, there was an increase in the concentration of nonwhites in Rockland County (New York State Commission for Human Rights, 1966).

Summary

The growth of nonwhite populations in Nassau, Suffolk, and Rockland counties represents a departure from the usual pattern of Negro concentration in urban centers, but even in this movement into suburbia, the nonwhites remained an isolated group. Numbers of nonwhite residents advanced in only a few communities, and there the proportions were markedly greater than in neighboring locations.

In all three suburban counties, further increases in the numbers and proportions of nonwhites are predicted. The percentage of nonwhites is expected to rise to 5 percent in Nassau County and 6 percent in Rockland County by 1970 (New York State Commission for Human Rights, 1965b, 1966), and it is predicted that Suffolk County will be 5. 5 percent Negro by 1975 (New York State Division of Human Rights, 1968). If the existing population patterns persist, there will be even greater concentrations of nonwhites in given suburban communities as the over-all increases occur.

TABLE 5

Distribution of Nonwhites in Selected Communities of Rockland County: 1960 and 1966[1]

Community	Total Community Population	1960			1966				% Inc. N.W.
		Non-White	% N.W.	% Total N.W.	Total	Non-White	% N.W.	% Total N.W.	
Spring Valley	6,538	675	10.3	9.4	12,892	2,510	19.5	24.2	271.8
Nyack	6,062	1,682	27.7	23.5	5,400	1,318	25.6	12.7	-23.8
Hillburn	1,114	552	49.6	7.7	1,011	508	50.2	4.9	- 8.0
Haverstraw	5,771	356	6.2	5.0	7,293	449	6.2	4.3	20.7
South Nyack	3,113	349	11.2	4.9	3,377	428	12.7	4.1	18.5
State Institutions	12,438	1,501	12.1	21.0	11,866	2,397	20.2	23.1	59.7
Rest of County (23 Other Census Tracts)	101,767	2,037	2.0	28.5	150,885	2,783	1.8	26.8	36.6
Total County	136,803	7,152	5.2	100.0	192,724	10,393	5.4	100.0	45.3

[1]Based on data from New York State Commission for Human Rights (1966).

Puerto Ricans in New York State

Puerto Ricans, estimated at more than a million in 1969, constitute 5.8 percent of the total population in New York State and are the State's second minority group. The largeness of the Puerto Rican population is due to heavy immigration, which was at its peak in the 1950's, and a relatively high birth rate.

Most of the State's Puerto Ricans have settled in New York City, their port of entry. A full 95 percent, more than 960,000, reside in the City; 1.8 percent live on Long Island; 0.9 percent live in Westchester and Rockland counties; and the remaining 2.3 percent are distributed throughout the State, in concentrations of more than 1,000 each in seven counties--Orange, Dutchess, Ulster, Sullivan, Erie, Chautauqua, and Monroe (New York State Division of Human Rights, 1969).

Because of their high birth rate and the continuing in-migration, the proportion of Puerto Ricans in the State can be expected to increase.

ETHNIC ISOLATION IN NEW YORK STATE SCHOOLS

The collection of ethnic and racial data on the school population of New York State is a recent innovation, the first effort of this kind having been the State Education Department's 1961 racial census of elementary school buildings. Since the 1966-67 school year, the collection of racial and ethnic data for both elementary and secondary schools has been a part of the Education Department's annual Basic Educational Data System programs (BEDS), and schools are currently asked to report enrollments in five ethnic categories--American Indian, Negro, Oriental, Spanish-Surnamed-American, and Other. Spanish-Surnamed-Americans are predominantly Puerto Rican in New York State, and so the latter designation is used in this study; the category Other is similar to the category White in the general census except that it does not include Spanish-Surnamed-Americans.

The BEDS data, covering only three years, reveal the same upward trends in the number of Negroes and Puerto Ricans and in the total school population that are shown by the long-range general census data. They show--as might have been expected in view of the higher nonwhite and Puerto Rican birth rate and the fact that fewer nonwhites and Puerto

Ricans attend private schools--higher proportions of Negroes and Puerto Ricans in the public schools than in the total population.

State-wide Increases in Minority Groups

Public elementary and secondary school enrollments in New York State rose from 3.25 million in 1966 to 3.41 million in 1968. Negro and Puerto Rican students combined accounted for 63.7 percent of the increase. The number of Negro students rose from 439,000 to 495,000, and the number of Puerto Ricans rose from 238,000 to 280,000 in two years from 1966 to 1968. The total school enrollment increased by 5 percent, but Negro enrollment went up 13 percent and Puerto Rican enrollment gained 18 percent. Accordingly, while Negroes made up 13.5 percent of the public school population in 1966, they accounted for 14.5 percent in 1968. Similarly, while Puerto Ricans constituted 7.3 percent of the total in 1966, they accounted for 8.2 percent in 1968. Table 6 shows the progression of the increases during the two-year period.

The 1968 percentage of Negroes in the public school population, 14.5, was 4.4 percentage points higher than the estimated percentage of all nonwhites, including Indians and Orientals, in the total population in 1967. The 1968 percentage of Puerto Ricans in the schools, 8.2, was 2.4 percentage points higher than the estimated percentage of Puerto Ricans in the total population in 1969.

Minority Concentrations

The effects of the increase in minority enrollments can be best understood by examining school districts in which there are minority concentrations. For this purpose, three-year data were assembled for forty-two districts: (1) All districts in the State having more than 20 percent Negro enrollment in 1968, except special districts with institutional schools (twenty-four districts);[*] (2) all districts in the State having one or

---

[*]Special districts receive pupils from all over the State for rehabilitation training. One special district, Echo Hills in Westchester County, was identified as imbalanced in the 1961 racial census; 45.7 percent of its pupils were Negro and 11.9 percent were Puerto Rican in 1968.

TABLE 6

Trends in New York State School Population: 1966-68[1]

	1966-67		1967-68			1968-69			% Increase 1966-68
	Number	%	Number	%	% Increase	Number	%	% Increase	
Total	3,251,654	100	3,336,678	100	2.61	3,406,658	100	2.10	4.77
Negro	438,585	13.5	462,992	13.9	5.56	494,919	14.5	6.90	12.84
Puerto Rican	237,916	7.3	256,094	7.7	7.64	280,275	8.2	9.44	17.80
Other[a]	2,575,153	79.2	2,617,592	78.4	1.65	2,631,464	77.3	.53	2.19

[1]Data from BEDS, NYSED, 1969.

[a]The term "Other" is used in the BEDS data to designate pupils who are neither Negro, Spanish-Surnamed-American (Puerto Rican), American Indian or Oriental. In this case only, Indians and Orientals, about 0.7 percent of the total, are included in "Other."

more schools with more than 31 percent Negro enrollment in
1966 or 1968 (40 districts); and (3) all districts that received
State Aid for Correcting Racial Imbalance in 1966, 1967, or
1968 (27 districts). *

Though the criteria for the selection of districts to be
analyzed refer only to Negroes in the schools, the forty-two
districts together comprehend 93 percent of all Negro and 96
percent of all Puerto Rican pupils in the public schools of New
York State in 1968.

The concentrations of these minority groups will be
examined in three ways: (1) by numbers, (2) by proportions
within districts, and (3) by proportions within districts as compared to surrounding districts.

Concentration by Numbers

In looking at concentration by numbers, attention will be
given to Negroes and Puerto Ricans as separate groups.

Of the 495,000 Negro school children in New York State,
85 percent were enrolled in eight school districts in 1968;
New York City alone had 356,000 Negro pupils, or 72 percent
of the total. Buffalo, the second largest school system, had
over 26,000, or more than 5 percent. Rochester, the third
largest district, had more than 13,600, or nearly 3 percent.
The three largest districts together accounted for 80 percent
of the State's Negro students. The districts with the next
largest numbers were Syracuse and Mount Vernon, with over
6,000, or nearly 1.3 percent, in each. Hempstead, a Long
Island district, had over 4,000, nearly 1 percent; and Yonkers
and Albany both had nearly 3,700, or 0.75 percent each.
Table 7 shows the number of Negro pupils in the eight districts cited and in the thirty-four other districts under study.
Fifteen of the other districts had more than 1,000 Negro
pupils; seven of these had between 2,000 and 3,000, and eight
had between 1,000 and 2,000.

The concentration of Puerto Ricans was more intense
than that of Negroes. New York City alone had nearly 261,000
Puerto Rican pupils, 93 percent of the 280,000 Puerto Rican

_____

*Six additional districts have received State Aid for Cor-
recting Racial Imbalance: one for a preventative program
(Roslyn), one because of religious isolation (West Hempstead),
one for in-service training of teachers (Scotia-Glenville), and
three for urban-suburban action exchange programs (Penfield,
Pittsford, and West Irondequoit).

TABLE 7

Negro Pupils in 42 Selected New York State School Districts: 1968[1]

District	Number	% of Enrollment	% of State Total	District	Number	% of Enrollment	% of State Total
New York City	356,392	31.9	72.01	Schenectady	950	7.3	a
Buffalo	26,356	36.8	5.33	Elmira	902	6.4	a
Rochester	13,679	28.9	2.76	Troy	899	12.3	a
Syracuse	6,365	20.9	1.29	Nyack	846	23.2	a
Mount Vernon	6,336	51.4	1.28	Ossining	845	15.4	a
Hempstead	4,159	71.4	.84	Bellport	796	18.2	a
Yonkers	3,698	12.0	.75	Middle Island	693	23.7	a
Albany	3,685	30.7	.74	Long Beach	617	9.8	a
Niagara Falls	2,986	16.2	a	Glen Cove	600	11.2	a
Newburgh	2,925	23.0	a	Beacon	598	17.6	a
Roosevelt	2,751	70.4	a	Kingston	583	5.3	a
New Rochelle	2,569	20.8	a	Southampton	442	23.8	a
Freeport	2,117	28.5	a	Geneva	319	9.4	a
Wyandanch	2,110	91.6	a	Rockville Centre	250	5.7	a
Westbury	2,008	39.8	a	Bridgehampton	210	55.6	a
Poughkeepsie	1,940	32.7	a	Suffern	73	1.4	a
Amityville	1,855	40.9	a	Peconic	6	22.2	a
Utica	1,715	11.8	a	Total 42 Districts	462,091	29.8	93.37
White Plains	1,637	18.3	a	All Other Districts	32,828	1.8	6.63
Malverne	1,378	47.4	a	State Total	494,919	14.5	100.00
Greenburgh	1,359	32.6	a				
Spring Valley	1,264	8.3	a				
Riverhead	1,260	29.7	a				
Peekskill	967	29.0	a				
Lackawanna	951	16.2	a				

[1]Data from BEDS, NYSED, 1969.
[a]Less than 0.7 percent.

pupils in the State in 1968. Among the forty-two districts under study are three other large city systems that had over 1,000 Puerto Rican pupils: Rochester with 1,553, Yonkers with 1,323, and Buffalo with 1,276. The district with the next highest number was Newburgh with 374, followed by Glen Cove with 295 and White Plains with 224. Ten of the districts had between 100 and 200 Puerto Rican pupils, twenty-two had Puerto Rican pupils numbering less than 100, and three had none. Table 8 lists all forty-two districts and shows the number of Puerto Rican pupils in each. In most of the districts, Puerto Ricans constituted a negligible proportion of the total pupil population. [*]

Concentration by Proportions Within Districts

Perhaps more important than numbers is the proportion of minority group pupils in a school population, shown for the same forty-two districts in Table 9, according to the proportion of Negroes and Puerto Ricans combined. The two groups are taken together because they share a common problem of estrangement from the main stream of society. [**]

As Table 9 shows, there were six districts in the State in which minority group pupils were the majority: that is, they exceeded 50 percent of the total public school population. Three other districts had between 40 and 50 percent minority group pupils; eight had between 30 and 40 percent, and ten had between 20 and 30 percent. A total of twenty-seven districts had more than 20 percent Negro and Puerto Rican students.

As Table 9 also shows, districts ranged in size from a handful of pupils in Peconic, a one-teacher district in Suffolk County, to over a million in New York City. Fifteen districts

---

[*]It should be noted that no systematic review was made to determine districts characterized by high Puerto Rican populations or Puerto Rican isolation in individual schools. Although 96 percent of the Puerto Rican pupils in the State are included in this sample, there may be districts that have more pronounced concentrations than those on the list.

[**]On proportion of Negroes alone, New York City would rank twelfth in the State instead of fifth. Similarly, Peekskill would rank fifteenth instead of eleventh, Beacon twenty-seventh instead of twenty-second, Troy thirty-first instead of thirty-fifth, and Glen Cove thirty-fourth instead of thirtieth. No other significant changes in rank order occur as a result of the combination of Negroes and Puerto Ricans.

TABLE 8

Puerto Rican Pupils in 42 Selected New York State School Districts: 1968[1]

Districts	Number	% of Enrollment	% of State Total	District	Number	% of Enrollment	% of State Total
New York City	260,963	23.3	93.11	Wyandanch	46	2.0	a
Rochester	1,553	3.3	.55	Geneva	45	1.3	a
Yonkers	1,323	4.3	.47	Schenectady	44	.3	a
Buffalo	1,276	1.8	.46	Roosevelt	43	1.1	a
Newburgh	374	2.9	.13	Riverhead	37	.9	a
Glen Cove	295	5.5	.11	Albany	30	.2	a
White Plains	224	2.5	a	Middle Island	25	.9	a
Mount Vernon	173	1.4	a	Niagara Falls	24	.1	a
Long Beach	171	2.7	a	Amityville	22	.5	a
Freeport	163	2.2	a	Greenburgh	21	.5	a
Beacon	162	4.8	a	Suffern	21	.4	a
Lackawanna	155	2.6	a	Nyack	12	.3	a
Utica	155	1.1	a	Poughkeepsie	11	.2	a
Peekskill	153	4.6	a	Troy	9	.1	a
Hempstead	102	1.8	a	Malverne	6	.2	a
Bellport	101	2.3	a	Elmira	5	a	a
Spring Valley	101	.7	a	Bridgehampton	0	0	0
New Rochelle	85	.7	a	Southampton	0	0	0
Ossining	85	1.6	a	Peconic	0	0	0
Westbury	73	1.4	a	Total 42 Districts	268,281	17.3	95.72
Rockville Centre	69	1.6	a	All Other	11,994	.6	4.28
Kingston	62	.6	a	State Total	280,275	8.2	100.00
Syracuse	62	.2	a				

[1] Data from BEDS, NYSED, 1969.

[a] Less than 0.1 percent.

69

TABLE 9

Selected New York State School Districts Ranked
by Proportion of Negro and Puerto Rican Students: 1968[1]

Rank	District[a]	County	Total Pupils	% Negro & P. R.	Rank	District	County	Total Pupils	% Negro & P. R.
1	WYANDANCH*	Suffolk	2,304	93.6	22	BEACON	Dutchess	3,393	22.4
2	HEMPSTEAD*	Nassau	5,828	73.2	23	PECONIC	Suffolk	27	22.2
3	ROOSEVELT*	Nassau	3,906	71.5	24	NEW ROCHELLE	Westchester	12,331	21.5
4	BRIDGEHAMPTON	Suffolk	378	55.6	25	SYRACUSE*	Onondaga	30,428	21.1
5	NEW YORK CITY		1,118,676	55.2	26	WHITE PLAINS*	Westchester	8,964	20.8
6	MOUNT VERNON*	Westchester	12,332	52.8	27	BELLPORT*	Suffolk	4,377	20.5
7	MALVERNE*	Nassau	2,905	47.6	28	LACKAWANNA	Erie	5,865	18.8
8	AMITYVILLE*	Suffolk	4,531	41.4	29	OSSINING	Westchester	5,473	17.0
9	WESTBURY*	Nassau	5,040	41.2	30	GLEN COVE*	Nassau	5,364	16.7
10	BUFFALO*	Erie	71,665	38.6	31.5	NIAGARA FALLS*	Niagara	18,426	16.3
11	PEEKSKILL*	Westchester	3,340	33.6	31.5	YONKERS	Westchester	30,794	16.3
12	GREENBURGH*	Westchester	4,174	33.1	33	UTICA	Oneida	14,581	12.9
13	POUGHKEEPSIE	Dutchess	5,937	32.9	34	LONG BEACH*	Nassau	6,279	12.5
14	ROCHESTER *	Monroe	47,372	32.2	35	TROY	Rensselaer	7,292	12.4
15	ALBANY*	Albany	12,010	30.9	36	GENEVA*	Ontario	3,383	10.7
16	FREEPORT*	Nassau	7,429	30.7	37	SPRING VALLEY*	Rockland	15,283	9.0
17	RIVERHEAD	Suffolk	4,240	30.6	38	SCHENECTADY*	Schenectady	12,928	7.6
18	NEWBURGH	Orange	12,720	25.9	39	ROCKVILLE CENTRE*	Nassau	4,373	7.3
19	MIDDLE ISLAND*	Suffolk	2,925	24.5	40	ELMIRA*	Chemung	14,126	6.4
20	SOUTHAMPTON	Suffolk	1,860	23.8	41	KINGSTON	Ulster	10,926	5.9
21	NYACK*	Rockland	3,651	23.5	42	SUFFERN*	Rockland	5,104	1.8

[1]Data from BEDS, NYSED, 1969.

[a]All districts with more than 20 percent Negro enrollment except special districts, districts with schools with more than 31 percent Negro enrollment in 1966 or 1968, districts receiving State Aid for Correcting Racial Imbalance in 1966, 1967 or 1968.

*Received State Aid for Correcting Racial Imbalance.

had more than 10,000 pupils, eleven between 5,000 and
10,000, fourteen between 1,000 and 5,000, and two less than
1,000. The district with the highest proportion of minority
group pupils, Wyandanch with 93.6 percent, had an enrollment
of 2,304. The second highest district, Hempstead, with 73.2
percent, had 5,828 pupils. New York, the largest district
with more than a million pupils, ranked fifth in proportion of
minority group pupils.

As for location, also shown in Table 9, the forty-one
districts outside New York City are located in seventeen
counties. The majority, twenty-six of the forty-one, are in
the New York City Metropolitan area: eight in Nassau County,
eight in Suffolk County, seven in Westchester County, and
three in Rockland County. Only six of the districts--Pough-
keepsie, Newburgh, Beacon, Geneva, Elmira, and Kingston--
are outside some metropolitan area, and four of these are in
the Hudson River Valley, within ninety-five miles of New York
City.

Thirteen of the districts, including New York City, are
urban centers in metropolitan areas. Four of these cities--
Mount Vernon, New Rochelle, White Plains, and Yonkers--are
in Westchester County. Five of the urban center districts had
over 30 percent Negro and Puerto Rican students: New York
City, Mount Vernon, Buffalo, Rochester, and Albany.

The districts with the highest proportions of minority
group pupils are on Long Island. Nassau and Suffolk counties
combined had thirteen of the twenty-seven districts with more
than 20 percent Negro and Puerto Rican pupils. Seven of the
sixteen districts on Long Island had more than 40 percent
Negroes and Puerto Ricans, and six other Long Island districts had between 20 and 40 percent.

This analysis clearly shows that concentrations of minority group pupils are not the problem of large city school systems alone. They exist in districts large and small, urban
and suburban, and in some smaller districts the proportions
of minority group pupils are many times larger than they are
in all but the very largest school districts.

Comparisons with Surrounding Districts

A further measure of the concentration of minority groups
lies in the contrast between the proportion of them in one
school district and that in neighboring school districts. Table
10 shows the proportions of Negroes and Puerto Ricans in the
forty-two selected districts in 1968, the proportions in the

TABLE 10

Comparison of Minority Proportions in 42 Selected School Districts with
Minority Proportions in Counties of Location and All Other Districts in Those Counties: 1968[1]
(Counties Arranged by Standard Statistical Metropolitan Areas;
Districts Ranked within Counties by Minority Proportion)

Area	% Minority[a]	Area	% Minority[a]	Area	% Minority[a]
NEW YORK CITY SMSA		Suffolk County (cont'd.)		Schenectady County	3.5
New York City	55.2	Bridgehampton	55.6	Schenectady	7.6
Westchester County	14.4	Amityville	41.4	6 Other Districts	.5
Mount Vernon	52.8	Riverhead	30.6	Rensselaer County	4.1
Peekskill	33.6	Middle Island	24.5	Troy	12.4
Greenburgh	33.1	Southampton	23.8	12 Other Districts	1.2
New Rochelle	21.5	Peconic	22.2	UTICA-ROME SMSA	
White Plains	20.8	Bellport	20.5	Oneida County	4.3
Ossining	17.0	64 Other Districts	5.3	Utica	12.9
Yonkers	16.3	BUFFALO SMSA		18 Other Districts	1.5
39 Other Districts	5.3	Erie County	13.7	OUTSIDE SMSAs	
Rockland County	6.9	Buffalo	38.6	Chemung County	4.0
Nyack	23.5	Lackawanna	18.8	Elmira	6.4
Spring Valley	9.0	27 Other Districts	.4	2 Other Districts	.5
Suffern	1.8	Niagara County	6.7	Dutchess County	8.2
6 Other Districts	4.6	Niagara Falls	16.3	Poughkeepsie	32.9
Nassau County	6.2	9 Other Districts	2.1	Beacon	22.4
Hempstead	73.2	ROCHESTER SMSA		11 Other Districts	2.9
Roosevelt	71.5	Monroe County	11.5	Ontario County	2.9
Malverne	47.6	Rochester	32.2	Geneva	10.7
Westbury	41.2	17 Other Districts	.9	8 Other Districts	1.1
Freeport	30.7	SYRACUSE SMSA		Orange County	10.6
Glen Cove	16.7	Onondaga County	6.6	Newburgh	25.9
Long Beach	12.5	Syracuse	21.1	17 Other Districts	5.3
Rockville Centre	7.3	17 Other Districts	.4	Ulster County	6.1
49 Other Districts	2.0	ALBANY-SCHENECTADY-TROY SMSA		Kingston	5.9
Suffolk County	7.6	Albany County	8.8	8 Other Districts	6.3
Wyandanch	93.6	Albany	30.9		
		12 Other Districts	1.2		

[1]Data from BEDS, NYSED, 1969

[a]Negro and Puerto Rican combined.

72

counties in which the districts are located, and the agglomera-
ted proportion in all other districts in those counties. The
counties are arranged by Standard Metropolitan Statistical
Areas so that these data may be compared with information
given at the beginning of this chapter on general population
trends in New York State. District enrollment figures and the
percentages of pupils in each of the two minority groups, Negro
and Puerto Rican, are shown in Table 42 in the Appendix.

With two exceptions, the proportions of minority group
pupils in the selected districts were, in 1968, several to many
times greater than those in surrounding districts. The most
striking examples are in Erie, Onondaga, Monroe, Albany,
and Nassau counties. In Erie County, Buffalo had 38.6 percent minority group pupils, and Lackawanna had 18.8 percent;
the other twenty-seven districts in the county together had
0.4 percent. In Onondaga County, Syracuse had 21.1 percent
minority group pupils; the other seventeen districts had 0.4
percent. In Monroe County, Rochester had 32.2 percent minority group pupils; the other seventeen districts had 0.9 percent. In Albany County, the City of Albany had 30.9 percent
minority group pupils; twelve other districts together had 1.2
percent. In Nassau County, eight school districts had minority group percentages ranging from 7.3 to 73.2, with highs of
73.2 percent in Hempstead, 71.5 percent in Roosevelt, 47.6
percent in Malverne, and 41.2 percent in Westbury. The
other forty-nine districts in Nassau County had 2.0 percent
minority group pupils.

The two exceptions to the generalization about district
contrasts within counties were in Rockland County and Ulster
County. In Rockland County, Nyack had 23.5 percent minority
group pupils, Spring Valley had 9.0 percent, and Suffern had
1.8 percent; the other six districts in the county had 4.6 percent minority group pupils, a higher proportion than in Suffern.
In Suffern, however, there was one school with more than 31
percent Negro pupils in 1966, for which reason it was included
in this study. The second exception in Ulster County arises
from a similar situation: Kingston, with only 5.9 percent
minority group pupils in 1968 had one school with more than
31 percent Negro pupils in 1966 and was included in this
study for that reason. The other districts in Ulster County
had 6.3 percent minority group pupils but no high concentrations in individual schools.

Another interesting contrast is evidenced in the proportion of minority group pupils in "other districts" in the upstate

metropolitan areas as opposed to those in the New York City
Metropolitan Area. In the four counties near New York City--
Westchester, Rockland, Nassau, and Suffolk--there were 5.3
percent, 4.6 percent, 2.0 percent, and 5.3 percent minority
group pupils, respectively. In four of the eight counties in
the other metropolitan areas--Erie, Monroe, Onondaga, and
Schenectady--the proportion of minority group pupils in the
other districts was less than 1 percent.

The contrasts between minority group proportions in high
concentration districts and in surrounding districts are further
evidence of what has been described as the polarization of the
American society into two societies, black and white (NACCD,
1968). The data already presented on trends in the general
population and data on trends in school district populations to
be discussed in the following section indicate that these contrasts will become more pronounced unless steps are taken
to counteract them. Some efforts toward mitigating the urban-
suburban contrast through pupil exchange are discussed in
Chapter 5.

Changes in School District Size and Minority Status

All of the forty-two districts under consideration experienced changes in enrollment between 1966 and 1968, the year in
which the most recent data available were collected: (1)
Thirty-four districts increased in total enrollment over the
two-year period; eight districts decreased. (2) Twenty districts lost white students; twenty-two districts increased in
numbers of white students. (3) Thirty-seven districts gained
Negro pupils; five lost Negro students. (4) Thirty-two districts added Puerto Rican students; eight lost Puerto Rican
pupils; and two remained without any. (5) The proportion of
Negro and Puerto Rican pupils increased in thirty-six districts; in six it declined.

Table 11 shows the total enrollment of each district for
the three successive years, the percentage of Negro and
Puerto Rican students in each year, and the direction of changes
in total enrollment and in the size of each of the ethnic groups.
Enrollment figures and proportions for each ethnic group in
each district are given in Tables 43, 44, 45, and 46 in the
Appendix.

The growth in 12 school districts is accounted for by increases in Negro or Negro and Puerto Rican enrollments
alone. Only two districts increased because of white gains

TABLE 11

Changes in School District Size and Ethnic Proportions
of 42 Selected School Districts: 1966-68[1]
(Districts Ranked by Percent Negro and Puerto Rican in 1968)

District	Total Enrollment			% Negro and Puerto Rican			Change in Numbers, 1966-68			
	1966	1967	1968	1966	1967	1968	Total	Other	Negro	Puerto Rican
Wyandanch	2,255	2,253	2,304	83.7	87.4	93.6	+	-	+	-
Hempstead	5,306	5,497	5,828	68.6	71.1	73.2	+	-	+	+
Roosevelt	3,676	3,846	3,906	53.4	60.0	71.5	+	-	+	+
Bridgehampton	404	389	378	50.5	50.6	55.6	-	-	+	0
New York City	1,084,818	1,105,549	1,118,676	50.2	52.0	55.2	+	-	+	+
Mount Vernon	12,059	12,964	12,332	46.0	48.7	52.8	+	-	+	+
Malverne	2,999	2,911	2,905	44.6	46.9	47.6	-	-	+	-
Amityville	4,496	4,499	4,531	36.4	37.5	41.4	+	-	+	+
Westbury	5,044	5,078	5,040	34.3	36.9	41.2	-	-	+	+
Buffalo	72,762	72,692	71,665	36.2	36.9	38.6	-	-	+	+
Peekskill	3,244	3,322	3,340	29.1	29.9	33.6	+	-	+	+
Greenburgh	2,989	3,073	4,174	36.7	38.2	33.1	+	+	+	+
Poughkeepsie	5,811	5,809	5,937	27.4	28.4	32.9	+	-	+	+
Rochester	45,365	46,570	47,372	28.4	30.1	32.2	+	-	+	+
Albany	12,991	12,674	12,010	28.4	29.1	30.9	-	-	-	+
Freeport	7,262	7,334	7,429	22.9	26.0	30.7	+	-	+	+
Riverhead	3,898	4,211	4,240	28.8	30.0	30.6	+	+	+	+
Newburgh	11,531	12,204	12,720	23.4	24.2	25.9	+	+	+	+
Middle Island	2,854	2,868	2,925	29.3	26.5	24.5	+	+	-	+
Southampton	1,784	1,710	1,860	21.7	23.9	23.8	+	+	+	-

(Continued)

TABLE 11 (Continued)

District	Total Enrollment			% Negro and Puerto Rican			Change in Numbers, 1966-68			
	1966	1967	1968	1966	1967	1968	Total	Other	Negro	Puerto Rican
Nyack	3,584	3,589	3,651	22.6	23.8	23.5	+	+	+	-
Beacon	3,173	3,227	3,393	22.9	23.4	22.4	+	+	-	+
Peconic	24	30	27	41.7	40.0	22.2	+	+	-	0
New Rochelle	12,273	12,581	12,331	17.9	19.7	21.5	+	-	+	+
Syracuse	30,650	30,862	30,428	17.6	19.4	21.1	-	-	+	+
White Plains	8,831	8,867	8,964	17.1	17.6	20.8	+	-	+	+
Bellport	3,849	4,023	4,377	19.0	21.1	20.5	+	+	+	+
Lackawanna	5,644	5,742	5,865	17.9	18.9	18.8	+	+	+	+
Ossining	5,183	5,525	5,473	14.3	15.0	17.0	+	+	+	+
Glen Cove	5,025	5,234	5,364	13.4	13.5	16.7	+	+	+	+
Niagara Falls	19,043	18,860	18,426	15.1	15.8	16.3	-	-	+	-
Yonkers	29,475	30,296	30,794	13.7	14.6	16.3	+	+	+	+
Utica	15,120	14,869	14,581	10.9	11.5	12.9	-	-	+	+
Long Beach	6,089	6,195	6,279	9.8	11.4	12.5	+	+	+	+
Troy	6,827	6,865	7,292	11.7	11.8	12.4	+	+	+	-
Geneva	3,195	3,325	3,383	10.9	10.4	10.7	+	+	+	+
Spring Valley	12,366	14,327	15,283	7.2	8.4	9.0	+	+	+	+
Schenectady	12,409	12,624	12,928	7.0	7.3	7.6	+	+	+	+
Rockville Centre	4,201	4,314	4,373	4.9	6.4	7.3	+	+	+	+
Elmira	13,870	14,151	14,126	5.6	6.3	6.4	+	+	+	-
Kingston	10,089	10,495	10,926	5.2	5.6	5.9	+	+	+	+
Suffern	4,286	4,908	5,104	3.2	3.0	1.8	+	+	-	-

[1]Data from BEDS, NYSED, 1969.

76

alone.   The decrease in five school districts is due to white
losses and in two others to white and Puerto Rican losses.
Negroes contributed to an over-all loss of students in only one
district.

The eight districts that ran counter to the statewide trend
of increased enrollments were the five city districts of Buffalo,
Albany, Syracuse, Niagara Falls, and Utica and three Long
Island districts, Bridgehampton, Malverne, and Westbury.
These eight districts had Negro and Puerto Rican enrollments
ranging from 10.9 percent to 50.5 percent in 1966.

Fifteen of the twenty districts that lost white pupils are
included in the sixteen districts with the highest proportion of
Negro and Puerto Rican students in 1968; all had more than 20
percent minority group enrollment in 1966.   The only district
of the top group to gain white pupils was Greenburgh, which
increased in over-all size by merging with another district.
The other five districts that lost white pupils were urban center districts that had substantial numbers, although somewhat
lower proportions, of Negro and Puerto Rican students--New
Rochelle, Syracuse, White Plains, Niagara Falls, and Utica.

The relationship between the proportions of Negro and
Puerto Rican pupils in the study districts and loss or gain of
white pupils in the study districts between 1966 and 1968 is an
interesting one.   With Greenburgh excluded because of its
merger, the correlation between rank order on minority group
proportions in 1966 and rank order on loss of white pupils over
the two-year period is 0.54 for the 41 districts (p < .01).   High
proportions of minority pupils are associated with high losses
of white pupils.

An increase in Negro pupils was the common experience
of most of the districts.   The five districts that lost Negro
pupils were the smallest suburban district, Peconic; two
other suburban districts, Middle Island and Suffern; and two
city districts, Albany and Beacon.   The loss of Negro pupils
lowered the proportion of Negroes in the district in only four
cases, Peconic, Middle Island, Suffern, and Beacon.

Except in New York City, Puerto Ricans made up a very
small proportion of the total school enrollments of the forty-
two districts.   Of the thirty-two districts that gained Puerto
Rican pupils, two, White Plains and Albany, reported none in
1966.   The districts in which Puerto Rican increases affected
the proportion of minority group pupils in the total school population to any marked degree--that is, raised it by more than
1 percent--were New York City, Rochester, White Plains,
Ossining, Glen Cove, Yonkers, and Rockville Centre.

The consequence of all of the changes that took place was the increase in the proportion of minority group pupils, Negroes and Puerto Ricans, in thirty-six of the districts and the decline of that proportion in six other districts.

The school district changes may be further analyzed in regard to the extent of the changes that occurred and the number of pupils involved. Table 12 shows the percentage changes in total enrollment, "Others," Negroes, and Puerto Ricans in the forty-two districts from 1966 to 1968.

The largest percentage increases in total enrollment were in three suburban districts, Greenburgh, Spring Valley, and Suffern. The Greenburgh increase, as noted elsewhere, was largely due to a merger with another district. The biggest numerical increases were 34,000 in New York City, 2,900 in Spring Valley, and 2,000 in Rochester. The largest percentage losses, 7.6 and 6.4, occurred in Albany and Bridgehampton; the largest numerical losses, 1,100 and 1,000, occurred in Buffalo and Albany.

Percentage losses for white pupils ranged from 1 percent to 59.2 percent. The highest was in Wyandanch, the district with the largest proportion of Negro pupils. A similarly high loss, 35.2 percent, occurred in Roosevelt, the third-ranking district in respect to proportion of minority group pupils. In four other districts, the white loss was 10 percent or more of the white enrollment in 1966; in nine districts it was between 5 and 10 percent. Numerically, the New York City loss was the greatest, 39,000 white pupils, and exceeded the increase in Negroes in New York City, though not the increase in the minority groups combined. White increases ranged from 0.2 percent to 50 percent; the largest percentage increase was in the smallest district. High percentage increases were coupled with high numerical increases in Spring Valley, which gained 2,400 "Others", and Suffern and Greenburgh, which gained about 900 "Others" each.

Increases in Negro enrollments, occurring in thirty-seven districts, ranged from 2.9 percent to 50.3 percent. The largest were in Spring Valley, 50.3 percent, and Roosevelt, 43.3 percent. Spring Valley is a fast-growing suburban school district, showing an increase in the population of white pupils amounting to more than 21 percent and an over-all increase of nearly 24 percent. Roosevelt, on the other hand, lost better than 35 percent of its white pupils while gaining 6 percent in total enrollment. In general, there is a tendency for large losses in white pupils to be associated with large increases in minority pupils, but, as evidenced here, the

TABLE 12

Changes in Total Enrollment and Ethnic Groups in
42 Selected School Districts: 1966-68[1]
(Districts Ranked by Minority Status in 1968)

| District | Total | Percent Change | | | District | Total | Percent Change | | |
		Other	Negro	P.R.			Other	Negro	P.R.
Wyandanch	+ 2.2	-59.2	+14.7	- 4.2	Beacon	+ 6.9	+ 7.6	- 1.5	+ 33.9
Hempstead	+ 9.8	- 5.0	+16.3	+ 56.9	Peconic	+12.5	+50.0	-40.0	a
Roosevelt	+ 6.3	-35.2	+43.3	+ 2.4	New Rochelle	+ 0.5	- 4.1	+18.2	+ 254.2
Bridgehampton	- 6.4	-16.0	+ 2.9	a	Syracuse	- 0.7	- 5.4	+17.9	+1450.0
New York City	+ 3.1	- 7.3b	+12.2	+ 15.2	White Plains	+ 1.5	- 3.5	+ 8.5	e
Mount Vernon	+ 2.3	-10.8	+15.7	+143.7	Bellport	+13.7	+11.7	+20.4	+ 42.3
Malverne	- 3.1	- 7.7	+ 3.5	- 14.3	Lackawanna	+ 3.9	+ 3.4	+ 3.7	+ 66.7
Amityville	+ 0.8	- 7.3	+14.6	+ 15.8	Ossining	+ 5.6	+ 2.5	+15.3	+1114.3
Westbury	d	-10.0	+17.6	+180.8	Glen Cove	+ 6.7	+ 3.3	+23.7	+ 57.8
Buffalo	- 1.5	- 5.2	+ 4.1	+ 20.9	Niagara Falls	- 3.2	- 4.5	+ 4.6	- 14.3
Peekskill	+ 3.0	- 3.4	+17.1	+ 29.7	Yonkers	+ 4.5	+ 1.6	+12.2	+ 77.6
Greenburgh	+39.6	+47.0	+24.2	+950.0	Utica	- 3.6	- 5.7	+15.0	+ 2.0
Poughkeepsie	+ 2.2	- 5.5	+22.2	+266.7	Long Beach	+ 3.1	+ 0.2	+38.7	+ 11.0
Rochester	+ 4.4	- 1.0	+14.4	+ 65.6	Troy	+ 6.8	+ 5.9	+14.2	- 10.0
Albany	- 7.6	-11.1	- 0.2	c	Geneva	+ 5.9	+ 6.2	+ 2.9	+ 15.4
Freeport	+ 2.3	- 7.8	+34.2	+ 83.1	Spring Valley	+23.6	+21.4	+50.3	+114.9
Riverhead	+ 8.8	+ 6.0	+14.0	+117.6	Schenectady	+ 4.2	+ 3.4	+13.1	+ 46.7
Newburgh	+10.3	+ 5.8	+19.0	+ 57.1	Rockville Centre	+ 4.1	+ 1.5	+26.9	+ 885.7
Middle Island	+ 2.5	+ 9.4	-17.1	+2400.0	Elmira	+ 1.8	+ 1.0	+16.8	- 16.7
Southampton	+ 4.3	+ 1.5	+14.2	-100.0	Kingston	+ 8.3	+ 7.4	+15.4	+169.6
Nyack	+ 1.9	+ 1.3	+ 6.3	- 7.7	Suffern	+19.1	+22.4	-35.4	- 8.7

[1]Data from BEDS, NYSED, 1969.

aNo Puerto Rican pupils in district.

bIncludes American Indians and Orientals

cChange from 0 to 30 pupils.

dLess than 0.1 percent.

eChange from 0 to 224 pupils.

relationship is only moderate and there are numerous exceptions to the trend.   The districts with the largest numbers of
Negroes had the largest numerical increases in Negro enrollment: 39,000 in New York City, 1,700 in Rochester, 1,000
in Buffalo, 1,000 in Syracuse, 900 in Mount Vernon, 800 in
Roosevelt, 600 in Hempstead, 500 in Freeport, and 500 in
Newburgh.

As for decreases in Negro enrollments, the highest percentage loss was in the smallest district and involved only
four pupils.   The districts in which the losses were significant
in terms of both numbers and proportions were Middle Island,
where the Negro enrollment dropped from 836 to 693, and
Suffern, where it dropped from 113 to 73.

Because their numbers outside New York City were small,
increases in Puerto Rican enrollment are drastically large
when expressed in percentages: many of the thirty-two districts in which Puerto Rican enrollment increased show gains
of several hundred percent.   In actual number, the New York
City gain was the greatest, over 34,000.   Rochester and
Yonkers gained about 600 each, White Plains and Buffalo about
200 each.

The enrollment changes in the forty-two districts affirm
the generalization that when there is a substantial concentration of Negroes in a school system, the proportion of Negroes
in that system is likely to rise through a combination of Negro
increases and white losses.   This generalization holds true
for suburban as well as urban districts.

The enrollment changes also make it clear that the achievement of integration and equal education will require continuing
effort.   The growth trends in the schools, as in the total population, augur greater, not less, concentration of minority
groups.

Isolation within Districts

The numbers and proportions of Negroes and Puerto
Ricans in a school population are but two indicators of possible
segregation.   In the last analysis, equality of educational opportunity must be measured, in part, by the racial or ethnic
composition of the schools.

To ascertain this mix of pupils, all elementary and secondary schools in the forty-two districts were placed in ten
categories according to the percentage of "Other" pupils enrolled: Category I, 0 to 10.9 percent "Others"; Category II,

11 to 20. 9 percent "Others"; and so forth through Category X,
91. 0 to 100 percent "Others. " Category I schools, with 0-10. 9
percent "Others, " are those with the highest proportion of
minority group pupils, at least 89 percent; Category X schools
are those with the fewest, 9 percent or less. A low proportion
of "Others" is indicative of racial or ethnic isolation; higher
proportions of "Others" indicate that some measure of ethnic
balance has been achieved.

In 1968, more than 50 percent of the Negro and Puerto
Rican pupils in the forty-two districts were in Category I, in
which they made up with more than 89 percent of the enrollments. Another 29 percent of the Negroes and Puerto Ricans
were in schools in Categories II through V, in which they made
up 89 percent to 49 percent of the enrollments. Altogether,
79 percent of the minority group children, 576, 000, attended
school where they were in the majority. The remaining 21
percent, some 154, 000 Negro and Puerto Rican pupils, were
distributed in schools with higher percentages of "Others, "
though only 1 percent of the Negro and Puerto Rican pupils
were in Category X schools with less than 9 percent minority
group pupils.

Table 13 gives the percentages and the actual numbers of
children in schools with varying proportions of "Others" in
1968 and similar data for 1967. In the forty-two districts
combined, the number of Negro and Puerto Rican pupils in
Category I, the most segregated schools, increased by nearly
24 percent in 1968. The numbers in the next two categories
declined slightly, but those in Categories IV and V increased.
The net result was an increase in the number of minority
group pupils in schools with less than 51 percent "Others"--in
schools that are racially imbalanced if an arbitrary 50 percent
dividing line is used as the criterion. Thus, there was an intensification of ethnic isolation in the schools of New York
State in 1968. The most significant fact shown by Table 13
is that the increase in the number of minority group pupils in
Category I schools alone was greater than the increase in
Categories I through V combined, approximately 70, 000 as
compared to 64, 000. This clearly indicates that ethnic isolation was intensified most severely in those schools that already
had large proportions of Negro and Puerto Rican pupils.

While statewide figures establish the magnitude of the
problem of ethnic isolation, it is again necessary to examine
the individual districts to determine just where and under
what circumstances it occurs.

TABLE 13

Distribution of Negro and Puerto Rican Pupils in 42 Selected School Districts in Schools with Various Proportions of "Others":[a] 1967 and 1968[1]

School Category Based on Percent of "Others" in Schools		Number of Negroes and Puerto Ricans		Percent Negro and Puerto Rican	
		1967	1968	1967	1968
I	0 - 10.9	296,576	366,361	43.5	50.2
II	11 - 20.9	87,118	74,566	12.8	10.2
III	21 - 30.9	49,496	45,024	7.3	6.2
IV	31 - 40.9	46,404	51,736	6.8	7.1
V	41 - 50.9	32,802	38,270	4.8	5.2
I - V	0 - 50.9	512,396	575,957	75.2	78.9
VI	51 - 60.9	40,514	30,905	5.9	4.2
VII	61 - 70.9	40,836	38,184	6.0	5.2
VIII	71 - 80.9	35,321	42,939	5.2	5.9
IX	81 - 90.9	39,898	34,105	5.9	4.7
X	91 - 100	12,126	8,282	1.8	1.1
I - X	0 - 100	681,091	730,372	100.0	100.0

[1]Data from BEDS, NYSED, 1969.

[a]Pupils not reported as Indian, Negro, Spanish-Surnamed-American, or Oriental.

Because New York City, having more than half a million Negro and Puerto Rican pupils, presents a situation unmatched by any other district, it will be treated separately. Attention will then be given to the forty-one other school districts studied.

Minority Group Pupils in New York City Schools

Table 14 shows the distribution of minority group pupils in New York City schools with varying proportions of "Others" in 1967 and 1968. In 1968, 55 percent of the Negro and Puerto Rican pupils were in Category I schools; nearly 85 percent were in Categories I through V combined. The 338,000 children in the Category I schools in the City of New York made up 44 percent of all Negro and Puerto Rican pupils in public elementary and secondary schools in New York State.

In one year, 1967 to 1968, the proportion of Negro and Puerto Rican pupils in Category I schools rose from 47 percent to 55 percent. Both white losses and Negro and Puerto Rican increases account for this intensification of isolation in New York City schools. The growth trends in New York City's school population leave no doubt that the isolation will be even greater when the next report is made.

Minority Group Pupils in Other Districts

Full information on the numbers and proportions of Negro and Puerto Rican pupils in schools in each of the forty-two districts is given by Category in Tables 47 and 48 in the Appendix. The following analysis of data on the forty-one districts outside of New York City will focus on Category I schools with an overwhelming majority of minority group pupils, schools in Categories I through V with a majority of minority group pupils, and changes in levels of isolation.

Overwhelming Majorities of Minority Group Pupils

In both 1967 and 1968, eight of the forty-one districts outside New York City had Negro and Puerto Rican pupils in Category I schools. Another district joined this group in 1968, while one eliminated Category I schools after 1967. All nine districts are listed in Table 15.

TABLE 14

Distribution of Negro and Puerto Rican Pupils in New York City
Schools with Various Proportions of "Others":[a] 1967 and 1968[1]

School Category Based on Percent of "Others" in Schools		Number of Negroes and Puerto Ricans		Percent Negro and Puerto Rican	
		1967	1968	1967	1968
I	0 - 10.9	270,313	337,902	47.0	54.7
II	11 - 20.9	79,985	68,176	13.9	11.0
III	21 - 30.9	42,660	37,135	7.4	6.0
IV	31 - 40.9	39,988	46,353	6.9	7.5
V	41 - 50.9	28,331	33,579	4.9	5.4
I - V	0 - 50.9	461,277	523,145	80.1	84.7
VI	51 - 60.9	29,829	18,391	5.2	3.0
VII	61 - 70.9	28,861	26,180	5.0	4.2
VIII	71 - 80.9	23,979	27,283	4.2	4.4
IX	81 - 90.9	25,779	18,986	4.5	3.1
X	91 -100	5,894	3,370	1.0	0.5
I - X	0 -100	575,619	617,355	100.0	100.0

[1]Data from BEDS, NYSED, 1969.

[a]Pupils not reported as Indian, Negro, Spanish-Surnamed-American, or
Oriental.

TABLE 15

Negro and Puerto Rican Pupils in Category I Schools in Districts
Outside New York City: 1967 and 1968[1]
(Districts Ranked by Minority Group Percent)

District	Number		Percent		Percent Minority Pupils in District	
	1967	1968	1967	1968	1967	1968
Wyandanch	709	2,156	36.0	100.0	87.4	93.6
Hempstead	2,481	2,619	62.5	61.5	71.1	73.2
Mount Vernon	1,256	1,751	19.9	26.9	48.7	52.8
Buffalo	16,832	16,614	62.9	60.1	36.9	38.6
Rochester	3,581	4,005	25.5	26.3	30.1	32.2
Albany	95	80	2.6	2.2	29.1	30.9
Newburgh	878	1,013	29.9	30.7	24.2	25.9
Niagara Falls	431	0	14.4	0	15.8	16.3
Utica	0	221	0	11.8	11.5	12.9

[1]Data from BEDS, NYSED, 1969.

85

Two of the nine districts in Table 15 are the suburban districts that have the highest proportions of minority group pupils, and seven are city districts that have total enrollments of over 12,000. Minority group enrollments in all these districts are large, ranging from more than 1,800 to nearly 28,000. All the districts show gains in minority-group pupils; all but one, Newburgh, show losses in white pupils.

In 1968 the proportions of minority-group pupils in Category I schools in these districts ranged from just over 2 percent to 100 percent. In six districts it was over 25 percent of the total minority population of the district. The extreme of 100 percent minority group pupils in Category I schools in Wyandanch corresponds to the high percentage of minority-group pupils in that district, nearly 94 percent. In Wyandanch and Mount Vernon, the proportions and numbers of pupils in Category I schools were substantially higher in 1968 than 1967.

Utica had no Category I schools in 1967 but had 11.8 percent of its minority-group pupils in Category II schools. As shown in Table 15, the same percentage was in Category I schools in 1968. By then the district had no Category II schools. This suggests intensified isolation in given schools. Niagara Falls, the one district that eliminated Category I schools, did so through a reorganization of school boundaries with State aid. This was accomplished in spite of a small increase in the proportion of minority-group pupils in the district.

Majorities of Minority-Group Pupils

Over the two years 1967-68, twenty-eight of the forty-one school districts had Negro and Puerto Rican pupils in Category I-V schools, schools with less than 51 percent "Others"-- schools in which, for all intents and purposes, the minority is the majority. There were twenty-seven such districts in 1967 and twenty-two in 1968. One new district showed increased isolation that brought it into the group of districts having schools in Categories I through V in 1968 while six districts had eliminated schools with more than 49 percent minority-group pupils. Table 16 lists the twenty-eight districts.

Of the twenty-two districts having schools with majorities of minority-group pupils in 1968, five had minority-group enrollments exceeding 50 percent of the total enrollment. For these districts, "majority" schools were, of course, inevitable unless there was a differential composition of the elementary school and secondary school enrollments, a greater

TABLE 16

Negro and Puerto Rican Pupils in Schools with Less
Than 51 Percent of "Others" by District: 1967 and 1968[1]

District	Number		Percent		Percent Minority Pupils in District	
	1967	1968	1967	1968	1967	1968
Wyandanch	1,970	2,156	100.0	100.0	87.4	93.6
Hempstead	3,689	3,943	92.9	92.5	71.1	73.2
Roosevelt	2,294	2,779	99.4	99.5	60.0	71.5
Bridgehampton	197	210	100.0	100.0	50.6	55.6
Mount Vernon	3,726	3,918	59.0	60.2	48.7	52.8
Malverne	454	730	33.2	52.7	46.9	47.6
Amityville	0	371	0	19.8	37.5	41.4
Westbury	326	774	17.4	37.2	36.9	41.2
Buffalo	19,820	19,811	74.0	71.7	36.9	38.6
Peekskill	169	368	17.0	32.9	29.9	33.6
Greenburgh	77	81	6.6	5.9	38.2	33.1
Poughkeepsie	640	1,062	38.7	54.4	28.4	32.9
Rochester	7,755	8,001	55.2	52.5	30.1	32.2
Albany	1,970	1,562	53.3	42.1	29.1	30.9
Newburgh	1,618	1,833	55.0	55.5	24.2	25.9
Nyack	274	0	32.0	0	23.8	23.5
New Rochelle	264	260	10.7	9.8	19.7	21.5
Syracuse	2,177	2,060	36.4	32.0	19.4	21.1
Lackawanna	869	867	80.1	79.4	18.9	18.8
Ossining	35	0	4.2	0	15.0	17.0
Glen Cove	96	115	13.6	12.8	13.5	16.7
Niagara Falls	570	324	19.1	10.8	15.8	16.3
Yonkers	1,219	1,366	27.6	27.2	14.6	16.3
Utica	201	221	11.8	11.8	11.5	12.9
Troy	277	0	34.0	0	11.8	12.4
Geneva	138	0	39.8	0	10.4	10.7
Elmira	206	0	23.0	0	6.3	6.4
Suffern	88	0	59.5	0	3.0	1.8

[1]Data from BEDS, NYSED, 1969.

proportion of minority-group pupils in the lower grades than in high school, for example. In the seventeen other districts with "majority" schools in 1968, the proportion of Negroes and Puerto Ricans in the total enrollment ranged from 12.9 to 47.6 percent.

In 1968, among the twenty-two districts, the proportions of minority-group pupils in schools with less than 51 percent "Others" ranged from 5.9 percent to 100 percent. Discrepancies between minority-group proportions in districts and in schools within districts are readily apparent in Table 16. For example, Buffalo had 38.6 percent Negro and Puerto Rican pupils, but more than 70 percent of these were in "majority" schools. Poughkeepsie, with 33 percent minority-group pupils, had 54 percent of them in "majority" schools. Newburgh had 26 percent minority-group pupils, but 56 percent were in "majority" schools; Lackawanna had 19 percent minority-group pupils with 79 percent in "majority" schools. In the cases cited, high proportions of each district's minority-group pupils were in schools characterized by ethnic isolation. In other districts, the proportions were smaller. Amityville, for instance, had 41 percent minority-group pupils, of whom only 20 percent were enrolled in "majority" schools; Greenburgh had 33 percent minority-group pupils, of whom 6 percent were in "majority" schools; New Rochelle had 21 percent minority-group pupils, of whom 10 percent were in "majority" schools. In these latter districts, ethnic isolation was less acute.

In eight of the school districts, the proportions of minority-group pupils in "majority" schools were higher in 1968 than in 1967. The sharpest increases were in Poughkeepsie, Westbury, Peekskill, Malverne, and Amityville, Amityville having had no pupils in "majority" schools in 1967. Eleven of the districts had lower proportions in "majority" schools in 1968 than in 1967. The biggest decreases were in Niagara Falls, from 19.1 to 10.8 percent; Albany, from 53.3 to 42.1 percent; and Syracuse, from 36.4 to 32.0 percent. These three districts received State Aid for Correcting Racial Imbalance, as did twelve other districts that continued to have "majority" schools. It should be noted that six city school districts with "majority" schools and large enrollments have never received State Aid for Correcting Racial Imbalance: Poughkeepsie, Lackwanna, New Rochelle, Newburgh, Yonkers, and Utica.

Six districts eliminated "majority" schools in 1968: Nyack, Ossining, Troy, Geneva, Elmira, and Suffern. The proportions of minority-group pupils in these districts ranged

TABLE 17

Districts with Change in Level of Minority Group Isolation: 1967 and 1968[1]

Decreases

District	Highest Category School	
	1967	1968
Malverne	IV	V
Nyack	V	VIII
Beacon	VI	VII
Peconic	VI	VIII
New Rochelle	IV	V
Bellport	VII	VIII
Ossining	V	VI
Niagara Falls	I	II
Troy	IV	VI
Geneva	IV	IX
Elmira	IV	VII
Kingston	VII	VIII
Suffern	V	X

Increases

District	Highest Category School	
	1967	1968
Amityville	VI	V
Peekskill	V	IV
Greenburgh	IV	III
White Plains	VIII	VII
Utica	II	I
Long Beach	VII	VI
Spring Valley	IX	VIII

[1]Data from BEDS, NYSED, 1969.

89

in 1968 from 1. 8 percent in Suffern to 23. 5 percent in Nyack.
However, the number of pupils in "majority" schools in these
districts in 1967 ranged from only 35 in Ossining to a high of
277 in Troy. The contrast with the numbers of pupils in "majority" schools in some other districts is obvious. Four of
these districts, Nyack, Geneva, Elmira, and Suffern received
State Aid for Correcting Racial Imbalance.

Changes in Levels of Isolation

The criterion for the level of isolation for a given district
is the highest category school in that district, that is, the
school with the largest proportion of minority-group pupils.
It does not involve the distribution of minority-group pupils
among category schools.

The level of minority isolation changed in 20 districts between 1967 and 1968; in 13 it decreased; in 7 it increased.
Table 17 shows the changes in level of isolation in the 20 districts where it occurred. Five of the thirteen decreases in
level of isolation are substantial, exceeding more than one
step--in Nyack, Troy, Geneva, Elmira, and Suffern. It should
be noted, however, that in the thirteen districts with decrease
in isolation, the number of pupils in schools with the higher
isolation levels in 1967 ranged from only 12 to 431; in only
one case was it over 300. All five districts except Troy received State Aid for Correcting Racial Imbalance.

Four of the seven districts in which the level of minority
isolation increased showed a loss of white students: Amityville, Peekskill, White Plains, and Utica. Long Beach and
Spring Valley, two other districts with increased levels, are
districts experiencing high percentage increases in minority
pupils.

SUMMARY AND CONCLUSIONS

In Chapter 2, attention has been given to population patterns in the Nation and in New York State that determine the
ethnic composition of the schools and to the current status of
school integration in the public schools of New York State.
Following are the most pertinent findings from this review:

1.   In a growing nation, the Negro population has been
increasing at a faster rate than has the white population.

Because of the higher birth rate and comparative youth of the Negro population, the proportion of Negroes in the country, already 11 percent, can be expected to continue to increase.

2.   Negro migration to the big cities, the high Negro birth rate, residential restrictions, and the exodus of whites to the suburbs have created large concentrations of Negroes in the urban centers of the Nation, where their proportions are much higher than in surrounding communities. Given the differential birth rates of whites and Negroes, the ethnic disparities between urban and suburban populations can be expected to intensify.

3.   Patterns of Negro concentration lead to increasingly large proportions of Negro pupils in some school systems and magnify the problem of integration. De facto segregation and racial isolation are increasingly prevalent in spite of Supreme Court rulings and efforts to assure equality of educational opportunity.

4.   New York State, which has in New York City the greatest aggregation of Negroes in the State and in the country, has had a threefold increase in its Negro population in 30 years. The number of nonwhites has grown from less than 600,000 to about 2 million, from less than 4.5 percent to more than 10 percent of the total population. In addition to its Negro minority, New York State has a Puerto Rican minority, which has been expanding rapidly. The more than one million Puerto Ricans in New York State make up nearly 6 percent of the total population. Given the relatively high birth rates of both Negroes and Puerto Ricans, the numbers and proportions of both Negroes and Puerto Ricans in the State can be expected to increase in the years ahead.

5.   Of all nonwhites and Puerto Ricans in New York State 75 percent and 95 percent, respectively, live in New York City. Concentrations of Negroes are also found in the urban centers of metropolitan areas throughout the State, in some suburban communities in the New York City Metropolitan Area, and in a few smaller cities close to New York City. In general, the smaller the population unit examined, the greater is the proportion of Negroes. That is, analysis by census tracts in large cities shows extremely high proportions of Negroes. With a continuation of current trends, the proportions of Negroes and Puerto Ricans in those areas in which they are now concentrated can be expected to rise. A particularly high rate of increase in the Negro population in Nassau and Suffolk counties will lead to an increasingly high proportion of the State's minority-group population on Long Island.

6.   The increase in the numbers and proportions of Negroes and Puerto Ricans in the State is reflected in an increase
in the numbers and proportions of minority-group pupils in the
public schools of the State. In 1968, Negroes and Puerto Ricans made up nearly 23 percent of the public school enrollment,
and this proportion can be expected to continue to increase.

7.   Reflecting the concentration of Negroes and Puerto
Ricans in certain areas, the largest numbers and proportions
of minority-group pupils are found in the large city school districts of the State; in a few suburban school districts in Nassau,
Suffolk, Westchester, and Rockland counties; and in a small
number of smaller city districts close to New York City. The
proportions of minority-group pupils in the smaller districts
are in some cases many times as high as those in the urban
districts. The proportions of minority-group pupils in districts showing high minority-group concentration are many
times as great as those in surrounding districts.

8.   During the two-year period studied, 1966-68, there
were increases in the numbers and proportions of the Negro
and Puerto Rican pupils in most of the forty-two school districts selected for analysis. In both urban and suburban districts having high proportions of minority-group pupils, there
was a concomitant loss of white pupils and in some cases a
decrease in total enrollment. High proportions of Negro pupils
were generally associated with white losses. Given the higher
birth rates of the minority groups, and the residential patterns
of Negroes, whites, and Puerto Ricans, the trend toward higher proportions of minority-group pupils in some districts can
be expected to continue.

9.   As the number and proportion of Negroes and Puerto
Rican pupils have risen, the number and proportion of minority-
group children in schools having more than 49 percent minority
pupils have grown. In one year, between 1967 and 1968, the
increase in the number and proportion of minority-group pupils
in nearly totally segregated schools (less than 11 percent
white) amounted to nearly 24 percent, or 70,000 pupils. The
proportions and numbers of Negro and Puerto Rican pupils in
schools with less than 51 percent white students showed increases, respectively of 3.7 percent or more than 64,000
pupils; the corresponding figures for minority pupils in 51
percent or more white schools showed a proportional decrease
of 3.7 percent or over 14,000 pupils between 1967 and 1968.
These facts, taken together, indicate that ethnic isolation in
the schools of New York State has increased and has been most
severely intensified in those schools that already had large proportions of Negro and Puerto Rican students.

10. The problem of ethnic isolation is of the greatest magnitude in New York City: more than half a million Negro and Puerto Rican pupils were in schools having more than 49 percent minority-group pupils in 1968; 338,000 pupils were in schools having more than 89 percent minority-group pupils. Growth trends in the New York City schools, with increases in Negroes and Puerto Ricans and attendant white losses, leave no doubt that ethnic isolation in the city will intensify.

11. There are school districts outside New York City that have equally high or higher proportions of minority-group pupils in schools having at least 89 percent Negroes and Puerto Ricans or having at least 49 percent minority pupils. Some of these districts have populations of more than 50 percent minority-group pupils, with the result that the achievement of an equitable ethnic balance by redistribution of pupils within the schools of the district is impossible. Though minority-group ratios within schools might be adjusted to conform to over-all proportions in these districts, accommodation with neighboring districts would be necessary to bring about an educationally desirable balance.

Other districts showing ethnic isolation--notably such city districts as Buffalo, Utica, Newburgh, Poughkeepsie, and Lackawanna--have high proportions of minority-group pupils in ethnically isolated schools but moderate proportions of minority-group pupils in their total enrollments. For these large districts, the possibility of achieving a more equitable ethnic balance in the schools appears to exist within the districts themselves.

12. Between 1967 and 1968, the level of ethnic isolation increased in some districts and decreased in others. In general, school districts that were able to reduce the level of ethnic isolation to any marked extent were those that had high minority-group concentrations in individual schools and a relatively low proportion of Negroes and Puerto Ricans in their total enrollments. When the proportion of minority-group pupils in a district is high, any lessening of ethnic isolation that occurs is apt to be undone as a result of the tendency for minority-group proportions to increase.

In summary, as Negro and Puerto Rican populations continue to increase and become more concentrated in given areas of the State, the problem of ethnic isolation in the schools becomes more intense. New and creative approaches involving interdistrict cooperation will be necessary if there is to be any enduring achievement of equality of educational opportunity.

CHAPTER **3** SOCIAL CLASS AND
ETHNIC STATUS:
RELATIONSHIP TO
INTELLECTUAL AND
EDUCATIONAL DEVELOP-
MENT AND RELATED
FACTORS

Robert P. O'Reilly

This chapter presents a review of selected research on
social class and ethnic relationships in relation to the following educational or psychological factors: intelligence, school
achievement, language development, special intellectual abilities, basic learning abilities, physical health, anxiety, achievement motivation, temporal orientation, self-esteem, and level
of aspiration. The intent is to provide a selective review of
major educationally relevant differences associated with social
class and ethnic group membership--as a background for interpretation of the research discussed in other chapters of this
volume.

One of the main purposes of this review is to identify more
or less typical differences in levels of intellectual and educational development associated with differences in ethnic group
membership or social class level. The review of other factors,
such as language development, special abilities, and basic
learning abilities, is intended to show some of the finer points
of the differences between students of different social class
levels and different minority groups. Knowledge of such differences is important when one attempts to understand why
typical measures of social class explain only part of the intellectual and achievement deficits of certain minority groups.
Findings of specific, probably largely culturally determined,
intellectual deficits associated with certain ethnic minorities
may also explain in part why certain kinds of compensations
typically made in educational programs have generally had only
slight effects on the educational development of students who
are members of these minority groups. Knowledge of gross

and specific educational deficits is also important when examining the findings of research relating racial and social class
isolation to intellectual development.

Further than this, knowledge of the relation of certain
personality variables to intellectual development is also important in the context of this study--if such factors have different implications as a function of social class level or ethnic
group membership. If this statement is true, as it seems to
be, for such educationally relevant factors as anxiety and
achievement motivation, then these factors become particularly relevant when the findings of the research on integration
and intellectual development are examined.

SOCIAL CLASS AND ETHNIC DIFFERENCES IN
INTELLECTUAL AND EDUCATIONAL DEVELOPMENT

Intelligence

Numerous studies document a low to low-moderate relationship between social class measures and IQ scores (correlations range from about .25 to 0.50). Differences between
social class groups vary over a range of one to two standard
deviations, or 15 to 30 IQ points (Jensen, 1969). It is usually
found that measures of IQ do not differentiate children of different social class levels under two years of age (Furfey, 1928;
Bayley and Jones, 1937; Knoblock and Pasamanick, 1960; Tyler,
1965), except in motor development (Jensen, 1969). After two
or three years of age, however, social class differences on
measures of intelligence become apparent, and they show an
increasing divergence with age (Dreger and Miller, 1968).

Racial differences occur in IQ test scores independent of
socio-economic differences, as documented recently by Jensen.
The results of a large number of studies show that there is a
median overlap of about 15 percent in the distributions of white
and Negro IQ scores, meaning that about 15 percent of the
Negro population exceeds the average IQ score for whites.
With social class differences controlled, the average difference
between Negro and white IQ scores reduces to about 11 points.
Negroes perform less well on tests of abstract abilities and
relatively better on verbal than on nonverbal intelligence tests
(Lesser, Fifer, and Clark, 1965; Jensen, 1969).

School Achievement

The fact that lower class children do not achieve as well as children in the upper class is generally substantiated in studies at the elementary school level (Engle, 1934; Knief and Stroud, 1950; Sheldon and Carillo, 1952; Granzow, 1954; Dimitz, Kay, and Reckless, 1958; Strodtbeck, 1958; Baker, Schutz, and Hines, 1961; Lovell and Woolsey, 1964; Cleveland and Bosworth, 1967; Hanson and Robinson, 1967), in junior high school and high school (Coleman, 1940; Sibley, 1942; Campbell, 1955; Miner, 1968), and among college students (Jenkins and Randall, 1948; Watson, 1965). The studies cited employed a variety of measures of school performance, including standarized achievement tests, school grades, teacher ratings, highest school grade attained, and average age for grade level.

Some evidence tends to indicate that social class background may be more important for achievement than intellectual ability. In studies in which the contribution of intelligence to achievement is controlled--that is, held constant--social class differences in achievement have been observed (Knief and Stroud, 1950; Campbell, 1955; Curry, 1962; Watson, 1965; Cleveland and Bosworth, 1967; Miner, 1968). The relative contributions of social class background and intellectual ability to achievement have been summarized by (McCandless, 1967):

> From the intelligence test differences between social classes, we would expect differences in school progress, middle- and upper-class children being expected to do better school work than lower-class children. The actual differences in academic achievement between social classes are even more dramatic than the differences in intellectual level. On the whole, lower-class children achieve less well in school than their intelligence tests predict they will, whereas middle- and upper-class children approach their academic potential more closely (p. 317).

There is some question about the effects of social class background on achievement for children having different ability levels. Curry (1962) compares the achievement performance of high and low ability sixth graders (IQs above and below 116) and reports social class differences in achievement in the low ability group but not in the high ability group. However, in a study of gifted children (McClelland, 1958), social class background differentiated subjects on a number of indexes of achievement and success after high school, although the sub-ject groups compared were equivalent on measured intelli-gence.

Racial differences in achievement (social class effects uncontrolled) are approximately of the same magnitude as the IQ score differences between whites and Negroes. The mas-sive data compiled by Coleman et al. (1966) indicate an aver-age difference of about one standard deviation between Negroes and whites in the Northeast at the sixth, ninth, and twelfth grade levels in the three areas of achievement shown in Table 18. Comparable data for Puerto Rican students are also shown.

The data in Table 18 indicate that the relative differences in verbal achievement of Negroes and whites are constant from the first grade through the twelfth. * This difference of about one standard deviation indicates that about 85 percent of Negro students begin school with verbal ability scores be-low the average score for whites and maintain this relative difference through the twelfth grade. Puerto Ricans begin with an even greater relative difference, though there is a tendency for this difference to decline slightly by the twelfth grade.

Although the relative differences between whites and Negroes shown in Table 18 remain roughly the same at differ-ent grade levels for the metropolitan Northeast, other data appear to indicate that these differences grow larger with successive grades. Table 19 presents data from the Coleman et al. report, showing the discrepancies in Negro and Puerto Rican grade level achievement relative to the achievement of whites in the metropolitan Northeast. These data appear to support the widely held thesis that Negro-white achievement differences show an increasing divergence with years in school. However, an examination of the relationship between grade equivalents and the corresponding standardized scores from the Coleman et al. report shows that this interpretation is inappropriate for certain Negro-white comparisons. ** For

---

*Data for earlier grade levels also indicate a difference of approximately one standard deviation in the achievement levels of whites and Negroes, metropolitan Northeast.

**Grade equivalents are based on norms and are somewhat analogous to mental age scores. For example, a grade equiv-alent of 3. 0 is assigned to the achievement score of the aver-age beginning third grader, and so on. The grade equivalents

TABLE 18

Verbal Ability, Reading Comprehension, and
Mathematics Achievement: Number of
Standard Deviations below the Mean for Whites
in the Metropolitan Northeast in Grades 6, 9, and 12[1]

	Verbal Ability	Reading Comprehension	Mathematics Achievement
Negro (Metropolitan Northeast)			
Grade 6	1.0	.8	1.1
Level 9	1.1	.9	1.0
12	1.1	.8	1.1
Puerto Rican			
Grade 6	1.7	1.4	1.5
Level 9	1.3	1.2	1.2
12	1.2	1.1	1.0

[1] Adapted from Coleman et al. (1966, pp. 274-75)

TABLE 19

Verbal Ability, Reading Comprehension, and
Mathematics Achievement: Number of
Grade Levels behind the Average for Whites
in the Metropolitan Northeast in Grades 6, 9, and 12[1]

		Verbal Ability	Reading Comprehension	Mathematics Achievement
Negro (Metropolitan Northeast)				
Grade Level	6	1.6	1.8	2.0
	9	2.4	2.6	2.8
	12	3.3	2.9	5.2
Change		(1.7)	(1.1)	(3.2)
Puerto Rican				
Grade Level	6	2.7	3.1	2.8
	9	2.9	3.3	3.4
	12	3.6	3.7	4.8
Change		(.9)	(.6)	(2.0)

[1] Adapted from Coleman et al. (1966, pp. 274-75).

example, the test score averages for Northern Negroes in
mathematics for the sixth, ninth, and twelfth grades (same
test at each grade level) were 22.0, 36.0, and 39, respectively; the corresponding scores for Northern whites were
34.1, 49.0, and 57.6, reflecting average Negro-white differences of 12.1, 13.0, and 18.6 points (all figures slightly more
than one standard deviation). The increases in the Negro-
white differences in scores were then 0.9 points between the
sixth and ninth grades and 5.4 points between the ninth and
twelfth grades. The corresponding grade equivalent differences by Coleman et al. are given as 2.0 years for the sixth
grade, 2.8 years for the ninth grade, and 5.2 years for the
twelfth grade (p. 275). Obviously, the achievement differences between Negroes and whites are relatively constant
from year to year, as shown previously in the Negro-white
and Puerto-Rican-white comparisons for the Northeast in
Table 18.

The approximately constant difference in the achievement
of Negroes and whites across grade levels is not maintained
when these groups are compared within geographical regions.
Figure 7 depicts the Negro-white achievement differences
within four geographical regions, based on the verbal ability
test data compiled by Coleman (1968, p. 20). The comparison
of whites in the urban Northeast with those in the rural South
shows the two groups beginning close together at the first
grade level and then diverging over the years of school. The
urban Negroes in the Northeast, compared with whites in the

---

shown in Table 19 do not actually reflect greater differences
in raw score means for the different ethnic groups with pro-
gressive grade levels. The disparity in the conclusions resulting from comparisons of differences among ethnic groups
in standard deviation and grade equivalent units is a function
of the fact that a standard deviation represents a smaller range
of grade levels at lower grades than at higher ones. The differences, however, are more apparent than real due to the
peculiar characteristics of the grade equivalent score. Similarly, comparisons of raw score increments or differences
between different groups at different grade levels (on the same
test) should not be made because of the noninterval characteristics of the scores. A more legitimate basis for making grade
to grade comparisons of group differences on the same test
would exist if such comparisons involved the use of percentile
ranks, standard deviation units, or standard scores (see Figure 7 in the subsequent discussion).

FIGURE 7

Achievement Levels in Verbal Skills
by Grade Levels, Race, and Region[1]

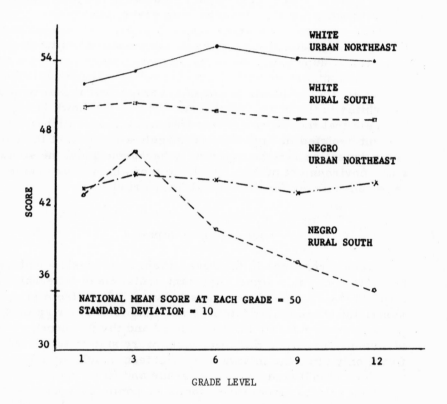

[1]From Coleman, J. S.   The Concept of Equality of Educational Opportunity.   Harvard Educational Review 38, 7-22
(1968).   Copyright by President and Fellows of Harvard College,
1968.   Reprinted by permission.

urban Northeast, begin further apart and remain about the
same distance apart, demonstrating again the constant grade
by grade differences between Negroes and whites in the Northeast. The most dramatic comparison, however, is that of
whites and Negroes in the urban Northeast with Negroes in
the rural South: here Negroes in the rural South and urban
North begin the first grade at about the same point below urban
whites in the Northeast; thereafter, Negroes in the rural
South increasingly diverge from both groups, ending up approximately two standard deviations below the average for whites
in the urban Northeast at the twelfth grade level.

     The regional comparisons shown in Figure 7 are among
the more dramatic illustrations of the results of cultural and
educational deprivation on certain ethnic minorities. The full
effect on Southern rural Negroes is rather staggering--placing
nearly all such students below the average verbal ability score
for whites in the urban Northeast. As will be shown later, it
is likely that the Negro-white differences in educational development depicted in Figure 7 are largely a function of the social
environment as reflected in family background and the social
class environment of the school, both of which offer decidedly
fewer advantages for the typical Negro student.

Language Development

     Recent research in the area of language development has
begun to illuminate some important social class differences.
Irwin (1948) reports differences between infants from professional and white collar families and infants of laboring class
parents in the number of sounds used and the frequency of use
of sound. However, the differences were statistically significant only after the infants were eighteen months of age.

     John (1963) compares first grade and fifth grade Negro
children selected from three socio-economic groups, a lower-
lowerclass group, an upper-lowerclass group, and a middle-
class group, on performance on measures of receptive and
expressive labeling. Social class differences were not found
among first grade children, but middle class fifth grade children achieved significantly higher scores on integrative tasks
than lowerclass fifth grade children. John concludes that acquisition of abstract and integrative language was hampered
by the living conditions in the homes of lowerclass children.

     Bernstein (1964), an English sociologist, propounds an
important new theory of social class language variation,

relevant to explaining the developing cognitive differences
among the social classes. He posited two major contrasting
types of communication codes, termed <u>restricted</u> and <u>elabo-
rated.</u> Restricted codes are employed in closed communication networks, in which the communication is primarily
support-providing, as in families, close friendship groups,
and English working class communities. Elaborated codes,
on the other hand, are used when specific information or meaning must be conveyed, as in giving directions to a stranger.
Elaborated codes are more complex, less redundant, and richer
in optional qualifications than restricted codes, which Bernstein
describes as syntactically redundant, elliptical, narrative, concrete, and relatively richer in vocal expressive features.

Restricted codes, or public language, were found to characterize the language of the lower socio-economic classes,
whereas elaborated codes, or formal language, were found to
characterize the language of the middle and higher socio-
economic classes. Bernstein apparently observed these class
differences in language in children as young as five years of
age, and he reports that the differences increased with increasing age.

Hess and Shipman (1965) conducted a series of investigations into the communications between Negro mothers and their
four-year-old children based on derivations from Bernstein's
theory. The mothers were divided into four different social
class levels: (1) college education, professional, executive,
and managerial occupational level with college education; (2)
skilled blue collar occupations; (3) unskilled or semiskilled
occupations with elementary school education; (4) unskilled
or semiskilled occupations with father absent or families supported by public assistance. The mothers were asked to teach
their children to do three tasks: to sort a group of plastic toys
by color and function, to sort blocks by two characteristics
simultaneously, and to copy five designs.

According to the authors, one of the most striking and
obvious differences between the environments provided by the
mothers was in language usage. Mothers from the middle class
gave protocols that were consistently longer in language pro-
ductivity than mothers from the other three groups. When the
quality of the language used by the mothers was assessed, it
was found that the middle class mothers used more abstract
words and more complex syntactical structure than did the
mothers of the other groups. When the mothers were asked
for responses to questions concerning what they would do in
dealing with hypothetical situations at school, upper class

mothers used a greater proportion of person-oriented statements while those of lower-status tended to use more status-
oriented statements. The classificatory behavior of the mothers
in the different social classes also differentiated the groups.
The middle class group was more descriptive and categorical,
whereas the low-status groups tended to employ simple rela-
tional classifications. According to the authors, these latter
responses of the latter group were usually given more quickly,
indicating less reflection and evaluation of alternatives, and
were often subjective. Children from middle class homes performed the sorting tasks much better than did children from
lower class homes, particularly in offering verbal explanations
for their sorts.

Hess and Shipman conclude that gross differences were
present in the verbal and cognitive environments offered by the
parents of differing social class levels. They identify one of
the educationally undesirable features in the interactions of the
working class mothers and their children as a tendency to act
without taking sufficient time for reflection and planning, a kind
of activity in which a particular act seems to be unrelated to the
act that preceded it or to its consequences, with the result that
the behavior lacks meaning. The authors describe some of the
possible effects of this kind of mother-child interaction as follows:

> . . . behavior is controlled by status rules rather
> than by attention to the individual characteristics
> of a specific situation and . . . behavior is not
> mediated by verbal cues or by teaching that relates
> events to one another and the present to the future.
> This environment produces a child who relates to
> authority rather than to rationale, who, although
> often compliant, is not reflective in his behavior,
> and for whom the consequences of an act are largely
> considered in terms of immediate punishment or
> reward rather than future effects and long-range
> goals (p. 885).

Strodtbeck (1965) discusses several factors affecting language development among the dependent poor in the great cities.
Comments elicited from Negro mothers receiving Aid to Families with Dependent Children indicated that the dependent, lower
class family could be characterized by (1) fear of neighbors,
(2) lack of social contacts because of fear, (3) frequent absence
of the father, (4) lack of organization of the roles of the family

members, and (5) disciplinary practices that seemed to be
based on a definition of good behavior emphasizing physical
inaction, verbal nonparticipation, and a state of being nonob-
servant. These factors appear to preclude establishment of
protracted verbal exploration possibilities of action on the part
of the family members, with the result that the family's language is characterized by restricted codes rather than elaborated codes.

Loban (1965) reports a study of the verbal learning of
children over a twelve-year period. He found that social class
was closely related to language development and that this relationship caused problems for the lower class child when he
was confronted with the demands of middle class society. Loban concludes:

> It . . . seems entirely possible that subjects from
> the least favored socio-economic categories can find
> themselves at a disadvantage in schools where the
> verbal linguistic skills of the middle class prevail.
> Such subjects may find themselves increasingly ill
> at ease and self-conscious to the point of avoiding
> oral performance. Such avoidance could, in turn,
> progressively affect performance in the related
> activities of reading and writing . . . (p. 128).

The lower class subjects in Loban's study exhibited a rigidity
of syntax, a limited and restricted use of structured possibilities for sentence organization, and a kind of condensed speech
in which certain meanings were restricted and the possibility
of their elaboration reduced.

In Great Britain, Jahoda (1964) selected primary and
secondary school boys from working class or middle class
homes. Matched pairs were formed at each age level, social
class level, and nonverbal intelligence level. At both the primary and secondary school levels, the vocabulary scores of
the working class children were significantly lower than those
of the middle class children. Moreover, the proportional differences between the fourteen-year-olds was greater than that
for the ten-year-olds.

The results of the research on language development generally indicate that the lower class disadvantaged child's language may be somewhat simpler in syntax, somewhat more
restricted in vocabulary, and somewhat poorer in descriptive
terms and modifiers than the language of the middle class child.
These and other differences apparently accrue from the gross

lack of verbal communication in the lower class home, as well as the nature of the communication. Lower class communication patterns tend to be characterized by commands and other short sentences and a heavy reliance on gestures (Deutsch, 1966). Although the exact functions of language in the development of complex thought are not yet clear, it does seem evident that language development plays an important role in certain kinds of problem-solving and concept-learning (Jensen, 1966), in learning to read (Ervin-Tripp, 1966), and in performance on tests of achievement and ability (Deutsch, 1966).

Special Abilities

The work of Guilford (1967) tends to show that the relationship of scores on special tests, such as clerical aptitude and the Thurstone Primary Mental Abilities tests, to occupational status is similar to that found in studies relating social class indexes to the more general ability factor measured by traditional intelligence tests. Dreger and Miller (1968), in a review of psychological studies of Negroes and whites, cite evidence of social class differences on tests of creativity, with upper status students scoring significantly higher on tests of originality and fluency.

Lesser, Fifer, and Clark (1965) measured verbal ability, reasoning, numerical ability, and space conceptualization in 400 young children grouped according to social class and ethnic group membership--Negro, Puerto Rican, Chinese, and Jewish. Significant social class differences were found, as shown in Figure 8--and there was no tendency for social class level to be associated with differential patterning of the four abilities measured in this study.

The most important results of the study were the findings of significant interactions between ethnicity and type of ability. Specifically, ethnic differences resulted in significant differences in both the patterning and the absolute level of each ethnic group. Absolute levels on the four abilities were significantly affected by social class within each ethnic group, but the ethnic patterns of ability levels remained essentially the same between social class levels. The ability patterns are as illustrated in Figure 9.

Differences in ability scores illustrated in Figure 9 are summarized as follows:

FIGURE 8

Mental Ability Scores for Two Social
Class Groups: Ethnic Groups Combined[1]

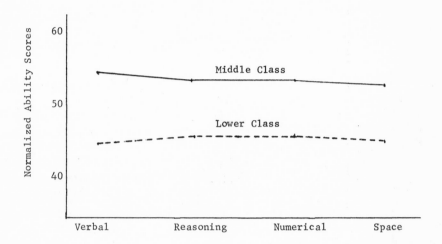

[1]From Lesser, G., Fifer, G., and Clark, D. "Mental
abilities of children from Different Social-Class and Cultural
Groups." Monographs of the Society for Research in Child
Development, Serial No. 102, 30. Chicago: University of
Chicago Press, 1965. p. 63. Copyright by University of Chicago
Press, 1965. Reprinted by permission.

FIGURE 9

Mental Ability Patterns by Ethnic Group[1]

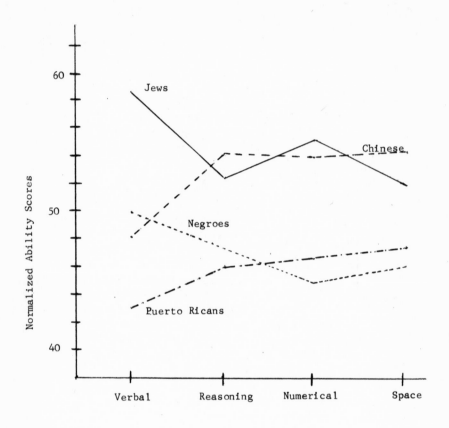

[1]From Lesser, G., Fifer, G., and Clark, D. "Mental Abilities of Children from Different Social-Class and Cultural Groups." Monographs of the Society for Research in Child Development, Serial No. 102, 30. Chicago: University of Chicago Press, 1965. p. 63. Copyright by University of Chicago Press, 1965. Reprinted by permission.

. . . (a) On verbal ability, Jewish children ranked
first (being significantly better than all other ethnic
groups), Negroes ranked second and Chinese third
(both being significantly better than Puerto Ricans),
and Puerto Ricans fourth. (b) On reasoning, the
Chinese ranked first and Jews second (both being
significantly better than Negroes and Puerto Ricans),
Negroes third, and Puerto Ricans fourth. (c) On
numerical ability, Jews ranked first and Chinese
second (both being significantly better than Puerto
Ricans and Negroes), Puerto Ricans third, and
Negroes fourth. (d) On space, Chinese ranked first
(being significantly better than Puerto Ricans and
Negroes), Jews second, Puerto Ricans third, and
Negroes fourth (p. 82).*

Additional findings of the study indicated two significant
interactions of social class and ethnicity on mental ability
levels but not on patterns. One of these indicated that the
social class factor produced more of a difference in ability
scores for Negroes than for the other ethnic groups. The
other interaction indicated that the mental ability scores of the
four ethnic groups were more alike within the middle class
group than in the lower class group. Based on their over-all
findings, Lesser, Fifer, and Clark reach the following conclusion:

These findings allow a reassessment of the various
proposed explanations of cultural influences upon
intellectual performance. The importance of the
mediators associated with ethnicity is to provide
differential impacts upon the development of mental
abilities, while the importance of the mediators associated with social class is to provide pervasive
(and not differential) effects upon the various mental
abilities (p. 83).

The results presented are inconsistent with the widely

---

*The ethnic ability patterns discovered by Lesser, Fifer,
and Clark were duplicated in another smaller sample of Negro
and Chinese children (Fort, J. G., Watts, J. C., and Lesser,
G. S., "Cultural Background and Learning in Young Children".
Phi Delta Kappan 50: 386-88 (1969).

held notion that, if certain disadvantaged ethnic groups could
be equated on a number of variables linked to social class
background variables, differences in intellectual performance
would virtually vanish. Clearly there may be more to it than
that. The evidence now available suggests that ethnic membership may be as salient as social class membership--or more
so--in determining the level and organization of children's mental abilities.

Direct evidence of either the cultural or hereditary factors
which may be responsible for this patterning of abilities by
ethnic group is not yet available (Jensen, 1968a). Indirectly,
however, there does seem to be reason to believe that such
patterning is at least in part due to cultural factors. It seems
likely that the Puerto Rican group would be subject to the greatest amount of interference in language development as a function of a bilingual family background as well as social and
economic disadvantagement (Lesser, Fifer, and Clark, 1965;
Coleman et al., 1966; Guilford, 1967), and this likelihood is
consistent with the fact that this group obtained the lowest mean
score in the verbal area. The Negro group must contend with
social and economic disadvantagement that may be peculiar
to it (Dreger and Miller, 1968), but there appears to be little
disadvantagement resulting directly from Negro dialects (Hall
and Mery, 1969). Preliminary observations by Fort, Watts,
and Lesser (1969) point to other cultural factors, such as an
emphasis on spatial activities and a corresponding relative
neglect of highly verbal activities in the Chinese family, extensive emphasis on verbal activities and occupations among
the Jews, and a relatively greater emphasis on verbal activities as contrasted with reasoning and numerical and spatial
skills in the Negro family.

In concluding this section on special abilities, it is of
some significance to note that the results of the research of
Lesser, Fifer, and Clark indicate that the Negro child is considerably more subject to the effects of social class differences
than are the other ethnic groups studied and that social class
exerts a more powerful influence for the Puerto Ricans than
for the Chinese. In attempting to explain this result, Lesser
and his associates offer two factors as an explanation:

> First, the lower class Negro group is more deprived
> in terms of . . . family stability. Second, the lower
> class Negro is a member of a more isolated lower
> class culture in which fewer models are available
> for educational aspirations. The lower class Negro

child is likely to lack contact not only with the cultural majority but with the middle-class Negro group
as well. In contrast, the Chinese child comes from
a more stable family unit . . . is a member of a
more unified cultural group in which value is placed
on education, and suffers less from isolation from
middle class models of his own ethnic origin. Thus
the disparity in the status of a middle- and lower-
class child in relation to the cultural majority is
perhaps much greater for Negroes than for Chinese
(p. 75).

Basic Learning Abilities

Research on basic learning abilities by Jensen (1968b) has
begun to illuminate some fundamental processes underlying the
ability to learn in different social class and ethnic groups.
Using tests that are largely independent of verbal mediational
processes and specific transfer from previous learning, and
thus largely independent of the cultural bias of traditional intelligence and achievement tests, Jensen analyzed the performance of children by social class and ethnic group. A
summary of the results relating basic learning ability to intelligence test scores for different social class groups is presented in Figure 10. These results show that basic learning
abilities are essentially unrelated to IQ scores in the low
socio-economic group but substantially in the high socio-economic group. This differential relationship by social class
level indicates that the learning ability measures and the IQ
test tend to measure the same function in the higher groups--
and IQ tests appear to be a poor index of learning ability for
lower class groups. The most important result reported,
however, is the finding that lower class children with low IQs
showed a wide range of learning ability scores, whereas the
middle class children with low IQs were invariably slow
learners.

In further findings reported by Jensen (1968b), a paired
associate learning test consisting of pictures of common ob-
jects was given to large numbers of children from Head Start
and to lower class and middle class children from kindergarten through sixth grade. The lower class group included
more than 90 percent Negroes. And results of the study
paralleled Jensen's earlier findings: lower and middle class
children differed only slightly on the learning ability tasks,

Figure 10

Summary Graph of Studies Showing Relationship between
Learning Ability (Free Recall; Serial, and Paired-Associate
Learning) and IQ as a Function of Socio-economic Status[1]

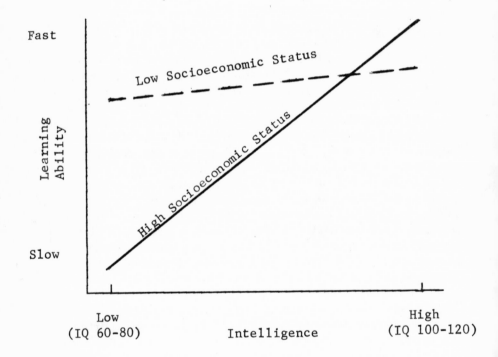

[1]From Jensen, A. R. "Social Class, Race and Genetics:
Implications for Education." American Educational Research
Journal 5: 34 (1968). Copyright by American Educational
Research Association, 1968. Reprinted by permission.

despite an average difference of 15 to 20 points in IQ scores
and even greater differences in school performance. In an
additional comparison, Head Start children with an average
Stanford-Binet mental age of four and a half were compared
with retarded adults with an average Stanford-Binet mental age
of ten, on the same learning task. The results showed that the
retarded adults were significantly slower learners than the
Head Start children.
 Interpreting these findings, Jensen explains:

 Basic learning abilities are measured by laboratory
 learning sets which involve little transfer from previous learning. Serial rote learning is a good example. A variety of short-term memory tests,
 including digit span, may prove to be the best means
 of measuring these basic abilities. Intelligence
 as measured by standard IQ tests consists of a res-
 ervoir of transferable knowledge and cognitive skills,
 most of which, I presume, have had to be acquired.
 The rate of acquisition is a function of the basic
 learning abilities and the opportunities afforded by
 the environment. In a good environment [middle
 class] we should therefore expect to find a very
 high correlation between learning ability and intelligence. Educability is the ability to learn school
 subjects by means of classroom instruction . . . .
 Raw learning ability is not directly converted to
 educability but serves educability through the agency
 of intelligence. To profit from ordinary classroom
 instruction, the learner must bring many developed
 skills to the situation: the voluntary control of attention, the perception of order, self initiated re-
 hearsal of newly acquired behavior, self reinforcement for successful performance, autonomous sym-
 bolic mediation, and a host of other processes . . . .
 In short, the learner himself must be able to act on
 the instructional input in order to master it. An intelligence test score is one indication of the degree
 to which a child has the equipment to act so as to be
 educable by ordinary means.
 It seems that it is in the lack of these cognitive
skills tapped by intelligence tests and required for
educability, rather than in basic learning abilities,

that culturally disadvantaged children differ from
typical middle class children. *

Jensen's results have been in some measure paralleled by
the findings of Cattell (1968) in the realm of crystallized and
fluid intelligence measures. His tests of fluid intelligence are
essentially nonverbal measures--of associative memory, fig-
ural relations, and intellectual speed, for example--and are
presumed to be the more direct measure of native intellectual
endowment. Crystallized intelligence is that which is measured by traditional intelligence tests and evidences the extent
to which the individual has acquired culturally relevant knowledge and skills. Cattell reports that his tests of fluid ability
do not differentiate among comparable samples from Britain,
Germany, France, and Italy and that there is only a slight correlation between fluid ability scores and social status. Measures of crystallized ability, on the other hand, tend to show
a higher degree of relationship to social status, comparable
to the degree of relationship found between social status and
other traditional measures of intelligence.
A partial explanation for the occurrence of large social
class differences in IQ and school achievement test results is
failure to recognize the basic learning abilities measured in
the tests used by Jensen and Cattell and a corresponding failure
of the school in adapting instructional procedures to social class
differences in ability patterns. One may speculate that, if the
schools continue to put heavy emphasis on cognitive (conceptual)
approaches to learning, social class differences will continue
to be evident and may even widen.

OTHER SOCIAL CLASS AND ETHNICALLY
LINKED DIFFERENCES

Other social class and ethnically linked differences relevant to effective learning in the school include such personality
variables as anxiety and achievement motivation, physical
health and educationally relevant attitudes, and values and aspirations. Certain limitations prevented more than a cursory,

---

*From Jensen, A. R., "Social Class, Race and Genetics:
Implications for Education". American Educational Research
Journal 5:36-37 (1968). Copyright by American Educational
Research Association, 1968. Reprinted by permission.

and to some extent unbalanced, review of these and other factors in this study. Such as it is, the review emphasizes most
heavily the relevant motivational factors associated with social
class, ethnic status, and intellectual growth or achievement.

Physical Health

Both Scrimshaw (1968) and Krech (1968) report that malnutrition, specifically the serious protein deficiency known as
kwashiorkor, may have a direct and irreversible effect on
brain development, resulting in permanent mental deficiency.
Less is known of the effects of milder degrees of malnourishment on mental development, the occurrence of which is more
common in the lower social strata of the United States. At
the very least, moderate degrees of malnourishment should
affect the child's ability to attend effectively in the instructional situation.

The results of studies on prematurity (Dreger and Miller,
1968) show that there is a 50 percent greater risk of prematurity among Negroes (50 percent) and among lower class whites
(somewhat less than 50 percent) than among middle class and
upper class whites, apparently related to nutritional factors.
The results of prematurity include marked neurological abnormalities among both white and Negro infants, and comparisons of premature and full term infants on Gessell's schedules
indicate significant differences in developmental levels, favoring the full term infants.

Anxiety

Since much is known about the relationships of anxiety to
achievement or intellectual development, it is appropriate to
first present a review of some of the basic factors present in
the anxiety-intellectual performance relationship. Somewhat
detailed treatment of this factor seems to be indicated because
anxiety is a key element in psychological theory and seems to
be more consistently and strongly related to school achievement and intellectual development than other nonintellective
characteristics (Ruebush, 1963; O'Reilly, 1969). Furthermore, anxiety is linked with social class (Ruebush, 1963) and
ethnic status (Phillips, 1966), and it appears that there is
reason to believe that anxiety plays a more detrimental role

in regard to the achievement of socially and economically disadvantaged groups than of the more advantaged segments of
society.

Anxiety and Achievement

There is an extensive amount of research indicating a
negative relationship between questionnaire and other indexes
of anxiety and intelligence and achievement test scores. Relatively recent reviews indicate that the negative relationship
between anxiety and achievement test or intelligence test performance exists at all elementary grade levels (S. B. Sarason
et al., 1960; Ruebush, 1963) and at the high school and college
levels (I. G. Sarason, 1960; O'Reilly, 1966). There are a
few exceptions to this general trend (Kerrick, 1956; Wirt and
Broen, 1956; Ruebush, 1963), and the extent of the negative
relationship varies from study to study (Ruebush, 1963; O'
Reilly, 1966). Recent longitudinal studies (Sarason, Hill, and
Zimbardo, 1964; Hill and Sarason, 1966) show that the negative relationship between anxiety and achievement test performance increased over the school years, was highest with
test scores involving verbal skills, and was unexpectedly high
when achievement levels were examined for students with very
high test anxiety and defensiveness scores (achievement differences between students showing high and low anxiety were as
high as two or three years in grade equivalent reading scores).
Although school or instructional variables have not been directly investigated in the work of Sarason et al. (1960), Sarason,
Hill, and Zimbardo (1964), and Hill and Sarason (1966), conclusions made on the basis of informal observation, correla-
tional patterns by grade level, and theorizing have led to
tentative identification of some of the dimensions that may
significantly increase anxiety in the learning setting and thus
affect the child's achievement and intellectual growth. Also,
a number of experimental studies tend to support the dimen-
sional analysis of Hill and Sarason and, at the same time,
suggest certain types of research concerning interactions of
anxiety and learning task variables on school achievement.

Anxiety and the Learning Task

The hypothetical and empirical relationships among anxiety, learning task variables, and intellectual performance are
somewhat illuminated by considerations of other personality
characteristics and behaviors of the child who is anxious in

school. According to Sarason et al. (1960), such a child pos-
sesses major unresolved dependency needs that require that
he maintain a reasonable level of positive rapport with significant adults, notably his teacher. He is presumed to be especially threatened by negative reinforcement of personal
inadequacies and by external pressure to perform learning
tasks in school without substantial emotional and cognitive support. These notions of the dependency needs of anxious children have been supported by informal classroom observation
(Sarason et al., 1960), objective research (Ruebush, 1963),
and clinical reports (Hill and Sarason, 1966).

The school learning dimensions linked to elicitation of
anxiety in school children by Sarason et al. (1960) and Hill and
Sarason (1966) include the social-emotional elements involved
in the student-teacher relationship and the presence of learning discontinuities in the organizational and curricular structure of the elementary school. Learning discontinuities more
specifically refer to "natural" variations in task difficulty resulting in part from discrepancies between the student's abilities and the requirements of school learning tasks, ordinarily
presented on schedule without careful attention to the readiness factor. There is some suggestive evidence to indicate
that the difficulty of school learning tasks tend to be "moderate,"
particularly when ability grouping is in effect (Atkinson, 1965).
Procedures used in the construction of standardized achievement tests and the well constructed teacher-made tests also
tend to result in mean item difficulties around 50 percent
(moderate difficulty). These definitions of task difficulty are
interpretable relative to abilities, and the latter are thus important considerations in studies and experiments focused on
anxiety and task difficulty. Other, perhaps more objective,
definitions of task difficulty may include some elements of the
test-like character of school tasks and tests proposed by
Sarason et al. (1960) and the cognitive and/or conceptual level
of requirements of different kinds of intellectual tasks. Again,
it appears that the latter elements of task difficulty are interpretable in relation to ability as well as anxiety.

Experimental analogues of elements of interpersonal dimension discussed by Hill and Sarason have been investigated
in a number of researches reviewed by I. G. Sarason (1960).
Some major generalizations were made on the basis of this
review: (a) highly anxious subjects were more affected in
their intellectual performance by motivating conditions or
failure reports than low subjects whose anxiety level was low;
(b) highly anxious subjects did not differ from subjects whose

anxiety level was low in their intellectual task performance under experimentally manipulated neutral or nonthreatening conditions, and (c) highly anxious subjects were found to be more self-deprecating, more self-preoccupied, less content with themselves, and more responsive to reassurance in experimental situations than subjects whose anxiety was low. More recent research (Winkel and Sarason, 1964; Diamond, 1965; Meisels, 1967) and reviews (Costello, 1964; Eysenck, 1964) consistently support the generalization that relatively mild threat and evaluative statements in the academic and test situations serve to elicit anxiety and effect a decrement in intellectual performance.

A number of studies have been reported by Sarason et al. (1960), which were directed chiefly at determining the relationship of test anxiety scores to performance on different kinds of tests or tasks. The experimental tasks used in these investigations were judged to differ in test-like character. Criteria applied in placing tasks near the least test-like end of the dimension included the following: (a) the game-like nature of the task; (b) the presence of a supportive individual in the test situation to whom the testee could turn for help; and (c) a lack of verbal and mathematical components in the test itself. Criteria used in placing tasks near the more test-like end of the dimension included these: (a) the use of stated time limits for completion of the task; (b) the presence of such verbal and mathematical components in the task as are found in standardized intelligence and achievement tests; and (c) the presence of an authoritative individual in the testing situation who might be perceived by the testee as serving a primarily evaluative function. An additional and important criterion related to the test-like dimension is ambiguity, which may be grossly defined as a lack of explicit structure in the task. For example, the open-ended responses required in the unstructured Rorschach testing situation would be expected to elicit anxiety and thus affect the quality of the responses made by the anxious testee. Based on this analysis of the test-like character of different tasks, test anxiety scores for different samples of children were related to performance on several tests or tasks judged to differ in regard to one or more of the defining characteristics of the test-like dimension described above.

In a study by Zwiebelson (1956) scores on two tasks, one more test-like than the other, are correlated with children's scores on the Test Anxiety Scale. As predicted, the correlations between test anxiety scores and scores on the more

test-like task were negative and significantly larger than those
obtained with the less test-like task.   Another study by Lighthall et al. (1959) indicates that children who are highly anxious in a test situation gain significantly more over time on a
less test-like task (Davis-Eels Games) than do children whose
anxiety level is low.   Other findings reported by Sarason et al.
indicated that (a) there was a tendency for highly anxious children to be more illogical or irrational in responses to Rorschach cards;   (b) in a figure drawing test, subjects scoring
high on anxiety drew figures that were more rigid, unsmiling,
and, in general, lacking in spontaneity;   (c) highly anxious
children were significantly more cautious on an embedded
figures test;   and (d) highly anxious children made significantly
more errors on a color naming task.

Related to the work of Sarason et al. (1960) on the test-
like nature of intellectual tasks are the studies of anxiety and
problem-solving reviewed by Ruebush (1963).   The findings of
twenty-one studies reviewed were consistent with those on anxiety and achievement test performance.   In general, the research shows that anxiety tends to impair children's performance on verbal and nonverbal problem-solving and learning
tasks.   Some of the tasks used in these studies included jig-
saw puzzles (Smock, 1957), the Witkin Ability Scale (Granick,
1955), and word completion and artificial language (Waite,
1942).   There is some suggestion that subjects characterized
by high and low anxiety do not differ significantly in their performance on learning and problem-solving tasks involving relatively simple cognitive processes, such as learning paired-
associates (Sarason et al., 1960) and simple discriminations
(Stevenson and Odom, 1965) but do differ significantly when
performance involves more complex cognitive process, such
as concept formation (Stevenson and Odom, 1965) and reading
comprehension as opposed to vocabulary growth (Neville,
Pfost, and Dobbs, 1967).

Amplification of the notion of task difficulty in anxiety research is provided in studies by Grimes and Allinsmith (1961)
and Gifford (1964).   In the Grimes and Allinsmith study, task
difficulty in the school learning task was defined in terms of
a complex concept termed structure.   Structured learning involves certainty in meaning;   definiteness of form;   sequential
introduction of the elements of the learning material so that
new learning is based on prior learning of fundamental facts,
skills, and principles;   and the provision of carefully defined
rules for proceeding in the learning task.   In a similar analysis
of the relationship of anxiety and learning task dimensions,

Gifford emphasized the relevance of appropriate practice in related tasks prior to performance of unfamiliar and more difficult tasks.

In their research, Grimes and Allinsmith assumed that the phonics and "look-say" approaches to reading instruction contained relatively disparate emphases on the dimension of structure. For example, the phonics, or structured, method is characterized by a gradual sequential development of skills for attacking words--such as sound-letter associations and rules for syllabication--taught through much drill and practice until the child begins to utilize the skills automatically in reading. Eventually, when the skills are thoroughly learned, the teaching of rules and skills is subverted to the more complex functions of comprehension and practice in reading. In the look-say, or unstructured, method, the teaching of skills and rules for attacking words is incidental to the actual process of reading, which begins with the recognition and memorization of whole words. Generally, skills taught by this method emphasize such procedures as making trial responses to unfamiliar words and making intelligent guesses based on contextual clues. From this analysis, it was predicted highly anxious and compulsive children would achieve at a higher level under structured methods of teaching reading than similar children under unstructured methods of teaching reading.

The sample for this study was composed of third grade boys and girls from two groups of schools, one of which emphasized phonics in reading instruction and the other of which emphasized the look-say method. Subjects were ranked high, low, and medium on compulsivity; anxiety; and combinations of anxiety and compulsivity and grouped for the structured and unstructured schools. The dependent variable was the discrepancy between predicted and attained achievement-- with IQ as a predictor, or control variable--on a standardized test measuring both reading and arithmetic skills. In addition to the control for IQ, an attempt was made to separate structure in the reading task from the possible effects of the social-emotional relationship between student and teacher on anxiety and achievement test performance. Observers judged teachers in the structured schools to be more impersonal and demanding, or relatively low on warmth and support, as compared to teachers in the unstructured schools.

The results indicated an interactive effect of anxiety and structured-unstructured teaching methods on achievement. Highly anxious children achieved at a significantly higher level in the structured schools than the similarly constituted group

in the unstructured schools. No significant effect of anxiety
on achievement was found in structured schools, but in unstructured schools, this effect was significant and in the predicted direction. The results also showed that anxiety and
compulsivity tended to combine to produce a further positive
effect on achievement in the structured schools.

Further support for the hypothesis that anxiety may not
interfere with performance in intellectual tasks under special
conditions was obtained in studies by Gifford (1964) and Hill
and Sarason (1966). Gifford gave anxious and nonanxious
fourth grade boys practice and no practice in the form of a
reading pretest and then administered another test that contained different reading material but was structured in the
same way. Anxious subjects performed at a significantly lower reading speed than nonanxious subjects on the second test
under the no practice condition, but there was no effect for
anxiety under the practice condition.

In the Hill-Sarason research, it was noted that instruction
tended to be discontinuous in the extent to which structure was
present in teaching reading at the primary and intermediate
grade levels of the elementary school. It was also noted that
the teacher-student relationship involved less reassurance
and involved a heavier emphasis on evaluation beginning approximately at the third and fourth grades. The results of
this research were consistent with observations indicating
instructional and interpersonal discontinuities in the reading
task. The absolute values of the negative correlations between
reading achievement and anxiety for the same students were
very low and nonsignificant at the second grade level but increased gradually from the third grade on. At the fifth grade
level, the correlation was approximately - .50 for a subsam-
ple of boys.

Anxiety, Other Intrapersonal Variables, and Intellectual Performance

There is growing evidence that the effects of anxiety on
achievement and other forms of intellectual performance are
partly dependent on ability and other intrapersonal variables.
The Grimes and Allinsmith study suggests that achievement
is facilitated in structured schools if the child is both anxious
and compulsive. The research of Hill and Sarason (1966)
shows that the predictive validity of anxiety scores is enhanced
if children's defensiveness scores are taken into account. A
number of studies, reviewed below, suggest that intellectual

abilities may be important determinants of the interfering
effects of anxiety on achievement and performance on intellectual tasks.

Sarason et al. (1960) conclude from their extensive research on children's anxiety that in the bulk of cases in which
there is a negative relationship between anxiety and intelligence, subjects scores on IQ tests fall within the average
range, 90-110. A similar conclusion is drawn from a longitudinal study by Hill and Sarason (1966). Feldhusen and Klausmeier (1962) clarify this relationship further in their report
on a study specifically designed to investigate the relationship
among IQ, achievement, and anxiety scores. In this study,
forty children with IQs of from 56 to 81, forty children with
IQs of from 90 to 110, and forty children with IQs of from 120
to 146 were used in an analysis of the relationships among
anxiety scores, IQ, and standardized achievement test scores.
Manifest anxiety scores reported for the high, average, and
low IQ groups were 12.0, 14.8, and 20.2, respectively. Differences between the average and low anxiety groups and the
high and low anxiety groups were significant. Correlations
between anxiety scores and achievement by IQ levels showed
that for subjects in the intermediate IQ range, three of four
correlations between anxiety and achievement were significant
and negative; for the low group, only one of the correlations
reached significance. The same comparisons for the highest
IQ group were nonsignificant.

A few studies with college students lend further support
to the results with children that suggest an interaction of anxiety and ability on academic performance. Denny (1962) hypothesized an interaction between IQ and anxiety on college
students' performance with a complex concept formation task.
Fifty-six males were used in an analysis of combinations of
anxiety (high-low) and intelligence (high-low). The results
indicated that high anxiety facilitated the performance of subjects with high IQs but impaired the performance of subjects
with low IQs. In a smaller study, Speilberger (1962) found
(a) that college students of low IQ earned poor grades, irrespective of anxiety scores; (b) that highly anxious students
in the mid-range of abilities obtained lower grades and had a
higher percentage of academic failure than students whose
anxiety was low; and (c) that the performance of students
superior in ability was apparently facilitated by anxiety.

Based on the studies reviewed here and elsewhere (I. G.
Sarason, 1960; Ruebush, 1963; Hill and Sarason, 1966), it
appears that anxiety relates negatively to indexes of school

achievement as well as to a variety of other indexes of intellectual performance. Recent evidence (Sarason et al. , 1960; Hill and Sarason, 1966; Phillips, 1966) supports the contention that anxiety has debilitating effects on intellectual performance but that the extent of this decrement seems to be a function of abilities of the subject as well as other intrapersonal variables and conditions present in the learning or testing task.

The learning task conditions under which anxious students may perform as well as, or perhaps even better than, nonanxious students include the presence of a warm, supportive teacher-student or administrator-testee relationship as opposed to an evaluative or achievement-motivating atmosphere and a nonambiguous or highly structured learning task in which task difficulty is made relatively low as a function of insuring that positive transfer occurs at various steps in the learning task and in which other well-known principles of learning are used. Such systematic structuring of the learning task is not ordinarily present in the school learning situation. The typical school learning situation may thus tend toward a moderate level of task difficulty. Such moderate levels of difficulty present in school learning and testing situations may create conditions productive of strong anxiety and avoidance reactions (Atkinson, 1965), and these factors may be more important in determining the effects of anxiety on intellectual performance than negative interpersonal elements of the learning situation (Grimes and Allinsmith, 1961).

For the socially and economically disadvantaged child, the typical school learning environment must present an unusually imposing set of stressful or anxiety-inducing circumstances. In general, students from the lower social strata lack the social behaviors appropriate to the typical school learning environment (Clausen and Williams, 1963), and thus they face a greater probability of social rejection, depending upon the prevalent socio-cultural context of the school (Phillips, 1966). A more important cause of debilitating anxiety for the disadvantaged student appears to stem from an initial and substantial discontinuity between his intellectual development in the family environment and the academic demands in the typical public school context. There is little reason to believe that such discontinuities are substantially mitigated by current educational techniques designed to compensate for an inadequate family background (Gordon and Jablonsky, 1968a), and for this reason it may be reasonably expected that learning discontinuities become increasingly relevant factors as the disadvantaged child continues in school.

For the lower class Negro child, the typical school learning environment may reasonably be viewed as even more stressful than it is for a lower class white child. Whether he enters a segregated school with middle class Negro teachers or a white middle class school, the Negro child is likely to be more subject to adverse stimulation as a function of social class disparagement in the former case (Proshansky and Newton, 1968) or as a function of conditioned anxiety associated with dominant white middle class figures in the latter case. Evidence from a series of studies by Katz (1964) provides convincing evidence that the white examiner or teacher is himself a threatening stimulus by the Negro student. When this source of arousal is added to all others potentially existing in the school or the individual--testing, social rejection, unfamiliar and difficult learning materials, lack of relevant educational training in the family--it becomes apparent that the Negro student may be subjected to many more sources of emotional interference than other disadvantaged groups. Although this question has received little study, there is evidence that relative to the typical white student, the typical Negro elementary school child is more anxious; experiences more failure, especially in the early elementary grades; has more pronounced feelings of inferiority, and shows more signs of maladaptive withdrawal from the academic situation (Phillips, 1966). There is also evidence that, among both lower class Negro high school students and lower class white high school students, anxiety tends to be associated with fewer planned years of schooling and a lower number of years perceived as necessary for first occupational choice (Schmalzreid, 1967).

Evidence that disadvantaged minority groups may be subject to more debilitating interference from anxiety than middle class white children comes from a study by Phillips and Mc-Neil (1968). The results of this study show that non-Anglos (Negroes and Mexican-Americans) were more anxious about school situations than Anglos, with the largest difference occurring for situations involving tests. It was suggested that the performance of non-Anglos on tests was probably penalized more by the effects of anxiety than Anglos. Furthermore, non-Anglo students were apparently more concerned about recognition from peers in school and from authority figures.

This last cited finding of the Phillips and McNeil study is coordinate with the assertion by Katz (1964) that authority figures, especially whites, are particularly relevant in inducing stress in the disadvantaged minority group students. To this may be added the possibility that the peer group functions as

a particularly relevant stressor for the disadvantaged minority group student. In reviewing the evidence on the relevance
of the peer group to the psychological well-being of the minority group student, Proshansky and Newton (1968) note:

> One of the most obvious factors contributing to possi-
> ble disruption in the racially mixed school is the atti-
> tudes which Negro and white children have toward
> each other. The children come to school bringing the
> attitudes about race which they have learned from par-
> ents and other adults in the community; these atti-
> tudes, in turn, have some influence over their behavior
> toward children of the other racial group. In a very
> early study [it was] found that Negro children in ra-
> cially mixed classrooms accepted white prestige but
> increasingly withdrew into their own group as a re-
> sponse to white rejection. Many other studies . . .
> support this finding. In a trenchant analysis, Katz
> . . . describes some of the factors influencing per-
> formance of the Negro child who enters a racially
> mixed school or classroom; in some situations,
> social rejection and isolation may produce such ef-
> fects as intellectual impairment and anxiety. It
> seems that the difficulties involved extend beyond
> simple "mutual suspicion" and resentment between
> the two groups. In most cases there are real dif-
> ferences in the form of intellectual development and
> scholastic performance of the Negro student in com-
> parison with his white classmate. Therefore, the
> Negro child in a racially mixed school is forced to
> cope with feelings of inferiority, which have some
> basis in reality, as well as those feelings induced by
> his status in and treatment by the dominant white
> society. *

To summarize, the findings of this review indicate that
the lower class student is more likely to be anxious than the
middle or upper class student. Because of his lack of intel-
lectually and socially relevant preparation in an economically

---

*Proshansky, H. and Newton, P., "The Nature and Mean-
ing of Negro Identification," in Deutsch, M.; Katz, I.; and
Jensen, A. R., eds., Social Class, Race, and Psychological
Development. New York: Holt, Rinehart and Winston, 1968.
pp. 211-12. Copyright by Holt, Rinehart and Winston, 1968.
Reprinted by permission.

deprived family, he is likely to enter school with less than the required equipment. The result is likely to be an intellectual and social gap, referred to as a psychological and intellectual discontinuity, leading very probably to rejection, anxiety, and then withdrawal or some more overt reaction. The socially disadvantaged student must also contend (probably unsuccessfully) with additional varieties of stress stemming from tests, reading material, and the intellectual and social authority of his teacher. For the disadvantaged Negro student, the teacher as an authority figure and the peer group may be more relevant as stress-inducing factors than for other minority students and may thus be more debilitating because of their motivational relevance. Vogel, Raymond, and Lazarus (1959), for example, found that stress was not induced unless the stressor directly threatened the central motivation of the individual.

Achievement Motivation and Temporal Orientation

The desire to perform competently in achievement situations is a basic and pervasive motive in human experience. The ubiquity of the need is evident not only in the towering intellectual products of a Spinoza or an Einstein, but also in the first faltering efforts of a toddler to walk unaided or of a preschool child to print his own name. To most humans--philosopher or carpenter, child or adult--the attainment of desired achievement goals, and the attendant approval (whether from self or others) accruing to such attainment, are important sources of satisfaction and security (Crandall, 1963, p. 416).

Although for most people, as Crandall states, a strong and well-developed achievement orientation has a pervasive and positive effect on the quality of life, for others achievement orientation is not well developed, for social and economic reasons. Under circumstances of social and economic deprivation, it is likely that even if an initial achievement orientation is present, circumstances will prevent its full development and bring about undesirable consequences for the development of the individual.

Katz (1968) reports that the results of a number of studies that showed that lower class Negro parents had inordinately high achievement aspirations for their children. Such

aspirations, however, were greatly discrepant with the amount
of effort lower class parents expended in supporting their children's achievement behavior. These high aspirations, however
unrealistic, were nevertheless transmitted to the children.
Indirect evidence further suggests that Negro boys whose level
of achievement is low develop a defense mechanism by way of
self-discouragement and self-criticism; they learn to impose
failure on themselves. Low academic achievement and self-
criticism are also found to be related to skewed perceptions
of reward and punishment.

Middle class parents, on the other hand, are relatively
more likely to create conditions appropriate to the development of achievement motivation. Such conditions include not
only the holding of high achievement aspirations for the child
but also the early initiation of independence training and the
selective use of negative and positive reinforcers designed to
strengthen independence and achievement-oriented behaviors
(Crandall, 1963).

An additional and important mechanism for the transmission of achievement-oriented behaviors from parent to child
is known as modeling or imitation. Bandura and Huston (1961)
explain that although part of a child's socialization takes place
by direct training, much of his repertory is acquired through
identification--which conclusion they drew by testing the hypothesis that children would learn to imitate behavior exhibited by an experimenter-model. Forty-eight preschool children performed a diverting two-choice problem of discrimination with a model who displayed fairly explicit, although
nonfunctional, behaviors during the trials. The results of the
study indicated that the children reproduced behaviors re-
sembling those of the model. And nurturance was not found
to influence imitative discrimination learning of discrimination. It seems that in reproducing the model's behavior, the
child rewards himself.

In a study of aggression through imitation (Bandura, Ross,
and Ross, 1961), the transmission of behavior through a process of social imitation was shown to involve the generalization of imitative responses to new situations in which the model
was absent. The results of this study provide strong evidence
that observation of cues producing certain behavior effectively
elicits responses for which the original probability of occurrence is very low or zero.

The significance of imitative learning in the development
of achievement behaviors linked to social class is evident
when one considers the types of models available to the lower

class child. And the lack of an appropriate achievement model
may be especially significant for the lower class Negro child,
who is far more likely to experience inappropriate or inadequate modeling than the white child (Wilson, 1967).

Still another aspect of orientation toward success in
achievement situations is the extent to which the individual
plans for, or orients himself toward, the future--his temporal
orientation. Current studies show that constriction in time
sense relates to lower class status and to such undesirable
behaviors as delinquency and low academic achievement.

LeShan (1952) investigated time orientation and social
class, employing 117 children of middle and lower socioeconomic status as subjects. Subjects were asked to tell a story,
and each child's time orientation was determined by the period
of time covered by the action of his story. The results demonstrated middle class subjects to be significantly more future-
oriented than lower class subjects. A similar study conducted
by Ellis et al. (1955) supported LeShan's findings.

Brandt and Johnson (1955) studied the time orientation of
adjudicated and nonadjudicated delinquent and nondelinquent
boys. Subjects were matched on the basis of social class.
The delinquents produced stories that had shorter time spans
than those of the nondelinquents. These findings were supported in a study that employed both adjudicated and nonadjudicated delinquent girls as subjects (Barabasz, 1968-69,
1969b).

Brock and Del Giudice (1963) found subjects who stole
money from the experimenter to be more constricted in temporal orientation than those who did not. His study also indicated that temporal orientation was not related to race, age,
sex, or IQ. The lack of significant correlation between temporal orientation and intelligence was supported by Barabasz
(1968).

Teahan (1958) investigated the future time perspective of
high and low academic achievers matched for age and socio-
economic status. The high achievers had received academic
grades in the upper quartile of their classes for the previous
two years, and the low achievers had been in the lower quartile
for the same period. It was concluded that high achievers
were more future-oriented than low achievers. It was also
noted that there was no significant relationship between time
perspective and intelligence.

Barabasz (1969a) conducted a similar investigation using
high achieving and low achieving college undergraduates as
subjects. The subjects were asked to tell stories concerning

several photographs, and the median length of the story plot
for each subject was employed as the measure of temporal
orientation. Significant differences were found between the
length of the plots of high achievers and the low achievers, indicating that the high achievers were more future-oriented.

The differences in the temporal future orientations of different social class and ethnic groups are probably largely a
reflection of the child's sense of control over the available reinforcers in the achieving society. Wilson (1967) implies that the
restricted time orientation of lower class students is realistic
in the sense that the future is less promising for them than for
the middle class students, whose orientation to the future is
continually reinforced by success in school and in other areas.
Therefore, it is easy to visualize the development of a future
temporal orientation in the middle class student, since he is
more likely to receive appropriate training, observe achievement-oriented models, be imbued with high but realistic educational and vocational aspirations, and probably most
important, experience a relatively high level of success in
school. The lower class student--particularly the lower class
Negro--is far less likely to experience such positive events
and thus is more likely to lack a sense of control over events
affecting him and less likely to plan for future contingencies.

Self-Esteem

As each child develops means for the evaluation of external
stimuli in the environment, he also develops an evaluative and
personal assessment of his own worth. This assessment is
described as the child's self-concept and is formed on the basis
of such referents as appearance, group membership, achievement, and aspirations. The value scale used by the child in
measuring his worth in terms of these referents is generally
that used by the larger society. For the lower class child and
for the Negro child, this value scale is more likely to result
in negative self-evaluations than for the middle or upper class
child or white child, partly for the reason that the values of the
white middle class family are usually representative of the
value scale used by the larger society.

The Negro child, especially, suffers the negative effects
of the dominant value system upon his view of self. He has
racial physical characteristics that are visibly at odds with
white, middle class norms. He is a member of a distinctive
racial group that has been viewed as inferior, either consciously

or subconsciously, since the introduction of slavery in the
American colonies, by the far more numerous white population.
The achievements of his race and his ancestors have been obscured by an educational and cultural system based on white
middle class values.   This sytem has also minimized his own
achievements, since he enters it disadvantaged by a lack of
knowledge and understanding of its values and requirements.
Because of discriminatory practices of the larger population
against the members of his racial group, he may realistically
aspire only to limited goals of future success.

     Educators have generally assumed that a child's view of
himself should be favorable.   For example, Newcomb, Turner,
and Converse (1965) state "it seems quite clear that one of the
individual's most basic and continuing needs is for a self-image
that is essentially positive" (p. 141).   Unfortunately, not enough
research exists to substantiate this assumption fully, and what
research does exist has been particularly hampered by methodological problems.   Measures of self-esteem have often been
highly subjective and have failed to recognize social class as
an important variable in instrument content.   Social class has
also been frequently neglected in research design, and researchers have viewed all differences between the levels of
self-esteem of Negro and white children as resulting from
racial differences.   Simpson and Yinger (1965) note that prejudice based on race and its effects on the Negro child may vary
greatly in relation to group cohesiveness, intergroup contact,
color variations within the group, surrounding group attitudes
toward prejudice, and experience with other intergroup patterns.

     One of the major factors affecting the development of the
Negro child's concept of self that has been rather thoroughly
examined is the development of an awareness or consciousness
of race.   Morland (1966) evaluated the ability of Southern and
Northern children of various age levels to identify themselves
as members of a distinct race and to recognize racial differences.   Subjects responded to a series of pictures depicting
Negroes and whites.   The ability to recognize the racial iden-
tity of the person depicted was found to increase from the age
of three to the age of six, the greatest occurring at the age of
four.   A study reported by Stevenson and Stevenson (1960) detected some degree of racial awareness as early as the age
of two.   Racial awareness is probably more apparent than real,
however, until the age of eight or nine (Proshansky and Newton,
1968); according to Vaughn (1963), the ability to categorize by
race seems to emerge at the age of seven.   These findings are
qualified by Goodman (1952), who found that although Negro and

white children used racial terms to describe and label others,
their use of such terms was often inaccurate.

As the child learns to identify in terms of racial labels,
he also learns the popular sterotypes used to describe racial
and ethnic groups (Proshansky and Newton, 1968). Negro and
white children begin to associate such terms as "dirty," "bad,"
and "ugly" with Negroes and such terms as "clean," "nice,"
and "good" with whites. For the Negro child, whites are established as superior, and in terms of this sterotype of supposed
white superiority, the Negro child may often subconsciously
reject his own race. Morland (1962) studied 407 young, Southern Negro and white children and found that 60 percent of the
Negro children preferred to play with children of the other race.
Only 18 percent of the Negro children preferred children of
their own race as playmates, and 22 percent expressed no preference.

Other studies have indicated that confronted by the sterotype of white superiority, the Negro child may even express
overt hostility toward other Negroes in greater measure than
he expresses hostility toward whites. Goodman (1952) found
that only 9 percent of the Negro children in her sample expressed hostility toward whites, whereas 24 percent expressed
hostility toward members of their own race.

In the famous Clark and Clark (1947) doll study, 253, Negro
children from two to seven years of age were individually presented with a white and a Negro doll and asked, "Which doll
looks nice? Which doll looks bad?" and "Which doll is a nice
color?" The white doll was selected by the majority of the subjects as the one that "looked nice" and had a "nice color." As
the age of the subjects increased, the preference for the white
doll decreased slightly, but a majority of all subjects at all
ages said that the Negro doll looked "bad."

Evidence conflicting with these findings of Negroes' hostility toward their own race was reported by Gregor and Mc-
Pherson (1966). They also reported, however, that whites
had a stronger preference for their own race than did Negroes.

Level of Aspiration

Considering the greater frequency of negative self-evalua-
tion among Negroes than among whites and the tendency of
Negroes to deprecate his own racial group, the level of aspiration of Negroes might be expected to be much lower than that
of comparable whites. Recent research, however, generally

indicates that the expressed educational and occupational aspirations of Negroes are actually higher than those of whites.

In a comprehensive study made by Reiss and Rhodes (1959), 21,000 students in the Northville, Tennessee, area served as subjects. The Negro students of the sample were found to place a much higher emphasis upon education than did their white counterparts. Age, sex, IQ, and socio-economic status were found to have less influence than race when comparisons of educational aspirations were made between whites and Negroes.

A study of the occupational goals of high school seniors in Kentucky was conducted by Lott and Lott (1963). They found that, with the exception of Negro girls, the occupational goals of Negro students were similar to those of white students. Negro girls concentrated their occupational aspirations among the professions, totally rejecting the role of housewife.

Sprey (1962) examined the aspirations of ninth grade students and found ambitious patterns of aspiration among Negro girls. A greater number of Negro girls were actively involved in planning for their future than were Negro boys. More Negro girls than boys were enrolled in college preparatory programs.

Gist and Bennett (1963) recorded the educational and occupational aspirations of Negro and white high school students in Kansas City. No significant differences between Negroes and whites were found in level of occupational aspiration, but Negroes did have significantly higher educational aspirations.

The great discrepancy between observed self-esteem and verbalized level of aspiration in the Negro child may be largely the result of wishful thinking or of a defensive reaction on the part of the Negro child. In regard to the college aspirations of Negro and white students, Coleman et al. (1966) report that while more Negro high school students than whites reported a desire to attend college, very few of these Negro students had seen a college catalogue or had written to a college for information. Katz (1968) suggests that verbalizations of educational and occupational goals by Negro students may be a psychological substitute for behaviors required to attain these goals, which they are unable to enact.

SUMMARY AND CONCLUSIONS

Substantial research effort has been expended to document the social and educational disadvantages of the American Negro child and of other children in similarly deprived ethnic and

social class groups. The results of this effort have been se-
lectively reviewed in the preceding pages. For convenience
of presentation, the research has been classified in terms of
major areas of disadvantagement related to school behavior
and learning.

Intelligence

Intelligence level, as measured by a wide range of group
and individual intelligence tests, generally shows a less than
moderate but positive relationship with indexes of social class
level. Moreover, ethnic differences in intelligence scores are
reported, which are only partly explained by typical indexes
of social class level. The picture is further complicated--or
illuminated--by recent evidence of a differential impact of
social class level within ethnic groups indicating that the lower
class Negro may suffer more debilitating effects on intellectual development than other lower class ethnic groups.

School Achievement

The evidence relating social status to school achievement
generally indicates that socio-economic status and intelligence
level contribute independently to school achievement. Negro-
white achievement differences are roughly on the order of one
standard deviation across the school years in the metropolitan
Northeast but increase with years in school when whites in the
metropolitan Northeast are compared with Negroes in the rural
South. Puerto Rican children are somewhat more educationally
disadvantaged than Northern Negroes. Regional differences
in Negro-white achievement comparisons appear to reflect different forms of inequality of educational opportunity.

Language Development

The survey of studies on language development generally
indicates that the lower class child's language may be somewhat simpler in syntax, somewhat more restricted in vocabulary, and somewhat poorer in descriptive terms and modifiers
than the language of the middle class child. Lower class communication patterns tend to emphasize commands and other
short sentences and a heavy reliance on gestures. Although

the educational significance of social class differences in language patterns is far from clear, it does seem evident that
language development plays an important role in certain kinds
of problem-solving, in learning to read, and in performance
on tests of achievement and ability. The findings thus provide
an important and provocative area for experimentation in the
educational programs of disadvantaged children.

Special Abilities

Scores on tests of special abilities and aptitudes are generally related to social class status in the same manner as
scores on traditional intelligence tests. However, recent
findings suggest that the effect of social class on abilities is
pervasive but undifferentiating, whereas ethnic group membership results in a patterning of special abilities in important
educationally relevant areas. The results of research in this
area are in need of extensive replication with additional samples of minority group children at different age levels; they
may eventually indicate that educational programs for disadvantaged children must take into account much finer differences
than those obtained from the gross measures of ability represented by the traditional IQ test.

Basic Learning Abilities

Measures of basic learning abilities, such as serial rote
learning, depend little on previous learning and verbal mediational processes, and thus theoretically are more indicative
than traditional IQ tests of native intellectual endowment.
Research on basic learning abilities reported by Jensen (1966)
has begun to illuminate some fundamental processes underlying the ability to learn in different social class and ethnic
groups. Using tests which are largely independent of verbal
mediational processes and specific transfer from previous
learning, and thus largely independent of the cultural bias of
traditional intelligence and achievement tests, Jensen found
that basic learning abilities were markedly less affected by
class and ethnic differences than were intelligence test scores.
A partial explanation for the occurrence of large social class
differences in school achievement has been the failure to recognize the basic learning abilities measured in the tests used
by Jensen and others, and a corresponding failure of the school

in adapting instructional procedures to capitalize on social
class differences in ability patterns. Although more definitive
research is required, the findings relating to basic learning
abilities suggest new approaches to the teaching of socially disadvantaged children.

Anxiety

Anxiety relates negatively to indexes of school achievement as well as a variety of other indexes of intellectual
performance. Since the typical school learning environment
may present an unusually imposing set of stressful and anxiety-
inducing circumstances for socially and economically disadvantaged children, these children, and especially disadvantaged
Negro children, may suffer inordinately from the negative
effects of anxiety upon school and intellectual performance.

Physical Health

The greater predominance of malnutrition and premature
births in the lower social strata and among Negro families
probably contributes to a greater predominance of neurological
abnormalities among these groups, thus affecting later intellectual development.

Achievement Motivation and Temporal Orientation

The development of achievement motivation is dependent
upon the modeling of observed adult behaviors and attitudes
and other special learning conditions. For disadvantaged
children and especially disadvantaged Negro children, the
available adult models in the home environment, though
stressing an inordinately high achievement aspiration, apparently do not foster the achievement-oriented behaviors required for academic success.

Current studies show that constriction in time sense--that
is, orientation of all or most of the child's thought and activities to the present--as opposed to a future orientation, relates
to lower class status and to such undesirable behavior as delinquency and low academic achievement. Other evidence
suggests that a constricted temporal orientation is a reflection
of continuously experienced failure in the academic context,
together with a corresponding weakening of commitment to
academic and other values ascribed to by the bulk of society.

Self-Esteem

It is generally assumed that a positive self-concept en-
hances and contributes to academic success. Racial stereotypes prevalent in society, however, generally deprecate
Negroes and contribute to a greater frequency of self-deprecating attitudes among Negro children than among white children. The relationship of these self-deprecating attitudes to
academic success, social class, and ethnicity is in need of
further illumination through research.

Level of Aspiration

While Negro children tend to verbalize higher academic
and occupational aspirations than do their white classmates,
these verbalizations are generally not accompanied by the behaviors required to attain the goals aspired to and are probably
merely psychological substitutes for such behaviors, which
the child is unable to enact.

Conclusions

This review has emphasized a number of potentially important socio-cultural differences among school age children,
some of which are firmly supported by research and others
of which still require considerable elaboration through research.
The firmly established "facts" relate generally to gross social
class and ethnic differences in educational and intellectual development. Such differences provide the basis for a general
understanding of the size or significance of the educational and
intellectual differences associated with social class and ethnic
membership. This evidence is also indicative of the potential
problems faced by the educators and supporting personnel involved in efforts to up-grade the educational development of
disadvantaged children in integrated school settings and otherwise.

The less established "facts" reviewed relate generally to
language development, basic learning abilities, and specific
intellectual abilities. It is, however, these least established
findings that form a potentially more useful basis for understanding the findings of research reviewed in subsequent chapters of this report. For example, findings reported by Jensen
in 1969, relating to social class and ethnic differences in basic

learning abilities, have a number of implications for understanding the generally massive failure of compensatory education programs. These findings, and others relating to abilities,
are relevant to the evaluation of the effectiveness of current
approaches to school integration.

Somewhat more established are the research findings
relating anxiety to educational and intellectual development.
Studies focused primarily on white school children have generally established that anxiety may have pervasive debilitating
effects on educational development, depending on the nature
of the school context and other characteristics of the student.
Much more needs to be learned of the potentially more debilitating effects of anxiety and related responses on the intellectual and educational development of minority group students.
However, the evidence now available is sufficiently provocative to suggest that anxiety and certain defensive orientations
play a psychologically significant role in newly desegregated
school settings as well as in those schools that may be considered disadvantaged as a function of social class composition.
Similarly, the research findings relating to temporal orientation, achievement motivation, and self-esteem have different
implications when examined in relation to school settings that
differ on the basis of racial and social class composition.

If anything, the findings reviewed in this chapter should
indicate the complexity of the problems that are likely to be
involved in efforts to facilitate the educational development
of disadvantaged minority group students, whether through
school desegregation, compensatory education, or both. The
disadvantaged Negro student cannot be typed simply as a student
with a relatively low IQ score; he is, rather, an individual who
is likely to display complex patterns of responses, behaviors,
and ability, the significance of which, in a variety of even more
complex behavior settings, is yet little understood. The
findings of Lesser et al., for example, show that Negro students displayed an ability patterning that differs considerably
from the patterns of other ethnic groups; the Negro sample
in this study was second only to the Jewish sample in level of
performance on the test of verbal abilities. Current efforts
toward compensatory education, however, appear to place
heavy emphasis on the development of verbal skills in disadvantaged Negro students, while underemphasizing or
neglecting other areas in which these students may have relatively little ability.

CHAPTER **4** MAJOR STUDIES OF
RACIAL AND SOCIAL
CLASS ISOLATION IN
THE SCHOOLS

Robert P. O'Reilly

The purpose of the present chapter is to present a critical
examination of major studies of the relationship between racial
and social class isolation in the schools and intellectual, educational, and attitudinal development in advantaged white and
disadvantaged minority student populations. Major sources
for the study of these relationships are the survey made by
Coleman et al. (1966), a number of reports in Racial Isolation
in the Public Schools (U.S. Commission on Civil Rights,
1967), and the reanalysis of the data of Coleman et al. made
by McPartland (1967). Together these reports constitute four
separate studies of racial and social class isolation in the public schools, three of which are based on the data from Coleman
et al. Three additional surveys of the relationship between
prior racial and social class isolation in the educational context and adult interracial attitudes and contact are reported in
the final section of the chapter. The source for the adult surveys was, again, the 1967 report of the Civil Rights Commission.

All studies reviewed were based on large and, in some
cases, nationally or regionally representative samples of
students and adults. All were designed to control for a number of extraneous sources of "noise" in order to create some
basis for causal analyses of the relationship between varying
degrees of racial and social class isolation in the schools and
intellectual and educational development, as well as other
student characteristics. The study of such causal relations
was not an entirely objective exercise in all studies reviewed;
in some instances it amounted to a search to uncover evidence
that would link segregation to severe educational deficiencies
in minority group students. A careful examination of the
evidence, however, fails to show that racial isolation, by

itself, is a prime cause of educational deficiency. The implications of the evidence are broader than would have been the implications of findings to the effect that educational deficiencies stemmed from the racial composition factor itself: what the evidence appears to show is that the predominant socio-economic context of the school and classroom exerts an important influence on the educational and intellectual development of the students. Negroes and certain other minority group members are thus recognized as decidedly disadvantaged, educationally and otherwise, because of the close correspondence between race and economic status.

The residue of the results of the studies reviewed in the present chapter also provide a substantial, though still tentative, basis for a number of recommendations concerning ways in which the social class status of the school and other relevant factors may be manipulated to increase the chances that Negro and other disadvantaged children may experience a more facilitating educational climate. Given the current national commitment to school desegregation, it is of considerable importance that all systematic knowledge be brought to bear on making the process of desegregation as psychologically and educationally effective as possible. A major purpose of this chapter, therefore, is to clarify the relevance of conditions that may be manipulated in the school to enhance the potentially facilitating effects of school desegregation. Such conditions include appropriate social class balance in the school and classroom at the appropriate grade levels. Other findings of the studies reviewed provide a source for additional recommendations concerning the types of general qualitative changes that may assist in facilitating the educational development of minority group students during the interim of segregated schooling.

It will be evident from this review and that presented in the subsequent chapter that school desegregation is no panacea leading to the sudden disappearance of the intellectual and educational gaps existing between the majority of students and those regarded as disadvantaged minority group students. The evidence in this and the subsequent chapter does indeed indicate that, under certain gross conditions, desegregation may result in worthwhile educational benefits for disadvantaged students, but knowledge of the process of desegregation is not yet so complete, nor is what is now known of the process so systematically applied, that any startling changes in educational development can be expected among desegregated minority group students.

The reader is encouraged to view the findings of this and
the subsequent chapter from an experimental point of view.
There are many large gaps in current knowledge of the process of desegregation, and what is "known" is subject to change
as a result of further, more sophisticated research. It is unnecessary, in any event, to justify the need for school desegregation on the basis of research findings; rather, it is proper
that recognition be given to the fact that the nation faces an
immensely complex and difficult socio-educational problem.
Commitment to a total solution has already been made--and the
results of the current body of research may assist in providing
a rational basis for the often slow and painstaking efforts required for the solution of this major social problem. Limited
as this knowledge is, at present, it is sufficient to increase the
chances of success and assist to obviate some of the more
serious errors that might render efforts at school desegregation either ineffective or damaging.

THE EQUALITY OF EDUCATIONAL OPPORTUNITY
REPORT

The survey of Coleman et al. was based on a national
probability sample of 4, 000 elementary and secondary schools,
including all district superintendents, principals, and teachers
therein and a total of 645, 000 students in the first, third,
sixth, ninth, and twelfth grades. Some 10 percent of the districts in the original sample refused to participate, and complete returns of all data were received from only about 60
percent of the sample. Although the nonresponse rate may
have affected certain of the results, there is little reason to
believe that the major relationships studied were seriously
affected (Jencks, 1969; Coleman et al., 1966, pp. 565-70).
The survey was directed, in part, toward determining the
relationships of a number of school and nonschool factors with
achievement. Those of concern in this review include the relationships between achievement as a dependent variable and
the independent variables family background factors, student
attitudes, individual and school social class level, school
characteristics, and racial composition of the school.
Data relating to the characteristics of the schools and
their personnel and socio-economic data for the neighborhoods
served by the schools were obtained from verbal tests given
to teachers and from questionnaire responses from teachers,

principals, and superintendents. Students provided information on individual socio-economic background, parents' education, educationally relevant items in the home, and academic
aspirations and attitudes about school. Measures of students'
verbal and nonverbal abilities were obtained at all grade levels
studied, and additional measures of reading comprehension
and mathematics achievement were obtained for the sixth,
ninth, and twelfth grades.

For the main analyses, the sample was classified on the
following characteristics: metropolitan or nonmetropolitan
location, presence in one of five geographical regions, elementary or secondary level, and membership in a certain racial
or ethnic group, designated as white, Puerto Rican, Indian-
American, Mexican-American, or Negro. Results of the analyses reported in this summary center primarily on Negro-
white comparisons in the metropolitan Northeast and, to some
extent, on Puerto Rican-white comparisons.

The analyses focused on in this summary involve between-
schools effects of such variables as individual and school social
class background, school facilities, teacher quality, and racial
or ethnic group membership, there being a total of some sixty
variables in the final analyses. The criterian or dependent
variable in most of these analyses was a verbal ability test,
a vocabulary test measuring verbal skills. Other analyses involved comparisons of attitudes for each ethnic group studied.

Examination of between-schools effects is analogous to
analysis in an educational experiment in which there are a
number of treatments--for example, A, B, C--and a certain
number of subjects within each treatment. If the treatments
differ in effectiveness, then the average scores of the subjects
within each treatment might be 80 for A, 65 for B, and 50 for
C--though there would also be variation in scores within each
treatment group. It is the between-group or between-school
differences (averages or means) that were of primary concern
in the Coleman et al. survey, the within-group variation in
scores being treated as "error" or unexplained variation in relation to school factors. Achievement variation among individuals (across schools or treatments) could be, and was, analyzed
in relation to nonschool, or family background, factors and student characteristics.

The main results of the survey are presented as proportions or percents of variance explained by a particular factor
or as average scores in a set of cross-tabulations in which
the factors under consideration were measured or classified
at different levels or for different groups. Before the results
of the survey are discussed, some explanation of the meaning

of variance is in order: The amount of variation in any set
of scores is technically known as the variance. If one takes
the difference between every score and the mean of the distribution of scores, squares each difference, sums them, and
then divides by the total number of scores, the resulting quantity is the variance, or a measure of the dispersion of scores
in the distribution. Since the variance is variation on an additive scale, the total variance (SS) of the score distribution
can be divided into a number of parts, each related to some
factor that contributes a certain proportion of the total variance. In the survey, there are two such major proportions of
variance: (1) the between-school variance (SS_b) and (2) the
within-school variance (SS_w). The total variance of scores is
then expressed as $SS = SS_b + SS_w$.

Parts of the survey focused primarily on SS_b variance,
that is, the part that could be explained by differences between
schools. The proportions of the total variance of verbal ability scores that could be explained by such differences is shown
in Table 20 for selected groups of the survey sample.

The between-school variance components reported in
Table 20, and the more complete estimates given in the report
of Coleman et al. (p. 296), indicate a range of from 5 to 35
percent over the various ethnic groups treated in the survey.
Generally, more than 70 percent of the variation in achievement for each ethnic group was variation within the same
student body, the within-group variance component being even
larger--from 80 to 90 percent--for Negroes and whites.[*] When
examined across ethnic groups and grade levels, as shown in
Table 20, there was no tendency for the between-school variance component to show the pattern of increase, which might
be expected if the influences of educationally relevant differences among schools were to become increasingly important
through the years of school. These results, plus the evidence
of an already sizeable between-school variance component at
the first grade level, indicate indirectly that the between-school
variance component itself is in part a function of initial and
continuing differences among schools in family background
factors and other differences--measured and unmeasured--

---

[*]This result held equally or more strongly for test scores
other than verbal ability. In general, the results cited here
for verbal ability are indicative of the results in other areas,
such as reading comprehension and mathematics achievement,
there being a high correlation among the achievement measures
used in the study.

TABLE 20

Percent of Total Variance in Individual
Verbal Achievement Scores that Lies between Schools[1]

Group	Grade Levels[a]				
	12	9	6	3	1[b]
Puerto Rican	22.4	21.0	31.3	26.7	16.7
Negro North	10.9	12.7	13.9	19.5	10.6
Negro South	22.5	20.17	22.6	34.7	23.2
White North	7.8	8.7	10.3	11.4	11.1

[1]Adapted from Coleman et al., (1966, p. 296).

[a]Changes in proportions of variance by grade level may be compared separately for grades 1-3 and 6-12. (Coleman et al., p. 296).

[b]Tests given shortly after the beginning of the school, thus reflecting the influence of nonschool experiences.

among students. Since the between-school variance component
is relatively small and includes the influences of nonschool
factors, it is evident that differences among schools in quality
of programs, teachers, and so on can explain only a relatively
small part of the total variance of school achievement. For
some minority groups, however, the between-school variance
component was large enough to be regarded as educationally
important at all grade levels. This was particularly notable
for Puerto Ricans, Indian-Americans, and Negroes in the
South. Indirectly, this is an indication that qualitative differences in schools make the most difference for those minority
groups that are most disadvantaged.

Relationship of Family Background Factors
to School Achievement

To determine the extent to which family background influences achievement, both within-school and between-school
variations were examined to elicit an estimate of the strength
of the relationship of social class and ethnic background to
achievement. The proportions of achievement variance attributable to family background, both within and between
schools, is shown in Table 21 for selected segments of the
sample. These data show that, on the average, the amount
of within-school variance accounted for by family background
and attitudinal factors, at each grade level, is roughly of the
same order of magnitude as the variance associated with between-school differences. For all groups examined in the
survey, the total variance of achievement associated with
between-school and within-school differences in family background and student attitudes was between 30 and 50 percent.
Furthermore, the between-school variance component was
found to be partially attributable to family background factors,
as shown in Table 21: approximately 16 percent of the total
between-school variance for Northern whites, 12 percent for
Northern Negroes, and 3 percent for Puerto Ricans at the
twelfth grade level.

The total variance attributable to all family background
factors alone, both between schools and within schools, ranged
from about 4 percent for Puerto Ricans in the twelfth grade to
36 percent for Oriental-Americans in the sixth grade. Examination of variance estimates for certain of the family background factors tended to show some decline in their relationship
to achievement (Coleman et al., 1966, Table 3. 221. 3. p. 300)

TABLE 21

Estimated Proportions of Achievement Variance Attributable
to Family Background and Related Differences
and Between-School Differences[1]

	Variance Source	
Grade 12	Between[a] Schools	Within and Between Schools
Puerto Rican	23.40	31.54
Negro North	11.19	31.04
Negro South	22.15	38.97
White North	8.25	27.12
Grade 9		
Puerto Rican	16.77	30.41
Negro North	8.96	30.48
Negro South	18.55	38.88
White North	8.31	39.56
Grade 6		
Puerto Rican	22.49	40.35
Negro North	11.86	26.39
Negro South	22.25	37.69
White North	12.77	35.77

[1]From Coleman et al. (1966, p. 299).

[a] Background factors are based on an index including urbanism, migration, parents' education, structural integrity of the home, family size, items in the home, reading material, parents' interest and parents' educational desires. Also included in the total relationship are child's attitudes, including interest in school, self-concept and control of environment.

from the sixth grade to the twelfth grade, suggesting that the
impact of the family on achievement is greater in the earlier
years of school than in the later years. This relationship was
particularly dramatic for Puerto Rican students.

One of the components of family background--parents'
interest in the child's schooling, based on the items "Talk
with parents about school?" and "Anyone read to you when
small?"--showed a greater increase in the strength of the relationship with achievement for whites and Oriental-Americans
with grade level than for the other groups. Although a clear-
cut interpretation of this result was not possible, it appeared
that both majority white parents and minority group parents
generally showed high interest in their children's education
but that minority group parents were probably less able to
translate their educational desires into effective support for
their children.

Further examination of the relationship of different family
background variables to achievement for different minority
groups showed that, at the sixth grade, educational items in
the home relative to economic level of the home had the highest relationship with achievement for minority groups whereas
parents' education had the highest relationship for whites. For
Negroes in the twelfth grade, length of time in an urban environment and size (small) of family showed approximately
the same degree of relationship to achievement as parents'
education. Structural integrity of the home (absence of the
father) showed essentially no relation to achievement for Negroes, but a strong relation for whites.

In general, these results indicate that family background
characteristics are highly important for student achievement
in the school and that each minority group has its own pattern
of relationship of family background variables to achievement.

Student Body Characteristics

Since the principal difference in the school environments
of minority groups and whites lies in the social class composition of the student bodies, relationships existing between
characteristics of student bodies and achievement have a number of important implications for education. Table 22 shows
the results of one of the survey analyses in which the relative
contributions of student body characteristics and school quality
to achievement were examined for different minority groups
across grade levels. Comparisons of the A column (variance

TABLE 22

Individual Verbal Achievement Variance Accounted for by School Characteristics (A) and by School Characteristics[a] Plus Student-Body Characteristics[b] (B): Family Background Controlled[1]

| | Grade Level | | | | | | | | | | | | | |
| | 12 | | | 9 | | | 6 | | | 3 | | | 1 | | |
	A	A+B	gain	A	A+B	gain	A	A+B	gain	A	A+B	gain	A	A+B	gain
Puerto Rican	6.7[c]	22.6	15.9	4.1	15.7	11.6	3.2	11.8	8.6	2.3	8.2	5.9	4.5	6.3	1.7
Negro North	3.1	7.7	4.6	1.5	4.6	3.2	.8	2.7	2.0	3.0	5.1	2.2	2.4	3.3	.9
Negro South	8.6	12.7	4.1	7.5	12.7	5.1	4.9	7.8	2.8	.8	1.4	.6	2.1	2.9	.8
White North	1.9	2.9	1.1	.7	2.3	1.6	.3	3.6	3.3	.3	1.5	1.1	.8	2.4	1.5

[1]Adapted from Coleman et al., (1966, p. 306).

[a]School characteristics are staff expenditures, library volumes, science laboratory facilities, extra-curricular activities, accelerated curricula, comprehensiveness of curriculum, tracking, movement between tracks, size, guidance counselors, school location.

[b]Student body characteristics are families with encyclopedias, student transfers, attendance, college plans, teacher perception of student body quality, hours of homework.

[c]All figures rounded to one decimal place.

accounted for by school characteristics) and the gain column
(additional variance accounted for by student body characteristics) show, in general, that the social class composition of
the student body (more positive educational backgrounds and
aspirations) related positively to achievement, independently
of the student's own background. Furthermore, this relationship was much stronger for disadvantaged minority group
students than for white students--and became increasingly so
at higher grade levels. This relationship was particularly
dramatic for Puerto Rican students, whereas achievement
scores for the highest achieving groups, whites and Orientals
(scores for the latter not shown), were only slightly affected
by variations in the social class composition of the student
body.

School Facilities and Curriculum

The results of the analyses presented in Table 22 show a
tendency for the relationship between school quality and verbal achievement to increase across grade levels for minority
group students, although this relationship was decidedly less
strong than the relationship between student body characteristics and achievement. Further analysis in which expenditures and pupil background were controlled indicated only
slight relationships between achievement and differences in
school facilities and curriculum--library volumes per student,
science laboratory facilities, presence of accelerated curricula, comprehensiveness of curriculum, promotion policies,
grouping or tracking, movement between tracks, school size,
number of guidance counselors, and urbanism of location. In
nearly all cases, the amount of achievement variance attributable to a particular index of facilities and curriculum was
less than 1 percent in all regions and for all groups. At the
elementary grade levels, it was apparent that the contributions
of facilities and curriculum to achievement could be ignored.
For all facilities and curriculum indexes combined, the largest
proportion of achievement variance contributed by school facilities and curriculum was 8.6 percent (inclusive of per-pupil
expenditures), and this was for Negroes in the South who were
notably more responsive to qualitative differences in schools
and student body characteristics than whites and Northern
Negroes. The corresponding contribution to achievement for
Northern whites was 1.9 percent.

Teacher Characteristics

In interpreting the results of the analyses relating teacher characteristics to achievement, it is important to note that other survey data showed important differences between teachers of majority whites and teachers of certain minority groups. Negro students are generally taught by Negro teachers, whites almost always by white teachers. Negro teachers scored lower than white teachers on a vocabulary test and were likely to have experienced the same segregated educational background as the students they were teaching.

Variables defining teacher quality used in the survey included educational level of teachers' families; teaching experience; localism of teachers' experience; level of education; vocabulary test scores; preference for teaching middle class, white collar students; and proportion of white teachers in the school. When the contributions of teacher characteristics to achievement were examined, with only background controlled, it was found that the effects of teacher quality increased as the grade levels rose. The effect of teacher quality on achievement was greatest for Puerto Rican students in the twelfth grade, and the effect for whites was negligible at all grade levels. The contribution of teacher quality was small at the first, third, sixth, and ninth grade levels for Northern Negroes but somewhat greater in the twelfth grade. Teacher variables with the greatest effects were teachers' family education level, teachers' own education, and teachers' score on the vocabulary test. All contributions were positive and generally similar for minority groups.

The relative contributions to achievement of school facilities and curriculum, teacher quality, and social class composition of the school may be estimated from the data given in Table 23. These data again show that adding differences in school quality increases the proportion of achievement variance accounted for only slightly but that adding the social class composition of the school affects the proportion of achievement variance accounted for substantially--particularly for minority group students. The effects of teacher quality and the student environment variables is again shown to increase across grade levels. By comparing the data shown previously in Table 22 in the column headed "gain" (achievement variance attributable to the addition of student body characteristics) with data shown in Table 23 in the column headed "T" (variance attributable to teacher quality), it becomes apparent that teacher quality is roughly as important

TABLE 23

Verbal Achievement Variance Attributable to Teacher (T), School Variables (S), and Student Environment Variables (E) in Grades 12, 9, and 6: Background Variables Controlled[1]

<u>Grade Level</u>

	12			9			6		
	T	T+S	T+S+E	T	T+S	T+S+E	T	T+S	T+S+E
Puerto Ricans	18.4[a]	20.0	26.4	9.7	11.4	16.3	8.1	10.8	14.0
Negro North	4.4	6.7	9.0	1.6	3.3	5.4	2.2	2.7	4.9
Negro South	10.0	11.7	13.9	7.7	11.2	13.3	5.3	7.8	9.0
White North	1.9	3.2	3.8	1.0	2.1	3.1	1.7	2.0	4.8

[1]From Coleman et al. (1966, p. 319).

[a]All figures rounded to one decimal place.

150

for achievement as the social class composition of the school and that both of these factors are far more important than in- dicators of school quality. These relationships are most pro- nounced for Puerto Rican students, considerably less pronounced for Northern Negroes, and far less pronounced for Northern whites. Indeed, white students appear to be almost negligibly affected by variations in school quality, social class composi- tion of the schools, and teacher quality.

Relative Effects of Racial Composition and Social Class

Initial regression analyses showed that achievement of Negroes was positively affected by increases in the proportion of whites in the school. Though this relationship was absent at the early elementary grades, it was stronger at the ninth and twelfth grade levels; it was not attributable to differences in facilities and curriculum. Further analyses showed that achievement differences associated with the racial composition of the schools were nearly wholly attributable to differences between schools in student social class background. Figures 11 and 12 show the results of further analyses in which student achievement was examined in relation to students' reports of the proportion of white students in their classes in the year preceding the survey and the grade level at which the students first attended an integrated school.

In examining Figures 11 and 12, it will be noted that there is a pattern of increase in achievement favoring students in classrooms of 50 percent or more whites as compared to those in classrooms in which whites constitute less than 50 percent. It will also be noted that there was a tendency for students who entered desegregated schools in the early grades to show some- what higher achievement levels than those who entered deseg- regated schools in later years. In the examination of these relationships, it will be recalled that increases in Negro a- chievement associated with increases in the proportion of white students in the school may reflect primarily the facili- tating effects of the more positive social class backgrounds of white students.

An additional important relationship shown in Figures 11 and 12 is the general lack of any positive relationship between the proportion of white students in the school and reading a- chievement until the proportion of white students exceeds 50 percent. The effect of integration in the school situation must be judged as relatively minor from the data in the Coleman

FIGURE 11

Average Reading Scores of Ninth Grade Negro Students by
Proportion of White Classmates in Previous Year of Schooling
and First Grade Level Interval at Which Integration
Took Place: Metropolitan Northeast[1]

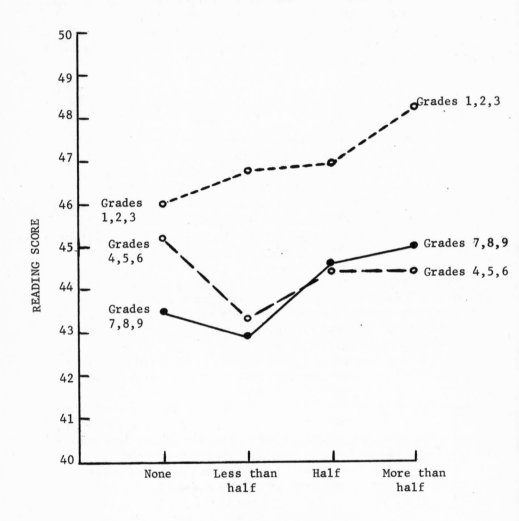

PROPORTION WHITE CLASSMATES
LAST YEAR

[1]Based on data from Coleman _et al._, 1966, p. 332.

152

FIGURE 12

Average Reading Scores of Twelfth Grade Negro Students by
Proportion of White Classmates in Previous Year of Schooling
and First Grade Level Interval at Which Integration
Took Place: Metropolitan Northeast[1]

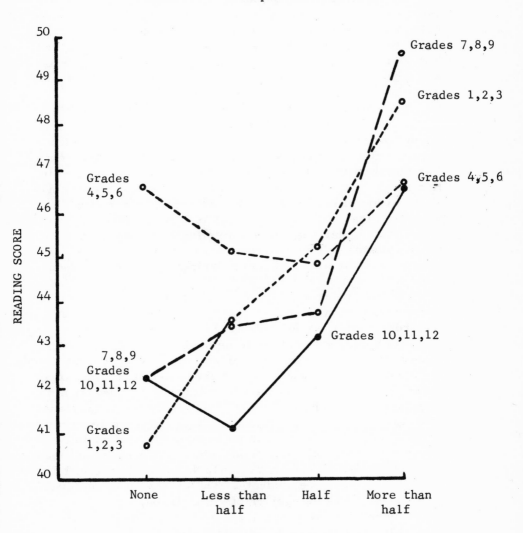

PROPORTION WHITE CLASSMATES
LAST YEAR

[1]Based on data from Coleman et al., 1966, p. 332

et al. study: for example, when the average ninth and twelfth
grade reading achievement scores for Negroes who experienced
classrooms in which less than 50 percent of the students were
white are averaged across grade levels (first grade level interval integrated) and compared with similar averages for Negroes who experienced 50 percent or more than 50 percent
white classrooms, the differences between the averages are
generally only a few score points in reading achievement.
Differences between the averages when integration was first
experienced at grades one through three, four through six,
seven through nine, and ten through twelve, also tend to be
minor, being of the order of one to three score points.[*]

The data presented in Figures 11 and 12, and additional
data presented by Coleman et al., give no indication of the
potential of the integrated situation for Negro achievement because social class composition of the school and classroom
was not simultaneously varied. Other results presented in
this report, however, indicate that the effect of social class
composition of the school appears to be more powerful than
any effect that might be attributable to racial integration per se.

Further analyses relating to effects of the proportion of
white students in the classroom also tended to show a relationship to interracial acceptance. White students who attended

_____

[*]As will become apparent from the findings of other reports reviewed later in this chapter, the relationship between
the proportion of white students in the school or classroom and
Negro achievement appears to be nonlinear. That is, when
the white proportion in the school or classroom is high, roughly 70 percent or more, achievement of Negro students is apparently facilitated. As the white proportion decreases, the
effect on Negro achievement becomes increasingly negative,
when these students are compared with Negro students in
schools and classrooms with high proportions of white students.
However, there may be no achievement differences between
schools or classrooms that are all Negro and those with fewer
than 50 percent white students. Thus the comparison made
here of two gross categories of "integration," above and below
the 50 percent white proportion, underestimates the "true"
size of the effect of white proportion in the school or classroom.
Caution is further advised in interpreting the tables of cross-
tabulations relating white proportion to achievement in the
Coleman et al. study, since social class and racial composition of the classroom are confounded, and there is no control
for possible ability differences between categories.

integrated schools at the early elementary grade levels were less likely to choose only white students as close friends than those who entered integrated schools at later grade levels.

Attitudes and Achievement

Expressions of student attitudes and motivation studied in the survey included the student's reported interest in school, his self-concept in relation to success in school, and his sense of control over his environment. Survey data indicated that both Negroes and whites expressed high interest in school and reported positive self-concepts. Negroes and Puerto Ricans, however, differed decidedly from whites in that they expressed a lower sense of control of the environment.

In contrast with previous research relating attitudes toward achievement, the results of the survey analyses showed that the attitudes described above were only moderately related to achievement, though were more strongly related to achievement than any other set of variables measured in the study. Table 24 shows the proportion of achievement variance accounted for by interest in school, self-concept, and sense of control combined, in contrast with the achievement variance accounted for by interest in school, self-concept, and sense of control combined, in contrast with the achievement variance accounted for by the strongest background variables. The data indicate that attitudes are somewhat more important for achievement than family background and, further, that these attitudes are generally more important for whites than for the minority groups identified.

Further analyses of the attitude variables showed a different pattern of relationship with achievement for whites and the minority groups, excluding Orientals. Interest in school showed the weakest relationship with achievement for minority groups (negative relationship for Puerto Ricans); self-concept related positively to achievement for all groups, but most strongly for whites; control of environment was most strongly related to achievement for minority groups, but only slightly related for whites. With family background controlled, self-concept again related most strongly to achievement for whites, whereas control of environment related most strongly to achievement for the minority groups--excluding Orientals who showed a pattern similar to whites. School factors were essentially unrelated to self-concept and control of environment.

The survey data thus show that the child's sense of control

TABLE 24

Achievement Variance in Verbal Skills Accounted
for by Three Attitudes and Eight Background
Variables at Grades 12, 9, and 6[1]

	Attitude by Grade			Background by Grade		
	12	9	6	12	9	6
Puerto Ricans	9.1	14.0	9.0	4.7	6.2	25.6
Negro North	17.5	20.1	13.3	11.0	11.4	10.3
Negro South	17.2	20.1	15.6	15.8	15.7	15.4
White North	29.1	31.1	24.2	24.6	22.4	15.6

[1]Adapted from Coleman et al. (1966, p. 321).

over his environment is one of the crucial differences separating whites and minority groups. The survey data further appear to show that the lower sense of control of minority group students proceeds partly from family background experiences. It is also likely that the school is in some way responsible for the differential relationship between sense of control and achievement for whites and minority group students. Further analyses, for example, showed that as the proportion of white students in the school increased, the minority group child's sense of control over his environment increased.

Summary and Implications

Major findings of the Coleman et al. survey are summarized as follows, including findings not directly treated in the previous review:

1. Most Negroes and whites attend schools that are largely racially segregated, though the majority is greater in the South than in the North.

2. Since Negroes are predominantly of the lower social classes, Negroes are likely to be isolated in school by race as well as by social class.

3. School facilities, curricula, and teacher quality tend to be somewhat better for whites than for minority groups.

4. There are large discrepancies between the school achievement scores of whites and minority groups, Southern Negroes and Puerto Ricans being the furthest behind whites. The achievement differences between white and minority group students hold true for verbal achievements, reading comprehension, and mathematics achievement, and in other areas as well. The discrepancy in achievement between whites and some minority groups grows with increasing grade level.

5. The analyses of the relation of school and nonschool factors to achievement yields the following major findings:

a. As has been found in the findings of many previous studies, students' family background contributes strongly to achievement. Although they are not directly analyzed in the study, there are apparently a number of indirect and interactive effects of family background on achievement, in addition to the direct effect estimated. For example, there is an apparent effect of family background on achievement through student attitudes, such as sense of control of environment. Further than this, it appears that the background factors that

contribute to achievement comprise a different cluster for each
minority group examined.

b. Relatively little variation in achievement is associated
with differences between schools in the regions studied. The
range is from 10 to 20 percent for Northern Negroes and
whites and from about 17 to 31 percent for Puerto Ricans, depending on grade level.

c. Of the total between-school achievement variation,
only a small portion is attributable to differences directly
under the control of the school; part of this variation is attributable to family background differences. Furthermore, there
is a tendency for family background influences on achievement
to decrease across grade levels, somewhat dramatically for
Puerto Ricans.

d. The two previous findings are further qualified by the
finding that differences in teacher quality seem to be increasingly important for the achievement of Puerto Rican students with
advancing grade levels. A similar relationship exists for
Southern Negroes and Northern Negroes, but it cannot be considered an important effect for the Northern Negro.

e. In addition to the presumed effects of school factors
and family background on achievement, the social class composition of the school relates fairly strongly to achievement at
the twelfth grade level for certain minority group students,
and this relationship is independent of individual student background. This relationship is only nominal at the primary
grade levels, where the influences of family background are
strong. In the ninth and twelfth grades, however, it appears
that school social class composition is roughly as important
for achievement as family background for certain minority
groups. This relationship is again much more dramatic for
Puerto Ricans than for Northern Negroes--it will be recalled
that family background influences seemed to decrease most
dramatically with grade level for Puerto Ricans.

f. Since minority group students appear to be more affected than whites by differences in school quality (some evidence existed that showed minority groups were slightly more
affected than whites by qualitative difference between schools
though the relationships were weak), teacher quality, and
social class composition of the schools, the implication exists
that minority group students are particularly sensitive to
variations on these dimensions.

g. Aside from the school and nonschool factors already
discussed in relation to achievement, attitudinal factors seem
to be particularly important in relation to achievement for

both minority group students and white students. One particular attitude, the individual's sense of control over his environment, is more strongly related to achievement for minority
group students than for whites; they are less convinced than
whites that they have such control but become more convinced
and achieve at higher levels if they attend integrated schools.

    6. There is a positive relationship between attendance at
schools with whites and achievement of Negro students, with
the following additional qualifications:

    a. It appears to be essentially absent when the proportion
of white students in the school is 50 percent or less.

    b. It appears to be primarily a function of social class
mixing rather than racial mixing.

    c. It is more likely to be strong if the Negro student has
entered an integrated school setting during the early elementary grades rather than later.

    The following variables appear, then, to relate in impor-
tant ways to the achievement of minority students (Northern
and Southern Negroes and Puerto Ricans):

    Family Background
    School Social Class Composition   Verbal
    Sense of Control (and other attitudes)   Achievement
    Teacher Quality

    One additional set of variables had a slight relationship
to achievement:

    Facilities and Curricula   Achievement

    Because of the nature of the survey by Coleman et al.,
which was cross-sectional, examining intact classes of different students at one particular time and which was not designed
for observation or direct manipulation of the major variables
studied, it is difficult to impute causation on the basis of the
results. A further and important difficulty with the study
centers around the use made of multiple regression as the
major analytical technique. When the variables studied tend
to be highly interrelated, as many were in the survey, the
importance of one variable relative to that of another included
in the same analysis may depend on such simple conditions
as first entry in the analysis: thus, if two variables are equally correlated with achievement and moderately correlated with
each other, the first variable entered in the analysis is likely
to be judged more important for achievement.

    A further caution concerns the interpretations that may
be made of correlations in the absence of other information.
In the survey, the correlation between teacher quality and
achievement was taken as indicating that teacher quality affects

the achievement of minority group students. An equally plausible interpretation is that more intelligent and highly educated
teachers tend to teach in schools in which the students are
brighter or achieve at higher levels. These and other criticisms have been covered in numerous articles, such as those
by Bowles (1968) and Jencks (1969).

Some final points of caution relate to the over-all success
of the survey in accounting for the variance of the achievement
of various groups of students. Only some 10 percent of achievement variance of white students could have been accounted for
by differences between schools. For Northern Negroes, the
percentage was not much higher, ranging roughly from 10 to
20 percent of the total variance of achievement, depending on
the grade level examined. If causal interpretations were valid,
then changing such variables as racial and social class composition and teacher quality would not appear to have any great
effect on Northern Negroes, although they might have a greater effect on Puerto Ricans. Obviously, it is important to take
steps to equate these differences wherever direct manipulation
is possible. It is even more important, however, to recognize
that most of the variation in achievement in the survey existed
within schools and was in part attributable to such factors as
student attitudes, particularly the sense of control for Northern Negroes, and family background. Even with these factors
taken into account, more than 50 percent of the variation in
student achievement remained unaccounted for. Thus, much
more needs to be learned about the causes of achievement and
intellectual development of minority group students before
highly definitive steps can be taken.

Despite these criticisms, the survey does provide some
limited bases for action in the case of minority group students.
And the additional studies reviewed in this section generally
substantiate the findings of the survey by Coleman et al.,
while allowing some further refinements, which may improve
chances of taking effective action.

RACIAL ISOLATION IN THE PUBLIC SCHOOLS:
A REANALYSIS OF THE COLEMAN DATA

In the report to the President of the United States entitled
Racial Isolation in the Public Schools (U.S. Commission on
Civil Rights, 1967a), the results of several studies that at-
tempted to replicate and extend the findings of the survey of

Coleman et al. are described. This section presents a summary of the major findings of the reanalysis of data gathered
by Coleman et al. for the sixth, ninth, and twelfth grades.
The main purpose of these further analyses was to study in
more detail the relative contributions of racial and social class
compositions of the school to the achievement of Negro students. *

    The analytical technique used in Racial Isolation in the
Public Schools (hereafter referred to as the RIPS report) in-
volved the construction of tables of cross-tabulations, of which
Table 25 is a slightly simplified example.

    The scores used in each cell of the cross-tabulations
were students' verbal ability test scores, the main dependent
variable in the survey of Coleman et al. This technique allows
the assessment of the independent effects of individual factors
on achievement, such as the social class of individual students: each factor is averaged across every other factor.
The technique further allows the assessment of whether or
not the effect of a given factor varies across the levels of
another factor, known technically as an interaction between
two variables: for example, the data might show an over-all
effect for proportion of white classmates (a "main effect"
averaged across the levels of every other factor) but not show
this effect for junior high school and high school unless integration first occurred at the elementary school level.

    Ordinarily, cross-tabulations are an initial step in the
analysis of variance. The results of such an analysis may
indicate statistical significance (reliability) for the effect of a
given factor or interaction as well as the relative importance
(size) of effects if two or more occur. It is important to note
that such analyses were apparently not performed on the data
in the RIPS report. Effects of individual factors and interactions were apparently judged through examination of the
average scores in the cells and the averages of blocks of
cells in the cross-tabulations. Conclusions about main effects, relative sizes of effects, and interaction effects must,
then, be considered with some caution.

    The initial set of cross-tabulations in the study was done
on ninth grade Negro students in eight geographical regions
in the country, sample sizes ranging from 926 to 8,246. One
of the initial tabulations controlled for school social class,
individual social status, and earliest grade in desegregated

---

    *The section of the report under discussion is McPartland's
reanalysis of the Coleman data, Appendices, Racial Isolation
in the Public Schools (1967, Appendix C-1, pp. 35-142).

TABLE 25

Explanatory Example of the Cross-Tabulation
Technique Used in the RIPS Report

Individual Student Social Class	Grade Level First Integrated	Proportion White Classmates Last Year			
		None	Less Than Half	Half	More Than Half
Low	Elem.	a			
	Intermed.				
	J.H.S.				
	Never				
Middle	Elem.				
	Intermed.				
	J.H.S.				
	Never				
High	Elem.				
	Intermed.				
	J.H.S.				
	Never				

aRepresents a score for each cell.

162

class. The remaining tabulations in these first analyses
eliminated the school social class factor. Succeeding analyses relating to achievement were done for sixth, ninth, and
twelfth grade Negroes in the metropolitan Northeast. This
group of analyses included the school social class factor measured in a variety of ways, one table including both school
and classroom social class factors. Sample sizes varied a-
mong tables, but they were generally large for the analyses
relating to achievement. For the one analysis that included
both school and classroom social class compositions, there
were a number of missing cells and large discrepancies in
cell sizes (Table 4.15, p. 84).

Several factors other than family background were controlled in the analyses, but sample size prevented simultaneous
control of all control factors included in the study. In essence,
the approach used leads to a preliminary establishment of the
effects on Negro achievement, independently, of racial and
social class composition of the student body; additional analyses lead to supplementary attempts to determine whether the
effects of the composition of the student body are washed out
by controlling factors related to school and teacher quality
and tracking and ability grouping. The most relevant analyses
for establishing the effects of racial composition per se--inde-
pendent of school and classroom social class effects--were
the tables that controlled for social class in the classroom.
The lack of a longitudinal control for ability in these analyses,
the inability to control simultaneously for racial and social
class factors in regard to the individual, school, and classroom, and the lack of control for school effects render any
findings of a separate contribution of racial composition of
the school and classroom to Negro achievement suspect.

These criticisms relating to controls in the RIPS study
should not lead to any serious equivocation about the existence
of facilitating educational effects associated with racial integration in the schools. What will emerge, in fact, in the
subsequent discussion of the findings of the RIPS report are
effects on achievement associated independently with racial
and social class compositions of the student body. What is
in doubt is the notion of racial composition of the student body
as a direct source of differences in achievement among Negro
students, not whether there is an additional source beyond the
social class composition of the student body. The effect of
student social class composition on educational development
among Negroes, it should be noted in advance, is less subject
to equivocation since its effect is consistently in evidence

when different indicators are used in otherwise similar analyses; for example, parents' education, material possessions in the home, reading material in the home, parents' educational desires, and the average verbal achievement level of the school.

It is also important to understand that the independent contributions of racial and social class composition of the school or classroom to Negro achievement are relatively large, being on the order of half a standard deviation or more, a fact that was less apparent in the Coleman analyses of the data than it is in the RIPS report. Few educational treatments tried in the schools have resulted in differences on this order (over what would normally be expected), and it is further apparent that applications of compensatory education in the schools have shown virtually no evidence of capability to effect educational changes on the order of the size of effect attributable to integration (see Chapters 6 and 7). One might further presume that the total effect of integration could comprise the even larger additive effects of both racial and social class compositions of the student body, if both were taken into account in planning desegregation. However, only more carefully conceived research can result in reliable judgements of the potential power of integration. One such study, reviewed later in this chapter (Wilson, 1967), shows that a longitudinal control for IQ removes the residual relation between racial composition of the school and Negro achievement, leaving school social class composition as the evident source of the facilitating effect of integration on Negro achievement.

With these cautions and considerations in mind, it is appropriate to proceed to a summary of the major relationships observed in the RIPS report.

1. Within the regional analyses, one table controlling for school social class indicates a minor effect on achievement for this factor and a larger effect for the racial composition factor. The remaining tables indicate a consistent effect for racial composition (school social class uncontrolled) and a more minor but consistent effect for earliest grade in desegregated class. Across different regional samples, achievement increases are negligible or inconsistent when, for the item "proportion of white classmates last year," the category "none" is compared with "less than half" or "half"; when the category "none" is compared with "more than half," achievement increments for Negro students are positive and more consistent and approach a value of half a standard deviation.

2. For Negroes in the sixth, ninth, and twelfth grade samples, metropolitan Northeast, where individual social class and school social class, and sometimes earliest grade in desegregated class, were controlled, the analyses showed relatively large contributions of both school social class and racial composition of the school to Negro achievement, generally half a standard deviation or more for both factors. The effect of the social class composition of the school may be nonlinear in its relationship with achievement: That is, when more than two levels of school social class composition are dealt with in an analysis, large achievement differences tend to exist between the high and low levels of the social class factors, whereas achievement differences between the low and intermediate categories of the social class factors tend to be generally small or nonexistent.

3. The residual effect of the racial composition of the school--that is, the effect of the racially segregated classroom independent of individual and school social class, school characteristics, and facilities and curricula--was further examined in a series of analyses in which the influences of the latter group of factors were controlled in different combinations. Under these conditions, it appeared that there was an independent or residual relationship between achievement of Negro students and the proportion of white students in the classroom. Although this finding is interpreted as indicating that racial segregation by itself exerts a damaging effect on achievement of Negro students, other interpretations also apply. On this crucial point, it must be remembered that no significance tests were applied in these analyses and that more sophisticated analyses of the same hypothesis failed to show that racial isolation by itself makes a significant difference in achievement (Wilson, 1967).

4. Examination of conditions within desegregated schools showed a slight relationship between interracial tension and achievement and between interracial tension and attitudes of Negro students. Additional evidence suggested that interracial tension is, in part, a function of the length of time the student has been in integrated schools, schools with students having relatively long experience of integration showing less racial tension. Desegregated classrooms are also associated with increases in the proportion of Negro students who have definite plans for college, who disagree with the statement "Good luck is more important than hard work for success," and who are likely to have close white friends.

5. Interracial friendships, which are apparently facilitated in integrated classrooms, also appear to reduce the
likelihood that Negro students will prefer to attend racially
segregated schools and increases the likelihood that Negro
students will make definite plans to attend college. Though
the relationships discussed in this item and the previous one
need further study, the data suggest that the development of
Negro-white friendships in the school context is psychologically important, possibly mediating in part the effect of interracial schooling on Negro students' achievement, racial attitudes, and sense of control over the environment.

Relationship of School Characteristics to Student Performance

Most of the relationships of school facilities and curriculum and school quality (an index) with achievement appear to
have been weak or inconsistent when examined across social
class variables and proportions of white students in the classroom. One relationship that appears to be consistent in the
survey is the positive relationship between indexes of teacher
quality and student achievement, and this relationship seems
to be more consistent for Negroes in the classrooms that are
more than 50 percent white. The results of the analyses in
the RIPS report on this point are similar to the findings of the
analyses of Coleman et al. on the same data for Negroes in
the metropolitan Northeast. According to both analyses,
school and teacher effects do not account for major portions
of achievement variance for Negroes in the Northeast, and
family background and social class composition of the school
appear to be more important.

Relationship of Integration to Achievement and Attitudes for White Students

1. With regard to the implications of integration for
white students in the metropolitan Northeast, the results of
the RIPS report relating to achievement indicated that, witn
family background and school social class controlled, there
was no apparent relationship between the proportion of Negroes in the school or classroom, or the grade level at which
integration was experienced, and the achievement levels of
white students. Parents' educational levels and educational

desires were strongly related to the achievement of white
students, and social class composition of the school was also
related to the achievement of white students, though independent of the proportion of white students in the classroom and
weaker than family background factors. The findings for college plans were similar to those for integration and achievement.

2. The findings on student attitudes showed that white
students were less likely to choose to attend an all-white
school if they had previously been in an integrated classroom.
This relationship tended to be stronger if the student had experienced integrated schooling in the elementary grades than
if he had experienced it at later grades. Other findings showed that the length and extent of the integration experience for
white students were similarly associated with the proportions
of whites who would choose all-white friends or prefer an all-
white school. As for the results for Negro students, the findings for white students suggest that positive racial attitudes
(less preference for all-white schools and all-white friends)
may be partly mediated by Negro-white friendships. All the
findings in which integration was related to attitudes of white
students were consistently more dramatic for students who
would be placed in the middle class or higher.

It should be recognized that many of the basic criticisms
made of the Coleman et al. study apply equally to the RIPS
report, which, after all, reanalyzed the same data. Thus,
the report is properly regarded as a study of relationships
for different students at different grade levels. The findings
of the RIPS report were encouragingly similar to those of
Coleman et al. Individual and school social class levels still
stand out as important factors related to student achievement.
School and teacher factors are found to be even more minimal
in their relationship with achievement than they are in the
Coleman et al. report. However, this disparity is probably
a result of the fact that some of the disadvantaged groups for
whom these factors were most important in Coleman et al.
were excluded in the RIPS analyses--Puerto Ricans, American Indians, and Southern Negroes. The inconsistency between the two reports on this point appears to be resolved on
the basis of the ethnic units treated.

The authors of the RIPS report apparently feel that one
of the more important findings of their study is the demonstration of a negative effect of racial segregation on Negro
achievement when other important sources of variation are
accounted for. In none of the analyses in which the residual

effect of racial composition on achievement was assessed, however, was it possible to control simultaneously the potentially confounding influences of all factors worthy of control. As with the Coleman et al. analyses, wherein it was concluded that the effect of racial composition was nearly or wholly attributable to social class composition of the student body, there is no clear-cut basis for judging the relative contributions of the racial composition and the social class composition of the student body. Caution is further advised because of the lack of control of student ability factors, which may have differed among the categories based on proportion of white students in the classroom.

Certain other findings of the RIPS reanalysis of the Coleman et al. data are properly regarded as contributing important new information concerning the conditions that are likely to contribute to success in the integrated situation. Beyond this, the report was unable to uncover any harmful effect of racial composition per se on the achievement and attitudes of white students; indeed, the converse effect seems to have been shown. From the point of view of a democratic society, integrated schools seem to have positive effects on the interracial attitudes of both whites and Negroes.

A STUDY OF INTEGRATION IN A CALIFORNIA COMMUNITY

As indicated at several points in the discussion of the Coleman et al. survey and the RIPS report, the methodology of these studies resulted in certain problems concerning the particular sources of the effect of integration on achievement. A study completed by Wilson (1967) for the U.S. Commission on Civil Rights provides further data on some of the major relationships studied in the survey by Coleman et al. and in the RIPS analysis of the Coleman et al. data. This study introduced a number of important refinements not present in the other reports. One of the more important refinements was the establishment of a quasi-longitudinal framework for studying relationships between factors associated with segregated schooling and student variables. Another refinement was the introduction of a control for intelligence--whereas student ability could not practically be controlled in the Coleman et al. and RIPS analyses and thus remains a major alternative explanation for the presumed effects of racial isolation.

Still another refinement, which requires more explanation, concerns Wilson's use of regression analysis, which avoids some of the problems experienced by Coleman et al. in their regression analyses. By selecting standardized partial regression coefficients as the measure of importance--rather than using increases in the squared multiple correlation (R^2), interpretable as a proportion of variance--and in effect including all independent variables simultaneously in the regression analyses, Wilson was in a better position to develop conclusions about the relative contributions of several factors to achievement. The simplified example given in Table 26 presents standardized regression coefficients for four factors in a single regression equation predicting achievement. The regression coefficients may be interpreted as indicating the strength of the independent relationships between factors A through D and achievement.[*] Depending on the ability to meet certain assumptions, an effect or causal interpretation may be made. In this case the regression coefficients represent relative sizes of effects interpretable as follows: given a unit increase in factor "A", the effect of A on achievement is roughly an increase of .37 units. Similarly, with every unit decrease in "B", there is a corresponding unit increase of about .19 units in achievement. Generally, standardized partial regression coefficients on the order of from .1 to .2 represent small but not necessarily unimportant effects; those of from .2 to .5 represent more substantial effects; and those greater than .5 are quite substantial and are far less frequently found in studies with large numbers of independent variables.[**] One further point should be made in preparation for interpreting Wilson's results, and that concerns

---

[*]The independence of each factor, A, B, C, and D, results from the fact that each regression coefficient is a "partial": that is, it represents the relationship between a given factor and achievement with the influences of all other factors included in the analysis removed. Thus if A, B, C, and D are intercorrelated (related to each other), a regression coefficient for achievement on A alone would represent a relationship including the influences of B, C, and D on achievement. The use of a partial regression coefficient effectively removes these confounding influences and may correspondingly allow evaluation of the "true" size of the direct effect of A on achievement.

[**] This interpretation must be used with considerable caution in this study since in a causal analysis a variable may

TABLE 26

Standardized Regression Coefficients for
Four Factors in Relation to Achievement[1]

Factor	Reg.[a] Coeff.	R^2	R^2 (increase)[b]
A	.369	55.4	55.4%
B	-.187	60.2	4.8%
C	.379	70.6	10.4%
D	-.109	71.4	.8%

[1]From O'Reilly (1969, p. 106). This is intended only as an explanatory example to aid interpretation of Wilson's analysis, which is more complex. The reader is also forewarned that the tests of significance applied in the study should be viewed with some caution (See Wilson, 1967, p. 176).

[a]Raw regression coefficients, which are included in Wilson's report, are not interpretable as relative effects.

[b]Measure of importance used in the Coleman et al. study and referred to as the proportion of variance attributable to a given factor. In the study from which these data are taken, if "A" is entered first, then "C" will appear less important, using the increase in variance (R^2/increase) as the basis for interpretation.

the interpretation of relative effects: such regression coefficients as those shown for factors A through D may be compared in relative size, using the absolute value of each coefficient, and it is thus possible to state that A is more important
than B, though small differences should not be emphasized.

Background of the Study

Since the area covered by the study may be analogous in
some measure to smaller urban areas in New York State, it
is worth giving some attention to economic and residential
factors associated with racial membership. Western Contra
Costa County, the geographical unit used in the Wilson study,
is an industrial urban area in the larger San Francisco-Oak-
land Metropolitan Area. As a result of in-migration, the
Negro population grew considerably over a twenty-year period, and twelve percent of the population was composed of
Negroes by 1960. The Negro population is centered primarily
in deteriorated areas. Average income in these areas is only
about half that in the more well-to-do white areas; the average
value of housing is only about a third. Because social class
and race are highly related, most Negroes live in neighborhoods that have a high percentage of lower class residents.
At the same time, the segregated Negro residential areas
tend to be less homogeneous with regard to social class (occupational level) than do white neighborhoods: that is, as a
result of segregated housing patterns, even Negroes in relatively high status occupations tend to live in areas in which a
high proportion of residents belong to the lower social classes.
Residence in racially segregated, largely lower class neighborhoods is usual for Negro students.
The racial composition of the schools usually reflects
the residential patterns described above. On the average,
white children attend nearly all-white, predominantly upper-
status schools. Negro children, on the average, attend
schools that have a much higher proportion of Negro and
lower status students. This pattern for Negroes is particularly

---

appear to have a slight effect due to the inclusion of other
variables that intervene between it and the variable affected.
The total effect of a particular independent variable (direct
plus indirect effects) may thus be considerably larger than its
direct effect alone. Procedures described by Blalock (1961)
are appropriate in this case but were not used in Wilson's study.

evident at the elementary grades, dropping off somewhat
sharply at the junior and senior high school levels.

From the area described above, Wilson, in 1965, selected
more than 5,000 students, stratified by sex, race, school, and
grade level. Random but disproportionate samples were drawn
from each stratum, and corrective weighting procedures were
applied in the analyses for disproportionate sampling. Measures were then taken for each student on neighborhood characteristics; social class level; race; family background characteristics relating to social class and ethnicity; a variety of
achievement and ability indexes; and indexes of self-concept,
attitudes, aspirations, and behavioral deviance. Intellectual
ability was controlled in the study by using IQ test scores obtained from students when they entered school at the early
primary grade levels. Students' ability scores taken at the
primary grade level were then used as the index of ability in
gauging the effects of schooling on their achievement and related variables at later grade levels. Achievement levels
occurring at later grade levels could then be attributed to
later environmental influences mediated by initial environmental effects and native endowment in ability. This procedure
effectively removed one of the more serious problems deficits
of the Coleman et al. and RIPS reports, the lack of control
for ability variables and early experience.

As indicated previously, the statistical technique used in
assessing the major questions of the study was regression
analysis. Cross-tabulations were also used to examine some
relationships. Like the Coleman et al. survey and the RIPS
reanalysis of the Coleman et al. data, Wilson's study was
directed at examining the relationships of various factors
associated with racial and social class isolation in the schools
with achievement and other behaviors of Negroes and whites
at different grade levels. Because of the methodological refinements instituted in Wilson's study, the results may be
taken as more definitive than those found with the Coleman
et al. data, although some important reservations remain,
which will be indicated later.

Nonschool Sources of Variation in Student
Ability and Performance

In regard to the contributions of family background variables and neighborhood characteristics to achievement of
Negro and white students, the intent of the analyses was, in

part, to determine whether certain background factors had any significance for achievement and could thus be removed from consideration or taken into account in the main analyses for the study. Achievement and intellectual differences between Negroes and whites by grade level were also further documented.

Table 27 shows the mean IQ scores for Negro and white students in the primary grades and in the sixth, eighth, and eleventh grades at the time the study was conducted. These data show a difference of 9 IQ points between Negroes and whites at the primary grades, which increased to 15 points at the eleventh grade. In grade equivalents, Negro students show a similar increasing lag behind whites in reading achievement: slightly less than 1 year in the first grade, 1 year in the third grade, and 1.7 years in the sixth grade.

To determine the relative contributions of background and school variables to achievement at the elementary school level, Wilson performed a series of separate analyses as follows:

1. Effects of the absence of the father on IQ by grade level, taking into account the following variables: IQ (first grade), family background, father absence versus father presence, sex, and race.

2. Effects of family background on primary grade IQ, taking into account the following variables: social class level of neighborhood, family background variables, individual social class level, racial composition of neighborhood, and race.

3. Effects of social class of neighborhood and segregated schooling on reading achievement, including the following variables: previous school social class level, previous attendance in segregated primary grades, extent of previous isolation by race and social class in neighborhood, family background, individual social class level, and race.

The investigation of the effects of the absence of the father on achievement was apparently included for the purpose of determining whether this family background factor, which is found very frequently among lower class Negro families, should be taken into account in the other analyses performed in the study. Wilson's analyses among lower class children, using several measures of educational development at various grade levels, failed to turn up any significant effects of the absence of the father among Negro and white students, a finding consistent with the findings of Coleman et al. for Negro students. Other studies of this relationship have been either

TABLE 27

Mean IQ Scores for Negroes and Whites by Grade Level[1]

Grade Level	N	$\bar{X}$ IQ Negroes	N	$\bar{X}$ IQ Whites
Primary	(1350)	102	(1495	111
Sixth Grade	(1507)	93	(1765)	105
Eighth Grade	(1722)	90	(2029)	104
Eleventh Grade	(623)	90	(934)	105

[1]From Wilson (1967, Tables 8-11, pp. 172 and 173).

negative (Weltz and Wilkinson, 1957; Birnbaum, 1966) or in-
conclusive (Kasdon, 1955; Crescimbeni, 1964; Kelly, North,
and Zingle, 1965; and Miner, 1968). Control of the frequency
of the absence of the father among the families investigated in
Wilson's study therefore appeared unnecessary.

The main results of the second analysis showed that neither the proportion of lower class children nor the proportion
of Negroes in the neighborhood seemed to have any relationship to the IQ scores of Negro or white children at the primary
grade level. The results of a regression analysis, controlling
for additional family characteristics, again failed to show any
effect of neighborhood on intelligence, as shown in Table 28.
This is an especially important finding. The possible effects
of race, individual social class, and the cultural level of the
home already appear to have had their effects on primary
grade IQ, as shown by the significant weights for these factors
in Table 28. Other findings showed that family background
factors tended to be more highly related to intellectual development for whites than for Negroes, apparently partly because
variation on social class is greater for whites than for Negroes.
Coleman et al. also found that family background tended to explain more variation in verbal ability for whites than Northern
Negroes (Tables 3.221.1 and 3.221.2, p. 299). The findings
of both studies suggest that social and economic aspects of
the family generally impinge more on the intellectual development of whites than Negroes.

The third set of analyses at the elementary grade level
examined whether the racial and social class composition of
both the neighborhood and the school at the primary grade
level had any effects on student achievement by the conclusion
of the elementary school years.

The results of the regression analysis, shown in Table 29,
indicate that primary grade IQ has the largest effect on later
educational development (B = .15), followed by lower class
primary school (in lower class primary school or not, B =
-.12), followed by family social class and related factors.
The results in Table 29 further show that when social class
composition of the primary school, primary grade IQ, and
family variables are held constant, attendance in a segregated
primary school and being in a lower class neighborhood during
the primary grades fail to show a relationship with achievement
at the sixth grade. Moreover, there is essentially no effect of
race by itself on achievement when other relevant variables
are held constant. In discussing the implications of these
findings, Wilson (1967) concludes:

TABLE 28

he Contributions of Nonschool Factors to Primary
Grade Intelligence[1]

Factor	Normalized Partial Regression Coefficients
Neighborhood Social Class	-N.S.
Family Background	
Lack of Supervision by Mother	-.05*
Number of Objects in Home	.12*
Number of Siblings	-.07*
Family Social Class[a]	-.17*
Race	
Negro	-.14*
White	.03*

[1]From Wilson (1967, Table 13, p. 176).

[a]Four occupational levels used.

*Statistically significant

N.S. = Nonsignificant

N = 2,066

176

TABLE 29

The Contributions of Primary Grade School and Nonschool
Factors to Reading Achievement at the Sixth Grade Level[1]

Factor	Normalized Partial Regression Coefficients
Lower-Class Primary School	-.12*
Negro Primary School	N.S.
Lower-Class Primary Neighborhood	N.S.
Negro Primary Neighborhood	N.S.
Primary Grade IQ	.15*
Lack of Supervision by Mother	-.04*
Number of Objects in Home	.07*
Family Social Class[a]	.08*
Race	
Negro	-.01*
White	---

[1] From Wilson (1967, Table 16, p. 180).

[a] Four occupational levels used.

*Statistically significant

N.S. = Nonsignificant

N = 2,078

The lack of any direct effect of neighborhood compo-
sition--either racial or socioeconomic--upon measured school achievement is of considerable consequence for policy and theory. One continuing
reservation about the relevance of proposals to alter
the demographic composition [racial and social class
composition] of schools is the question as to whether
continuing residential segregation might structure
the effective environment of students so that their integration in schools makes no difference. These
data are inconsistent with this reservation. On the
contrary, these data suggest that the effect of neighborhood segregation on achievement is entirely through the resulting segregation of neighborhood
schools on social class lines. Restructuring the
composition of schools, even in the absence of residential rearrangement, can be expected to have an
effect upon the academic achievement of students
(p. 180).

Relative Effects of Racial and Social Class Composition on the Achievement of Negroes and Whites

In regard to the contributions of racial and social class
isolation to achievement and intellectual development, examined for both whites and Negroes at different grade levels,
the results of the analyses document further the notion that
the effect of racial segregation on Negro achievement operates
through the concomitant segregation along social class lines.
The negative effect of social class isolation is also evident
for whites but appears to be a more minor contributing factor
than for Negro students.

A series of initial cross-tabulations, which may have
been considerably affected by sampling errors, tended to
show that the verbal reasoning scores of eighth grade whites
were negatively affected by prior attendance in schools of
lower social class levels, but racial composition had no effect. Table 30 shows the relative contributions of racial and
social class isolation to achievement for white and Negro
students separately. Comparison of the coefficients in the
first row shows that as the social class status of the school
increases, student achievement increases--but the effect is
about twice as great for Negro students as for whites. School
racial composition, on the other hand, fails to show any

TABLE 30

The Contributions of Racial and Social Class Isolation
to Eighth Grade Achievement (DAT Verbal Reasoning Percentiles)[1]

Factor	Normalized Partial Regression Coefficients	
	Negro[c]	White[d]
Lower-Class Intermediate School[a]	.20*	.10*
Negro Intermediate School[b]	N.S.	N.S.
1st Grade IQ	.31*	.32*
Lack of Supervision by Mother	N.S.	-.04*
Number of Objects in Home	.07*	.16*
Number of Siblings	-.09*	-.05*
Family Social Class	N.S.	.15*

[1]Adapted from Wilson (1967, Tables 21 and 24, pp. 184 and 186).

[a]Three school social class levels used (0-19, 20-49, 50-100 percent lower class).

[b]Three levels of racial isolation (0-9, 10-49, 50-100 percent Negro).

[c]N = 905

[d]N = 1,204

*Statistically significant

N. S. = Nonsignificant

relationship to achievement for either Negroes or whites. It may also be noted that the relationship between IQ at the first grade and achievement at the eighth grade is about the same for Negroes and whites. Family social class, however, is significantly related to achievement only for whites. These results are in accord with those of Coleman et al. and may be interpreted as indicating differential sensitivity of Negroes and whites in relation to the social class context of the class-room and the social class context of the family.

The later effects of social class isolation experienced at different stages in the students' schooling may be judged from the results shown in Table 31. The first column shows the coefficients for social class composition of the school at the junior high, intermediate, and primary grade levels, in re-lation to achievement. The major finding to be observed in this regard is that the relationship between the social class composition of the school and achievement is stronger at the intermediate grade level than at the junior high school level. The next two columns show the same relationships for eleven-th grade intelligence scores, with the exception of the primary school level, for which data on social class composition were apparently not available. The results for these two columns again show that the experience of upper or lower social class composition in the school at the senior and junior high school levels fails to relate to IQ scores, in this instance, at the eleventh grade. Whereas having attended a predominantly upper status intermediate school was facilitating for both Negroes and whites in relation to eighth grade achievement, however, this relationship with the intermediate grade exper-ience holds up for whites only when examined at the eleventh grade level, failing to be replicated for Negroes.*

The results of the analyses relating achievement to level of school social class composition and to the time at which these levels were experienced clearly lead to the interpretation that segregation at the elementary school level may effect subsequent school achievement. Segregation at the junior and senior high school levels apparently has only a slight effect, if any. Since the social class composition of the school tends to be of a much lower status for Negroes than for whites, Negro students are at a decided educational disadvantage.

---

*The lack of a consistent relationship for Negroes at the high school level may have been a result of the higher dropout rate for Negroes, resulting in a group of mostly high achieving Negroes (see Wilson, 1967, p. 189).

TABLE 31

The Contributions of Social Class Isolation Experienced at
Different Grade Levels to Educational and Intellectual Development[1]

Factor	8th Grade DAT[b] Negroes and Whites	11th Grade IQ[c] Whites	11th Grade IQ Negroes
Lower-Class Senior High School[a]	---	N.S.	N.S.
Lower-Class Junior High School	.06*	N.S.	N.S.
Lower-Class Intermediate School	.11*	.11*	N.S.
Lower-Class Primary School	N.S.	---	---
1st or Primary Grade IQ	.30*	.24*	.22*
Lack of Supervision by Mother	-.04*	-.05*	N.S.
Number of Objects in Home	.13*	.10*	.13*
Number of Siblings	-.05*	-.06*	N.S.
Family Social Class	.13*	.22*	.12*
Race	.12*	---	---

[1]Adapted from Wilson (1967, Tables 28, 29, and 30

[a]Two school social class levels at senior high; three levels for the remaining grades.

[b]Verbal reasoning score, Differential Aptitude Test.

[c]Henmon-Nelson IQ

N's are 2049 for 8th grade DAT; 533 for 11th grade IQ, white; 315 for 11th grade IQ, Negro.

*Statistically significant

N. S. = Nonsignificant

This is a direct result of racial segregation in the schools and proceeds from the fact that Negro students are far more likely than whites to attend segregated schools at the elementary levels and to be members of the lower class stratum, the correlation between race and class status being reported by Wilson as .77.

Segregation and Other Educationally Relevant Variables

The final set of findings reported by Wilson was concerned with the relationship of racial and social class composition of the school to educational aspirations, academic sense of control, self-concept, and delinquent behavior. The major findings in these areas, summarized briefly, were as follows:

1. Academic self-concept--belief that one can get A's and B's--was essentially unrelated to race and social class but was strongly and significantly related to achievement level.

2. Sense of control--"Planning is useless since one's plans hardly ever work out."--was significantly related to verbal achievement, race, the social class composition of the school, and sex. A lack of a sense of control over events seemed to be associated with the following factors: low achievement, male sex, Negro race, and predominantly lower class schooling. The most important factor in this respect was verbal achievement level.

3. Among white students, academic self-concept and verbal achievement were equally strong predictors of aspiring to attend college. Previous social class composition of the school, family background variables, family social class, and being male also contributed significantly to college aspirations, but less strongly than achievement. Among Negroes, the same set of variables contributed much less strongly to college aspirations, although verbal achievement and academic self-concept were the strongest predictors.

4. The lower relevance of achievement and academic self-concept in determining college aspirations of Negroes suggests a distorting defensive process, since it is known that Negro students are far more likely than whites to be low achievers. Among Negroes who attended lower class schools, the discrepancy between professed college aspirations and the likelihood of academic success was most pronounced. Paradoxically, Negroes were the more likely to reject manual occupations.

5. Data from police records for a two-year period show-ed that 53 percent of Negro adolescent boys and 26 percent of white adolescent boys had official police records of offenses. The most important correlates of the tendency to be nondelin-quent, that is, not to have a police record, were perceived importance of school grades, verbal achievement, and attend-ing an upper status school. Family social class level and be-ing in a broken home were not significantly related to the be-havioral deviance criterion.

The results of this final set of analyses in Wilson's study suggest a pattern linking attendance in racially and socially isolated schools with maladaptive defensive responses ex-pressed in attitudinal orientations as well as in antisocial be-havior. Lack of school success, which is partly determined by the effects of early experience in the home and the contin-uous experience of isolation from upper status students during the elementary school years, progressively weakens the in-dividual's feeling that he can attain valued long-term rewards. His sense of commitment to the future is correspondingly weakened, and he becomes less constrained to meet the im-mediate educational demands. Increasing alienation from academic values is reflected in withdrawal from schoolwork and school-related activities. The student thus has more op-portunity to engage in delinquent acts. In these analyses, it is clear that the quality of schooling is as important a factor in determining antisocial behavior in lower status Negroes as are the continuing but more indirect influences of individual ability. Neighborhood factors and family structure fail to show any independent influence on the development of delin-quent behavior.

Conclusions and Implications

The conclusions and implications stated below are taken directly from Wilson's report.

1. Allowing for individual differences in personal background, neighborhood context and mental ma-turity at the time of school entry, variations in elementary school context [social class composition of the school] make a substantial and significant dif-ference in subsequent academic success at higher grade levels.

2. Socioeconomic and racial characteristics of
students' agemates in the local neighborhood have
no independent effect upon the academic achievement
of students attending similar schools.

3. The social class composition of the school . . .
affects the academic development of both Negro and
white students in either racially integrated or racially segregated situations.

4. Given similar social class compositions, the
racial balance of a school has slight [or no] bearing
on the academic performance of students.

5. Social-class segregation of students, through
its effect upon the development of academic skills,
has ramifying consequences for students' subjective
sense of competence and belief that they can plan
and control their futures.

6. Failure to succeed in school weakens students'
bonds to established institutions and social norms,
freeing them to engage in delinquent activity. Segregation, moreover, affects official delinquency
rates . . . through its effect [on] competence, morale, and subsequent behavior[s] . . . (pp. 202-3).

Wilson further concludes:

In broad outline, we see that the unequal inheritance
[social class background] with which students enter
school which should become less salient as students
progress through school if schools in fact maxi-
mized individual potential, is in fact aggravated because of segregation.

     Three guidelines to policy are implicit in the
results of this study: (1) Considering conclusions
3 and 4 above, together, strategems to achieve
racial balance in schools must simultaneously amel-
iorate social-class imbalance if they are to equalize
the educationally relevant milieu.

     (2) From conclusions 2 and 3, while residen-
tial integration may be a desirable social goal in
its own right, the effectiveness of school integration is not dependent upon concomitant changes in
neighborhood patterns.

     (3) The large initial differences in social in-
heritance of children entering school are not per-
ceptibly ameliorated by standard school programs

of remedial reading, special classes for the "mentally retarded" which take place in segregated
schools, and grouped classes within schools
(p. 203).

Two additional broad implications of Wilson's results are
brought out in Table 32, which shows the regression coefficients for different levels of school social class composition
in relation to educational and intellectual development. A-
cross the analyses in Wilson's study, either two or three
school social class levels were used: (1) 0 - 19 and 20 - 60
percent lower class students in the school and (2) 0 - 19,
20 - 49, and 50 - 100 percent lower class students in the
school. When the regression coefficients for these school
social class levels are examined, it is apparent that there is
a generally consistent and positive "effect" on achievement
when the percentage of lower class students in the school is
less than 20 and that there is a negative "effect" when the percentage exceeds 20 percent. This trend breaks down for Negro
students at the high school level, who, at that point, constitute
a select group. The effect of social class composition of the
school on performance is further modified by the length of
the experience, the elementary school level appearing to be
the most effective point for the initiation of integration. The
point at which "percent lower class students in the school"
assumes a negative value in relation to achievement cannot
be determined precisely from the data given in Wilson's report. However, these and other data given in this volume
clearly suggest that the effect of integration on the achievement of lower status students, both Negro and white, ranges
from being slightly positive to being slightly negative when
the percentage of lower status students ranges from 30 to 50.
When the percentage of lower status students exceeds 50,
there does not appear to be any marked increasing negative
effect associated with increasing proportions of lower status
students in the school.
    All in all, the data indicate that the typical integrated
school context is effective for the disadvantaged student when
the advantaged student population is very much the majority.
Since this trend is consistent in the studies under consideration, as well as in less representative studies of integration
(Jaquith, 1967; Sullivan, 1968), it appears that there is a
sufficiently strong basis for the formulation of policy concerning educationally desirable proportions of upper and lower
status students in the typical integrated school.

TABLE 32

Contributions of Different Levels of School Social Class Composition
to Student Achievement Examined across Analyses[1]

Analyses	Race	N	% Lower-Class in School		Normalized Parti Regression Coefficients
A		640	0	- 19	+.05[a]
(Intermediate on	White	525	20	- 49	-.05
Eighth Grade)		39	50	- 100	-.02
B		17	0	- 19	+.18[a]
(Intermediate on	Negro	502	20	- 49	+.02
Eighth Grade)		368	50	- 100	-.06
A + B$_1$	White	1,430	0	- 19	+.04[a]
(Junior High on	and	619	20	- 69	-.03
Eighth Grade)	Negro				
A + B$_2$	White	632	0	- 19	+.06[a]
(Intermediate on	and	1,004	20	- 49	-.04
Eighth Grade)	Negro	413	50	- 100	-.04
C$_1$		224	0	- 19	.00[b]
(Senior High on	White	309	20	- 69	.00
Senior High)					
C$_2$		298	0	- 19	.00[b]
(Junior High on	White	235	20	- 69	.00
Senior High)					
C$_3$		265	0	- 19	+.05[b]
(Intermediate on	White	250	20	- 49	-.05
Senior High)		18	50	- 100	-.03
D$_1$		30	0	- 19	-.02[b]
(Senior High on	Negro	285	20	- 69	.00
Senior High)					
D$_2$		5	0	- 19	---[b]
(Junior High on	Negro	310	20	- 69	.00
Senior High)					
D$_3$		2	0	- 19	---[b]
(Intermediate on	Negro	179	20	- 49	-.03
Senior High)		134	50	- 100	+.04

[1]Adapted from Wilson (1967, Tables 21, 24, 28, 29, 30).

[a]Eighth Grade, Differential Aptitude Test, Verbal Reasoning.

[b]Eleventh Grade Henmon-Nelson IQ.

Some Points of Criticism

At the outset of this discussion of Wilson's study, it was shown that a few important refinements not present in previous studies of interracial education had been introduced. It was further indicated that these refinements allowed greater confidence in interpretations of relationships as possible causal effects and causal chains. Although causal interpretations may appear plausible at this point, a number of cautions appear in order, and may now be considered.

The analysis of causal relations using a regression model requires a number of assumptions. Some major assumptions that apply in Wilson's analysis are as follows:

1. The relationships between the causal variables and achievement are linear and additive.

2. Reciprocal causation between any independent variable and achievement (the dependent variable) can be ruled out.

3. Outside variables causing achievement are either small in magnitude and relatively numerous, or if there are a few additional major causes of achievement, these variables are uncorrelated with any of the independent variables included in the analysis.

4. Measurement errors included in the independent variables are negligible.

First, it appears that the direct effect of school social class composition may be nonlinear in its relationship with achievement, and the value of its regression coefficient may thus be underestimated. Moreover, the relationship between this variable and achievement may be partly obscured by the assumption of a linear function.

Moreover, since an analysis of the causes of achievement in the school context is somewhat analogous to tracing the paths of individual bugs in a swarm, caution must thus be observed in interpreting the values and significance of the regression coefficients in Wilson's study. The inclusion of a new causal variable, correlated with the current list of independent variables, can result in considerable modification of the current set of relationships. Such modification could have been caused by adding measures of teacher behavior and other variables relating to the process of instruction that differed between schools of different social class levels. Possible differences between schools and classrooms relating to instruction were not treated in Wilson's analysis.

A third point of criticism concerns Wilson's reliance on direct path coefficients, which allow assessment of direct, but not total, effects of causal variables. If other techniques had been used (see Blalock, 1961), estimates of total effects of particular variables would have been possible. The effect on Wilson's study was very probably an underestimate of the total effect of certain variables, such as social class composition of the school, which had a direct effect and conceivably at least one indirect effect on achievement--through its effect on intellectual development. Since there were probably many direct and indirect effects, relative comparisons of regression coefficients may be made only tentatively until better evidence is available.

The possibility that some relationships might change radically if other variables were included in Wilson's analyses is suggested by the fact that the total amount of achievement variance accounted for by all factors combined in any analysis was relatively low. Multiple correlations (R) across all analyses ranged from a low of .27 to a high of .60, with a median R roughly between .44 and .45. Thus the degree of prediction of the variance of any dependent variable ranged from about 7.3 percent to 36 percent. The largest amount of predicted achievement variance in any analysis was 36 percent (R = .60), and this analysis included primary grade IQ, which appears to have accounted for roughly a third of the predicted variance of achievement. Even excluding this somewhat risky calculation of the contribution of IQ to achievement, it is apparent that, as with the analyses of Coleman et al., a large amount of the variation in achievement remains unexplained.

EFFECTS OF DESEGREGATION BY CLASSROOM AND BY SCHOOL

The third work to be reviewed in this chapter is a reanalysis of the Coleman et al. data by McPartland (1967). In contrast with studies previously treated, McPartland's research specifically attempted to determine whether the effects of interracial schooling proceeded from desegregation at the school level or the classroom level.

Data analyzed for the study were obtained from 5,075 ninth grade Negroes in New England and the Middle Atlantic States. Students were cross-classified on three major dimensions: (1) family background based on mother's education and educational items in the home, at six levels; (2) the

proportion of white students in the school, at four levels--
0-19, 20-49, 50-69, and 70-99 percent; and (3) the proportion
of white students in the classroom, at four levels--none, less
than 50 percent, 50 percent, and more than 50 percent.

The dependent variable for the analysis was the student's
score on the verbal ability test used in the Coleman et al.
study, expressed in standard deviation form. The analytical
procedure used in the study allowed assessment of the amount
of increase in student achievement obtained when the student
moved from one level of racial isolation by school or class
to the next level--for example, from the 0-19 percent level
to the 20-49 percent level of white students in the school--each
level under consideration being averaged across the levels of
the variables not under consideration.

The results of the main analyses in McPartland's study
are shown in Table 33. The left-hand side of the table indicates the type of comparison being made and the number of
comparisons (in parentheses). The right-hand column shows
the increment in achievement (standard deviation units) averaged across levels of the proportion of white students in the
school or classroom, for each level within these categories.

The first figure in the right-hand column of Table 33
shows that the average increase in achievement across four
levels of the proportion of white students in the classroom is
.16 standard deviations. The next two figures, both .13
units, show that controlling for either family background or
proportion of white students in the school reduces the average
effect of the proportion of white students in the classroom
only slightly.

The next four figures in the right-hand column of Table
33 show the increments in achievement by the level of the
proportion of white students in the school, for students matched on family background (proportion white classmates uncontrolled). These data show that there is a regular trend of
increase in achievement through the level of 70-99 percent
whites in the school. The datum .02 achievement units shows
the average effect of these increments associated with proportion white in the school, when both family background and
proportion of white classmates are controlled. Thus, on the
average, the effect of the proportion of white students in the
school on achievement is largely through the proportion of
whites in the classroom. This is shown more clearly by the
final set of achievement increments by proportion of white
classmates. Here the data show that only those students in

TABLE 33

Effects of Proportion of White Students in the Classroom and
Proportion of White Students in the School on Ninth
Grade Negro Student Achievement[1]

	Achievement Increment in SD's
Proportion White Classmates (3)	+.16[a]
Proportion White Classmates (family background controlled) (18)	+.13
Proportion White Classmates (family background and percent white in the school controlled) (72)	+.13
0-19% white in school (18)	+.07
20-49% white in school (18)	+.16
50-69% white in school (18)	+.19
70-99% white in school (18)	+.34
Percent White in School (family background and proportion white classmates controlled) (72)	+.02
No white classmates (18)	-.03
Less than half white classmates (18)	-.02
Half white classmates (18)	+.03
More than half white classmates (18)	+.09

[1]Adapted From McPartland (1967, p. 12).

[a]N = 5,075 for each achievement increment.

classes more than 50 percent white experience any meaningful facilitating effect from the experience of desegregation.

Taken together, McPartland's data show that integration
at the classroom level is a key factor in the relationship between desegregation and achievement and that there is an
additional facilitating effect if the desegregated school is predominantly white. Apparently, Negro achievement is facilitated by interracial contact at both the classroom and student
body levels, but there is only a very slight relationship between integration and Negro achievement in the absence of
integration at the classroom level. Further analyses performed in the study showed that the relationship between
classroom racial composition and achievement was maintained
when possible selection processes in the school, such as
tracking and program of study, were controlled.

It should be recalled that, using the same data, Coleman
et al. found that the relationship between racial composition
and achievement in Negro students was largely, if not entirely, a function of social class composition of the school. Mc-
Partland's findings are thus, at least in part, a result of the
influences of social class composition of the school and classroom, as opposed to racial composition.[*] In any event, Mc-
Partland's findings add one more significant dimension to
knowledge of the process of desegregation. And it is apparent
that efforts at school desegregation should take place at the
classroom level if any effect is to be expected.

ADULT CONSEQUENCES OF RACIAL ISOLATION
IN THE SCHOOLS

This final section of the present chapter is a review of
three surveys of the relationship between racial isolation in
the schools, on the one hand, and interracial attitudes and
contact among Negro and white adults, on the other hand. The
first survey dealt with racial attitudes and related factors

---

[*] A personal communication from McPartland concerning
this point (April, 1970) indicated that further analysis of the
data had resulted in the finding of roughly equivalent effects
for both racial and social class compositions on achievement
of Negro students. A similar finding was apparent in the
reanalyses of the Coleman et al. data in the U.S. Commission
on Civil Rights report (1967).

among Northern Negroes who had experienced different degrees of racial isolation in the schools. The second survey
examined essentially the same questions in a national sample
of white adults. The third survey examined interracial attitudes and related factors among Negro and white adults who
had graduated from high school in Oakland, California. All
three surveys are reported in the Appendices of the RIPS
report (U.S. Commission on Civil Rights, 1967).

Negro Adult Survey

A representative sample of 1,624 men and women, aged
seventeen to fifty-four, living in metropolitan areas of the
North were interviewed. Questions were asked in five general categories: educational history, family background,
occupational history, race relations, and attitudes about self
and others. The principal objective of the survey was to
compare Negro adults who had attended racially desegregated
schools with Negro adults who had attended racially segregated schools. Attending a desegregated school was defined
as being in an elementary school with a student composition
of more than 50 percent white for five years. All respondents
who had not attended schools thus defined as desegregated
were considered to have attended segregated schools. Over-
sampling was done to ensure a large sample of Negro adults
who had attended racially desegregated schools.

Results of preliminary data analysis showed that 81.7
percent of the respondents who had attended segregated
schools had been born in the South, whereas 71.4 percent of
those who had attended desegregated schools had been born
in the North. A control was devised for this difference, and
respondents were further categorized into five divisions, as
shown in Table 34.

In this appraisal of the study, attention will be given to
only the first four groups shown in Table 34. There were no
differences among these groups, on the average, in family
background, except those born in the South who had slightly
lower educational attainments than those born in the North.

The primary objectives of the study were to determine
occupational, income, aspirational, and attitudinal differences
between Negro adults who had attended desegregated schools
and Negro adults who had attended segregated schools. Analysis of data collected was limited to cross-tabulations in
which regularities among proportions associated with

TABLE 34

Number of Respondents by Region of Birth
and Type of School Attended[1]

	No.
1. Born in North, attended desegregated elementary school	282
2. Born in North, attended segregated elementary school	215
3. Born in South, moved North before age 10 and attended desegregated elementary school	113
4. Born in South, moved North before age 10 and attended segregated elementary school	126
5. Born in South, moved North after age 10 and attended segregated elementary school	832
No answer on one or more parts of question	56
SUBTOTAL	1,624
Spouses of respondents who attended desegregated schools	115
TOTAL	1,739

[1]From RIPS report (1967b, p. 212).

193

segregated and desegregated schooling were of primary interest. Most of the tables were in a form similar to that shown in Table 35.

The categories of Table 35 are read as follows: "North desegregated (North)" is born in the North and attended a desegregated elementary school in the North. The "(N)" is the sample size in a particular cell, and the percent sign indicates the proportion of the people in the cell who reflect one side of the attitude posed by a particular question or who more frequently exhibit some characteristic presumed to be a consequence of interracial schooling as opposed to segregated schooling. To study relationships with this procedure, one examines relative proportions by cells. For example, if the variable to be examined is "proportion with white friends," one would attempt to determine whether the proportions tend to be higher for those who had attended desegregated schools than for those who had attended segregated schools. Levels of education, age, and sex, depending on the particular analysis, were included as controls.

This discussion should make it evident that with the technique and methodology used in the survey, one is studying relationships between dimensions--in this case the relationship between segregated versus desegregated schooling and interracial attitudes. In the RIPS report, however, the existence of such relationships is taken as evidence of a causal sequence in which more positive racial attitudes and other "effects" proceed from attendance in a desegregated school as opposed to attendance in a segregated school. Specifically, it was expected that examination of variations in cell proportions would show that the desegregated educational experience, relative to segregated schooling, would be associated in a causal way with more positive attitudes toward whites, higher incomes, living in desegregated neighborhoods, and having white friends.

To bolster such conclusions, particularly implications of causality, necessary steps were neglected. For example, no significance tests were run, and the continuum of school experience in various segregated-desegregated settings by proportion of minority group included therein and number of years in schools was not considered in sufficient detail. No controls were made of parental racial attitudes--though such a control seems necessary to the determination of the precise effects of desegregated or segregated school settings on pupils (Proshansky and Newton, 1968). A further problem stems from frequent and wide variations in the sample sizes within cells. Relationships noted in the survey may thus reflect in

TABLE 35

Percent of Negro Adults...[Variable to be Examined]...
by Education, Type of School Attended, and Region of Birth[1]

| Education | Region of Birth and Type of School Attended | | | | | |
	North Desegregated (North)	North Segregated (North)	South Desegregated (North)	South Segregated (South)	South Segregated (North)
Some High School	% (N)	% (N)	% (N)	% (N)	% (N)
High School Graduate	% (N)	% (N)	% (N)	% (N)	% (N)
College	% (N)	% (N)	% (N)	% (N)	% (N)

[1]From RIPS report (1967b, pp. 215-20).

195

part the effects of sampling errors. More stable results would have been obtained if the sampling had been done within segregated and desegregated categories, rather than basically on a geographical basis.

With these criticisms in mind, the major relationships noted in the study can be summarized as follows:

1. The proportion of "main family earners holding a white collar job" was fairly consistently related to the experience of desegregated schooling, with the tendency leveling off at the college level.

2. Income levels over $6, 500 per year (the sample median) did not appear to relate consistently to segregation or desegregation of schooling.

3. Residence in predominantly white neighborhoods was consistently and appropriately related to the experience of desegregation in school.

4. Preference for a desegregated neighborhood was consistently related to the experience of desegregated schooling, and there was a tendency for the relationship to be higher if the experience began in the North.

5. Willingness to pioneer to white neighborhoods appeared to be relatively independent of desegregated or segregated schooling, the proportions in the "South Desegregated (North)" category averaging from five to ten percentage points lower than those in the other three categories.

6. Being a parent with children in desegregated schools was consistently related to the experience of desegregated schooling, and there was a slight tendency for the relationship to be stronger if the experience began in the North.

7. Being a parent with children in predominantly white schools was related to the desegregation experience, but this relationship did not reflect a majority tendency as it did in the previous item. In other words, Negroes tended to prefer balanced interracial school settings rather than those in which their children would be members of a small minority.

8. The proportion of respondents reporting "desegregated schools create hardships for Negro children" was slightly though consistently related to the experience of segregated schooling, there being a tendency for the relationship to be higher if the experience had begun in the South. The younger group, aged seventeen to thirty-three, had a higher incidence of "yes" responses than the older group, aged thirty-four to fifty-four, and evidenced a more consistent relationship to the experience of desegregated or segregated schooling.

9. "Having no close white friends" was consistently and appropriately related to segregation and desegregation, the relationship growing stronger as the levels of education descended. The results for this item appear to provide clear indications that the relationships noted in the study may also reflect the possible influences of factors other than the segregated or desegregated educational experience, for example, the respondents' inheritance in educational background, interracial attitudes, and opportunity for interracial contact accruing from the family experience and place of residence. Since background experiences related to the development of positive interracial attitudes are also more likely to occur in association with desegregated as opposed to segregated schooling, the relationships noted may not necessarily directly reflect the influence of desegregated versus segregated education.

10. Respondents who had attended desegregated schools and also reported that they had "played with white friends" were more likely to report current association with white friends. This relationship, however, was not strong or entirely consistent in relation to segregation versus desegregation. For those who reported they "did not play with whites, " the tendency to have current close white friends was less strong in both the desegregated or segregated categories. The appropriate conclusion seems to be that having played with whites exerts an important influence on later Negro-white friendships, independently of the dimension of segregated versus desegregated schooling.

11. Possession of high self-esteem did not appear to be consistently related to desegregation versus segregation but was somewhat related to "having a close white friend." At the college level, the relationship between self-esteem and segregation versus desegregation or having or not having a "close white friend" was entirely inconsistent.*

White Adult Survey

The data from this survey were based on a national sampling of the opinions of 1, 309 white adults obtained by the

---

*Additional relationships included in the examination of self-esteem are not discussed here because of the many inconsistencies in the results. Moreover, conclusions about self-esteem that are presented must be regarded with considerable caution because they appear to be highly subject to sampling errors.

National Opinion Research Center in the summer of 1966.
Questions related to family background, educational history,
and attitudes about race relations and civil rights. The first
major objective of the survey was to determine whether desegregated versus segregated education was related to interracial contact reported by whites--reports of having a close
Negro friend, having a Negro visit at home, and living in
neighborhood with Negroes. The second major objective of
the study was to determine whether desegregated versus
segregated education was related to the extent to which whites
professed positive interracial attitudes.

Data were presented in nineteen cross-tabulations of
percentages, in a form somewhat similar to that used in the
Negro adult survey. Three educational levels (grade school,
high school, and college) and two regions of birth (North and
South) were used as controls in all comparisons.

Controls were necessary because of the nature of the
data. Northern, well-educated, and younger respondents
were the more likely to report having attended schools with
Negroes. Males were slightly more likely than females to
report interracial schooling. A complication was introduced
by the determination of a "liberal-conservative" political dimension, based solely on the response to one item: "A lot of
professors and government experts have too much influence
on too many things these days." A liberal "No" appeared to
have some relation to previous attendance at a desegregated
school, particularly among the better educated. For this
reason political attitudes were used as a control in some of
the analyses.

The major findings of the survey relating to interracial
contact and interracial attitudes follow:

1. In almost all comparisons within regional, educational, and sex categories, white respondents who had experienced
desegregated education as opposed to segregated education
were more likely to have had Negro friends, to have invited
Negroes into their homes, and be currently living in an interracial neighborhood. Controlling for age and education in
the North did not diminish the relationships. In the South,
these trends were found only for those who had resided outside the region.

2. The survey also computed percentages of approval
among respondents who had experienced desegregated or
segregated schooling and (1) were willing to accept a Negro
on the block, (2) were willing to accept an equal-status Negro
on the block, and (3) thought that a Negro had a right to live

anywhere. In addition to the desegregated or segregated
dichotomy, responses were examined in terms of whether or
not the respondent had a Negro friend and whether or not he
lived in a biracial neighborhood and in terms of sex and age.
In almost all cases more than 50 percent of the Northern
respondents, whether having attended segregated or desegregated schools, answered positively to all three questions.
Percentages of agreement were often in the 70's and 80's.
Southern respondents who had attended desegregated schools
not in the South also had an acceptance rate of more than 50
percent across most categories.

High school and college graduates indicated a greater
acceptance of having an "equal-status Negro on the block"
than they did of having merely a "Negro on the block" or of
the proposition that "a Negro had a right to live anywhere."
Apparently college and high school graduates believed that a
Negro's having a status commensurate with the neighborhood
had a bearing on his right to live there.

When Northern male and female grade school and college
level respondents who had attended desegregated schools were
compared with Northern male and female grade school and
college level respondents who had attended segregated schools,
those who had attended desegregated schools were found to be
more acceptant of interracial housing. This relationship held
for Northern high school level females but not for Northern
high school level males. For the South, males and females
who had experienced desegregated schooling were more acceptant of interracial housing than those who had experienced
only segregated schooling.

Respondents who had attended either desegregated or
segregated schools and had a Negro friend were more acceptant of interracial neighbors than respondents who had attended
either a segregated or a desegregated school and had no Negro
friend. Respondents who had a Negro friend and had attended
a segregated school were much more acceptant of interracial
neighborhoods than respondents who had attended a desegregated school but had no Negro friend. Respondents who had
attended a desegregated school and had a Negro friend expressed about the same degree of acceptance as respondents
who had a Negro friend but had attended a segregated school.
Having a Negro friend thus appears to be more related to
acceptance of interracial neighborhoods than is attending a
segregated or desegregated school.

With the exception of Northern respondents who had only
a grade school education, the percentages of respondents who

were acceptant of interracial neighborhoods were greater for
those who had lived in a biracial neighborhood than for those
who had attended desegregated schools but lived in all-white
neighborhoods. When these findings are juxtaposed with the
findings about Negro-white friendships, it appears that interracial living is more salient in relation to Negro-white friendship and positive interracial attitudes than is desegregated
schooling. However, there does appear to be some independent
effect for desegregated schooling. For example, the survey
showed that respondents who had lived in an all white neighborhood and who had attended a desegregated school were more
acceptant of biracial neighborhoods than respondents who had
lived in an all-white neighborhood and had attended segregated
schools.

3. The survey queried white respondents who had attended
either segregated or desegregated schools in order to find out
whether they differed in attitude toward discrimination and
desegregated schooling. Both male and female respondents
who had attended either segregated or desegregated schools
in the North and South were highly acceptant of equal job opportunities for Negroes. However, when asked if they favored
a law to enforce equality of job opportunity, only about 50 percent of the Northern respondents indicated acceptance and less
than 50 percent of the Southern respondents indicated acceptance. Respondents from desegregated schools were slightly
more positive than respondents from segregated schools. The
survey further showed that respondents from desegregated
schools were more acceptant of "having a Negro to dinner"
than respondents from segregated schools. Among respondents
who had attended a segregated school, "having a Negro friend"
was related to greater acceptance of "having a Negro to dinner."
This same relationship also held for high school and college
level respondents who had attended desegregated schools. In
regard to Negro attendance in all-white schools, Northern
respondents were highly favorable, from 70 to 83 percent in
agreement, regardless of whether they had attended desegregated or segregated schools. For the South, those who had
attended desegregated schools were much more highly acceptant of the enrollment of Negro students in an all-white school.
Respondents who had attended a segregated school and had no
Negro friends were less acceptant of having Negroes in an
all-white school than were respondents who had attended desegregated schools or respondents who had a Negro friend.

4. As a final point of interest, the survey attempted to
determine whether respondents who had attended either

desegregated or segregated schools felt differently about Negro
protest. Respondents were asked whether they (1) approved
most Negro protest, (2) thought most protest was peaceful,
and (3) thought protest helped the Negro causes. The responses
to all three questions were highly colored by the respondents
levels of education. College people were far more positive
about all three categories than were either the high school
people or the grade school people. Only among college level
respondents was there any substantial relationship between
positive attitudes toward protest and prior attendance at a
segregated or desegregated school. Even among the college
group, which displayed the most approval, protest was not
highly popular, as shown by the fact that positive responses
only slightly exceeded 60 percent in any category.

The results of the survey of white respondents indicate
that more positive attitudes about biracial housing, equal job
opportunity, social contact, and school desegregation are related to having had some kind of contact with Negroes. Respondents who had attended desegregated schools were generally more acceptant than respondents who had attended
segregated schools. However, other forms of contact with
Negroes were also related to positive attitudes. In several
instances, respondents who had attended segregated schools
and had a Negro friend had more positive attitudes than those
who had attended desegregated schools but lacked Negro
friends. Within the groups having had segregated or integrated
school experiences, friendship with Negroes seems to exert
an important effect on the development of positive interracial
attitudes. Another possible influence on the development of
positive interracial attitudes and interracial contact is the biracial neighborhood. Other interpretations of the influences
of desegregation, interracial friendship, and residential setting on interracial attitudes also apply. For example, it may
be that positive interracial attitudes influence choice of residence and thus attendance in a desegregated school as well as
the formation of interracial friendships. Or the relationships
noted may reflect a circular process--attitudes creating the
conditions for the development of interracial friendships,
those leading to a higher level of positive interracial attitudes,
and so on. It should also be noted that contact within the
neighborhood or school does not appear to be a necessary
condition for the development of positive interracial
attitudes.

Oakland, California, Survey

The study under consideration in this section is a small study excerpted from the larger study of "Race and Education in the City of Oakland" conducted for the U.S. Commission on Civil Rights. The objective of this smaller study was to ascertain how Negro and white children who were educated in the same school system of Oakland, California, differed in terms of the consequences of being in segregated and desegregated schools.

The sample for the study consisted of 1,429 pupils, the 40 percent in the 1965 graduating class who had attended public schools in Oakland continuously from first grade. All members were excluded who either had Spanish surnames or were not either Caucasian or Negro. The resulting population was stratified as follows: desegregated Negroes (at least four years in an elementary school having 20 to 50 percent Negro concentration from 1950 to 1960); segregated Negroes (four years in an elementary school with at least 70 percent Negro concentration in 1950 and 85 percent in 1960); desegregated white (same as desegregated Negro); and segregated white (four years in an elementary school, all white between 1950 and 1960). Each group, with the exception of segregated whites, was sampled in total. Response rates ranged from 65 percent to 84 percent for each group, the average being 71 percent. Depth interviews sampled educational aspirations, occupational aspirations, racial attitudes, and family background. The control variable used in the study was the educational level of the household head, which was categorized four ways; no schooling to eight years, from nine to eleven years, twelve years, and thirteen or more years. Analyses for the study were completed only on Negro respondents.

A summary of the findings follows:

1. Respondents who had attended a desegregated school were consistently more positive than those who had attended a segregated school about sending their own children out of the neighborhood to a desegregated school.

2. Except in cases in which the household head had 12 years of schooling, respondents who had attended a desegregated school were more willing to move to an all-white neighborhood even if it might create some trouble.

3. Respondents who indicated that there were white people whom they considered friends were more consistently found among those who had a desegregated educational experience.

4. Except in cases in which the household heads had had only eight or less years of education, respondents who had attended desegregated schools, as opposed to those who had attended segregated schools, consistently felt that they could trust a white man as much as another Negro.

5. Respondents who expressed "frequent" fear of the occurrence of expressions of white prejudice were more consistently found among those who had had a segregated educational experience, except in cases in which the household heads had 13 or more years of education. For the latter group, there was a slight tendency for this response to be related to a desegregated educational experience.

6. Respondents who expressed "frequent" fear or anger in relation to social interaction with whites were consistently more likely to have attended segregated schools. The overall percentages for the response of "frequently" were small, indicating that a small proportion of the population was involved.

The results of the study can be summarized as having shown that Negroes who had attended desegregated schools, as opposed to those who had attended segregated schools, were more likely to respond that they were willing to send their children to interracial schools, live in biracial neighborhoods, have white friends, and be somewhat more at ease in biracial settings and contact situations.

Summary and Critique of Adult Surveys

The three studies reviewed were undertaken in order to survey Negro and white opinions about various facets of interracial acceptance and contact. Respondents were asked about their feelings toward equal job opportunities, biracial neighborhoods, desegregated schooling, and social relationships between members of different races. They were also asked if their experiences included interracial friendships and living in a biracial neighborhood. Responses were analyzed according to whether or not the respondent had attended a desegregated school. The suggestion was left that if there were differences between respondents who had attended a desegregated school and respondents who had attended a segregated school, the differences could be attributed to having different school experiences.

The implication that segregated or desegregated school experience results in different responses and behaviors may

be inaccurate insofar as these surveys are concerned, because the surveys failed to control for a number of other factors that might also have influenced the responses of the survey
participants. In effect, the investigators made the assumption
that the only important difference between respondents was
whether or not they had attended a segregated or desegregated
school. But one can reasonably hypothesize that the attitudes
of the respondent's parents, for example, might be important
in molding his subsequent responses. One may hypothesize
further that the background of a Northern Negro attending a
desegregated school is somewhat different from that of a
Northern Negro attending a segregated school. The Northern
Negro in the desegregated school is likely to live on the border
of a Negro neighborhood or in a biracial neighborhood--and
the fact that his parents have chosen to live in this particular
place may indicate that they have positive, or at least neutral,
attitudes about coming into contact with whites. Also, their
choice of residence may indicate that they have a relatively
high social status. A respondent coming from such a background may have a point of view and set of experiences very
different from those of his counterpart who lives a more
rigidly segregated life and has parents with a different set of
attitudes. These two respondents are different at the outset,
and it is impossible to tell how much of the differences in
their responses is a result of their attendance at a desegregated or segregated school.

　　Another difficulty with the surveys is that the number of
respondents falling into certain categories is frequently so
small that not much credence can be given to generalizations.
A further weakness of the surveys is that interracial experience was examined mostly in retrospect, and the accuracy of
the findings are thus dependent on memory and on subjective
interpretation.

　　In the case of the Negro and white adult surveys conducted
by the National Opinion Research Center, it is reasonable to
question the validity of the method employed to classify respondents into the segregated or desegregated categories.
As has been explained, respondents who had attended an elementary school for at least four or five years (depending on the
survey) in a desegregated setting would be classified as having
attended a desegregated school; all other patterns of school
attendance were classified in the segregated category. Thus,
if a respondent were to have attended a desegregated elementary school for two years and then spend six years in a desegregated secondary school, he would still be classified in

the segregated category. His responses would be thrown in and counted equally with the responses of another participant who might have spent his entire school career in a segregated setting. It is impossible to tell how frequently such ambiguous classifications were made, but it seems likely that the results may have been skewed.

The foregoing criticism may explain why the results frequently did not show wide disparities between respondents who had attended desegregated schools and respondents who had attended segregated schools. Often considerably less than 10 percentage points separated the two groups. Nevertheless, there was a consistent trend indicating that respondents who had attended desegregated schools had more positive attitudes toward interaction with members of a race other than their own and more often accepted and desired contact with members of the other race. The results also clearly indicated that the factor of friendship with a member of another race may act as a mediating variable that crosses the segregated-desegregated barriers and is related to positive attitudes about members of another race. It can be concluded that experiences that provide for interracial contact are likely to be related to positive changes in attitudes and desire for contact with members of a different race--and a desegregated school is one of the means of providing interracial contacts. Further study of the conditions under which desegregation in the schools is related to either negative or positive changes in interracial attitudes and contact is needed.

IMPLICATIONS AND CONCLUSIONS

Without reiteration of the many methodological criticisms that have already been made of the studies reviewed in this chapter, a series of generalizations will be presented, many of which were supported in more than one study. Precise causes of achievement, attitudes, and other educationally relevant variables have not been determined. For example, one might be tempted to conclude that, if a group of lower class Negro students were transferred to a predominantly upper status white school, some substantial effect would accrue to the achievement levels of the integrated Negro minority. However, any effects of social class composition of the school in this hypothetical situation would not result from some osmotic process whereby the Negro minority takes on the

characteristics of the majority group but would probably be
a slow and cumulative process resulting most directly from
complex social and cognitive interactions in the classroom
setting. Virtually nothing is known of the nature of the interactions of these phenomena in the biracial classroom, and
such interactions are undoubtedly further modified by events
in the community and family. The generalizations that follow
are thus properly interpreted as tentative formulations related
to certain gross conditions, which in all likelihood should be
created or modified in order to provide the kind of school
setting wherein a facilitating educational climate can be made
possible for the disadvantaged student. There is no guarantee
that such facilitation would occur, except perhaps on the average. The statements made are limited to Northern Negroes
and whites, with the exception of occasional reference to
Puerto Ricans when justified by the data available.

    1. It appears unlikely that efforts to upgrade such fac-
tors as teacher and school quality will have any major effects
on educational development among disadvantaged minority
group students, with the possible exception of Puerto Rican
and Southern Negro students. Such potential changes refer
to manipulations made along traditional lines, such as upgrading the curriculum; hiring more intelligent, more educated teachers; and improving school facilities. Of the factors
most easily manipulated in the school, those defining teacher
quality appear to be potentially more effective in the development of procedures that would enhance the educational opportunities available to minority group students, irrespective of
racial and social class integration. However, for Northern
Negroes, improvements in teacher quality are likely to have
only minimal effects, and improvements in traditional indexes of school quality are likely to have even more minimal
effects. Findings reviewed in this chapter and later chapters
indicate that a fundamental reorientation of educational approaches is necessary if the school itself is to have any
practical effect in the matter of improving educational opportunity among such disadvantaged groups as Negroes.

    2. The social class composition of the school has been
established as an educationally relevant dimension, having
substantial potential influences on achievement that are independent of the influences of teachers, curricula, and facilities. Whether through accident or intent, schools that have
predominantly lower status students thus constitute an undesirable educational milieu, which becomes increasingly
relevant for the educational development of some groups of

disadvantaged students with increasing years in school. Negro
and Puerto Rican students are more responsive to differences
in the social status of the school and are disproportionately
more affected by such differences because they are far more
likely to attend schools in which their classmates are predominantly from lower status families.

3. For disadvantaged Negro and Puerto Rican students,
the potential positive influences of attendance in schools with
upper status whites is likely to be more evident if the experience begins at the elementary school level. Correspondingly,
racial and social class isolation in the schools is more severe
at the elementary level because of the prevalence of the neighborhood school policy.

4. Because of the association between socio-economic
status and ability, and the even closer association between
socio-economic status and school achievement, school practices which tend to group students on the basis of ability and
prior achievement are also likely to result in the creation of
academic programs along social class or ethnic lines, or
both, thus resulting in essentially the same educationally
debilitating situation as that created by the existence of schools
isolated by race and social class. Since the probable negative
effects of social class composition work primarily through the
classroom and ability grouping and tracking are very widespread practices, the implications of the research findings in
this area should be considered in relation to any practices
that tend to result in homogeneous social class groupings in
classrooms in all schools.

5. Manipulation of the social class composition of the
schools--that is, transfer of lower status minority group
students to upper status schools--for the express purpose of
achieving equality of educational opportunity is likely to be
educationally effective for the disadvantaged minority group
student if at least three initial conditions are met:

a. The proportion of lower status students in the school
does not exceed 30 to 40 percent.

b. The transfer of lower status students to predominantly
upper status schools occurs initially at the elementary school
level--the earlier the better.

c. The proportion of lower status students in any given
classroom is a reflection of the first condition, which is unlikely to create appropriate educational conditions for the
transferred minority group student unless the proportion of
lower status students in individual classrooms is relatively
low.

6. Positive changes in educationally relevant attitudes in minority group students, particularly a sense of control over the environment, are more likely to occur if such students attend predominantly upper status schools. Since the sense of control over one's environment and other academically relevant attitudes may contribute to achievement independently of other factors, such as family background and school social class composition, they constitute additional factors that may be subjected to educational and psychological manipulation. Two factors that appear to affect sense of control in complex ways are school success and attendance in predominantly lower status schools. A complex of psychological factors, including sense of control, academic success, antisocial acts, temporal orientation, academic motivation, and commitment to middle class values appear to be affected in part by attendance in predominantly lower status schools as opposed to attendance in predominantly upper status schools. Although the relationships among these variables are in need of more definitive study, it appears that the failure of the schools to provide equality of educational opportunity is part of a complex set of causes resulting eventually in the much higher rate of antisocial behavior and academic failure existing among disadvantaged minority group adolescents and adults.

7. The social and economic background of the disadvantaged minority group student does not appear to exert any effect on achievement independently of ability factors, family background, and school social class composition. This finding suggests that the local social and economic context of the student's life will not interfere with the level of academic success that might be expected when disadvantaged students are transferred to predominantly upper status schools.

8. Evidence of the contribution of the racial composition of the school to educational development among Negroes is either inconsistent or very equivocal. Strategies for school integration must then take into account social class balance of the school if any effect is to be expected on the educational development of disadvantaged minority group students. Integration strategies that reflect the local distribution of ethnic minorities (in some instances a majority) may be irrelevant if the goal of such strategies is the creation of equality of educational opportunity. It is probable that integration strategies would be generally harmful to the educational development of all student groups involved if the result of such strategies were the creation of schools in which the school population was nearly 50 percent lower status students. The creation of such

schools may result in negative effects on the educational development of lower status students with previous experience
of a facilitating educational climate in which the social class
balance was within the appropriate range. Over-all achievement may possibly be even further decelerated with increases
in the proportion of lower status students beyond the 50 percent point, although this question needs further study.

    9. It is evident from the results of all studies reviewed
that the achievement level of disadvantaged minority group
students still remains substantially below that of advantaged
whites, even when they attend upper status, predominantly
white classes and schools. One factor that appears to exert
a major initial and continuing influence on educational development in Negro and white students alike is initial intelligence
level. Similarly, family social class level appears to exert
an important influence on student achievement, although more
for whites than Negroes. The years prior to school attendance
are thus an important point for educational intervention for
disadvantaged minority group students. It may also prove
possible to circumvent some of the continuing influences of
family status on intellectual and educational development
through appropriate strategies.

    10. The review of findings relating desegregated and
segregated schooling to interracial attitudes and contact must
be considered as suggestive only, because of the serious methodological weaknesses in the studies examined. One particularly important relationship does appear to stand out from the
Coleman et al. data: the establishment of Negro-white friendships may be an important factor through which some of the
possible effects of the integrated school environment are
translated into a reorientation of the lower status Negro student toward academic values and active participation in the
predominant academic environment. The suggestive findings
in this area tentatively establish the development of interracial
friendship and understanding as one of the important conditions
in the development of a facilitative educational climate for the
disadvantaged Negro student.

    11. The educational implications of the research findings
that establish the social class composition of the school as an
educationally relevant dimension are interpretable in relation
to the current instructional procedures of the schools emphasizing group processes in the learning situation. Instructional
procedures that de-emphasize the role of the classroom group
in instruction may produce a different set of values in the relationship between individual and group social status and
achievement.

CHAPTER **5** STUDIES OF INTEGRATION
AT THE LOCAL LEVEL

Howard D. Berkun and
Robert P. O'Reilly

The purpose of this chapter is to present a critical review
of certain studies of school integration initiated and evaluated
by local school districts. Basically, these studies examined
a number of issues of particular relevance to the school districts in which they were initiated; their common major purpose was to answer the question whether integration facilitates
educational development in Negro children relative to the educational development of Negro students in de facto segregated
schools. It is probable that the initiating force for many of
these local experiments in school integration was in part the
findings of Coleman et al., which indicated that segregated
schools, whether segregated de jure or de facto, constituted
an educationally undesirable situation. The studies examined
here present evidence somewhat different from that provided
by Coleman et al., in that schools newly integrated as a result
of a local decision were being examined rather than schools
representing existing variations in the proportion of white students resulting from educational policy or regional representation of the major racial and socio-economic groups of the
nation, or both. The reports reviewed in this chapter are thus
much more relevant to the planning of those concerned with initiating integration programs in areas of the nation in which
there is no direct legal press to create equality of educational
opportunity through school desegregation.*

---

*No regular distinction is made in this chapter between
the "desegregated" school and the "integrated" school. Although conceptual distinctions are relatively easily made between the two terms, it is impossible to make such distinctions
on the basis of the information made available in research reports. Generally, the term "integration" is used to refer to
racial mixing existing in the schools reported in the studies

This chapter is also concerned with studies of the relationship between interracial education and interracial acceptance, though relatively few hard data were available relating directly to this issue. The present review thus brings together various theoretical positions, a few studies that are directly relevant to the problem, and those studies that partially reflect on or are parallel to the problem. The question of interracial acceptance appears to be of increasingly crucial significance as interracial education continues to be a major goal of American education and as student groups in many locales become more vocal in their requests for equality and a share in making the decisions that affect them in the schools. Moreover, an understanding of the nature of social interaction between students and teachers and among students is particularly crucial in an educational system that places very heavy reliance on group processes in the transmission of information, learning, attitude development, and socialization.

This review is organized into a number of major sections and subsections. The first major section of the review deals with studies of integration and achievement of Negro students, considering separately elementary and secondary school levels, types of transfer programs, the length of the integration experience, and the influence of school social class composition and the proportion of white students in the school. Other major sections deal with the effect of integration on the achievement of white students and on the quality of the instructional program and the relationship of integration and interracial acceptance.

In preparing this review, efforts were made to gather studies of school integration in which attempts had been made to institute at least minimal controls--equating for initial ability, initial achievement, differences between schools, and so on. Ideally, studies of integration should be based on the formation of equivalent comparison groups, using randomization procedures, which are then assigned by chance to treatments or variations on the integration theme. Additional controls might still be required for essentially irrelevant factors, such as community characteristics and quality of schools, facilities, and teachers. Moreover, measurements of potential effects should be taken at appropriate time intervals. Since refined experimental control is the exception rather than the rule in studies conducted in the school context, the researcher usually

---

reviewed, and the term "desegregation" to refer to the decision-making process prior to the accomplishment of integration.

resorts to statistical control or obtains as many measurements
of relevant factors as he can. In both of these instances the
procedures involve a complex sorting-out of effects and relationships in the context of many variables operating simultaneously, frequently in confusing ways, as in the Coleman et al.
analyses. The studies examined in this chapter may be generally characterized as considerably less sophisticated than
studies conducted according to the research models outlined
above, and so the reader should view the findings of many of
the studies with caution.

It has already been noted that the studies examined in this
chapter generally tended to proceed from local needs. As a
result of this, the integration variable has been manipulated
in several ways. Most of the studies compare students who
were integrated with those who were not. In some instances,
however, a study has been reported that examines achievement
for a group before integration and after integration without using
a comparison group. In addition, in at least one study, the two
groups under examination were both integrated. Efforts will
therefore be made in the course of the review to inform the
reader of situations in which the variables have been handled
in ways that preclude reasonable comparability of integrated
and nonintegrated groups.

ACHIEVEMENT OF NEGRO STUDENTS
IN INTEGRATED SCHOOLS

This section presents a review of studies of the achievement levels of Negro students under a variety of conditions of
integration. The criterion of achievement in nearly all instances examined is derived from scores on standardized tests,
which include norms based on the performance of the general
population to which the tests are directed. Most of the studies
compare the achievement levels of integrated Negro students
with comparable students in segregated school settings, and a
few compare the achievement growth of integrated Negroes
with the achievement growth to be expected without integration,
on the basis of elapsed time and test norms. There is some
variation among studies in the meaning of the term "segregated,"
but it may generally be taken to imply an overwhelming predominance of Negro or Negro and Puerto Rican students. Segregated schools are generally predominantly lower status and
are thus referred to as "disadvantaged." The majority-white

schools into which Negro and Puerto Rican students are integrated tend to be predominantly middle class or upper middle
class, having only small proportions of socially and economically disadvantaged students.

Integration at the Elementary School Level

For many communities, the intensity of segregation is
greatest at the elementary school level. Segregated housing
patterns and adherence to the notion of the neighborhood school
combine to produce elementary schools that are highly segregated. As a result, studies of integration have been most numerous at the elementary school level. In one of the earliest
studies undertaken, Samuels (1958) compared achievement in
a number of segregated and desegregated schools. He found
that although desegregated first and second grade Negro students initially fell behind their segregated counterparts, they
eventually caught up. Integrated Negro students in the upper
primary grades surpassed their segregated counterparts in
achievement. After desegregation of the Louisville schools,
Stallings (1959) examined scholastic performance. He found
that in the second year of desegregation, the achievement of
Negro children improved by amounts greater than would be
normally expected; examination of records for the nine previous school years revealed no examples of similar gains. His
results appear to pertain to both elementary and secondary
school children, since the two groups were lumped together
in the data analysis. In addition, Stallings grouped all Negro
students together, whether in segregated or integrated settings,
and analyzed their achievement--and it appears that the community atmosphere created by the existence of some integration may have had a general motivational effect on the whole
Negro student population.

Another study similar to Stallings' was reported by Hansen
(1960), Superintendent of the Washington, D. C., schools.
According to his study, the achievement of Negro pupils at both
the elementary and secondary levels improved after four years
of integration over what it had been before integration. Once
again, there was no comparison between a group of Negro students that was integrated and a group that was not. The results
simply indicated that after integration, achievement was substantially improved relative to achievement levels recorded
for previous years. It must be noted, however, that Washington, D. C., does not have many schools in which the percentage

of whites is high and that, in the years following desegregation, substantial efforts were made to up-grade the system's instructional program. Thus, the effects of integration cannot be clearly separated from other relevant factors operating at the same time.

Wrightstone, McClelland, and Forlano (1966) report another study in which the effects of integration were examined without being related to nonintegration. In the integration program under study, highly segregated Negro and Puerto Rican elementary schools, grades one through six, were paired with highly segregated white elementary schools to produce a combination that would be racially balanced. Pretest and posttest achievement differences were then examined on the basis of whether the students had been formerly in predominantly Negro and Puerto Rican schools or in predominantly white schools. Analyses of Metropolitan Achievement Test (MAT) scores indicated greater growth in reading ability on the part of the Negro students from predominantly white schools (Puerto Ricans included) than on the part of those from predominantly Negro and Puerto Rican schools, although the growth was not always equivalent to the amount that would be expected to occur on the basis of elapsed time. This was especially true among the slower students. The students in the upper quartiles showed the greatest amount of growth, many exceeding the amount expected according to elapsed time. Scores on the MAT arithmetic problem solving subtest showed greater gains for integrated Negro students in grades three, four, five, and six than would have been expected on the basis of elapsed time. Since Negro students are generally shown to fall further and further behind in terms of grade level scores, these data may be viewed positively.

Another report produced by the Metropolitan Council for Educational Opportunity (1968) is similar to the Wrightstone report in that there was no comparison group of segregated students. In this case, the achievement scores of sixty-six Boston elementary grade students who were bused to outlying schools were compared to the achievement scores that could have been expected according to elapsed time. The children showed improvement in arithmetic, but the most dramatic gains were found in language; after an elasped time of six months, the integrated students showed gains of nine months in reading, thirteen months in spelling, and nine months in vocabulary.

In a more controlled study of integration in New Rochelle, Wolman (1964-65) found no significant differences in achievement between equivalent groups of integrated students and segregated students in grades one through five (MAT reading scores). Apparently, Negro children in this bracket achieved at the same rate whether integrated or not. This was not the case, however, in the kindergarten, where integrated Negro children scored significantly higher on the MAT reading readiness test.

In another study of integration at the elementary school level, Long (1968) carefully controlled a number of variables ignored in many other research designs. Using kindergarten and first and second grade students whose intelligence and social class background were controlled for and who attended schools that were comparable in facilities, personnel, and educational programs, Long found no significant differences between integrated and nonintegrated Negro students. His results indicated essentially the same negative findings as those reported by Wolman, with the exception that, at the kindergarten level, the results for integrated Negro students were also negative. Accordingly, he found that integration per se was not related to higher achievement but that intelligence and student social class background were.

Like New Rochelle, Berkeley (Sullivan, 1968) also had a number of elementary schools having large concentrations of Negro students, 250 of whom were transported to less utilized schools in Berkeley's foothills and hills. After the duration of the school year, transferred and nontransferred students were given achievement tests, and the results showed higher average gains for the students who had been bused. In addition, the bused children made greater gains than they had in previous years, and their gains were greater than would have been expected on the basis of average measured intelligence.

Syracuse undertook several integration projects at about the same time. The first was a federally sponsored program for elementary school children; the second was a locally initiated junior high school program; and the third was a locally initiated elementary school program. In reporting on the third project, Jaquith (1967) indicates that one of two highly segregated Negro elementary schools was closed and that the students were bused to other schools with existing unused classroom space. By random selection methods, two groups were constituted from the bused students and the students who were left in the one remaining highly segregated elementary school. When reading achievement scores were examined, there were some instances of statistically significant improvements for the bused students. In addition, during the second year, the amount of growth in reading achievement for

the bused children was about double that of the control group.
Results of this project and the other ones convinced Syracuse
School Board members and school officials that pupil transfer
to promote integration was a necessary undertaking.

Mahan (1968) reports on the results of busing in Hartford,
Boston, Rochester, and White Plains, of which only the results
of the Hartford project will be reported here because the Boston
and Rochester studies are covered separately and information
about achievement in White Plains is very incomplete. According to Mahan, Hartford's Project Concern was aimed at
determining whether Negro students from highly segregated
elementary schools, 85 percent or more nonwhite, would improve in achievement if they were bused to white schools in
five towns outside Hartford. The design of the project was such
that two randomly selected groups of Negro students were established and comparisons were made between those who were
bused and those who remained in segregated settings. Mahan
reports that when the two groups were given achievement tests,
the students bused to the suburbs showed a "growth pattern in
achievement and mental ability that was clearly and significantly superior to their controls. . ." (p. 298). In addition to
this, the achievement growth of the bused students exceeded
normative expectations and reversed the trend of Negroes falling
further behind national grade level norms. As Mahan indicates,
these results are based upon only a one year trial, and final
judgement must be reserved until more time has passed and
there is an opportunity for the results to be replicated.

In November, 1965, the schools of Buffalo, New York,
transferred 560 kindergarten through seventh grade children
from two inner city, highly segregated schools to seventeen
peripheral schools in which the student population was predominantly white (Dressler, 1967). Prior to transfer, all
second grade children were given the paragraph meaning and
word meaning sections of the Stanford Achievement Test (SAT),
Primary Level. The average scores on the tests were 1.8
and 1.7 respectively, whereas the grade norm was 2.2. In
November, 1966, fifty-four of the transferred students attending peripheral schools were retested; at the same time,
sixty randomly selected third grade students who had remained in the segregated settings were retested. The segregated group had had a slightly lower median achievement
level initially, and other aspects of their score distribution
were dissimilar to the experimental group score distribution;
consequently, it cannot be assumed that the two groups were
equivalent at the outset of the study. Even so, it should be

mentioned that the transferred students made far greater gains
than did the remaining segregated students. It is also true that
the average difference between the scores of the segregated
students and the norms became much greater; for the transferred students, this difference grew only slightly on the paragraph meaning test and diminished slightly on the word meaning
test.

Rochester is another school system than has undertaken
a number of programs to improve racial imbalance within its
schools. The earliest of these was an open enrollment program begun in 1963 and subsequently taken up for examination
by Rentsch (1966). Under the open enrollment plan, approximately 500 kindergarten through sixth grade students were
transferred from schools with an average nonwhite enrollment
of 90.3 percent to eighteen schools having an average nonwhite
enrollment of 1.6 percent. When Rentsch decided to pose some
research questions about the project, it had already been under
way for a year, and it was necessary for him to make a number
of adjustments that resulted in some problems in equivalence
of the groups compared in the study. Rentsch took the existing
group and constituted the population for his study in two different ways. Under the first procedure, he took students who
had applied for and received transfer and a like number who had
applied for but not received transfer. Following this, he employed statistical techniques that would account for various
differences existing between the two groups at the outset. Under
the second procedure, he took a group of kindergarten through
fifth grade transferred students and matched them with a similar group of students who had not been transferred. When comparisons on reading achievement were made for groups
constituted by the first procedure, some significant differences
were found in favor of the transferred students. However,
when the data were compared for the groups constituted under
the second procedure, no significant differences were found,
and the suggestion is left that in reality there were no differences in reading achievement between students who transferred
and students who remained in a segregated setting. No differences in arithmetic achievement were found except at the
fifth grade level, where transfers scored significantly better--
but it should be noted that fifth grade testing took place only
four months after the initiation of the program.

A second Rochester program, begun at the time the open
enrollment study was under way, involved the busing of students from a highly segregated inner city elementary school
to the almost totally white suburban school district of West

Irondequoit (Rock et al., 1967). The program began in September, 1965, when twenty-five first grade children from an inner city school were bused to six neighborhood elementary schools in West Irondequoit. The following year, September, 1966, a second group of twenty-five first graders began the same experience. In both instances, experimental and control groups were randomly selected from a pool of from sixty to seventy incoming first graders who had been judged as average or above average achievers by their kindergarten teachers. Initial achievement differences were taken into account by making adjustments on the basis of initial achievement scores. An evaluation took place at the end of the first and second years for the first group and at the end of the first year for the second group, using the Metropolitan Readiness Tests, the MAT Primary I Battery, the MAT Primary II Battery, and the Science Research Associates (SRA) reading achievement tests for the first group only.

The results showed that the second group of experimental first graders began their integrated schooling behind their controls on the Metropolitan Readiness Tests. By May, the experimental group equalled or exceeded the control group in terms of grade placement on every subtest of the MAT Primary Battery. Except for control group performance in arithmetic achievement, both the experimental and control groups performed at or above grade placement on all subtests. In terms of statistical significance, the experimental group outperformed the control groups on both the word discrimination and arithmetic subtests of the MAT.

The data on achievement of students in the first group at the end of the first year were composed of the results of two test batteries. On the MAT, there were no significant differences between the experimental and control groups. On the second test, the SRA reading achievement tests, there were significant differences in favor of the experimental group in language perception, reading comprehension, and reading vocabulary.

When this first group was again tested at the end of the second year, only the MAT was used. At this time, there were significant differences in favor of the experimental group on the arithmetic subtest. All other differences were nonsignificant. With exception of control group performance in arithmetic, both groups scored above grade placement on all sections of the achievement tests. The data indicate that select (higher ability) students in an integrated setting do slightly better than select students in a segregated setting and that both do relatively well.

In the most recent study undertaken by Rochester (Rock, et al., 1968), comparisons were made between students in integrated city schools, students in integrated inner city schools, and students in integrated outer city schools. The comparisons were made on the basis of the scores received on the various achievement tests given in each of the grades. The tests were initially given in October, 1967, and then again in May, 1968. The October, 1967, scores served to identify initial differences between the various groups. Covariance adjustments were made for the initial differences in achieve- ment levels between the groups. The assumption is made that the various groups become equal and that the differences noted on the posttest are the result of the differing treatments received by the various groups. In this case, it is assumed that by accounting for initial differences and then providing an integrated or segregated treatment, it is possible to de- termine whether students do better in an integrated setting or a segregated setting. However, many other factors may impinge on the integrated-segregated factor and prevent a clear-cut answer. Such factors as teacher quality, building facilities, programs, and school social class composition could account for some, or even all, of the differences that were found. A truly rigorous study would have to control for these other influences, but in many school situations it is not possible--and the study under discussion reflects this fact. Even within these limitations, the study provides, some re- sults that merit consideration.

In the report, the comparisons between segregated students and integrated students were made in answer to a series of questions. The first question: How does the achievement of Negro pupils attending a segregated school having small class size (mean class size of 14.5 in grades K-3) compare, first, with the achievement of Negro pupils in racially integrated classes at an inner city school and, second, with the achieve- ment of Negro pupils in racially integrated classes in outer- city schools? The results of the comparisons are as follows: There was no instance in which Negro students, as a group, in segregated small classes attained significantly better scores than did the Negro students in larger integrated classrooms. In the inner city schools, integrated students achieved signifi- cantly better reading scores in the first grade and significantly better work knowledge and reading scores in the second grade than did students in small classes. Negro students who trans- ferred to outer city schools achieved significantly better scores in reading at the third grade level than did Negro students in

small classes in the segregated school. All other comparisons
of achievement on the various subtests of the MAT given in
the first and second grades and the New York State tests given
in the third grade were nonsignificant.

Another question: How does the achievement of Negro
pupils in racially integrated classes in outer city schools compare with the achievement of Negro pupils in classes almost
completely Negro at an inner city school? The inner city
school children who attended classes that were almost all Negro
attended two schools. The first school, Number Two, was
new and somewhat integrated, although a majority of the
students were Negro and many of the classes remained segregated. The second school, Number Four, had a 98 percent
Negro enrollment according to the 1966 racial census. At
the first grade level, students transferred to the integrated
outer city schools did significantly better on the arithmetic
subtest of the MAT than did students in the segregated settings.
At the third grade level, the transfer students did significantly
better on the reading section of the New York State Achievement Test than did students in the segregated settings.

At the fourth grade, transfer students from school Number
Three were combined with transfers from school Number Two.
This became the transfer group to be compared to students
in segregated classes in school Number Two. School Number
Four was not used. In this case, the Iowa Achievement Tests
were used, and the segregated students in school Number
Two did significantly better than the transferred students in
vocabulary, capitalization, arithmetic concepts, and arithmetic problem-solving. The testing in the fifth grade showed
no significant differences on the Iowa test between the transfers and the students remaining in segregated classes in
school Number Two. In the sixth grade, the New York State
tests were used and school Number Four was again used.
No significant differences were found between students who
transferred and students who remained in a segregated setting.
The over-all results indicate that somewhat greater gains
were made by transferred students who were compared to
students remaining in a segregated setting. In the fourth grade,
students in segregated classes in school Number Two outperformed transfer students on several subtests. In no case did
students in the most highly segregated school, school Number
Four, outperform transferred students.

Another question: Within the same school, how does the
achievement of Negro pupils in racially integrated classes
compare with the achievement of Negro pupils in classes

almost completely Negro in enrollment? The scores received
by kindergarteners revealed no significant differences between
the two groups. Similar results were obtained when the children in the first grade were given the MAT. In the second
grade, a number of differences were found, the children in
the integrated classrooms scoring significantly better in word
knowledge, word discrimination, reading, and spelling. In
the third grade, no significant differences were found between
the two groups on the New York State tests of reading and
arithmetic achievement. The analysis of the data for the fourth
grade showed that the integrated students performed significantly better on the Iowa tests of vocabulary, spelling, arithmetic concepts, and problem-solving. In the fifth and sixth
grades, there were no differences between the two groups on
the Iowa and New York achievement tests.

   When the results of all these elementary school studies
were reviewed, there was only one instance in which there
was superior achievement on the part of students in a segregated school as compared with students in an integrated school.
In all other cases, either there were no significant differences
in achievement between students in an integrated setting and
students in a segregated setting or students in an integrated
setting outperformed students in a segregated setting. Over-
all the results indicate that the Negro student in an integrated
elementary school setting has a better chance of higher achievement than his segregated counterpart.

Integration at the Secondary School Level

   Studies of integration at the secondary school level (grades
seven through twelve) do not appear to be as numerous as
studies at the elementary level. In spite of this, it has been
possible to gather together several studies that provide information about the effects of integration on Negro achievement
at the secondary school level.

   Hansen (1960), in his review of achievement since the
integration of the Washington, D. C., public schools, claims
that substantial gains "resulted from integration." These
findings are based on two kinds of data. The first study compared SAT achievement scores of successive groups of students who were in the eighth and ninth grades during a five-
year period. The assumption was made that year by year,
students in a particular grade are basically alike and that if
their scores tend to increase abruptly at a particular time,

it is because of something that the school is doing. Within
this framework, scores made by students in the eighth and
ningh grades during a five-year period showed a substantial
improvement over what they had been for a previous five-
year period. The second study, involving students beyond the
ninth grade, compared the percentile scores on the Iowa Test
of Educational Development obtained at one point with the percentile scores obtained two years later. Since percentile
scores measure position relative to others in the same classification, obtaining higher scores after two years indicates
greater performance than would normally be expected. And
in this study, fairly substantial gains in basic social concepts
and correctness of expression, amounting to as much as a
gain of 23 percent in percentile ranks were made in almost
all cases during this two-year period. Once again, however,
caution is advisable in interpreting the results because some
of the assumptions made may not be tenable. In addition, there
was no unintegrated control group that could be used for comparison. Furthermore, the extent of integration must have
been somewhat limited in terms of the number of whites per
classroom, since 76 percent of Washington's students were
Negro at the time the study occurred.

In Syracuse, the effects of integration on thirty junior
high school pupils were studied by comparing their achievement during the year before integration and the year after integration. Jaquith (1967) reported that, "it shortly became
obvious to all concerned that most of the 30 students so transferred showed a significant and in several cases, a dramatic
improvement in their levels of educational achievement" (p.
4). All these students had been sent to a predominantly white,
high-achieving, junior high school. No statistical data are
provided, nor is there an indication of what measures were
used, but Jaquith reports that on the basis of these results
the Board of Education decided to draw up plans designed to
further eliminate segregated schooling.

Sullivan (1968), in his report of an integration project
undertaken by the Berkeley school system, concludes that
". . . average teacher grades achieved by the tenth grade students who experienced the newly desegregated seventh and
eighth grade school and the desegregated separate ninth grade
campus of the high school were generally better than the
average of those who did not" (p. 150). It was also found that
those students who had been integrated in the earlier grades
continued to improve in their average grades over those who
had not been integrated. Though these findings give some

information about the effects of integration on Negro achievement, it must be pointed out that teacher grades are not a
good basis for comparing treatment groups, and it is also quite
possible that the comparison groups were not equal to begin
with.

In a somewhat more controlled study, conducted by Banks
and DiPasquale (1969) in the Buffalo school system, segregated
students in the fifth, sixth, and seventh grades were tested
with the SAT in June, 1967, and then again in June, 1968, a
selected group of 1,200 having been bused to schools in which
the student population was primarily white, has been in integrated classrooms for a year. Testing in June, 1967, and
June, 1968, yielded scores for 3,051 pupils divided as follows:
white students in integrated schools, Negro students in integrated
and Negro students remaining in segregated schools. To be
included in the final analysis a student had to have taken both
the pretest and posttest. Adjustments in the final scores were
made, using covariance procedures, on the basis of differences
between groups on the initial test.

The findings indicated that the integrated Negro students
made greater gains in achievement than their segregated
counterparts. No significance tests were done on the differences,
however. Of interest also is a further comparison of growth
rates, which was based on a redivision of white students in
the integrated but largely white schools. This comparison
was made between the growth rates of white students who were
in an integrated school but remained in segregated classes,
0 to 5 percent Negro, and the growth of Negro students in integrated classes of from 10 to 30 percent Negro. The segregated whites started the year ahead of integrated Negroes and
ended the year ahead of them, but there was no significant difference between the rates of achievement growth for the two
groups. Instead of falling further behind white students in
grade level achievement, as is often the case, the group of
Negro students in classes of from 10 to 30 percent Negro
maintained their position, growing at a rate equivalent to that
of the segregated white groups.

As can be seen from the reviews of the preceding studies,
the evidence about the effects of integration on Negro students
achievement at the secondary level is hardly sufficient to attempt to make any definitive statement. All that can honestly
be said is that there is generally no indication that the achievement of integrated Negro students is less than that of their
segregated counterparts, and there is some indication that
they achieved at higher levels. Obviously, what is needed is

a number of rigorous studies that will yield results that can be interpreted with greater confidence.

Negro Achievement in Open Enrollment Programs

Open enrollment has been one of the methods used to decrease racial segregation within a school system. Under this plan, students are free to transfer to any school in the district providing the school has room for them. Depending on the situation, the transportation costs may be borne either by the school system or, by the parents of the child. Naturally, the latter arrangement inhibits pupil transfer, since the parents of children most likely to benefit from transfer are usually poor. A number of cities have established open enrollment programs, but only two appear to have studied the effect of integration on the achievement of pupils participating in this program. In the first of these studies, Wolman (1964-65) analyzed the achievement scores of students who voluntarily transferred under New Rochelle's open enrollment program. She found that the transfers in grades one through five "showed a pattern of growth consistent with those for comparable socioeconomic and ethnic groups" (p. 30): that is, there appeared to be no facilitating effect for open enrollment. At the kindergarten level, transfers showed significantly higher achievement on the Metropolitan Readiness Tests than, did two nontransfer groups with whom they were compared.

Rochester is another school district that has had an open enrollment program, under a plan whereby the school district pays the transportation costs for transfers. When the plan was first offered, many more students than could be accommodated applied for transfer. While this was no doubt disappointing to many, it enabled Rentsch (1966) to work out a reasonable design to analyze the program a year after it had begun. He was able to develop comparison groups by sorting out Negro pupils who had applied for transfer and been denied and Negro pupils who applied for transfer and received it. Covariance procedures were used to factor out the influence of initial achievement differences on final performance. The results, discussed more fully in a previous section indicated that there were no significant differences between the achievement levels of the integrated Negro children who transferred and the segregated Negro children who applied for transfer but were denied.

A later Rochester study by Rock et al, (1968) was concerned
with 273 kindergarten through sixth grade students bused on
a volunteer basis from an inner city school to sixteen outer
city schools. The bused students were compared to the students who remained in almost completely Negro classes in the
school the transfers left. This school was new, had special
programs, and had a number of white pupils who had voluntarily
transferred in. Both groups of students were tested at the
beginning and at the end of the year. The first grade transfers
did significantly better in arithmetic achievement on the MAT.
At the third grade level, the next level at which test information was available, the transfers did significantly better in
reading achievement on the New York State Achievement Tests.
In the fourth grade, the transfers from the one inner city
school Number Two, joined by the transfers from another city
school were compared to students remaining in high segregated
classes in school Number Two. This last set of results indicated significantly better achievement for the segregated students in school Number Two on the Iowa tests of vocabulary,
capitalization, arithmetic concepts, and problem-solving.
Analysis of the scores for grades five and six indicated no
significant differences between groups.

The results of the analyses of the data for the fourth grade
thus yielded results that were inconsistent with the other results of the study, as well as other studies, which consistently
failed to find any instance in which segregated students were
superior to integrated comparison groups. To determine
whether there were any other differences between the fourth
grade integrated and segregated groups relating to achievement, data on social growth and work habits were reviewed:
the students' teachers assigned grades ranging from A to E
for social growth and for work habits. The data on social
growth and work habits for all the grades except the fourth
showed that the percentage of students receiving A's and B's
did not differ greatly between the two groups; in the fourth
grade however, there was a large difference between the percentage of segregated students who were given A's and B's
and the percentage of integrated students who were given A's
and B's, the difference clearly favoring the segregated students.
Since these differences are conceivably related to achievement
and were not taken into account in the covariance adjustment,
this instance of superiority for the segregated group over the
integrated group may not be interpreted with any confidence.

The results of the studies of Negro achievement under
open enrollment programs, although few in number, generally

fail to show that integration facilitates educational development
of Negro students.

Negro Achievement in Transfer Programs Within Cities

In addition to open enrollment programs, which are usually
system-wide, there are other programs that involve transfer
to achieve racial integration. Some involve closing schools
and transferring students whereas others involve reassigning
pupils to integrated schools. Even when the programs are
voluntary, they differ from programs of open enrollment in
that they are not conducted on a system-wide basis, although
they may form part of a district-wide plan designed to eliminate
segregated schooling eventually.

Johnson (1967), Superintendent of Schools in White Plains,
reports approaching the problem of de facto segregation by
closing an elementary school that was predominantly Negro
and busing the students to schools in the outer parts of the city.
He states that the integrated Negro children made satisfactory
peer adjustments and showed gains in academic achievement.

In a study containing more of a research dimension,
Wrightstone, McClelland, and Forlano (1966) report on a project that involved integration through the pairing of several
schools in Queens, New York. The schools had included the
first through the sixth grade, but were changed to include either
grades 1-3 or grades 4-6, all continuing to maintain their kinder-
gartens. The degree of student achievement was established
by the gains students made between the initial testing at the
time of integration and the final testing two years later. Since
there was no comparison group, the success of the program
may only be judged on the basis of the growth in achievement.
On this basis, it appears that all students did as well as they
would have if they had remained in a segregated setting and that
many of them made greater gains than would be normally
expected.

More conclusive evidence about the effects of inner city
busing programs is provided by Jaquith's (1967) report of the
Syracuse effort. In that city, the Board of Education decided
to close two of the three predominantly nonwhite schools and
bus the children in these schools to predominantly white schools
located throughout the city. In order to determine the effects
of integration on Negro achievement, a randomly selected
group was drawn from the transfers and a second randomly
selected group was drawn from the students remaining in the

one predominantly Negro school. The two groups of students
were compared on amount of achievement growth, and it was
found that the transfer group showed some statistically significant improvement in reading achievement. As discussed
previously, Jaquith reported that, during the second year, the
transfer group advanced in reading achievement at a rate about
double that of the control group.

Results similar to these are reported by Sullivan (1968),
Superintendent of Schools in Berkeley. Berkeley engaged in
a program to transport 250 Negro students from segregated
schools to underused, predominantly white schools. The
achievement of the bused children was compared to that of
children remaining in the segregated schools and to their own
achievement in previous years. In reporting the findings,
Sullivan states that the bused children made higher average
gains than those who were not bused and higher gains than they
themselves had averaged in the previous years. Moreover,
these gains were apparently greater than would have been predicted on the basis of average measured intelligence. In
another manipulation of the data, all the scores received on
the paragraph meaning section of the SAT were classified according to whether they fell in the lower third, the medium
third, or upper third of all scores--the paragraph meaning the
subtest of the SAT correlating highly with total score. When
the scores of Negro students in the predominantly Negro schools
were examined, it was found that more than 66 percent of them
fell in the lower third on this achievement measure; in the two
different integrated settings, only 33 percent and 43 percent of
the Negro students fell in the lower third of the achievement
distribution. These results strongly point to superior achievement on the part of Negro students in integrated schools.

The Buffalo, school system conducted two programs involving the transfer of Negro students from their predominantly
Negro schools to predominantly white schools. In the first
study, reported by Dressler (1967) and reviewed earlier in
this chapter, 560 kindergarten through seventh grade children
were transferred from their schools, one of the schools being
closed and the overcrowding in the second being reduced.
Before this transfer, both transfer and nontransfer students
in the second grade were tested on the SAT paragraph meaning
and word meaning subtests. When these groups were in the
third grade, 54 of the transfer students were retested along
with 60 randomly selected students who had remained in the
segregated school. Although some reservations about the
comparability of the groups may be held, it is apparent that

the transferred pupils made significantly greater gains than
did the pupils remaining in the segregated school.

In the second Buffalo study, reported by Banks and Di-
Pasquale (1969) and reviewed more extensively in a previous
section of this chapter, 1,200 Negro students were bused from
largely Negro schools to predominantly white schools. When
the achievement growth rate of white students in classes containing from 0 to 5 percent Negroes was compared to the
achievement growth rate of Negro students in classes containing from 10 to 30 percent Negroes, there was no significant
difference. As was mentioned earlier, this finding is of particular interest, since it seems contrary to usual findings that
the Negro growth rate does not keep up to the growth rate of
whites.

The studies discussed above fail to indicate that transfers
that may be nonvoluntary retard the achievement growth of
Negro students. In fact, the evidence presented in these studies
points toward increased achievement on the part of Negro students who have been bused out of predominantly Negro schools
and into predominantly white schools elsewhere in the city.

Negro Achievement in Programs of Busing
to the Suburbs

In what seems to be the most recent integration technique,
Negro students attending predominantly Negro inner city schools
are bused out to the suburbs to predominantly white schools.
The programs are based on agreements drawn up by the city
and suburban boards of education. Usually they provide for
the busing of only a small number of inner city children, the
costs for this program being borne by the city board of education. The suburban boards generally have the option of ending
their participation if they feel that the program is not working
out. Three programs of this kind were undertaken in the Boston,
Hartford, and Rochester areas. Though in several instances
the suburban boards began the programs with large segments
of their communities in opposition.

The evaluation of the programs is not yet complete, but
there is enough information to make some preliminary judgments about their success. The program in the Boston area
compared the achievement gains of bused Negro students against
expected gains based on elapsed time. This evaluation indicated very substantial gains in the language achievement of the
transferred students; after six months had elapsed, the

transferred students had gained nine months in reading, thirteen months in spelling, and nine months in vocabulary knowledge.

Hartford's Project Concern conducted an evaluation that
took place after one year and involved comparisons between
bused children and children who remained in their segregated
inner city schools. The achievement growth pattern of the
transferred students was significantly better than that of their
segregated counterparts. In addition, the achievement growth
of the bused children exceeded the amount of growth that would
be expected to occur on the basis of elapsed time. Thus,
during the time these children were in an integrated setting,
they were doing more than simply keeping up.

Rochester has had a busing program for a number of years
and therefore has had a chance to conduct a lengthier evaluation. The evaluation of the program with the West Irondequoit
Central School District took place over a two year period, the
first group being evaluated at the end of the first and second
years of participation and the second group being evaluated
after the initial year of participation. The results, discussed
in greater detail earlier, showed greater achievement for
the bused children than for those who remained in their segregated inner city schools.

The studies done on the effects of busing Negro students
to suburban schools indicate, on an over-all basis, superior
achievement on the part of the bused students. Though in a
number of instances there were no significant differences on
a particular achievement subtest, there was no case in which
the achievement of segregated Negro students was significantly
better than the achievement of the bused students. The achievement question would be more conclusively answered by the
replication of these kinds of studies over longer periods of
time.

The Effect of Length of Integration
on Negro Achievement

The material in this section will compare the results of
integration programs evaluated at the end of one year with the
results of integration programs evaluated at the end of two
years or at the end of both the first year and the second year.
Unfortunately, the literature has not revealed any substantial
studies of longer than a two years' duration. The results obtained from Hartford, Buffalo, Berkeley, and Boston programs

and one of the Rochester projects are all based on evaluations
that covered elapsed time of from six months to one year.
The Boston program, the only one evaluated before the end
of one year, had the further disadvantage of lacking a control
group. The findings of superior achievement were based on
the fact that the transferred students exceeded normative
achievement expectations. In the remaining studies, transferred students were compared with students who had not been
transferred, and the over-all results indicated superior achievement on the part of the transferred students.

The Syracuse (Jaquith, 1967), Rochester-West Irondequoit
(Rock et al., 1967), and Louisville (Stallings, 1959), programs
were all evaluated at the end of both the first year and the
second year, while initial open enrollment programs in Queens
(Wrightstone, McClelland, and Forlano, 1966) Rochester
(Rentsch, 1966), and New Rochelle (Wolman, 1964-65) were
evaluated only after more than a year had passed. The Syracuse study showed some statistically significant improvements
in reading achievement levels for a group of transferred students matched against a control group remaining in a predominantly nonwhite school, at the end of the first year; at the
end of the second year, the achievement in reading for the
transferred group was about double that of the control group.
The transferred students in Rochester-West Irondequoit
study showed significantly greater achievement in some areas
than did their controls, though at the end of the first year,
there were no significant differences between the mean MAT
scores of the experimental and control groups. At the end of
the second year, the transferred students scored significantly
better on the arithmetic subtest of the MAT, differences in
scores on all other sections being nonsignificant--but since
the arithmetic section was not used in the initial testing, it
is impossible to tell whether this difference developed only in
the second year. In the Louisville study, no difference was
found after the first year in the rate of achievement of newly
integrated Negro students over the previous years. During
the second year, however, the rate of Negro achievement
substantially increased, exceeding gains made in previous
years. The studies in which evaluations were conducted at
the end of both the first year and the second year tend to point
to better achievement with the passage of more time in an
integrated school environment. This conclusion is also supported by the results found by Sullivan (1968) in the Berkeley
study in which tenth grade Negro students who had been in an
integrated setting for three years had higher average grades

than tenth grade Negro students who had been in an integrated setting for only one year.

In the Queens' study the evaluation was conducted two years after the participating schools had been integrated. The criterion was achievement growth in relation to enrollment in a predominantly Negro and Puerto Rican school or in a predominantly white school. Students who had been in a predominantly Negro and Puerto Rican school and were transferred to mixed schools grew in reading achievement but not always as much as they should have according to elapsed school time. This finding is not unusual, however, since it often occurs even in situations in which integrated Negro students make significantly better scores than their segregated counterparts. It appears that the integrated students are relatively better off because they do not fall as far behind as the segregated students. In arithmetic achievement, Negro students in grades three, four, five and six showed greater gains that would have been expected on the basis of elapsed school time. This finding coincides with the findings of the Rochester-West Irondequoit study showing significantly better arithmetic achievement on the part of transferred students at the end of two years of integrated schooling.

In the New Rochelle study, Wolman (1964-65) obtained the same results using the reading comprehension section of the MAT as were obtained in the Rochester-West Irondequoit study. She too found no significant differences in reading comprehension between integrated and nonintegrated Negro students. Interestingly, in another study in which the evaluation was conducted two years after it was initiated, Rentsch (1966) obtained nonsignificant differences between the reading achievement of transferred Negro students and Negro students who remained in segregated settings.

The results of these studies are far from being in any way conclusive. The studies that show superior achievement on the part of transfer students at the end of one year indicate that the most substantial gains were made in the language and reading areas. The Syracuse evaluation, which was conducted both at the end of the first and second years, also indicated substantial reading improvement. The other longer studies for which detailed information is available (Wolman and Rentsch) show that after two years, there were no significant differences in language and reading achievement between integrated and nonintegrated students. Apparently, the area in which differences may be reliable after two years is arithmetic achievement. Obviously, no firm conclusions can be drawn.

The Effect of School Social Class Composition
and the Proportion of White Students in the
School on Negro Achievement in an Integrated School

Most of the studies that have been reviewed on the preceding pages do not include any information about the effects
of student body characteristics on Negro achievement. Where
comparisons between Negro achievement in integrated schools
and Negro achievement in segregated schools are made, it is
assumed that any differences that appear are a result of integration versus segregation in the school environment. However, when the Negro child moves from a segregated school
he moves not only into a racially integrated environment but
also into a socially more advantaged context. As is well documented, there are a number of differences in the beliefs and
attitudes associated with different social classes and these
differences extend to ideas about school. The problem remains
then, to determine to what extent differences in achievement
and other differences result from racial integration itself and
to what extent they result from other factors associated with
the social class background of the student body.

The most direct evidence concerning this question is
provided by the Berkeley study reported by Sullivan (1968).
In an effort to eliminate overcrowding and produce a better
racial balance, 250 Negro students were bused to predominantly white schools in the Berkeley hills and foothills. The
Berkeley hill schools were predominantly white and appeared
to have the highest social class composition. The foothill
schools had more of a racial mixture and were between the
hill schools and the predominantly Negro, inner city schools
in level of social class composition. All the SAT reading scores
for the district were examined, and it was determined where
the cut-off points were for students falling in the lower third,
the medium third, and the upper third of the distribution.
Negro scores were separated from "other" scores, and both
were classified on the basis of whether they fell in the lower
third, medium third, or upper third of the distribution. Table
36 shows district-wide performance for Negro and "other"
students in the Berkeley schools.

Tables 37, 38, and 39 present the same breakdown as
does Table 36, for schools manifesting different levels of integration and different social class characteristics: predominantly Negro schools, lowest social class level; integrated
foothill schools, intermediate social class level; and hill schools,
highest social class level and lowest proportion of Negro

TABLE 36

Percentages of Students' Reading Scores Falling into Low,
Medium, and High Thirds in the Berkeley Grade Schools:
All District Grade Schools[1]

	Low	Medium	High	Total
Negro	58.7	33.8	7.5	100 (N = 2809)
Other	13.1	36.2	50.7	100 (N = 4283)
Total	31.3	35.2	33.4	100 (N = 7047)

[1]Adapted from Sullivan (1968, p. 153).

TABLE 37

Percentages of Students' Reading Scores Falling into Low, Medium, and
High Thirds in the Berkeley Grade Schools: Predominantly
Negro Schools with Compensatory Consumption[1]

	Low	Medium	High	Total
Negro	66.2	29.2	4.5	100 (N = 2028)
Other	43.8	40.5	15.7	100 (N = 395)
Total	62.4	31.1	6.5	100 (N = 2423)

[1]Adapted from Sullivan (1968, p. 153).

TABLE 38

Percentages of Students' Reading Scores Falling into Low, Medium, and
High Thirds in the Berkeley Grade Schools: Integrated Schools
(Foothill Schools) in Racially Mixed Residential Areas[1]

	Low	Medium	High	Total
Negro	43.3	44.1	12.6	100 (N = 562)
Other	14.6	39.4	46.0	100 (N = 1207)
Total	23.6	40.9	35.5	100 (N = 1769)

[1]Adapted from Sullivan (1968, p. 153).

TABLE 39

Percentages of Students' Reading Scores Falling into Low, Medium, and High
Thirds in the Berkeley Schools: Predominantly White Schools (Hill Schools
Integrated by Negro Students Bused from Lower-Social-Class Areas)[1]

	Low	Medium	High	Total
Negro	33.4	45.2	21.4	100 (N = 234)
Other	8.2	34.3	57.5	100 (N = 2660)
Total	9.9	35.5	54.6	100 (N = 2899)

[1]Adapted from Sullivan (1968, p. 153).

students. It is evident from examination of Tables 37, 38 and 39 that the predominantly Negro schools had a much greater percentage of their Negro students falling in the lower third of the distribution. The actual figures indicate that 66.2 percent of the Negro students in the predominantly Negro schools fell in the lower third of the distribution, whereas only 33.4 percent of the Negro students in the hill schools fell into the lower third. The foothill schools had 43.3 percent of their Negro students falling into the lower third, between the percentages for the hill schools and the predominantly Negro schools but still substantially less than the 66 percent found in the predominantly Negro schools.

The figures for the upper end of the distribution are also revealing. As Table 37 indicates, only 4.5 percent of the Negro students in the predominantly Negro schools had scores that placed them in the upper third of the distribution. Schools in the foothills, on the other hand, had 12.6 percent of their Negro students in the upper third, and the hill schools had 21.4 percent of their Negro students in the upper third of the distribution.

The findings reported above are impressive on several accounts. First, of course, the integrated Negro students generally did considerably better than their segregated counterparts. Second the findings appear to provide evidence about the gross effect of school social class composition on Negro achievement, for though Negro students in the integrated foothill schools did better than Negro students in the segregated schools, the performance of both was substantially surpassed by the performance of the Negro students in the hill schools, which had the highest social class composition. These findings appear to demonstrate again a facilitating effect by social class composition of the school on Negro achievement; however, this effect is confounded with the effect of integration per se since the hill and foothill schools had different proportions of non-white students. It should be recognized, moreover, that in drawing conclusions, it is assumed that differences in the quality of the hill and foothill schools and other educational factors did not exist and that the caliber of the Negro students who transferred to the hill and foothill schools was also equal. Within the framework of the assumptions, the conclusions are consistent with the findings of other studies that have shown that school social class composition has a substantial effect on student achievement.

An examination of the remaining studies that provide some data on the proportion of Negroes in the school or classroom

offers additional, though indirect evidence of the influence of
social class composition of the student body on achievement.
Like the Berkeley study, the remaining group of investigations
to be examined did not directly utilize measures of social
class.   However, with the exception of the Queens study, it
is known that the integrated school situations represented a
substantial shift in school social class composition for the
transferred Negro minorities.   The findings of Coleman et al.
suggest that this is one of the most powerful factors influencing
Negro achievement, but other factors such as teacher quality
may also have contributed to integrated-segregated Negro
achievement differences.   At best, the current analysis provides additional evidence consistent with the hypothesis relating school social class composition to student achievement.

For purposes of this examination, the studies to be considered have been divided into two groups on the basis of
evaluation of gains in achievement.   The first group consists
of those studies that show either no significant differences as
a result of integration or some significant differences as a
result of integration.   The second group is comprised of
studies that show more extensive and more consistent achievement differences as a result of integration.   Both groups of
studies are then examined in relation to the proportion of Negro
students in the school or classroom, under the assumption
that the proportion of Negro students is a rough index of the
proportion of lower status students in the school.

Within the first group, the Rochester study reported by
Rentsch (1966) was one in which the over-all analysis showed
no significant differences between the integrated students and
the segregated students.   In this study, the proportion of Negro
students in each of the receiving schools averaged about 8 percent; it is impossible to tell what the percentages were within
integrated classrooms, but it is surmised that they too were
relatively low.   The Rochester-West Irondequoit study (Rock
et al., 1967) showed findings that can be described as mixed.
In many instances, the differences were nonsignificant, but
some showed significantly better achievement for the integrated
students.   There is no specific report on the proportions of
Negro students in each of the six receiving schools, but analysis
of what data there are indicates that they must have been
small.   The study covered only students in the first and second
grades and never dealt with more than forty-four Negro students distributed in six elementary schools.   It appears that
these students could have made up, at most, no more than 2
or 3 percent of any of the student groups.   It also appears that

in most instances they did not constitute more than 10 percent of the population in their particular classrooms.

The Rochester report of the expanded open enrollment program (Rock et al., 1968) is another study that shows some significant differences along with many nonsignificant differences. In this study the average Negro student enrollment per school was 12.5 percent, ranging from 1.5 percent to 24.3 percent-- though again no information was available about the percentages of Negro students within classrooms. The final study falling into the first group is the Queens study reported by Wrightstone, McClelland, and Forlano (1966). As was stated earlier, achieve- ment comparisons in this study were based on whether students failed to come up to or exceed normative expectations. The results indicated that normative expectations for language were not met and that, in several instances, the normative expectations for arithmetic were exceeded. In this study the make-up of the average student body was apparently of a lower status than others included in this group: 8.8 percent Puerto Rican, 43.5 percent Negro, and 47.7 percent "other." There was no specific information about the percentages of Negroes within each particular class, but the total school percentage indicates that they must have been somewhat high in most instances.

The studies in this first group showed percentages of Negro students fairly close to the extremes of the integration continuum--three near the lower end, less than 10 percent Negro, and the fourth near the upper end, approaching 60 per- cent Negro. The studies in the second group are characterized by more extensive achievement differences on the part of in- tegrated students--and they will be analyzed to determine whether percentages of integrated Negro students were any different from the percentages in the first group.

Johnson (1967), in his report of the White Plains integra- tion project, indicates that Negro student achievement increased after integration took place. Since there was no control group for comparisons and no hard data are included in the report, the extent of improvement is unknown. Johnson does, however, state that, after integration, each school in the district had a minimum of 10 percent Negro students and a maximum of 30 percent.

The report by Jaquith (1967) on the Syracuse project also indicates substantially improved achievement on the part of integrated students. In this project the number of Negro stu- dents was held to three or four per class, implying that if the average class size was about twenty-five, the percentages of

Negro students ranged from 12 to 16. The Hartford project
(Mahan, 1968), which also showed significantly improved
achievement on the part of its integrated students, involved
only classes having Negro enrollments of less than 25 percent.

In the Buffalo study, in which the issue was directly studied,
it was found that in classes between 10 and 30 percent Negro,
the achievement growth rate of Negro students was equivalent
to that of white students. In addition, no differences were
found between the achievement growth rates of classes from
30 to 75 percent Negro and classes from 75 to 100 percent
Negro. The data suggest that schools with more than 30 percent of Negro students are, in effect, disadvantaged.

Because data are not available on the proportion of Negroes
within classrooms and because other information is also lack-
ing--about social class levels of minority and majority students for example--definitive conclusions about specific factors influencing achievement levels of Negroes in the integrated
school setting are not possible. The results, however, are
consistent with the findings of other more extensive studies
(Coleman et al., 1966; Wilson, 1967) in that they indicate that
high proportions of (lower status) minority group pupils in
integrated schools settings are associated with inconsistent
or negative results in relation to the educational effectiveness
of school integration. When the proportions of disadvantaged
Negro students in integrated schools fall in the range of from
10 to 30 percent, approximately, the results tend to indicate
facilitating effects on achievement. There is also the bare
suggestion from the data that very small proportions of Negro
students in integrated schools may not be educationally desirable, although this question is much in need of more definitive
study.

In the final analysis, it is difficult on the basis of the
studies reviewed here to make any definitive statements about
the effects on achievement of time, school social class composition, and the proportion of Negro students in the school.
There is some indication that Negro achievement increases
with time in an integrated school. Moreover, the Berkeley
study appears to provide some indication that the social class
composition of the school affects Negro achievement, since
Negroes attending integrated schools with a higher social class
composition did better on the average.* It also appears that

---

*A publication by Sullivan and Stewart (1969) suggests
that Negro students within Berkeley's integrated schools were
tracked. How much this policy may have contributed to

schools having a disadvantaged Negro population of from 10 to
30 percent, the remaining proportion generally composed of
more advantaged whites, may be more effective in facilitating
the achievement of Negro students than schools in which the
Negro student population is a majority or a tiny minority.
This tentative conclusion is supported by the analysis of Coleman et al. and the RIPS report, which tended to show improved
achievement for Negro students when the proportion of white
students in the classroom exceeded 50 percent. Although more
complete data are required, it is likely that the relationship
between the proportion of white students in the classroom and
Negro achievement is the result of a complex of factors, such
as the social class levels of both whites and Negroes in individual classrooms and over-all school racial balance.

WHITE CHILDREN IN INTEGRATED SCHOOLS

Until now the major concern of this review of integration
studies had been to determine the effect of integration on the
achievement of Negro students. But the effect of integration
on the large number of white students who are part of it and
whose achievement may also be affected by it is also a consideration. In fact, one of the major arguments advanced by
opponents of integration centers around the deleterious effects
integration is presumed to have on white achievement. The
argument is advanced that standards are lowered and programs
deteriorate as a result of integration. And so a review will
now be made of available studies that provide information
about the effects of integration on white student achievement
and on school programs.

When integration does not already exist, it may be brought
about in either of two ways: the first is by transferring Negro
students to predominantly white schools, and the second is by
transferring white students to predominantly Negro schools.
Of the two methods, the transfer of Negro students to white
schools is the more prevalent by far. Nevertheless, two studies
gathered for this review report either the second method or

---

segregated classrooms within "integrated" schools cannot be
determined from available publications. In any event, the application of tracking in the integrated schools in Berkeley
renders suspect any judgment concerning the effects of the
social class composition of the classroom on Negro student
achievement.

a combination of both the first and second methods. The review covers, first, those studies in which the white students
remained in their home schools, and second, the two studies
in which whites traveled from their home schools.

Among all the school district projects reviewed here,
White Plains was one of the earliest to employ the first method
to bring about the integration of their schools. In his report
on the project, Johnson (1967) states that the achievement of
White students who had been in all-white or mostly white
schools before integration was in no way impeded by the transfer of Negro students. This same conclusion was drawn by
Jaquith (1967), who stated that the receiving schools in the
Syracuse project experienced no drop-off in the level of achievement. Mahan (1968), in his report of the Hartford project,
also indicates that there was no evidence of a drop in achievement among white students when Negro children were placed
in formerly all-white classes. This statement is somewhat
stronger than either of the two preceding ones, since it specifically refers to what happened to white students in the particular classes that were integrated rather than to what occurred
on a school-wide basis. In Berkeley (Sullivan, 1968), the
same kinds of data were gathered, and it was found that white
students in classes with bused Negro children continued to
score high and make large gains in achievement.

In a recent Buffalo project (Banks and DiPasquale, 1969),
achievement of white students was examined on a school-wide
basis rather than by looking only at classes in which integration was in effect. Thus, results reflect the achievement of
white students both in integrated classrooms and in white
classrooms. The results indicate that white students had a
very satisfactory growth rate. The mean achievement growth
for white students was 1.23, exceeding the 1.0 increase that
would be expected according to elapsed school time.

The Queens study (Wrightstone, McClelland and Forlano,
1966) included data on both white students who were integrated
in their home schools and white students who experienced integration by traveling to predominantly Negro schools. When
the achievement gains of the white pupils who were integrated
in their home schools were evaluated from the point of view of
elapsed time, the gains at the median for all grades exceeded
the gains that would be expected on the basis of elapsed time
(gains ranged from seven months to two years). All the studies
that involved the transfer of Negro students to predominantly
white schools fail to indicate any adverse effects of integration
on white student achievement.

As mentioned before, two of the studies examined the effects of white transfer on white student achievement. In the Queens study, predominantly white schools were paired with predominantly Negro schools, and this made it necessary for some pupils of both races to transfer. It also meant that, in the final evaluation, white pupils who had transferred to establish integrated schools could be compared to white pupils who remained in their home schools during the integration process. Thus, both sets of pupils were experiencing integration, under different circumstances. When the median grade score gains of white students in each grade were compared with the gains expected on the basis of elapsed time, it was found that the white students in each grade exceeded the expected gains. When the median grade score gains of the white students who traveled were compared to the median grade score gains of the white students remaining in their home schools, it was found that the students who remained at home showed greater gains at all grade levels. It is not clear why this occurred, but it does appear that those students who traveled also found themselves in schools with greater percentages of Negro students.

A second study that examined this question was conducted in the Rochester school system and reported on by Rock et al. (1968). In this study, the achievement of white students who voluntarily transferred to an inner city school in order to establish integration was compared to the achievement of white students experiencing integration in their predominantly white outer city schools. The inner city school was a new one, featuring some new instructional programs. A group of randomly selected white transfer students and a group of randomly selected white students remaining in their integrated home schools were used for the comparisons. Adjustments were made for any initial achievement differences found between the two groups, and when the final comparisons were made, there were no significant differences in the achievement of the two groups except at the fourth grade level. At this level the students who transferred into the inner city school scored significantly better on the Iowa vocabulary test and the Iowa arithmetic concepts test.

The findings of these two studies concur with those of the first group of studies in indicating that white student achievement does not appear to be adversely affected by integration. In both instances, the white students made substantial achievement gains. In Queens, the gains in achievement at the median substantially exceeded normative expectations.

The additional question whether white student achievement is affected by transfer to formerly segregated schools is not yet answered. In the Queens study, achievement of whites may have been affected adversely by transfer, but in the Rochester study the opposite seems to have been true. In both instances the transferred students found themselves in schools with large percentages of Negro students. Perhaps information on the attitudes of the two groups of transferees might suggest reasons for the observed differences. In any case, final conclusions will have to await more studies of this kind.

The over-all data gathered from the studies that employed either of the integration methods, busing Negro students in or busing white students out, indicate that white student achievement did not suffer because of integration. During the integration period, whites continued to make the usual gains in achievement. If this question is to be studied any further, future investigators would do well to examine in detail variations in school social class composition, school morale, school quality, and other variables that may affect white student achievement, independently of any presumed effects of race. It appears that most investigators have been somewhat myopic in their failure to establish white control groups under varying conditions of integration.

QUALITY OF INSTRUCTIONAL PROGRAMS
IN INTEGRATED SCHOOLS

Another issue raised opponents of integration is that school programs are down-graded as a result of integration. One of the major claims has been that integration results in a large increase in the proportion of time given to disciplinary problems, which affects, at least, the quantity of instruction available, if not also the quality. This position is not unreasonable, since research does tend to show that a disproportionate share of available instructional time is given over to discipline in disadvantaged Negro schools (Katz, 1964). Opponents also point to the lower average achievement levels of Negro children, suggesting that this condition alone results in a general down-grading of the quality of school programs. Objective evidence on this proposition is difficult to obtain, and it is thereby necessary to make judgements on the basis of more indirect information.

In 1963, Wey (1964) surveyed a number of Southern school systems in an attempt to find out how desegregation was proceeding, and particularly whether academic standards had been lowered as a result of integration. Out of forty respondents, only two southern educators felt that a lowering of standards had accompanied integration. In addition, many felt that the instructional program was better than it had been before desegregation. In his report of the Washington, D.C., schools before and after desegregation, Hansen (1960) also speaks about the general up-grading of the total school program. He claims that fewer problems developed and that more in-service programs were offered to teachers.

The Queen's project (Wrightstone, McClelland, and Forlano, 1966) also attempted to determine whether integration had any effects on the school programs. On the positive side, principals and teachers indicated that benefits had accrued from the project in consequence of greater availability of textbooks and other materials and new curriculum implementation and adaptation, including emphasis on Negro history. On the negative side, more than half the teachers felt that smaller classes in neighborhood schools would create a better learning situation. They also cited discipline as one of their biggest problems--though the significance of this finding is questionable because discipline is one of the chief problems usually cited by teachers in general.

Comments made by teachers in the Rochester open enrollment program (Rentsch, 1966) indicate that the instructional program continued in almost the same manner after the change in enrollment policy as it had before. However, some new programs dealing with developing better social relations among pupils and learning about minority group contributions to the country may have brought many new positive learning opportunities into the curriculum. Teachers did not indicate that the instructional program was in any way impaired, although some did say that in many cases the achievement levels of the transferring students were noticeably lower than those of the children who had been in the school previously. Most teachers seemed to be able to accept this situation and work within it; a number of teachers felt that they had to alter their disciplinary procedures, but none mentioned that their doing so necessarily brought down the quality of the educational program.

Banks and DiPasquale (1969) queried Buffalo teachers and principals who had participated in a transfer program. They did not ask them directly whether or not they thought the quality of the instructional program had suffered, but they did ask them to indicate whether they thought that achievement levels had been affected. About one-half of the principals and one-third of the teachers stated that achievement levels had gone down. One of the principals expressed the opinion that the drop in achievement levels was not so much a result of the integration program as of the change in the social class composition of the school, the more affluent students moving out. A great proportion of the principals felt that disciplinary problems had increased, though only a minority of the teachers agreed; and 29 percent of the teachers thought that the incidence of disciplinary problems had decreased either slightly or significantly. The results are somewhat contradictory, because while making these negative observations, 75 percent of the principals and 85 percent of the teachers felt that the program was educationally sound, had demonstrated positive results, or was a good idea. It is perhaps reasonable to conclude that on an over-all basis, teachers and principals did not feel that a busing program was detrimental to their instructional program.

While the evidence presented in the studies cited above is relatively crude and subjective, it does generally suggest that instructional programs are not greatly affected by integration. There is no doubt that certain problems occur when integration is effected--but teachers appear to feel that these problems are within the scope of their abilities. In addition, certain positive effects on the instructional program were reported to accompany the onset of integration. Many school staffs mentioned the development of programs dealing with the history of the black peoples and the contributions of minority groups and also increased opportunity for learning experiences involving members of a different race or social class. Given present societal conditions, such new content takes on considerable importance and represents a positive improvement in the curriculum of the school.

As was indicated earlier, the evidence lacks objectivity. Any final conclusions about the effects of integration on school programs will have to be made on the basis of evidence gathered by more objective measures. This might involve, for example, observations of the amount of material covered in the year before integration and in the year after integration. Also, some measurement of the depth of topic coverage would be in order. If enough of these kinds of measurements were taken, it would probably be possible to draw some firm conclusions. For the moment, however, it will be necessary to work with the present highly subjective data, which suggest that school programs are not adversely affected by school integration.

THE INTEGRATED CLASSROOM: POTENTIAL FOR PROMOTING POSITIVE INTERRACIAL ATTITUDES AND ORIENTING THE DISADVANTAGED STUDENT TOWARD ACHIEVEMENT

Since little direct evidence is available about social interaction in interracial classrooms, it is necessary to obtain some view of the possible nature of the process from the research completed in racially unspecified classroom settings. What evidence there is suggests that newly integrated classrooms may have substantial potential for either facilitating or debilitating the psychological and intellectual growth of entering minority group students. Informal studies (Coles, 1968) and reports of the desegregation process in the schools (Mack, 1968; Crain, 1969) suggest that the experience may be stressful for students and teachers and for various adult groups involved in the process. Although not much is known of the social interaction process as it occurs in the integrated classroom, recent reports (Katz, 1964; 1967; Coleman et al., 1966; U.S. Commission on Civil Rights, 1967) suggest that interracial classrooms may facilitate the development of positive interracial attitudes, and they also provide a partial explanation for the fact that desegregation works to the academic advantage of the integrated minority group student.

In a review of fourteen studies of the social context of the classroom, Clausen and Williams (1963) revealed the now well-known generalization that most economically and socially deprived segments of the population typically rear children who may either lack motivation toward educational opportunities or be unable to translate such motivation into effective behavior. These children are further disadvantaged in cognitive abilities and academic skills and are unfamiliar with the bulk of the material treated in the classroom. Moreover, they are likely to be disapproved of by teachers, school administrators, and their peers because of their speech, attitudes, and behavior. Disadvantaged minority group children may be further affected by negative attitudes toward the self, as demonstrated by Proshansky and Newton (1968) in their survey of the literature relating to Negro self-rejection:

readily absorbing cultural judgments about his race and learning in a rudimentary way about his limited opportunites and
prejudice against him, the Negro child is likely to learn to
reject himself.

Evidence indicating that socially and economically disadvantaged children may experience greater negative teacher-
student interaction than their more advantaged compeers is
shown in a few studies. Davidson and Lang (1960), for example, studied fourth, fifth, and sixth grade students' perceptions of their teachers feelings toward them and related this
variable to their level of achievement, tendency to view themselves favorably, and social class level. The results showed
that children who had favorable self-images were likely to
perceive their teachers' feelings as being more favorable than
children who had negative self-images; children's perceptions
of their teachers' feelings as favorable were found, in turn,
to be positively and significantly related to their level of academic achievement and expressions of desirable behavior in
the classroom. A related study by Hoehn (1954) further
showed that the contacts of teachers with lower class students
were decidedly more frequent and more negative than their
contacts with middle class students. Of considerable significance in the Davidson and Lang study was the additional finding of a positive and significant relationship between student
social class level and student perception of the teacher's
feelings toward him as favorable, irrespective of achievement
level. These findings suggest that the low-achieving student
with a disadvantaged background is more likely to be further
disadvantaged by his teacher's affective behavior.

Several investigations summarized by Glidewell et al.
(1966) generally substantiate the notion that the teacher holds
a powerful position in the social structure of the classroom,
which affects on the social-emotional climate, students performance, students' social positions, students' attitudes and
values, and students' behavior. The great ability of the classroom teacher to influence the process of interaction in the
classroom and the typical ways in which such influence occurs
should be an important consideration in attempts at school
desegregation.

Perhaps of equal importance to success in the desegregation process are the characteristic ways in which children
interact in the social context of the classroom. Substantial
evidence gathered by Glidewell and his associates shows that
children tend to accept or choose others from their own or
higher social class levels. There appear to be a number of

limits to this tendency: for example, children near the limits
of the modal social group may be accepted, and children from
the lower social classes who have middle class orientations
and behaviors may also achieve general social acceptance in
the classroom.   These findings are of particular interest within the context of school desegregation because of the hypotheses
advanced about the effects of individual classroom social status
on mental health, in respect to such factors as self-esteem,
intellectual development, feelings of inferiority, rejection,
and school achievement.   The positive and negative effects of
the classroom interaction process have been described as a
circular event by Glidewell et al. as follows:

> . . . If a child is fortunate enough to be strong and
> healthy, intelligent, upper-middle class, and pos-
> sessing well-developed interpersonal skills, he is
> likely to have a high self-esteem and a capacity to
> perceive accurately the nature of the approaches
> and responses of others to him . . . . As the skillful
> child develops more acceptance, power, and com-
> petence in the classroom, he appears also to develop
> still greater self-esteem. Under some conditions,
> he also develops more willingness to take risks by
> trying new approaches to people and tasks. His new
> approaches can modify his position in the system.
> As the risks--small or large--turn out to be profit-
> able, self-esteem further increases and his position
> in the social system becomes more satisfying. A
> circular, self-perpetuating interaction process thus
> becomes established . . .
>
> Turning to the other extreme, consider the
> child who enters the classroom with less vigorous
> health, with limited intellect, inadequate interper-
> sonal skills, from the lower classes. He is likely
> to have a low level of self-esteem and relatively
> high anxiety. The data indicate that he is likely to
> initiate interaction with his peers and the teacher
> with awkwardness and he is likely to induce re-
> sponses which are, at best, a restrained embarass-
> ment, or at worst, hostile ridicule . . . . he is
> likely to respond with some degree of either aggres-
> sion or withdrawal, or both in alternation. If he re-
> sponds with aggression, he is likely to promote
> counteraggression. If he responds with withdrawal,
> he is likely to promote some form of passive

rejection or counterwithdrawal. . . . His utilization of
his intelligence is likely to be reduced. Again, a
self-sustaining circular process is established
(pp. 247 and 248).*

Empirical support for the process described by Glidewell
et al. has been obtained primarily in the elementary school
classroom setting. Viewed in relation to the process of desegregation, it appears that the white, middle class environment presents substantial obstacles to the effective adaptation
of the newly integrated student. Even when any potential racial
difficulties are discounted, it appears that the typical Negro
student may be reacted to by white middle class teachers and
students alike with some kind of hostility (Katz, 1964). The
evidence suggests that the well documented inferior educational experience of the Negro student (Katz, 1964; Coleman
et al., 1966; Mack, 1968) plus the inferior socio-economic
position of the great majority of Negro families (Pettigrew,
1969) may place the newly integrated Negro student at a double
disadvantage in the school setting. The inability of the typical
Negro student to meet the academic and social standards of
the middle class white majority may directly initiate rejection
by teacher and peer group alike, leading to the defensive responses described by Glidewell et al. The results can be expected to be further rejection by the peer group more
defensive behavior by the Negro, and eventually withdrawal
from the dominant white group and its academic and behavioral
norms.
  The process described above may, in part, account for
the fact that desegregation, as it is currently being carried
out, does not necessarily facilitate the educational and psychological development of the Negro child. But according to
Katz (1964, 1967), the racially balanced classroom can generate both favorable and detrimental effects on the performance
of minority group students as a function of three salient dimensions: (1) social threat posed by contact between the majority

---

*From Glidwell, J. C., Kantor, M. B., Smith, L. M., and
Stringer, L. A. "Socialization and Social Structure in the
Classroom," in L. W. Hoffman and M. L. Hoffman, eds.,
Review of Child Development Research, Vol. II. New York,
Russell Sage Foundation, 1966. Pp. 221-256. Copyright by
Russell Sage Foundation. Reprinted by permission.

group and the subordinate minority group; (2) low expectancy
of success as a result of being faced with white academic
standards; and (3) fear of failure arising from anticipation
of disapproval, disparagement, or rejection by the white peer
group and teacher in academic matters. The effects of the
operation of these factors include debilitating anxiety, the results of which may be substantial decrements in intellectual
development and achievement performance (Hill and Sarason,
1966; O'Reilly, 1969) or motivational damage manifested
either in withdrawal from the achievement situation or in defensive setting of future goals at unrealistically high or low
levels (Atkinson, 1965).

In his series of laboratory studies employing small groups
of college students, Katz (1964, 1967) was able to support a
number of aspects of his interpretations of the biracial learning setting. In an early set of studies, the performance of
biracial pairs of students was examined in cooperative problem-solving tasks (1964). In a later set of experiments, a
number of possible sources of the Negro's fear of social or
academic failure were manipulated. The findings of the
earlier studies disclosed that in work teams composed of
Negro and white students, Negroes were passively compliant,
rated their performance as inferior even when it was not,
and expressed less satisfaction with the team experiences than
did their white companions. In the later studies by Katz and
his associates (1967); attempts were made to determine
whether the biracial learning setting could be manipulated to
overcome the motivational deficits experienced by the Negro
students by manipulating such dimensions as the race of the
adult leader, the nature of the interaction between Negro and
white students, and such additional stressors as task difficulty, instructions, and threat of shock. The results of these
studies indicated that the generalized threat posed by the
white adult leader and peer group and the specific threat posed
by the academic task--as perceived by the Negro student--
may seriously affect his performance. Of considerable interest were the findings indicating that these sources of threat
could be directly manipulated to induce greater performance
in Negro students relative to the level induced in a segregated
learning setting. Thus, Katz concluded that when anxiety
factors are minimized, the biracial learning setting may
actually have a facilitating effect on Negro intellectual achievement. The factors responsible for such an effect are presumed to be the greater prestige value of evaluation by white

adults, the valid challenge of white norms to Negro performance, and control over such additional motivational factors
as anxiety.

On the basis of these studies, it appears that the difficulties experienced by whites and Negroes in the integrated
school setting may be extensive and even harmful--particular-
ly for the Negro student. Given the inadequate background of
disadvantaged minority group students for appropriate and
adaptive response in white middle class classrooms and the
relative intractability of widely held racial prejudices (Proshansky, 1966), it seems unreasonable to expect that interracial classrooms will generally facilitate the achievement
of Negro students or effect positive change in interracial acceptance. Nevertheless, recent evidence on the effects of
desegregation generally tend to show positive results, though
the results are somewhat mixed.

One of the early reviews of research on school desegregation, by Weinberg (1965), failed to show any general positive effects of the integrated school setting on interracial
social acceptance. One report showed that although the Negro
student was a participant in social activities in the college
setting, he tended to feel rejected by the white majority.
Findings of studies in the high school setting showed a lack
of change in racial attitudes after seven months of desegregation, in one instance, and a negative effect on white students'
acceptance of Negro students after nine months of desegregation, in the other instance. On the positive side, Weinberg
reports a number of informal findings that suggest that desegregation increased the number of friendly interracial associations among the students.

Research findings reviewed by Proshansky (1966) reveal
a somewhat more positive picture of the potential of the desegregated setting for modifying interracial attitudes. In one
of the studies cited--a study conducted by Singer in 1964--the
racial attitudes of two fifth grade classes, each from a suburb
of New York City, were compared. One class was from a
community in which integration had been established thirteen
years earlier, with a great deal of care for appropriate
arrangements in the school setting. The comparison group
attended an all-white school in a community that was similar
except that there were virtually no Negro residents. The results showed that the children in the integrated school held
significantly more positive attitudes and embraced fewer
negative stereotypes in regard to Negroes than the students
in the all-white school. They also had a greater desire for

personal contact with Negroes, and they had more familiarity
with, and greater positive affect toward, Negro celebrities.
There were, however, still manifestations of racial prejudice
in each group, perhaps the result of parental influence. In
two other studies reviewed by Proshansky--studies conducted
by Witmore in 1957 and Campbell in 1958--the effects of desegregation on the attitudes of white high school students toward Negroes were found to be positive; they apparently
sprang from changes in adult norms for Negro-white relations
in one instance and from classroom contact and friendship
with Negroes in the other instance. In the former case it was
found that the direction of attitude change was associated with
the students' perception of the racial attitudes of their parents
and friends.

Pettigrew (1968) noted the distinction made in the Coleman
report between merely desegregated schools and those that
are integrated. Merely desegregated schools can be either
effective or ineffective according to the context of interracial
acceptance or interracial hostility, as shown by the greater
variance of test scores of Negroes in desegregated classrooms, as contrasted with segregated classrooms; some
students are doing extremely well while others are not. And
the Coleman data suggest interracial acceptance as one of the
relevant variables. In schools in which teachers reported no
racial tension, Negro students evidenced higher verbal achievement, more definite college plans, and more positive racial
attitudes than comparable Negro students in merely desegregated settings.

Other studies of desegregated school settings tend to show
positive effects on interracial attitudes and social acceptance.
In a study of perceptions of Negro adolescents with and without white friends in integrated urban high schools, Webster
and Kroger (1966) found that Negroes with white friends had
more favorable self-images, reported higher levels of aspiration, and scored higher on measures of social competence
and personal independence. Wrightstone, McClelland and
Forlano (1966) studied interracial social acceptance among
more than 5,000 elementary school students in eight desegregated schools in the New York City Public School System.
Observations of social interaction in fifty randomly selected
classes were made nearly two years after the initiation of
desegregation. Sociometric preferences were gathered for
the initial and second year of the studies during the middle
and concluding parts of each school year. The results of
direct observations of student and teacher behavior generally

indicated that children did not discriminate along ethnic lines
in such activities as holding hands for games or choosing part-
ners for teams. Similarly, teachers did not use ethnicity as
a basis for choosing students for certain activities and did not
relate in either a friendly or hostile manner on the basis of
ethnicity. The results of the analyses of the sociometric data
for the first year showed a small decline in the tendencies of
Negroes to select other Negroes as a first choice and a corresponding increase in their tendencies to select whites as
first choice. Whites, however, preponderantly selected other
whites as a first choice, and this tendency remained stable
during the first year. When the choices of whites for the first
and second years of the program were examined, there was
a small increase in the proportion of Negroes selected as first
choice by whites, and this tendency remained stable for the
second year.

In a study of a busing program in the Buffalo shcools,
Banks and DiPasquale (1969) distributed attitude questionnaires
to a random sample of the principals, teachers, and students
involved in the program. There were some serious problems
with return of the questionnaires, particularly from Negro
parents and students, which probably had a biasing effect on
the results for this group. Analyses of parent responses indicated that the great majority of both Negro and white parents
were favorable toward the busing program. Negro students
(97 percent) overwhelmingly expressed "good" or "very good"
attitudes toward white students, and white students gave identical
responses regarding their attitudes toward Negroes.

Informal reports from White Plains and the Metropolitan
Council (METCO) of Boston indicated generally satisfactory
adjustment of Negro and white students in these school integration programs. Purl (1968), in a study of an integrated elementary school in California, found that minority group children
achieved social acceptance, but that for Negroes, acceptance
seemed to be determined more by achievement than for Mexican-
American children.

In its review of the evidence from national survey data
(Coleman et al. , 1966), as well as other small scale studies,
the RIPS report (1967a) includes the following observations
concerning the effects of racially segregated and racially integrated schools on the attitudes and preferences of Negroes:

1. Negro students who had attended integrated schools
were more likely to express a preference for continuing attendance in integrated schools than were Negro students who had
attended racially isolated schools.

2.   Attendance at racially integrated schools appeared to have an important influence on the tendencies of Negroes to prefer interracial neighborhoods, to hold more trusting attitudes toward whites, and to send their children to desegregated schools.

The effects of Negro experience in the integrated setting appeared to be reflected in adult behavior and preferences in that it was found that Negroes who had attended desegregated schools were more likely to have children in interracial schools and reside in interracial neighborhoods than those who had not. It was also found that whites who had previously attended racially integrated schools had more positive preferences for interracial neighborhoods and schools, expressed a greater willingness to have Negro friends, and were more favorable toward nondiscriminatory practices relating to Negro employment than whites who had attended all white schools. Furthermore, the results of the national survey data show that the preference of white students for interracial schooling was even more likely if prior attendance in a desegregated school had begun in the early elementary grades than if attendance had begun in later grades.

It was further reported that racial isolation in the schools also fostered attitudes and behaviors that perpetuated isolation in other areas of American life. Negroes who had attended segregated schools had developed attitudes that alienated them from whites. White adults with similarly isolated backgrounds tended to resist desegration in many areas--housing, jobs, and schools.

Not all intergroup contact in schools and other settings leads to increased acceptance, as some of the studies previously cited have shown and as Pettigrew (1969) concluded in his review of the research. Chesler, Wittes, and Radin (1968) found that desegregation in a Northern Midwest school had a number of undesirable effects on interracial understanding. The study involved ninety Negro children in the second, third, and fifth grades who were bused to several predominantly or entirely white schools. Data from observations and self-reports led to the following conclusions (paraphrased from Chesler, Wittes, and Radin, 1968, pp. 2-4):

1.   The negative reactions of the white children ranged from deliberate ignoring to name-calling, physical provocation, and aggression.

2.   Most Negro children reported a systematic and consistent pattern of rejection.

3. The causes for rejection by whites appeared to revolve around (a) generalized fear; (b) jealousy in that they felt Negroes received favored treatment; and (c) fright at the way some Negroes taunted and defied school rules and authorities.

4. Whites who expressed nondiscriminating, unprejudiced feelings and attitudes frequently learned their group's disapproval and were pressured to conform to the normative standards of rejection and disdain of the integrated Negro minority.

5. With few exceptions, white children appeared to end the school year with the same negative attitudes toward Negroes that they had at the beginning.

6. In summary, the children by themselves did not appear to be forming positive interracial relationships and positive attitudes toward racial association. There were occasional indications of the beginning of acceptance and friendship, but the over-all pattern of distance, caution, and rejection remained at the end of the school year.

Chesler and his associates implicated both teachers and parents as primary causes of the failure of desegregation in this instance. It appeared that some teachers held attitudes that would contribute to the exacerbation of negative interracial attitudes. Moreover, some teachers seemed to have seriously limited ability to cope effectively with the changed situation they met in the form of an interracial classroom. Parents of whites, however, were probably a more serious problem in this instance, since they appeared to maintain consistent and unyielding cognitive and affective support of their children's negative racial attitudes. Previous studies (Proshansky, 1966) suggest that changes in the racial attitudes of parents may be a necessary condition for positive changes in children's interracial attitudes in the classroom situation.

Research reported by Proshansky (1966), Katz (1967), and others directly implies that the integrated classroom does not necessarily promote positive interracial attitudes or orient the disadvantaged student toward achievement values. Their work and the additional studies cited above appear to confirm this position. If integration alone were the key to producing more positive interracial attitudes and a stronger orientation toward achievement on the part of disadvantaged students, all the studies would have indicated growth in these areas. Since the results relating to this hypotheses were often negative, the appropriate conclusion appears to be that positive growth in these areas occurs only in cases in which integration is accompanied by other factors. The Katz studies, for example, suggest that an atmosphere combining low social threat and

high expectation of success can have a facilitating effect on the
intellectual performance of Negro students.

　　With appropriate training procedures and other manipulations, it should prove possible to circumvent or reduce the
educationally and psychologically undesirable experiences that
are likely to affect the newly integrated student for a considerable period of his schooling. For example, enough is known
about the learning conditions that contribute to the development
of debilitating anxiety to make it possible to create therapeutic
approaches to instruction (O'Reilly, 1969). Similarly, opportunities for positive interracial contact can be systematically created for the disadvantaged minority student. Teachers
can be trained to inhibit negative affective reactions toward
students who exhibit "undesirable" behavior linked to social
class. With the addition of effective training in teaching procedures and instructional materials for disadvantaged students,
the stage may be set for more systematic utilization of classroom social interaction directed toward theoretically probable
positive consequences for the intellectual and psychological
development of the socially and economically disadvantaged
student. It seems reasonable to contend that, if these and
other factors had been given careful attention in the studies of
integration examined in this report, differences favoring integrated students would have been far more substantial.

SUMMARY AND CONCLUSIONS

　　This chapter of the study has examined in part, the results of studies on school integration programs initiated and
evaluated by staff members and consultants in local school
districts. Typically, these studies examined issues of particular relevance to the districts in which they were initiated,
but they were generally similar in their focus on studying the
relationship between integration and educational development.
The differences and similarities among these studies allow
some tentative identification of conditions that may mediate
the effects of school integration on educational development.
Such conditions include the grade level at which integration
was experienced, the duration of the experience, the social
class composition of the integrated school, the proportion of
white and Negro students in the school, and the type of transfer program used. To a limited extent, the conditions examined in these studies were similar to those examined in Chapter

4, and thus allow further documentation of the findings of that
review. Studies at the local level also contributed additional
information on the integration process not available from the
more representative and more sophisticated studies reviewed
in Chapter 4. Of particular importance is the information
made available on the decision to initiate school integration
where de facto segregation was in existence, as contrasted
with research on fortuitous variations in racial isolation in
the schools, as in the Coleman et al. study, which are depen-
ent on an existing situation rather than a direct manipulation
of integration. In addition to examining the relationship between integration and achievement, a second group of studies
provided data on changes in interracial acceptance that may
occur with the initiation of integration programs in the schools.
The results of these studies are suggestive of the nature of
the social and educational interactions that are likely to occur
under different conditions associated with the process of school
integration.

While the studies in this section provide some new evidence
about the integration process, they are, at the same time,
beset with certain methodological problems that preclude drawing firm conclusions about the effects of racial integration
per se. The first problem arises from the fact that evaluations
of the effects of integration were conducted, at most, only two
years after the programs were initiated. The second problem
results from the use of integrated and segregated comparison
groups that were, typically, equated only in terms of ability.
Or initial achievement. Such factors as school social class
composition and school quality are potentially important determinants of achievement among disadvantaged children, and
since they were not specifically investigated in these studies,
it is impossible to determine the particular sources of any
differences found between segregated and integrated comparison
groups. As a result, when the findings show superior achievement for "integrated" students, it must be taken to mean that
integration produced a number of important changes in the
educational milieu--any one, or all, of which could have contributed to the differences between integrated and segregated
groups.

Within this framework a number of generalizations about
the findings of the studies may be drawn:

1. Integrated Negro students, as a group, achieved at
least as well as their segregated counterparts, and in many
cases, achieved at higher levels. Though segregated students
sometimes achieved as well as integrated students, or the

differences between integrated and segregated groups were
only minimally significant in only one instance--which is of
questionable validity--did segregated student groups achieve
at a significantly higher level than integrated students. Moreover, these results are strengthened by the fact that they were
obtained under a wide variety of conditions. Superior achievement was found at both the elementary level and the secondary
level, although the evidence on the secondary level was less
conclusive because of a dearth of studies. Findings of superior
achievement for integrated students were also obtained in
programs that involved busing either to the suburbs or within
the city and in studies of one and two years duration.

2.   The investigation into the relationship between the proportion of white students in the classroom and the achievement
of Negro students yielded findings that were roughly similar
to those of Coleman et al. and the RIPS report: that is, any
positive association between the proportion of white students
in the classroom and achievement for Negro students generally
does not appear to be present or meaningful from a practical
point of view until the proportion of white students exceeds
50 percent. It is likely that the Negro proportion indicated
as desirable for planning the integrated school would expand
or contract depending upon other factors, such as the level of
social class background, ability, and academically related
attitudes of both the minority Negro groups and the majority
white groups. Though this conclusion may provide some lati-
tude, the over-all results of these studies and the Coleman
et al. study and the RIPS report clearly indicate that the experience of integration generally facilitates educational development among Negro students when the integrated white student group is very much the majority.

3.   One study provided indirect information about the
effect of school social class composition on achievement in
integrated schools. In that study integrated Negro students in
schools with a higher social class composition achieved at
higher levels than Negro students in integrated schools with a
lower social class composition. Both groups of students
achieved at higher levels than did segregated Negro students.
Some reservations must be made about the study, and it can
only be said that there appears to be a tendency for Negro students in integrated schools with a high social class composition to do better than Negro students in an integrated school
whose social class composition is lower.

4.   The evidence presented in these research studies gives
no reason to believe that white student achievement suffers

under integration.   The educational problems that may exist
because of integration may frequently have a greater effect
on the teacher than on the white student.   Integration often
means that teachers are faced with students whose achievement
is behind that of their classmates, and their different behavior
patterns are likely to create the need to alter some aspects of
the teacher-student interaction process.   Though teachers have
reported the need to practice some new instructional behaviors,
the reports of the schools give few indications that their instructional programs have suffered as a result.   One noticeable
change has been the alteration of the curriculum in many of
these schools to include more study of minority group contributions to society and to provide activities designed to promote
interracial understanding.   Most of these efforts, however,
have been minimal, and these largely ignore the body of research
on racial and class differences that could provide a much more
systematic basis for program development in integrated schools.
     5.   Investigations of the relationship between interracial
schooling and interracial acceptance indicate that the integrated
school does not necessarily bring about improved interracial
understanding, acceptance, and friendship.   The more representative analyses of the data of Coleman et al. and the surveys reviewed in Chapter 4 suggest that the integrated school
is effective in bringing about increased positive rapport between
Negroes and whites and that this impact of integration is last-
ing.   However, the general body of research on social interaction in the classroom and smaller studies of desegrated
school settings suggest that the effect of school integration on
interracial acceptance may be either positive or negative, depending upon a number of variables, including teacher and
parental support of the integrated school and the manipulation
of certain factors to change the conditions of learning and the
nature of the peer group interaction in the classroom.   Though
schools involved in studies of integration at the local level did
relatively little to create systematically an ideal classroom
atmosphere, they, nevertheless, found that the subjective reports of students, teachers, and principals indicated that one
of the major strengths of their integration programs was an
increase in interracial understanding.   Although these reports
are subjective, they and objective research findings, together
suggest clearly that the processes of instruction and social
interaction in the integrated classroom can be manipulated in
ways that may substantially facilitate the educational and
psychological development of disadvantaged Negro students, as
well as other groups of socially and economically disadvantaged
children.

6. Even though the studies often indicate superior achievement on the part of integrated Negro students, it must still
be noted that integrated Negro students generally remain behind the white majority in achievement. Integration, on an
over-all basis, does help the Negro student to close some of
the achievement gap that is found between white and Negro students, but it does not appear to have the potential to close the
gap completely. It appears that if this gap is to be closed,
integration must be accompanied by a number of additional,
specific programs designed for the disadvantaged learner.

The efforts of local school officals to initiate integration
programs and, at the same time to evaluate them are to be
applauded. It is evident, however, that local efforts to evaluate
school integration programs have not contributed much new
knowledge of interracial education. The findings of Chapters
4 and 5 indicate that new kinds of research must be undertaken
if knowledge of the integration process is to progress beyond
knowledge of a few conditions that provide relatively gross
guidelines for planning the integrated school. Since many of
the potentially significant studies of school integration will
continue to occur as local events--the evaluative effort being
thought of afterward or, in any event, poorly conceived--
there is a need for a flexible but standard approach for studying the process of integration. More reactive evaluative approaches, in which several significant factors may be simultaneously and periodically monitored, might well yield the
kinds of detailed information that to date have been largely
lacking. Studies indicating that integration is effective must
now appear to be generally redundant, except under a special
circumstances; integration programs that "fail" may contribute more to understanding multiethnic education, if the
process of failure has been systematically observed.

CHAPTER **6** COMPENSATORY
EDUCATION AND
INTEGRATION

Katherine S. Bluegrass
and Ruth Salter

Integration seeks to assure equality of educational opportunity for members of minority groups by eliminating segregation within the schools. Compensatory education seeks to overcome deficiencies in the disadvantaged so that they may profit
from educational experience and participate more fully in the
economic and social life of an affluent America. Because
minority groups are those most likely to suffer economic and
cultural deprivation, compensatory education has been most
frequently directed toward minority group members--Negroes,
Puerto Ricans, and Mexican-Americans. It is therefore appropriate to give attention in this study to compensatory education programs, the results they are achieving, and their relation to the immediate issue--integration.

The current national focus on the education of the disadvantaged is the consequence of a number of factors:

1. The civil rights movement
2. The persistence of poverty in a land of plenty
3. The growing demand for intellectual talent and the
diminishing need for unskilled labor in a technological society
4. The decline of the cities, the concentration of the un-
employed in urban centers, and the tension of the ghettos
5. Increasing welfare rolls and mounting tax burdens.

All these factors have prompt interest in compensatory
education programs and support for them. And the assumption
is made that special educational programs for the deprived
will break the cycle in which the poor are caught--school failure, school drop-out, minimal employment or unemployment,
and economic dependency--and will benefit the disadvantaged
and the entire nation. In short, compensatory education is the
outgrowth of both humanitarian concerns and practical economic
considerations.

Underlying the current commitment to compensatory education is a general ideational orientation without which the
formulation of compensatory education programs as a possible

solution to the problem of disadvantagement would not have
occurred. This orientation is a combination of faith in individual human potential and belief that human behavior is predictable and can be directed and modified, the latter belief
being fundamental to all education.

From a theoretical point of view, compensatory education
is a product of the environmentalist school of thought. Members of this school adhere to the postulate that the human mind,
a _tabula rasa_ at birth, may take a limitless number of forms,
depending upon the environmental circumstances experienced
in the course of its development. They hold that it is the interaction of the organism with the environment, not genetic inheritance, that determines intellectual functioning and most of
human behavior. It follows that as the environment can be
controlled and structured, so can human development be controlled and directed. As phrased by Gordon and Wilkerson
(1966), it is the posture of the enironmentalist-interactionist
to perceive--

> the developmental process as malleable, to regard
> intelligence as nonstatic and variable, to see motives
> and attitudes as determined and modifiable by ex-
> perience, and to recognize all achievement as the
> product of the individual's characteristics in con-
> tinuous and dynamic interaction with those elements
> of the environment which are effective at a given
> time (p. 26).

In the case of the disadvantaged, it is believed that environmental deprivation (economic, social, and cultural) is directly responsible for retarded intellectual development and
academic accomplishment. The negative relationship between
deprivation and achievement has been documented in numerous
studies, and a previous chapter of this report has enumerated
some of the specific effects of disadvantagement on school
children. Children of poverty enter school poorly motivated
and lacking in cognitive skills and often fall further and further
behind their middle class peers.

Compensatory education programs are directed toward
overcoming the environmental deficiencies and negative experiences of disadvantaged children and altering their usual
course of development. Four approaches to compensatory
education, all of which may be incorporated into a single program were noted in the RIPS report (1967a):

1. Remedial instruction: giving intensive attention to students whose achievement is poor. Remedial efforts include reducing teacher-pupil ratios and class size, providing extra help during and after school hours, counseling, and using special materials to teach and improve basic skills.

2. Cultural enrichment: broadening the horizons of the poor by exposing them to activities usually beyond their reach. Cultural enrichment programs may include field trips, concerts, plays, and visits to museums, other schools, and colleges.

3. Building self-esteem: overcoming negative attitudes that inhibit learning and cause failure. Efforts to promote self-esteem and confidence range from providing educational experiences that will bring success and recognition to instituting courses in Negro history. Attention may be given to the outlook of teachers as well as pupils.

4. Parental involvement: enlisting parental cooperation to promote pupil achievement. Efforts to work with parents include both assuring them of the school's concern for their children and offering suggestions by which they may help to improve their children's academic performance.

Compensatory programs have been introduced at all educational levels from preschool through college. They have such diverse objectives as raising capacity to learn, teaching a specific occupational skill, and turning a functional illiterate into a reader. Compensatory programs are indeed so varied and so numerous as to preclude any thorough review of them, past or present, within the context of this report. The examination of compensatory programs in this chapter focuses on preschool education, the newest frontier for compensatory education; some of the landmark programs that have served as models for other programs; and programs instituted under Title I of the Elementary and Secondary Education Act. In examining these programs, consideration will be given to their measured effects and the extent to which they have changed the school performance of the disadvantaged. Finally, the effects of some integration programs on pupil performance will be examined and compared with the effects of compensatory education programs initiated in the public schools.

PRESCHOOL COMPENSATORY EDUCATION

The current emphasis on preschool education in compensatory programs for the disadvantaged is based on the assumption

that the early years of life contribute heavily to the development of intellectual potential and future academic achievement
and the fact that, even at school entrance, there are substantial
differences between children of low socio-economic background
and their middle class peers. Research findings on the effects
of stimulus deprivation and other factors on intellectual development have led to an educational paradigm in which programed
preschool experiences are expected to make up for deprivations
in the home environment that are assumed to handicap the child
in the school setting. In general, preschool programs have
three kinds of objectives--cognitive, affective, and physical.
Specific programs differ in emphasis and in technique.

Project Head Start

The largest single compensatory education program ever
undertaken was Project Head Start, initiated in 1965 by the
Office of Economic Opportunity. Launched on a nationwide
scale, the program was designed to prepare young disadvantaged
children for school through a full array of educational, medical,
nutritional, and social services. It was intended to overcome
in a brief time the cognitive, psychological, physical, and familial handicaps that may impede the learning of the disadvantaged
child as he enters school. By the spring of 1969, nearly 3 million youngsters had been served by Head Start, more than 2
million in summer programs and nearly 800,000 in full-year
programs (Lewis, 1969).

To date, two studies using national samples have dealt
with the effects of Head Start on cognitive and psychological
development. One is a subsection of the study by Coleman
et al. (1966) entitled Equality of Educational Opportunity; the
other is the report by the Westinghouse Learning Corporation
and Ohio University (1969) entitled The Impact of Head Start.
The first came immediately after the first summer of Head
Start operation; the second was made when the program had
been under way for more than three years.

Equality of Educational Opportunity.

The evaluation of Head Start made by Coleman et al. utilized data collected for the broad-scale study of educational
opportunity. Three samples of first grade pupils were randomly
selected from the total first grade population: (1) children who
had attended Head Start summer programs in the summer of

1965 (approximately 9,000); (2) children in the same schools who had not participated in Head Start or in any similar program (approximately 6,000); and (3) children in communities in which Head Start programs did not exist and who had not participated in any similar program (approximately 12,000). The latter two samples served as control groups for comparison purposes, based on indexes of achievement and educational motivation.

The achievement measures used were three subtests of the Inter-American Tests of General Ability: a picture vocabulary test giving a score for verbal ability and association and classification tests yielding scores for nonverbal ability. Educational motivation, or desire to learn, was determined by teacher responses to questions on pupils' classroom behavior and interest in school activities.

The results of the achievement tests showed the following:

1. Head Start participants of a given race did not perform as well as nonparticipants of the same race. The poor children who attended Head Start programs did not catch up with their classmates.

2. Head Start Negroes in Southern states had higher test scores than Negro nonparticipants attending the same schools.

3. Head Start Negroes in metropolitan communities outside the South and Head Start whites in the metropolitan South who did not attend kindergarten showed positive effects when compared with nonparticipants who had also not attended kindergarten.

4. With race, region, kindergarten attendance, and socioeconomic status controlled, the scores of the poorest Head Start participants were consistently higher than those of comparable children in the same schools. Specifically, Negroes of low socio-economic status--particularly those in rural areas --were those who had benefitted most.

5. In general, differences between experimental and control groups were small.

Analysis of teacher ratings showed the following:

1. Head Start participants of the lowest socio-economic status had higher ratings than did nonparticipants.

2. There was a tendency for all Negro participants to be more highly motivated than nonparticipants.

3. For whites, differential motivational effects were found for Head Start participants of the lowest socio-economic status in some regions.

4. Generally, the effects of participation were more noticeable in the area of educational motivation than for achievement test performance.

In summary, the Coleman et al. data did not reveal any
over-all successes for Head Start but indicated some modest
benefits for the poorest children, particularly Negroes, in
some locations. It should be noted that the analyses of the effects of Head Start are based on differences in mean scores,
but the study gives no indication of the significance of the differences reported. Perhaps this disadvantage stems from the
fact that the sample sizes are so large that almost any difference would be statistically significant--and those found were
small. The study has the further disadvantage of not having
had pretreatment data that would assure the initial equivalence
of the groups compared and thus more confidently indicate
changes resulting from the program. While the Coleman et al.
study was done when Head Start was just beginning, recently
implemented on a crash basis, the findings for regional and
ethnic differences in program effectiveness are not inconsistent
with those reported three years later in the nationwide study
conducted by Westinghouse and Ohio State.

The Impact of Head Start

The Westinghouse-Ohio State evaluation, undertaken in
1968 at the request of the Office of Economic Opportunity, focused on cognitive and affective development and compared
Head Start children in the first, second, and third grades with
comparable children who did not attend Head Start. To obtain
the study population, a total of 104 Head Start centers were
randomly selected from among the 12,927 centers operating
during the period from September 1966 to August 1967. Populations of Head Start children and a control group of children
who were eligible for, but did not attend, Head Start were then
identified in the geographical areas served by each center. In
each area, random samples of eight Head Start children were
drawn at each of the three grade levels and matched with control group samples on race, sex, and kindergarten attendance.
There was a total of 3,963 subjects: 1,582 from the first grade,
1,535 from the second grade, and 846 from the third grade.
(Not all programs had children in all three grades.)
In the analysis of the data, distinctions were made between
full-year and summer programs. Reflecting the distribution
of such programs in the country, 70 percent or seventy-five
of those in the study were summer programs and 30 percent,
or twenty-nine, were full-year programs. After analysis of
the total sample in each category, the programs were subdivid-
ed for analysis by geographic location, community size, and
ethnic composition.

Standardized tests--the Illinois Test of Psycholinguistic Abilities (ITPA), the Metropolitan Readiness Tests (MRT), and the Stanford Achievement Tests (SAT), Primary Batteries I and II--were used to measure cognitive development. Three instruments developed especially for the project were used to assess affective development. Two were projective tests, the Children's Self Concept Index (CSCI) and the Children's Attitudinal Range Indicator (CARI), the latter covering attitudes toward peers, home, school, and society. The third was the Classroom Behavior Inventory (CBI), a rating scale completed by the teachers, which assessed motivation for school achievement. All test and rating data were collected in the first two and one-half months of the 1968-69 school year. In addition, all parents were interviewed to obtain attitudinal, social, and economic data, and information was collected on the Head Start programs and the elementary schools attended.

A covariance random replications model, using socioeconomic status as the covariate, was used in the data analysis, the .05 level of probability being used as the critical region for rejecting the null hypothesis. Results were cross-checked and, in general, confirmed by a nonparametric approach.

Specific findings. The specific findings leading to the first three conclusions on cognitive and affective efforts are summarized below by type of program.

    I. Summer programs (75 in number)
        A. Total sample
            1. ITPA: No significant differences on total test or subtests at any grade level. Observed differences in total score at each grade level favored controls. Total raw score of Head Start children on the average from about one-half to about two-thirds of a standard deviation below norms for chronological ages.
            2. MRT, Grade 1: No significant difference on total score; control mean higher. Controls significantly higher on two subtests, Word Meaning and Listening. Head Start total readiness score at the 44th percentile, slightly below national average.
            3. SAT
                a. Grade 2: Battery median of controls significantly higher than battery median of Head Start children. Significant differences favoring controls on three subtests. Head

Start children more than one-half year below national norms in grade equivalents;
percentile ranks on subtests ranged from
29 for Vocabulary to 9 for Spelling.

b. Grade 3: No significant differences on
total or subtest scores; battery median of
the controls higher. Head Start children
almost one full year below grade level on
national norms; percentile ranks ranged
from 21 for Language to 10 for Arithmetic
Computations.

4. CSCI: No significant differences in grades 1
and 3; controls were significantly higher in
grade 2.

5. CBI: No significant differences at any grade
level.

6. CARI: In grade 1, Head Start children's attitudes toward "Home" significantly more positive
than those of controls. No other significant
differences found at any grade level.

B. Subgroups: Subgroup analysis by geographic location, community size, and ethnic composition
of centers permitted 893 comparisons between
Head Start and control children on six different
measures. Altogether, 61 significant differences,
45 favoring controls. Of the differences, 45 on
cognitive measures, controls superior in 34 instances. On the affective measure, 16 differences
equally divided between Head Start and control
children. Significant differences favoring Head
Start children appeared only for centers in the
Southeast and centers having mostly Negro participants. Out of a possible 76 comparisons, Head
Start children in mainly Negro centers superior
on only four cognitive and two affective comparisons, and those in Southeast centers superior on
only one cognitive and two affective comparisons.

II. Full-year programs (29 in number)

A. Total sample

1. ITPA: No significant differences on total
language score at any grade level, but significant differences in favor of Grade 2 Head
Start children on two subtests, Visual Sequence and Manual Expression. Scaled scores
for Head Start children about one-half standard
deviation below normative group mean.

   2.   MRT: Head Start children significantly higher
        on Total Readiness and on Listening.   Total
        Readiness score of Head Start children at 51.74
        percentile of national norms.
   3.   SAT
             a. Grade 2: No significant differences on
             the battery median or on any subscores.
             Head Start children about one-half year be-
             low national norms in grade equivalents.
             b. Grade 3 (six centers only): No signifi-
             cant differences between Head Start children
             and controls. Head Start children one full
             year or more below in national grade equiv-
             alents, percentile rankings ranging from 6
             on Arithmetic Computation to 23 on Lan-
             guage.
   4.   CSCI: No significant differences at any of the
        three grade levels.
   5.   CBI: No significant differences at any grade
        level.
   6.   CARI: No significant differences at any grade
        level.
B. Subgroups: Of a total of 350 comparisons between
    Head Start children and controls, 40 significant
    differences. Head Start children superior on 34
    cognitive and 2 affective comparisons, more than
    10 percent of all comparisons. Controls had sig-
    nificantly higher scores on two cognitive and two
    affective measures. For Head Start centers in
    the Southeast, 10 significant differences, all on
    cognitive measures. For centers in the West, 6
    significant cognitive differences; for centers with
    mainly Negro participants and centers in core
    cities with more than 50,000 population, 5 signifi-
    cant differences. On the Metropolitan Readiness
    Tests, 10 favorable significant differences in
    grade 1, and on the ITPA, 14 favorable significant
    differences in grade 2. (No subgroup analysis at
    grade 3 because of insufficient cases.)

Major conclusions. The analysis of the data led to four major
conclusions:
   1. Summer Head Start programs appeared to be ineffective
in producing any gains in cognitive and affective development
that persisted into the elementary grades.
   2. Full-year Head Start programs appeared to be ineffective in terms of affective development but were somewhat

effective in producing gains in cognitive development that
could be detected in the first, second, and third grades. Programs were of greatest effectiveness in the Southeast, in core
cities of over 50,000, and in all-Negro centers.

   3. On language development and scholastic achievement,
Head Start children were still in a disadvantaged position with
respect to national norms.

   4. Head Start parents approved of the program and its
influence on their children and participated in center activities.

Discussion: The critical factor in this evaluation of Head
Start is the incidence of statistically significant differences
between Head Start and control group children. The minimal
number of such differences in the summer programs and the
superiority of the control group children in the majority of
cases in which differences were found clearly support a negative conclusion about the effectiveness of Head Start. It is interesting that, in their summations, the evaluators chose to
emphasize lack of difference favoring the Head Start children
and to give relatively little data on differences favoring the
controls.

   The more positive findings on the effects of the full-year
program on cognitive development are generally equivocal.
One consideration is the extent of the differences between Head
Start and control group children, for while statistically significant, the differences found were small in magnitude and
were, in fact, questioned by the investigators in regard to
practical significance. For example, the comparisons on the
Metropolitan Readiness Tests, the sole basis for a finding of
Head Start superiority for the total full-year sample, indicate
a mean raw score for Head Start children of 51.74 and for
controls of 48.46 (a difference of approximately .15 standard
deviations on the national norms). This difference is less
than one-half a standard deviation, which is defined by some
as the minimum difference that is "educationally worthwhile,"
In the subgroup analyses, in only one instance, the miscellan-
eous racial-ethnic category, does the total MRT score difference reach this level of practical significance. When the other
standardized test scores are analyzed in a similar way, differences approaching or exceeding a meaningful magnitude are
found in a number of the subgroup analyses.

   A major limitation of the Westinghouse-Ohio State study,
recognized by the evaluators, is that it is a post hoc study
providing no data on the comparative standings of the Head
Start children and the controls before they entered the program.

Matching on sex, race, and kindergarten attendance and using socio-economic data in a covariance analysis does not control for initial differences in capacity or development. Thus, the use of the term "gains" in the conclusions suggests more information than is actually available.

Another limitation of the study is the lumping together of programs without regard to possible program distinctions that might have had differential effects. The evaluators question the adequacy of the implementation of the program--and this implicitly suggest that the lack of more positive findings may reflect poor implementation. Subgroup variations in success also suggest the possibility of differential implementation according to locale and community size. Another implication that might be drawn is that Head Start was more effective with certain types of pupils than others. This implication likewise suggests that initial capacity and level of development, as well as input, may be critical to outcomes.

The main thrust of the Westinghouse-Ohio State report was its final recommendation that summer Head Start programs be phased out and that full-year Head Start programs be retained and improved. It was specifically suggested that it would be advisable (1) to offer programs of longer duration, extending downward to infancy and upward into grade school; (2) to vary procedures in accord with pupil characteristics; (3) to concentrate on the remediation of specific deficiencies; and (4) to train parents to become more effective teachers of their children. Asserting that the benefits of full-year Head Start programs could not be described as satisfactory, the report urged more extensive research into new procedures and techniques for remediating disadvantagement in young children.

Innovative Preschool Programs

The topic of programing for the preschool, the basic issue raised by the Westinghouse-Ohio State report, is one that has been and is currently the subject of much controversy. Research into effective procedures of early intervention for the disadvantaged child began well in advance of Head Start, and educational and research psychologists proposed some radical departures from traditional approaches. Some innovations proposed by them have been made a part of some Head Start programs and of other preschool programs. A number of the better known program researches are discussed in the following section.

Peabody Early Training Project

One preschool program for disadvantaged children that has received nationwide attention is the Early Training Project conducted at George Peabody College in Tennessee (Klaus and Gray, 1967). In it an attempt was made to develop an intervention approach that would affect school performance; the attempt was based on research on social class, cognitive development, and motivation. The project had a total of 86 subjects in two experimental and two control groups. One control group was located sixty miles away from the other groups and was included to assess diffusion effects in the local community. All subjects were Negro children born in 1958; their families were judged to be disadvantaged on the basis of home setting, parents' education, and parents' occupation. Children were randomly assigned to experimental and control groups.

One experimental group of children, starting at the ages of from three and one-half to four and one-half, participated in three, ten-week summer programs; the second experimental group of children, starting at the ages of from four and one-half to five and one-half, attended two such summer programs before entry into the first grade in 1964. (There was no kindergarten in the community.) Between summer sessions and during the first year of elementary school, a program of home visitations was conducted for the experimental group.

The project was concerned with both attitudes toward achievement and aptitudes for achievement. Efforts were made (1) to encourage motivation toward achievement, persistence, delay of gratification, interest in organized activities, and identification with achieving role models; (2) to develop perception--the ability to make discriminations in visual, auditory, and other modalities; and (3) to teach concept development--using colors, roles, numbers, size, direction, position, and the like--and verbal expression. While the program used much of the equipment and adhered to many of the activities of a traditional nursery school, reinforcement techniques using material as well as psychological and affective rewards were systematically and extensively employed to bring about desired behaviors. Parental participation was enlisted through home contacts in which the visitor assisted the parents in using specific techniques for furthering their children's educational progress.

Specific findings. Periodic evaluations through 1966, when the children were finishing second grade, showed the following results:

1. Stanford-Binet, seven administration (1962-66):
    though there were no significant differences among
    the groups on the initial testing, there was a signifi-
    cant difference (p < . 05) between the experimental
    groups combined and the control groups combined at
    the end of second grade.   The first experimental group
    (T_1) showed a significant gain of 14. 4 points in mean
    IQ (87. 6 - 102. 0) at the end of the first summer
    session and then a loss of 5. 6 points over the next
    winter.   The two control groups also made significant
    IQ gains on the testing following their initial experi-
    ences in a formal educational program, that is, at
    the end of the first grade.   All four groups showed a
    loss in IQ from the end of first to the end of second
    grade.   The net changes over the four years were as
    follows:
        Experimental T_1: + 3. 6 pts. (87. 6 - 91. 2)
                     T_2: + 3. 5 pts. (92. 5 - 96. 0)
        Control T_3: + 2. 5 pts. (85. 4 - 87. 9)
                     T_4: - 2. 1 pts. (86. 9 - 84. 8)
2. Wechsler Intelligence Scale for Children, three ad-
    ministrations (1964, 1965, and 1966): The experimen-
    tal group children were superior to the controls on all
    three administrations.   Substantial gains of from 8
    to 10 IQ points were made by all four groups between
    the first and second testings.
3. Illinois Test of Psycholinguistic Abilities, three ad-
    ministrations: The ITPA was administered before
    entry into the first grade and at the end of first and
    second grades.   The language age of the experimental
    groups combined was significantly greater than that
    of the control groups on the first two testings but not
    on the third.   The language age scores of the experi-
    mental groups dropped substantially on the last testing,
    while those of the local control group went up moder-
    ately.   The distal controls had the lowest scores on
    the ITPA.
4. Peabody Picture Vocabulary Test (PPVT), nine ad-
    ministrations (1962-66): Alternate forms of the test
    were used for each administration.   There were no
    significant differences between groups on the initial
    testing.   On the second testing, the first experimental
    group (T_1), which had then completed one summer
    program, had a significantly higher mental age score
    than did the three other groups combined.   This signi-
    ficant difference was not sustained on the next testing.

After the second summer program, there were significant differences between the experimental group children combined and the controls combined on all testings.

5. Reading readiness tests: Both the Metropolitan and
the Gates reading readiness tests were given at the
beginning of the first grade. The two experimental
groups had significantly higher scores than the control groups on all subtests of the batteries except the
Sentence section of the MRT. The experimental
groups were significantly different from each other on
one subtest; the local control group was superior
(p < .05) to the distal control group on three subtests.

6. Achievement tests: Metropolitan Achievement Tests
were given at the end of the first and second grades.
The experimental groups had significantly higher grade
level scores than did the controls on three of the four
Primary I subtests at the end of first grade and on two
of the five Primary II subtests at the end of second
grade. In four cases the significant differences between experimentals and controls were the result of
lower scores on the part of the distal control group.
The SAT Primary I Battery was given twice, in February and again in May of the last evaluation year. On
both testings the grade equivalent scores of the experimental groups were significantly higher than those of
controls combined on two subtests, Word Reading and
Paragraph Meaning. In three instances this was the
result of significantly lower scores on the part of the
distal control group. There were significant
differences between the local and distal control groups
on both administrations of two other subtests, Word
Study Skills and Arithmetic. In all the achievement
subtests, the mean scores were somewhat below grade
level for the time of administration. The highest
subtest score on the MAT at the end of the second
grade was a mean of 2.85 for the second experimental
group on Spelling. The other subtest scores for the
experimentals ranged from 2.32 to 2.75. The local
control group had means of from 2.29 to 2.65 while
the distal control group had grade equivalent means
between 1.98 and 2.20. On the SAT administered in
May of the second grade, the range of subtest means
were as follows: experimentals, from 1.92 to 2.38
and from 1.88 to 2.36; local controls, from 1.89 to
2.29, and distal controls, from 1.64 to 2.01.

7. Affective measures: On Kagan's Matching Familiar
Figures Test, a measure of cognitive style given at

the end of the preschool period, the experimentals were significantly more reflective than were the controls. On other measures of self-concept, reputation among peers, delayed gratification, motivation toward achievement, and social perception there were no sustained significant differences.

Summary. The Early Training Project demonstrated the posibility of modifying the IQ and language performance of disadvantaged children through a preschool intervention program. Differences in readiness and achievement between experimental and control group children in the first and second grades were attributed to the early intervention. The differential in the performance of the local control group and the distal control group was seen as a consequence of diffusion in the local community where experimental and control group families were in immediate contact. The possible effects of differing school situations and teacher variables were also acknowledged. The decline in IQ scores at the end of second grade was regarded as evidence of the need for sustained efforts to counteract familial deficiencies (Klaus and Gray, 1967).

Perry Preschool Project

Another early intervention program that has received considerable attention is the Perry Preschool Project operated by the public schools of Ypsilanti, Michigan. This project was designed to determine, through longitudinal evaluation, the effects of a cognitive program upon the intellectual development and educational performance of culturally deprived Negro children diagnosed as educably mentally retarded. The program provided morning preschool classes, afternoon home visits through which mothers were involved in the education of their children, and group meetings for the parents. One distinguishing element of the preschool classes was the teachers' use of "verbal bombardment," a method of drawing the child's attention to his environment by a steady stream of questions and comments. The curriculum has been described as permissive and teacher-structured, emphasizing verbal stimulation and interaction for cognitive rather than social development (Weikart, Kamii, and Radin, 1964; Weikart, 1967). All subjects in this project were drawn from the immediate school district; eligibility was based on IQ and a cultural deprivation rating that took into account parental occupations, parental education, and home density (rooms per person).

Subjects were divided into two groups matched on these criteria and roughly balanced with regard to sex and percentage of working mothers. The groups were arbitrarily designated experimental and control.

Specific findings. In 1962-63, the initial year of the project, there were two sets or waves of experimental and control groups: Wave 0 made up of four-year-olds and Wave 1 made up of three-year-olds. Additional groups of three-year-olds were added to the project in subsequent years. Evaluative data for the first three Waves (0, 1 and 2) are available on a number of measures:

1. Stanford-Binet
    a. Waves 0, 1, and 2: The Stanford-Binet was administered as a pretest, a posttest, and a follow-up measure. The three waves of experimental group children made substantial IQ gains in the first year of preschool: Wave 0, 12.7 points; Wave 1, 11.5 points and Wave 2, 20.4 points. All three were significantly different from their controls at the end of one year of preschool.
    b. Wave 0: The Wave 0 experimentals, thirteen children who entered the project as four-year-olds, were not significantly different from their controls at the end of kindergarten or the first grade. Through a combination of losses for the experimentals and gains for the controls, the groups were almost identical in mean IQ at the end of the second grade. The net change over the years had been 7.1 points (from 78.4 to 85.5) for the experimentals and 8.9 points (from 75.0 to 83.9) for the controls.
    c. Waves 1 and 2: The Wave 1 and Wave 2 children who had entered the program as three-year-olds were significantly different from their controls at the end of one year. The significance level was higher for the thirteen Wave 2 experimentals than for the 10 Wave 1 experimentals ($p < .001$ as compared to $p < .05$). Though the Wave 1 experimentals were still superior to the controls at the end of the second preschool year, the significance level had dropped to a marginal point ($p < .10$). Continuation of the Wave 0 pattern of diminishing differences between experimentals and controls was cited but not documented.
2. Leiter International Performance Scale: Arthur Adaptation: This test was also given as a pre-post measure,

but at varying intervals--which beclouded initial differences and gains. After an interval of two years,
at the end of kindergarten for Wave 0 and at the end
of preschool for Wave 1, there were no significant
differences between experimentals and controls. At
the end of one year of preschool, the Wave 2 experimentals scored significantly higher (p < .001) than
their controls.

3. Peabody Picture Vocabulary Test: At the end of kinder-
    garten, the Wave 0 control children had a higher mean
    IQ on the PPVT than did the experimentals (76.8 ver-
    sus 74.7), but the difference was not significant. The
    experimental group children in Waves 1 and 2 were
    significantly superior to their controls (p < .01):
    Wave 1 at the end of two years of preschool and Wave
    2 at the end of one year.

4. Illinois Test of Psycholinguistic Abilities: The ITPA
    was given as a posttest measure to Waves 0 and 1
    after two years. At the end of kindergarten, Wave 0
    had higher scores on six out of nine subtests with one
    difference being significant. At the end of preschool,
    Wave 1 had higher scores on seven subtests with two
    differences attaining significance. Both Waves 0 and
    1 had significantly higher scores on Auditory Vocal
    Association, a subtest which is highly verbal and
    conceptual. In contrast, the Wave 0 controls had a
    significantly higher score on Auditory Vocal Sequenc-
    ing (a digit-span test on a non-conceptual level). This
    conceptual superiority of the experimentals was con-
    sidered a highly significant outcome for the program.

The following additional results apply only to the Wave 0
children who were tested through second grade:

1. Gates Reading Readiness Test: On reading readiness
    at the end of kindergarten, the Wave 0 experimentals
    had higher scores than their controls on all subtests.
    There were significant differences on two subtests:
    Picture Directions and Word-Card Matching.

2. California Achievement Tests: California Achieve-
    ment Tests in Reading, Arithmetic, and Language
    Skills were administered to Wave 0 subjects at the
    end of first and second grades. The mean percentile
    ranks of the experimentals were significantly higher
    (p < .05) on all three subsections in the first grade
    and in Reading and Arithmetic in the second grade.
    Mean percentile ranks on the total test were significantly

higher for Wave 0 experimentals in both years (a rank of 22 as against a rank of 5 in the first grade and a rank of 18 as against a rank of 3 in the second grade).

3. Pupil Behavior Inventory: Teacher ratings on a 34-item inventory were obtained for the Wave 0 children in kindergarten and in the first and second grades. Mean scores on five factors--Classroom Conduct, Academic Motivation, Socio-Emotional State, Teacher Dependence, and Personal Behavior--were higher for the experimentals in all but two instances. Controls in kindergarten and the first grade scored higher on teacher dependence.

4. Ypsilanti Rating Scale: A teacher rating scale covering academic potential, social development, verbal skills, and emotional adjustment was developed for the project and used for Wave 0 subjects in kindergarten and the first and second grades. The scores of the experimentals were consistently higher each year, significant differences occurring (p < .01) on all factors except academic potential in the second grade.

Summary. The Perry Preschool Project resulted in substantial differences in the learning capacity of its participants, but the IQ gains tended to disappear over time. The relatively successful performance of children with one year of preschool on readiness and achievement tests led the evaluators to conclude that, although preschool experiences did not make a sustained difference in the measured intellectual level of disadvantaged children, they appeared to provide a basis for improved academic performance. However, in a further analysis of the test scores of the Wave 0 experimentals the authors noted the existence of two subgroups: five achievers whose mean percentile rating for achievement was at the 37th percentile and five nonachievers whose mean was at the 2nd percentile. The IQ scores of the achievers had been maintained and improved after their initial upward spurt while those of the nonachievers returned to their pretreatment level. Recognizing the limitations of such small samples, the evaluators suggested that the structured preschool program might be effective for some children and another approach needed for others (Weikart, Kamii, and Radin, 1964; Weikart, 1967).

Baltimore Early School Admissions Project

Another experimental preschool program, initiated in 1962, was the Baltimore Early School Admissions Project. This project was also aimed at discovering whether early school experiences could overcome barriers to school learning believed to be attributable to environmental factors. The program, which started with two groups of thirty four-and five-year-olds in two early admission centers, included enrichment activities and parental involvement and made use of both regular staff and volunteers. A preliminary evaluation made in 1963 after the first five months of program operation showed that the twenty eight children remaining in each of the centers, had made 20-point gains and 17-point gains, respectively, on the Columbia Mental Maturity Scale. The children's scores on a Verbal Maturity Scale developed in Baltimore showed 15-point and 9-point gains. The pre-post mean scores differences were all significant at the .001 level. No comparisons were made with control groups (Wilkerson, 1965). The Baltimore Early Admissions Project was extended beyond an initially planned three-year period and to serve several hundred pupils under Title I of the Elementary and Secondary Education Act.

The Bereiter-Engelmann Program

Another preschool program, which has been the focus of much controversy, was developed by Carl Bereiter and Sigfried Engelmann at the University of Illinois (Bereiter and Engelmann, 1966). The program is based on an analysis of the cognitive behaviors a child should attain by entry into first grade if he is to succeed in school. The investigators assert that if the disadvantaged child is to make up for deficiencies he must progress at a faster than normal rate in a specially devised, highly structured program directed toward specific objectives. In its initial format the Bereiter-Engelmann program consisted of three daily classes of fifteen to twenty minutes each in basic language skills, reading, and arithmetic, each small class being taught by its own special teacher. The only other major educational activity was singing which, through specially written songs, gave additional practice in the class skills.

The participants in the first implementation of the program were fifteen Negro children in a school district with an extremely low income level, who were selected on the basis of school difficulties exhibited by older siblings and the judgement that their homes were educationally unfavorable. Their median age was four and one-half years at the beginning of the program, and their scores on two subtests of the ITPA were at about the three-year level. The ITPA and the Stanford-Binet were given in the course of the nine-month program, and the Wide-Range Achievement Test was administered at the end of the school year.

Some limited reporting of the results of the program are available as follows (Bereiter and Engelmann, 1966):

1. Stanford-Binet: The Stanford-Binet was first administered two months after the start of the program to avoid "the irrelevant six-to-eight point gain that is expected merely from the children's becoming adjusted to schooling." The mean IQ was then about 93. On a retest after seven months of school the mean IQ was slightly above 100 (p. 54).

2. ITPA: On a full-test administration of the ITPA at the end of six weeks in the program, the children showed 6-month gains in the verbal reasoning and grammar subtests previously given (Auditory-Vocal Automatic and Auditory-Vocal Association). Their ability to use descriptive language (Vocal Encoding) was then about one year below level. Ten weeks later, they had gained about 1 year on Vocal Encoding and an additional 3 or 4 months on verbal reasoning and grammatical usage. At the end of seven months of schooling, subjects' scores on all verbal subtests except vocabulary were approximately normal and their scores on Vocal Encoding were 6 months above average.

3. Wide-Range Achievement Test: After nine months of the program, eleven of the fifteen children scored at or above beginning first grade level on the reading section of the Wide-Range Achievement Test: eleven scored at or above beginning second grade level on arithmetic and only one scored below first grade level.

Additional achievements not covered by the standardized tests included solution of equations with unknowns, solution of complex deduction problems, and reading of stories with phonically regular vocabularies. It was noted that many of these activities were performed at a higher level than would have been expected from measured IQ's.

Visitors reacted to the children as if they were gifted rather than disadvantaged. And it was the opinion of the evaluators that the children's performance on the kinds of tasks

they had been taught was a better criterion of success than
gains on general measures of learning capacity.

No statistical analyses of test scores were reported, and
there were no comparisons with a control group. Furthermore,
no follow-up data were reported for this experimental group.

New York State Study of Prekindergarten Programs for the
Disadvantaged

A four-year study of prekindergarten programs for the
disadvantaged in New York State attempted to assess the effectiveness of different types of preschool programs (Di Lorenzo,
Salter, and Brady, 1968). Eight school districts developed
their own half-day programs to improve capacity to learn, language development, self-concept, motor development, and attitudes toward school. The programs incorporated many elements of a traditional nursery school program, but there was
variation among the programs in their use of structured activities for cognitive objectives. Two districts included nondisadvantaged children in their classes as part of their program
treatments. Subjects, three and one-half to four and one-half
years in age, were identified as disadvantaged on the basis of
father's occupation or receipt of public assistance. Children
in each district were matched on the basis of sex, race, IQ,
and socio-economic status and randomly assigned to experimental and control groups. There were three successive waves
of subjects, a total of more than 1,800 children. Wave 1 was
followed into the second grade, Wave 2 into first grade, and
Wave 3 into kindergarten. The evaluative instruments used
were the Stanford-Binet Intelligence Scale, the PPVT, the
ITPA, and the MRT and MAT. Data for each year of program
operation were analyzed by treatment, socio-economic status,
district, race, and sex. On pre-post test measures (the
Stanford-Binet and the PPVT) changes in mean scores were
compared.

The disadvantaged experimentals were significantly different from their controls on the Stanford-Binet, the PPVT,
and the ITPA in each of the three years; six of these differences
were significant at the .05 level, three at the .10 level. The
significant differences in IQ resulted, in part, from lower
scores for the controls. There were only two significant differences between the nondisadvantaged experimentals and their
controls over the three years and both were at the .10 level;
one favored the experimentals, the other the controls.

In general, the programs were effective for both boys and
girls. They were also effective for both white and nonwhite
disadvantaged children but were more effective for the whites.
The gain scores of white children on the Stanford-Binet, for
example, were greater than those of the nonwhites in each of
the three years.

Examination of the results by district showed that not all
the programs were effective. Four of the districts accounted
for 21 out of 26 significant differences between disadvantaged
experimentals and controls in the course of three years, total
number of possible significant differences being 75. Three of
the programs that produced significant differences were described as structured and cognitively oriented. One offered
specific instruction in reading readiness and beginning reading;
another made use of Bereiter-Engelmann pattern drills and
planned discussion groups for language development.

Follow-up testing at the end of kindergarten for Waves 1
and 2 showed that the disadvantaged experimentals as a total
group had significantly higher scores on the MRT. There were
no significant differences between the nondisadvantaged experimentals and controls. Covariance analyses were used in
these analyses with Stanford-Binet and PPVT pretest scores as
covariates. Analysis of these results by district disclosed that
there were three districts in which the disadvantaged experimentals were significantly different from their controls on
reading readiness, two with Wave 1 subjects and one with Wave
2 subjects. In two of these districts, there had been no significant differences between experimentals and controls at the
end of prekindergarten, suggesting the possibility of latent effect for the preschool experience. Analyses of readiness test
results by sex showed that disadvantaged experimental girls
did better than both the control girls and the experimental boys.

Wave 1 subjects were followed into first grade in only the
one district, where there had been significant differences between the experimentals and controls at the end of prekindergarten. On the Metropolitan Achievement Tests, Primary I
Battery, there was no significant difference between the two
groups, though the experimentals had been superior to the controls on reading readiness at the end of kindergarten.

Summary

The large, comprehensive evaluations of broad-scale
early intervention programs have generally shown minimal,

if any, improvements for disadvantaged children. These studies are handicapped methodologically by their lack of pre-post
measures and longitudinal data. It is doubtful, however, that
any tightening of the research design would alter the outcomes.

Small-scale studies of specific programs and techniques,
on the other hand, have frequently shown some meaningful
changes in learning capacity and language development. Although the gains made through preschool have sometimes dis-
appeared in the early grades, the over-all results suggest a
number of ways to affect the achievement levels of disadvantaged children. Unfortunately, these innovational procedures
have not been fully explored or widely applied.

COMPENSATORY PROGRAMS AT THE ELEMENTARY
AND SECONDARY LEVELS

Compensatory education programs are by no means completely new, but have been evolving over a number of years.
In this brief review of compensatory programs at the elementary and secondary levels, attention is given first to some of
the forerunners of current efforts, then to two programs outside regular school auspices, and finally to programs supported
under Title I of the Elementary and Secondary Education Act.

Forerunners of Current Compensatory Programs

Many of the first compensatory programs for the disadvantaged were developed in the great cities of the Nation where
the problems of low achievement, school dropout, and unemployment among youth were most extensive. Among such programs were the Demonstration Guidance Project and Higher
Horizons Program in New York City, the All-Day Neighborhood
School, also in New York City, and the Banneker Project in St.
Louis, Missouri.

Demonstration Guidance Project

Faced with de facto segregation, the Commission on Integration of the New York City Board of Education ". . . sought
ways of reversing the process of apparent deterioration in
ability and achievement among minority group school children
and the subsequent limitation of educational opportunity"

(Hillson and Myers, 1963, p. v). And the Demonstration Guidance Project was a direct outcome of the Commission's work. It was a pilot project designed to identify and stimulate culturally deprived children to pursue higher educational and vocational goals.

The project started in September 1956 with 717 pupils in the seventh, eighth, and ninth grades in a junior high school in a depressed area. The evaluation continued until June 1962, when students in all three classes had graduated from the predominantly middle class George Washington High School. The final project population, after moving and transfers, was 329. The majority of the project participants were Negroes and Puerto Ricans from disadvantaged backgrounds. Latent academic aptitude was a criterion for selection, and although the participants represented the upper half of the student body in their junior high school, most ranked low in both IQ and scholastic achievement.

The project provided a saturation program of compensatory education on the junior and senior high school levels. It included curriculum modifications, reduced-size classes, remedial instruction, cultural enrichment activities, counseling and clinical services, and contact with parents (Wilkerson, 1965).

The counseling and clinical services appeared to be among the most highly emphasized aspects of the treatment. Individual counseling was devoted to personal and emotional problems, as well as academic achievement, reasons for failure, need for tutoring, interpretation of test results, selection of school subjects, and post-high-school plans. The counselors furnished the teachers with detailed information about the background and personal needs of the students, enabling them to achieve a better understanding of the attitudes and reactions of the students and to adapt instruction to meet individual needs. In providing clinical treatment for pupils with more severe problems, the clinicians aided them in practical matters, finding them part-time jobs, giving them monetary help, setting up better sleeping arrangements and places for study, and improving their relationships with their parents (Hillson and Myers, 1963).

The report on the Demonstration Guidance Project included a number of individual case studies and an enumeration of the school accomplishments of the participants. The attainments of the project pupils are compared with those of preproject students from the same junior high school who were in the classes of 1957, 1958, and 1959 at George Washington High School.

Specific outcomes of the project can be summarized as follows:

1. Of the final 329 project participants, 108 received academic diplomas, 147 graduated with general diplomas (an indication of holding power rather than academic achievement), and 3 earned commercial diplomas. Dropouts totaled 75.

2. The dropout rate for project students was 22 percent, below the average rate for the school and one-third lower than the rate for the rest of the city.

3. The number of academic graduates was two and a half times that in the three preproject classes: 108 as against 43.

4. Of the 108 academic graduates in the project--
    a. No failures were reported for 44, failures having been reported for 14 preproject students.
    b. Grade averages of 80 percent were reported for 37, such grade averages having been reported for only 11 in the preproject groups.
    c. Further education was undertaken by 96 (89 percent).
    d. IQ's below 100 had been previously reported for 38 and of 90 or below for 16.
    e. Reports showed that 36 were retarded one year or more in arithmetic at the beginning of high school.
    f. Reports showed that 13 were retarded one year or more in reading at the beginning of high school.

5. In graduating classes of 800 to 900, project students ranked first, fourth, and sixth in 1960; fourth in 1961; and second, fourth, and ninth in 1962. The highest-ranking students in the preproject classes placed fifty-first in 1957, sixty-fifth in 1968, and two hundred twenty-sixth in 1959.

6. A total of 168 project participants went on to higher institutions of learning, as against 47 of the preproject students (three and one-half times as many). Of these, 96 were academic graduates, and 72 had received general diplomas.

Further evidence of the success of the project was found in staff reports of improved pupil conduct and attitudes and in the positive reactions of both students and teachers to the project. The report also noted that not all results were satisfying. For example, among the academic graduates were

19 pupils who had IQ's of 110 and above who were not able to achieve 80 percent averages, and there were other pupils of adequate IQ's who did not attain the academic diploma of which they were capable (Hillson and Myers, 1963).

The report on the Demonstration Guidance Project suggests a high degree of success. However, the generally positive evaluation rests on the counting up of individual accomplishments rather than any systematic study of the effects of the program on all of its participants. The comparison of project and preproject students is open to question because there is no indication of the initial comparability of the two groups except on previous attendance at the same junior high school. Even the size of the preproject group is not specified, with the result that the comparisons of absolute numbers, as with the numbers of academic graduates, has limited meaning. In spite of the limitations in the evaluation, the Demonstration Guidance Project offered some tentative indication that the school performance of disadvantaged children could be improved.

Higher Horizons Program

The Higher Horizons Program was conceived as an extension of the Demonstration Guidance Project. Begun in September, 1959, with 12,000 children and expanded to include 64,000 at its conclusion in 1962, the program sought to serve children of all ability levels. The major purpose was "to develop techniques for the identification, motivation, enrichment and education of culturally disadvantaged children, and to perfect means for stimulating them and their families to pursue higher educational and vocational goals" (Wrightstone et al., 1964, p. i). The underlying premise of the program was that "improvement in a child can best be effected by direct influence upon the child, the teacher and the parent" (Wrightstone et al., 1964, p. 3). To this end, the program focused on intensive individual and group counseling, cultural and occupational experiences, remedial services, and parent education. The counseling and guidance services were intended to raise students' aspirations and to provide greater opportunity for employment and further education. The teachers were encouraged to improve their expectations of the students and their own ability to teach disadvantaged children.

Several hundred specialized personnel were added to the staffs of the project schools. The extra teachers were used as curriculum assistants, teacher training specialists, or subject matter specialists (particularly in reading). Each teacher was expected to spend a good part of his time on parent and community education, cultural activities, and in-service training, as well as on curriculum improvement and remedial work.

Wrightstone et al., of the New York City Bureau of Educational Research, conducted an extensive evaluation of the Higher Horizons Program for the Board of Education through a grant provided by the U. S. Office of Education. On the elementary level, eight Higher Horizons schools were selected as representative of the thirty-one schools in the program on the basis of third grade Otis Alpha IQ scores, reading comprehension scores, ethnic composition, geographic location, and size of school population. These eight were matched with eight control schools on a one-to-one basis. The Higher Horizons experimental schools tended to have smaller classes, lower teacher and pupil transiency, a greater percentage of regular teachers, and more professionals per pupil than the control schools. At the junior high school level, ten of the thirteen experimental schools were matched with ten control schools on size, ethnic composition, and IQ. The experimental and control group students in both elementary and junior high schools were administered an extensive array of standardized tests, rating scales, inventories, and questionnaires.

It should be noted that while Higher Horizons was intended to duplicate the apparently successful Demonstration Guidance Project, it never did actually replicate that program. One major difference between the two programs was that the Demonstration Guidance Project specifically worked with students who were identified as having academic potential while Higher Horizons was open to students of all ability levels. In addition to this, although per pupil expenditures and the number of personnel provided were higher for students in Higher Horizon schools, when compared to students in regular schools, they were still substantially lower than they had been in the Demonstration Guidance Schools. Finally, the Demonstration Guidance Project concentrated on secondary students while Higher Horizons was implemented at both the elementary and secondary level.

The results of the evaluation were as follows:
1. Scholastic aptitude and achievement
   a. After the elapsed treatment period, no significant differences were found between the I.Q. scores of experimental and control students at either the elementary or secondary levels.

b. For the junior high pupils, the experimental
    group did not achieve higher reading scores
    than the controls over a two-year period. A
    similar finding was reported for the mathema-
    tics achievement scores.
c. For elementary schools students, the reading
    gains made by the Higher Horizon pupils be-
    tween the third and sixth grades were not sig-
    nificantly different from those made by the
    control pupils. In arithmetic achievement,
    Higher Horizon pupils scored significantly high-
    er than controls on computation and problem-
    solving.

2. Personal and social development: There were no
    significant differences between Higher Horizons and
    control students on social, school and personal atti-
    tudes, self-image, or educational and vocational
    aspirations (ninth grade). There was some improve-
    ment in behavior, as measured by teacher judgment.
    Attendance improved at all levels. Higher Horizons
    tended to reduce the truancy rate, but there was no
    consistent pattern in the suspension rate.

3. Professional staff reactions: Concerning the effec-
    tiveness of the program, positive evaluations were
    positive by the teachers and especially by the prin-
    cipals. They felt the program most successful in the
    provision of cultural opportunities and extra remedial
    guidance services.

Indications of success for the Higher Horizon Program
are found solely in the positive attitudes of participating teachers and principals. Except for improved attendance, some
alteration in classroom behavior, and gains in arithmetic
achievement at the elementary level, this compensatory education program failed to demonstrate fulfillment of its objectives.
The educational and vocational goals of the pupils were not
altered, achievement was not stimulated, and attitudes and
self-image remained poor.

All-Day Neighborhood School Program

The All-Day Neighborhood School Program was organized
in New York City as an attempt to counteract the deleterious
effects of a ghetto neighborhood environment. Fifteen elementary schools were selected in economically impoverished
areas; seven schools with a majority of Negro pupils, four

schools with a majority of Puerto Rican pupils, and four schools with a majority of Negro and Puerto Rican pupils. Each school was assigned seven teachers with special training in child development and home and school relationships. They assisted the regular teachers during the school day and conducted an after-school program that included activities related to school work. The program cost an average of $70,000 per school, which was about $60 per student in excess of normal costs (RIPS report, 1967).

In 1965, the program was evaluated by independent researchers from New York University who compared the participants to control group students in similar schools that did not have compensatory education programs. The reading level, IQ, and academic achievement of the experimental group were not measureably improved. A follow-up of these students in junior high school revealed no significant differences between the participants and the control groups (RIPS report, 1967).

Banneker Project

The Banneker Project began in St. Louis, Missouri, in September of 1957 and by June of 1966 involved 23 elementary schools with Negro majorities, which enrolled more than 14,000 students. The project goal was to improve academic achievement by raising the expectations of teachers, the motivation of students, and the aspirations of parents. In 1967, the U.S. Commission on Civil Rights undertook an evaluation to determine the measureable results of the program upon the academic performance of Negro students. The evaluation procedure involved comparing the standardized test scores of project schools with (1) national testing norms and (2) the test scores of schools with Negro majorities not in the project and the test scores of schools in St. Louis with white majorities.

In the comparison of the Banneker schools with national norms, eighth grade reading scores in 1957-58 were 1 year below the national norm. In 1960-61, the scores were only 1/2 year below norm. However, by the school year 1965-66, when some of the eighth grade students had been in the program for seven years, the eighth grade reading scores in the majority of the Banneker schools had dropped to 1 year or more below the national norm. Furthermore, between the years 1962-63 and 1965-66, the standing of most Banneker schools in relation to other schools in the city with Negro and white majorities did not improve.

Efforts to improve achievement by means of altering expectations, aspirations, and motivation of teachers, pupils,
and parents were unsuccessful in the Banneker Project. The
initial achievement goals of the project schools were not sustained relative either to national norms or to other schools
within the system (RIPS report, 1967).

Other Compensatory Programs

Some compensatory programs have functioned outside
the bounds of regular elementary and secondary school systems.
Two of those that have achieved notable results are Upward
Bound, a program sponsored by the Office of Economic Opportunity, and Case II: MODEL, a special project of the Institute for Behavioral Research.

Upward Bound

Upward Bound is a national college preparatory program
designed ". . . to generate the skills and motivation necessary
for college success among . . . tenth to twelfth grade students . . . from low income backgrounds and inadequate
secondary school preparation" (Office of Economic Opportunity,
1965, p. 1). In the summer of 1965, pilot programs were
conducted on 18 college campuses. The number of programs
was expanded to 220 colleges, universities, and residential
secondary schools in 1966. These programs served 20,000
students.

The program treatment involved two phases: (1) A six-
to eight-week residential summer session planned to remedy
poor academic preparation and to increase the students'
chances for admission to and success in college and (2) a
follow-up program conducted during the regular academic
year to sustain gains made during the summer. The academic
content of both phases was not intended to parallel regular
secondary school work. Both phases included experiences
intended to lead to enrichment experiences.

Data from six of the original programs indicate that 80
percent of the Upward Bound students went on to education
beyond secondary schooling; 78 percent entered college, as
against the usual 8 percent. Data on college retention show
that Upward Bound participants had the same dropout rate as
all other college youths (Gordon and Jablonsky, 1968a).

Case II: MODEL

Under the aegis of the Institute for Behavioral Research, 28 young men at the National Training School for Boys were included in a one-year program to improve their academic behavior and prepare them to return to school. The boys ranged from fourteen to eighteen years of age and had an average IQ of 93.8. "Eighty-five percent were school drop-outs, and only three had never been sentenced and institutionalized before" (Gordon and Jablonsky, 1968a, p. 275).

The program was based on presenting a structured learning environment utilizing reinforcement to maintain students' interest and to program them for success. These objectives were to be attained by (1) structuring each curriculum unit at the level at which the individual could perform successfully step by step and (2) providing direct pay-off for achievement. The extrinsic immediate reinforcement used was money, which the student earned when he performed on tests at 90 percent or better. The student's earnings paid for his room, food, clothing, gifts, and fees for special classes. The student without sufficient funds went on relief--sleeping on an open bunk and eating from a metal tray. No student was on relief for more than two weeks.

The intermediate findings of Case II are impressive. The average increase in IQ was 12.09 points. "For every 90 hours of academic work, there was an average increase of 1.89 grade levels on the Stanford Achievement Test and 2.7 grade levels on the Gates Reading Survey (p. 276).

Title I, Elementary and Secondary Education Act

Title I of the Elementary and Secondary Education Act of 1965 provides the largest single source of funds for compensatory education. It has reached some 10 million youngsters at the cost of approximately $4 billion, of which roughly $340 million were allocated to New York State (NYSED, 1968a). The Title I program has been directed at schools in areas of concentrated deprivation. The legislation gives the states and school systems wide freedom in developing their own programs. Reports on these programs are available for 1965 and 1966. In general, the reports are not encouraging. Gordon and Jablonsky (1968a) summarize their evaluation of the program as follows:

1. Money was so rapidly allocated that the quality of program-planning and development was severely limited.

2. Many programs were operative for too brief a time to be evaluated effectively.

3. Many programs received insufficient funds to operate adequately.

4. Difficulty was experienced in locating appropriate specialized personnel.

5. Most programs could not report appreciable improvement in academic achievement for the target populations.

6. Generally, the programs increased the quantity of services offered but not the content or the quality.

Economic deprivation is the major qualification for Title I participation. Deprived children are defined as those children between the ages of five and seventeen who come from families whose incomes are less than $2,000 according to the 1960 U. S. census or from families who received Aid for Families with Dependent Children under Title IV of the Social Security Act even though their incomes were more than $2,000. Of the 48.5 million children enrolled in elementary and secondary schools, 12.4 percent fell into this category. Of these, 6.7 percent resided in New York State, and 71.5 percent of these deprived children were enrolled in schools in the six largest cities of the State.

A report on the first two years of experience with Title I in New York State (NYSED, 1968a) shows general over-all gains in achievement for children in the programs funded under Title I and concludes that Title I is effective. The nature of the study and the format of the data, however, make any firm conclusions respecting these programs difficult. In some cases, the programs served disadvantaged children who had much ability but achieved at a low level. The study offered no comparison data or means of determining the significance of any gains made. Without the inclusion of control groups in these programs, there was no way of ascertaining whether an eight-month gain in seven months was the result of specialized treatment or might have occurred with no treatment at all. It can only be concluded from the data presented in the NYSED study that Title I programs have failed to demonstrate a general rise in achievement in respect to grade level.

On the national level, among programs reporting positive findings, the tendency was reported toward improved morale, higher teacher expectations, improved self-perceived climates for learning, improved attendance, and reduced school dropout rates. The over-all national development of compensatory education under Title I programs, however, has not yet resulted in any measurable improvement in the academic achievement of children from disadvantaged backgrounds as against the achievement of their more advantaged peers (Gordon and Jablonsky, 1968a). In all fairness, however, all programs initiated under Title I should not be lumped together in making judgments since the Title I section of ESEA has fostered a variety of programs. They must be examined on an individual basis to determine which efforts were successful and which were not. The New York State evaluation cited a number of programs that had been examined on an individual basis. Among them was a program instituted by the City School District of Tonawanda. The District conducted a comprehensive reading program in five reading centers for 305 students ranging in age from 6 to 18 years. The program was designed to upgrade the reading ability of children not reading at a level commensurate with their IQ's. At the conclusion of the 10-month program, gains in ability ranged from one and one-half to three years. During the year, 10 percent of the children returned to regular classes and were reported to be achieving at a satisfactory level.

The latest annual report of The National Advisory Council on the Education of Disadvantaged Children (1969) deals with the procedure of examining individual projects. Under contract to the National Advisory Council and the U.S. Office of Education, the American Institutes of Research reviewed 1,000 of the more than 20,000 individual Title I compensatory programs and collected detailed data on 400 of them. The following criteria were used in screening the projects:

1. Only compensatory programs whose directors had measured achievement through standardized tests were included in the AIR report. Ratings, classroom grades, and even special tests prepared by teachers were considered too unreliable and subject to bias by program personnel to provide an accurate index to achievement gains.

2. An improvement in achievement scores was not considered sufficient by itself to identify a "successful program." The achieved gain had to exceed that made by a control group over a comparable period of time, or that to be expected on the basis of normative data, and had to be statistically significant.

3. The terms "successful" and "unsuccessful"
    have a highly restricted meaning as used
    in this report; they denote only programs
    which produced pupil gains in language or
    number skills. If, for example, a program
    succeeded in improving pupil attitudes but
    failed in the formal, "cognitive" or academic
    area during the period observed it was con-
    sidered unsuccessful.
4. Language skills meant achievement in such
    areas as reading, speaking fluency and word
    recognition; "number skills" usually implied
    arithmetic and, in some cases, mathematics
    (p. 20).

Of the 400 projects qualifying for more intensive review,
21 were designated as successful. These 21 projects were
matched with one or more unsuccessful projects that were
similar in terms of objective and age of pupils, in order to
determine what makes one project successful and another unsuccessful. On the basis of the comparisons made, the following criteria seemed to distinguish successful programs
from unsuccessful programs:

For pre-school programs
1. Careful planning, including statements of
    objectives
2. Teacher training in the methods of the pro-
    grams
3. Small groups and a high degree of individu-
    alization
4. Instruction and materials closely relevant
    to the objectives
For elementary school compensatory programs
1. Academic objectives clearly stated
2. Active parental involvement, particularly
    as motivators
3. Individual attention for pupils' learning
    problems
4. High intensity of treatment
For secondary school compensatory programs
1. Academic objectives clearly stated
2. Individualization of instruction
3. Directly relevant instruction (pp. 23-24).

It seems, therefore, that the concept of compensatory education--particularly as manifested in Title I--is a viable one, provided the individual programs that are developed follow the criteria previously discussed. As the National Advisory Council points out, these criteria are basic to good program construction no matter what program is involved. It can therefore be expected that successful use of Title I funds is within the realm of possibility for all districts that are presently receiving these funds.

COMPENSATORY PROGRAMS AND INTEGRATION: COMPARISONS

Of special interest and pertinence to the improvement of educational opportunities for disadvantaged children are several studies that have examined the relative effectiveness of (1) compensatory programs in racially or socially segregated schools and (2) programs of racial or social integration without compensatory educational services. All the studies located indicate that racial and social integration of the schools alone is at least as effective as compensatory programs alone, if not more so, in improving the educational achievement of disadvantaged students. The environment of the racially or socially isolated school with an overwhelming majority of deprived students evidently defeats the purpose of presently existing compensatory programs.

Since 1962, the school system of Berkeley, California, has provided an extensive program of compensatory education for disadvantaged children in the de facto segregated schools of the city (Sullivan, 1968). This program has incorporated reduced class size, an expanded staff of educational specialists, improved teaching materials, individual tutoring, parental and community involvement, after school study halls, preschool programs, flexible grouping, improved teaching techniques and special training for the teaching staff. By 1965, the program had produced no noticeable effect on the achievement levels of disadvantaged fifth grade children who had received the compensatory services for four years, as compared to the achievement levels of fifth grade students in the same schools before the compensatory services had been introduced (RIPS report, 1967).

As reported previously in Chapter 5, Berkeley's public schools have also initiated a program of racial integration involving the busing of children from predominantly Negro elementary schools to predominantly white schools and to socially and racially mixed schools having no compensatory services (Sullivan, 1968). In the spring of 1967, scores of all students in the city in the first grade through the sixth grade on the paragraph meaning section of the SAT were compared by type of school program and school racial composition. Of special interest are the comparisons of the scores of the following three groups of students: (1) Negro students remaining in segregated, predominantly Negro schools but receiving compensatory educational services; (2) Negro students transferred to underused, predominantly white schools and receiving no compensatory services; and (3) Negro students transferred to or attending racially mixed schools and receiving no compensatory services. Table 40 presents the results of these comparisons in terms of the percentages of students from each group receiving scores in the bottom, middle, and upper third of the entire city elementary school population.

As indicated by Table 40, an over-all pattern of much higher reading achievement occurred among those Negro students who attended both the predominantly white and the racially mixed schools where no special provisions were made for compensatory education, as compared with the Negro students who remained in the segregated, predominantly Negro schools and received extensive compensatory services. These substantial results must be viewed with some caution, however, since the research report (Sullivan, 1968) does not clearly indicate whether or not the bused children were initially academically equivalent to those who remained in the segregated schools.

The Seattle Public Schools adopted a limited busing program during the 1965-66 school year in order to reduce the class size at two schools having a majority of Negro students, as part of a new compensatory program in those schools (RIPS report, 1967a). A group of 242 children, most of whom were Negro, were transported to other schools in the city that had larger class sizes and no special compensatory programs. At the beginning and end of the school year 17 first grade students in the transfer group were compared with 25 first grade students in the control group that remained in the predominantly Negro schools, on the basis of reading test scores. The transfer students, who had received no compensatory education during the year, showed slightly higher gains in reading than did the control students, who had received all the supposed benefits of an intensive compensatory educational program.

TABLE 40

Percentage of Students' Paragraph Meaning Subtest Scores
(Stanford Achievement Test) Occurring in Each Third for Three Student Groups[1]

Negro Student Groups	N	Percentage of Scores in:		
		Bottom Third	Middle Third	Upper Third
Segregated, with Compensatory Programs	2028	66.2	29.2	4.5
Transported to White Schools, No Compensatory Programs	234	33.4	45.2	21.4
Attending Racially and Socially Mixed Schools, No Compensatory Programs	562	43.3	44.1	12.6

[1]Adapted from Sullivan (1968), p. 153.

One of the earliest and most extensive programs of compensatory education for disadvantaged children was the Education Improvement Program of the Philadelphia Public Schools established in 1963 (RIPS report, 1967a). Initiated at the first grade level, the program was gradually expanded until in 1965 approximately 30,000 students in impoverished areas from first grade through high school were involved. An evaluation of the effectiveness of the compensatory program in comparison with traditional programs in other schools having a majority of Negro students and in schools integrated by busing was conducted by the U.S. Commission on Civil Rights (RIPS report, 1967a):

> To evaluate the effectiveness of this program, the Commission used existing test data and compared the achievement histories of three groups of Negro children: those in nearly all-Negro schools participating in the program; those in non-participating nearly all-Negro schools; and those bused to nonparticipating majority-white schools. The Negro children who were bused to the majority-white schools were of the same social class level as those in EIP (Education Improvement Program) schools which were nearly all-Negro; the students in the nearly all-Negro non-participating schools were of a somewhat higher social class level (p. 133).

The reading achievement levels of these three groups were traced from the end of first grade. The median achievement level of the children in the participating schools having a majority of Negro students consistently fell further behind that of the children in the other two groups over the two-year period.

At the beginning of the evaluation, the children in the non-participating predominantly Negro schools, who were of a slightly higher social class than the other two groups, had a slightly higher reading achievement level than the children in the other two groups. By the end of the evaluation, the Negro students bused to the nonparticipating white schools had raised their achievement level sufficiently to close this gap, but the students in the participating predominantly Negro schools had not.

In 1962, the public schools of Syracuse, New York, established programs of compensatory education in three predominantly Negro schools of the city, two elementary schools and

one junior high school.   These programs incorporated small
class size, special instructional materials, extra guidance
counselors, and remedial specialists (Jaquith, 1967). Approximately $100 more per pupil was expended by the school sys-
tem in these three schools than in the other schools of the district (RIPS report, 1967a).   A comparison was made of the
reading achievement scores at the third, fourth, and fifth grade
level of Negro students attending the two elementary schools
participating in the compensatory programs and of Negro students attending predominantly white schools of the city having
no compensatory services.   The median achievement levels of
both groups at the beginning of the study were approximately
equal but by the fifth grade the median achievement level of the
children receiving compensatory education was approximately
1/4 grade level behind that of Negro children attending integrated schools and receiving no compensatory services.

In 1965, a limited program of integration through busing
was initiated at the first, second, and third grade levels in
the Syracuse city schools.   Approximately 80 Negro students
in these three grades were transported from the predominantly
Negro elementary schools to a predominantly white school with
a record of high achievement (Jaquith, 1967).   An evaluation
of the effects on reading achievement of this program of integration as opposed to the effects of the compensatory programs in the predominantly Negro schools was conducted with
a small sample of students.   The transported students, who
received no compensatory services, achieved, over the course
of one year, at a rate double that of the children in the predominantly Negro school providing compensatory education.

In the same city, at the junior high school level, 30 pupils
from the predominantly Negro junior high school were transferred to a predominantly white school with a record of high
achievement (Jaquith, 1967).   When a comparison was made
of their own achievement in previous years, during which they
had participated in compensatory education programs, these
students showed significant gains.   Each of the students was
individually interviewed concerning what he considered to be
the reason for his improvement.   The results of these interviews indicated that the peer models available to the students
at the junior high school having a high achievement level were
more important in stimulating academic achievement than had
been the compensatory education programs in the predominantly Negro school.

Another study was conducted by the Rochester Public
Schools (Rock et al., 1968) to evaluate the relative educational

effectiveness of several types and degrees of compensatory
programs and racial integration. One object of this study was
to determine how the achievement of Negro pupils attending a
predominantly Negro school having small classes compared
with the achievement of Negro pupils in larger racially integrated classes both in an inner city school and in a suburban
school. Very few of the numerous comparisons of achievement
that were made for these three groups showed significant differences. They generally indicated, however, that Negro
pupils achieved at higher levels when in larger classes that
were integrated than when in smaller classes that were almost completely Negro.

Caution should be observed in evaluating the conclusions
of studies comparing the relative effectiveness of compensatory education and integration for the educational development
of Negro students. The appropriate conclusion seems to be
that integration is consistently more effective in raising the
achievement levels of Negroes than are a variety of applications of compensatory education. This conclusion does not
mean that the notion of compensatory education is invalid;
rather, it raises questions about the manner in which current
programs of compensatory education are being conducted.
Furthermore, the assumption of a lack of "compensatory
education" in the predominantly white schools in which the
Negroes experienced integration may not be valid. It is
possible that these schools could have provided compensatory
education in a number of ways through the quality of their
teachers, facilities, and curricula. Since qualitative differences between schools may be confounded with integration,
part of the assumed effect of integration could have been the
result of such differences, and other differences as well,
such as social class composition of the school and differences
in family background between integrated and nonintegrated
Negroes--and possible Hawthorne effects.

Although the effects of integration have generally been
more pronounced than those of compensatory education, the
size of the changes in achievement produced through integration indicate that integration itself is not sufficient to raise
the achievement of disadvantaged minority students to national
norms. Research is needed to evaluate the relative effects of
programs that will combine the advantages of integration and
the most efficacious techniques of compensatory education.

COMPENSATORY EDUCATION AND INTEGRATION:
SUMMARY AND CONCLUSIONS

Compensatory education programs, conducted at all educational levels from prekindergarten through high school, have been pedagogical experiments aimed at overcoming or circumventing the environmental and experiential deficiencies of the disadvantaged child, particularly the urban Negro child. The specific formats of the programs have been highly diversified, but they have generally incorporated remedial instruction, cultural enrichment activities, and efforts to overcome attitudes presumed to inhibit learning.

Project Head Start, the largest compensatory program undertaken, was designed as a national program and conducted on either full-year or summer basis to offer disadvantaged preschool children appropriate preparation for primary school. A major evaluation of Head Start compared the achievement of Head Start participants with that of similar children who had not attended the program. Summer programs failed to show any effect on achievement; full-year programs were minimally effective in raising the achievement level of the participants.

Head Start was most effective in the Southeast in scattered programs in the central cities and in programs having mainly Negro participants. Over-all achievement levels of Head Start participants did not approach national norms for the standardized tests of language development and scholastic achievement. Gains that were made tended to disappear after the children had entered a traditional primary program.

Two other compensatory programs directed toward preschool disadvantaged children were conducted in Baltimore, Maryland, and Ypsilanti, Michigan. In Baltimore, 60 children from four to five years old received enriched educational experiences and showed a substantial amount of growth during a five-month observation period; the significance of this growth is unknown, however, for no comparisons were made with a control group. For Perry Preschool Project of Ypsilanti, which served three- and four-year old children, an evaluation following some of the children into second grade indicated that marked growth in IQ and language development were not sustained.

A review of the highly structured Bereiter-Engelmann program suggests that it was highly effective, although deficiencies in data reporting suggest that any conclusions must

remain tentative. And the New York State study of prekindergarten programs also appears to indicate positive
results for programs that emphasize structure and cognition.

The Demonstration Guidance Project, designed to stimulate deprived children to pursue their education after high
school, involved approximately 700 academically able junior
high school students whose achievement was low. The program contined through high school, and according to the report issued, highly gratifying results were obtained. On this
basis, New York City initiated the Higher Horizons Project,
composed of the basic elements found in the Demonstration
Guidance Project, extended to some 64,000 students by the
time of its conclusion in 1962. Though the new program was
basically the same, there was a smaller per pupil expenditure,
and elementary school students and less academically able
students were included. Higher Horizons did not result in
superior academic performance on the part of project students
except in the area of arithmetic achievement at the elementary
school level. Another one of New York City's programs, the
All-Day Neighborhood School Program, was similar to Higher
Horizons in that it also failed to reveal any significant differences between the participants and a control group. In this
project, additional teachers were supplied to aid regular teachers during the day and to run special school-related programs
after school. A similar large-scale program initiated in St.
Louis, Missouri, known as the Banneker Project, also resulted in generally negative findings with a sample of some
14,000 elementary school students.

Upward Bound was among the more successful programs
of compensatory education, in which academically promising,
disadvantaged high school students spent from six to eight
weeks on a college campus in a program designed to overcome academic deficiencies and generate the skills and motivation necessary for college success. Data on this program
indicated that 78 percent of the participants entered college
and that the dropout rate for them was no greater than that
of other college youths.

Project Case II: MODEL was another promising compensatory education program. The goal of the program was
to improve the academic behavior of 28 training school boys,
85 percent of whom were school dropouts, and to prepare
them to return to school. Students participated in a structured learning experience that could be conducted on an individual basis, and they received a direct monetary pay-off
for test performance of 90 percent or better. Standardized
tests administered at the end of a year showed dramatic
gains in both IQ and achievement.

The largest expenditure in compensatory education has been allocated through Title I of the Elementary and Secondary Education Act of 1965. Available evidence suggests that Title I programs in general have had little positive impact on the level of educational retardation exhibited by minority group students and other disadvantaged children. One national study of Title I screened some 1,000 projects, and then, having selected 400 for intensive review, finally selected 21 programs designated as successful in accordance with moderately ambitious criteria. This study attempted to serve the further useful function of tentatively identifying program components that differentiated successful and unsuccessful Title I programs. The results of this effort are no more illuminating than any standard text on curriculum, but, nevertheless, constitute good advice to teachers in the disadvantaged school.

Based on the large-scale evaluations now available, it must be concluded that current large-scale applications of the concept of compensatory education have failed to show any real promise of reducing the intellectual and achievement deficits of disadvantaged children (Jensen, 1969; Gordon and Jablonsky, 1968a). In contrast, several studies that have compared disadvantaged Negroes in traditional compensatory education programs with Negro students transferred to schools having a majority of white students have showed integration to be more effective. Despite the apparent superiority of the integration as an approach, it is evident, as at Berkeley, that disadvantaged Negroes achieve at considerably lower levels than more advantaged whites. Continuation of compensatory education seems to be a logical necessity even when integration has been achieved, since integration generally results in a facilitative manipulation along only a few educationally relevant dimensions.

One of the notable problems in the application of current concepts of compensatory education has been in determining the extent to which the programs should impinge on the disadvantaged child's life. Typically, compensatory programs are supplementary to the regular school program or may comprise a few short weeks of concentrated effort. Important also is the period at which the program intervenes in the child's life. It is important, in this connection, to recognize that the educational and intellectual deficiencies of the disadvantaged child have been accruing since infancy--or perhaps earlier--and that programs of short duration are thus unlikely to have much of an effect. There is now some support for the nation that certain types of compensatory programs,

if begun very early (as early as 15 months) and continuous over
a number of years, may substantially reduce predictable intellectual deficiencies. It may also prove desirable to continue certain types of compensatory efforts once the child
has reached school age, in order to allay the continuing influences of a deprived background.

Another general criticism of current approaches to compensatory education centers around the global nature of program objectives and the corresponding global nature of approaches. Such concepts as self-esteem, language development, and academic motivation are frequently little understood by program directors and teachers alike. The resultant
lack of definition leads to a plethora of nonstandardized and
varied activities having varying degrees of relationship to the
program objectives, assuming that even the objectives are
clear. Attention to behavioral concepts and systematic instructional approaches related to program objectives should
facilitate the design of effective programs that may be appropriate for wider application. There is, of course, a related
need for application of more systematic approaches to program evaluation that time series observations of behaviors
derived from program objectives.

Still another general criticism of compensatory education
derives from a pervasive lack of recognition of the specific
psychological, intellectual, and learning deficits typically
displayed by the disadvantaged child. Most compensatory
approaches designed for general application have been no
more radical than any educational program available to the
advantaged student. And the Coleman et al. report clearly
indicates that improvements along traditional dimensions of
school and teacher quality are likely to have only minimal effects on disadvantaged Negroes and only slightly greater
effect on Puerto Ricans. The research review presented in
Chapter 3 indicates some of the basic differences between
social class and ethnic groups that might well be taken into
account in selecting an appropriate instructional methodology.
For example, it has been demonstrated that lower class
children use language in a concrete fashion and are not likely
to be able to deal initially with the abstract manipulations
of language that are more familiar to children of the middle
class. Moreover, Jensen (1966, 1968) has indicated potential differences in the ways in which middle class and lower
class children are likely to respond to the same reinforcement techniques--and Project Case II: MODEL made extensive

use of techniques based upon principles established through research including direct monetary pay-off, somewhat radical by middle class standards but effective with the disadvantaged student, and should incorporate the techniques that are most effective with him.

A number of additional, potentially useful leads for the improvement of educational opportunities for economically and socially disadvantaged children are contained in the literature reviewed in this and other reports. At this point, however, racial and social integration appear to offer the most consistent and the greatest promise for improvement in educational development among disadvantaged Negroes and other minority groups, as compared to other treatments tried in experimental settings or in the regular school setting. Moreover, it appears that the potentially positive effects of integration on educational development among minority group students can be approached more systematically than they have been thus far, with perhaps even greater facilitating effects. Yet, for various reasons that will be discussed in Chapter 7, it seems a logical necessity to continue placing part of available educational resources into research and field testing of approaches to compensatory education. The findings of Title I evaluations suggest that one effective approach may be nothing more complicated than systematic teaching, coupled with an adequate plan for evaluation. The findings of some studies suggest applications of certain principles of reinforcement; other studies suggest highly structured approaches to instruction; still other studies suggest a focus on parental involvement in the learning process. There remains the fact that many thousands of children now in the public schools, and thousands more in the future, require effective help largely administered in the school context.

In the final chapter of this volume, an attempt is made to explore some of the larger implications of the findings of the study for the education of disadvantaged children in the public schools of New York State and elsewhere. Certain of the larger problems that have emerged in past experiences in compensatory education are further clarified, and a number of recommendations are made in the interest of improving the educational opportunities of disadvantaged children in both integrated and segregated school settings. Beyond this, an attempt is made to show how the concept of compensatory education can be made viable in the integrated school, without defeating the basic purposes of integration.

7

GENERAL IMPLICATIONS AND RECOMMENDATIONS

Robert P. O'Reilly

Whites--particularly those who have only recently attained a modest measure of affluence--have great difficulty in understanding the meaning behind the symptoms of Negro frustration as evidenced in the recent wave of racial riots (NACCD, 1968) and the more recent instances of active protest in the schools and in other areas of American life, (Kruger, 1969; Urban Crisis Monitor, 1969). It is generally believed that the economic, educational, and social status of the Negro has been advancing steadily (Kruger, 1969) and that legal efforts in the cause of integration have had a substantial positive effect upon the extent of racial isolation in the schools. However, a recent analysis of the employment status of Negroes in the United States (Kruger, 1969) indicates that, at the present rate of improvement in regard to income, parity with white incomes can be expected in 805 years. Turning to progress in school integration, the analysis by Sullivan and Stewart (1969) of the impact of Federal and State laws and policy relating to school desegregation indicates only minor progress over the past fifteen years. The results of the analyses in Chapter 2 of this volume show a substantial and continuing increase in racial isolation in the schools in New York State --and this is a pattern that exists in other industrialized states in the North, the border states, and certain cities in the South (RIPS report, 1967a). One may go on to list scores of inequities relating to the economic, social, and educational positions of Negroes and other minority group members, but the main point seems clear: Negroes are at the bottom of American society, educationally and economically--and there has been no essential improvement in their relative status since the 1940's (West, 1968; Kruger, 1969).

The persistence--and in some respects, worsening-- of the gap between Negroes and whites has no doubt contributed greatly to social unrest in the United States. It is not generally our nature to continually endure frustration, as the U.S. National Advisory Commission on Civil Disorders (1968) states:

. . . for many minorities, and particularly for
the children of the ghetto, the schools have failed
to provide the educational experience which could
overcome the effects of discrimination and deprivation.

This failure is one of the persistent sources
of grievance and resentment within the Negro
community. The hostility of Negro parents and
students toward the school system is generating
increasing conflict and causing disruption within many school districts (p. 25).

And the Commission describes the dangers to American
society resulting from the failure to integrate the schools:

We support integration as the priority education
strategy; it is essential to the future of American
society. In this last summer's disorders we have
seen the consequences of racial isolation at all
levels, and of attitudes toward race, on both
sides, produced by three centuries of myth,
ignorance and bias. It is indispensible that opportunities for interaction between the races be
expanded (p. 25).

Since the Commission's report in 1968, there has been
growing evidence of predicted racial cleavage occurring directly in the schools, as the sense of grievance at the Nation's response to Negro demands has filtered down to the young. The
Urban Crisis Monitor (1969) reports some 2, 000 disorders in
the Nation's high schools between November and February,
1968-69. Racial conflict is reported to be at the heart of the
ugliest and most violent of the protests surveyed and is apparently the major cause of disorders in high schools in the large
cities.

The cost of racially and socially isolated schools also
includes the enormous effect of violence and crime on the
economy and on the lives of thousands of individuals every
year. In 1969 the National Commission on the Causes and
Prevention of Violence concluded that the United States clearly
led other stable nations in number of homicides, rapes, rob-
beries, and assaults. The Commission further noted that the
roots of violence and crime lay in class status. Given the
close correspondence between social class and race, one would
then expect Negroes to contribute disproportionately to the

extent of crime recorded in the United States. As noted in the Wilson (1967) study, the failure of the schools to provide quality education for all appears to be one of the major factors contributing to the high rate of delinquency among lower-status adolescents, whether Negro or white.

It is evident from the findings of this study that an enormous waste of human resources resulting partially from racial isolation in the schools can partially be remedied through quality education in the integrated school setting. The findings of this study focus attention on the disadvantaged Negro child, the equally disadvantaged Puerto Rican child, and other children who generally experience frustration and failure in the school setting. However, it is not only minority groups that will benefit from the educational and social changes that will result from the achievement of quality and equality in education. White and other advantaged children will thereby obtain a greatly expanded opportunity to experience the diversity in behavior and custom that has always been part of the American cultural scene. Sullivan and Stewart (1969), in reporting on the process of integration at Berkeley, described numerous instances of interracial interaction among children, parents and teachers that constitute social experiences that cannot be gained firsthand in the isolated white middle class school. For example, some 500 adult volunteers are currently participating in the educational process in Berkeley. White parents who formerly feared the effect of integration on their children's achievement are now helping Negro children to read, write, or do arithmetic.

The general failure to achieve real progress in the elimination of segregation in the schools, whether de jure or de facto, thus represents a loss to the enrichment of American culture, while at the same time it has increased the level of interracial distrust among both major racial groups. A reflection of this distrust is found in the Negro separatist movement, which calls for among other things, the establishment of quality education in segregated school settings. Riessman (1966) has correctly analyzed this response as a capitulation to the negative response of whites to moves to initiate desegregation in the schools in various parts of the Nation. The call for separatism is further analyzable as a normal defensive response to the overwhelming frustration that Negroes must have experienced as a function of viewing the record: "If you are not going to help us (as it now must appear), then we will do it by ourselves."

It is, however, not at all evident that quality education

can be initiated now or in the near future in segregated school
settings.   The findings of the Coleman et al. study and the RIPS
reports certainly do not support this notion.   Rather, the general body of evidence relating to school integration indicates
that improvement in the educational development of Negro
students can be expected within a relatively short time following the placement of the child in an integrated school setting.
There appears to be no other educational treatment that comes
as close to meeting the demand for improvement now as effective integration.

The question remains how integration in the school is
to become a reality in view of the past record of progress and
this study was not initiated or designed to answer that question.
The implications of the study that remain to be discussed and
the recommendations deal primarily with research and practice
in selected areas.   A number of guidelines that should assist
in enhancing the chances of success in initiating school integration programs are implicit in the findings reported in
Chapters 3 through 6.   These may now be enlarged upon and
added to in the expectation that judgements based on research
will be given careful consideration in decisions involving
school integration.   Three particular sources that may assist
in the planning of school integration programs are (1) the previously mentioned RIPS report, (2) a recently released book
by Sullivan and Stewart (1969), in which the experience of
integration in Berkeley is described in considerable detail,
and (3) a volume edited by Robert L. Green entitled, Racial
Crisis in American Education (1969).

Sullivan and Stewart's book should be of particular use
to school administrators and members of boards of education,
as well as community leaders involved in decisions to integrate
the schools.   The RIPS report is an excellent source for a
variety of plans and proposals relevant to initiating desegregation in the schools, particularly in large urban centers.   It is
also an excellent source on the issue of Federal and State laws
relating to de jure and de facto segregation in the schools.   The
book edited by Green is a good source of recommendations concerning integration in relation to teaching alternatives, teacher
characteristics, text books and curricula, racial attitudes,
language development, and other meaningful topics.   To this
group may be added a number of recommendations offered by
Urie Bronfenbrenner (1967) in an article that deals with the
special educational and psychological needs of the newly integrated minority student, and a series of papers by Mark Chesler
and others (Chesler, 1969;   Chesler, 1966;   Chesler and Barakat,

1967; Chesler and Fox, 1966, 1967) that are relevant to the
current issue of interracial conflict in the schools. This last
topic, dealt with only briefly in this volume, is a crucial consideration in the schools. Additional useful sources will be
found in the bibliography.

The implications and recommendations discussed below
fall into four main areas. The first section utilizes some
limited data on the economic status of minority groups in New
York State in order to determine the extent to which racial
isolation also means social class isolation in the schools in
different areas in the State. The implications of the correspondence between racial and social class isolation in the
schools for policy and planning relating to school desegregation are also discussed. The next section deals with the influence of group processes on learning and social interaction
in integrated and disadvantaged school settings. Recommendations are made for changing the content, structure, and approaches to instruction and interaction in both settings. The
third section presents a number of suggestions for improving
research and program development in the disadvantaged
school, and analyzes some of the major faults of previous
efforts to up-grade the educational process in inner city
schools.

SOCIAL CLASS IMPLICATIONS OF RACIAL
ISOLATION IN THE SCHOOLS

The results of major studies reviewed in this report
generally substantiate the observation that the typical racially isolated school is one that is also isolated on the basis
of social class. Some brief considerations of data available
on the economic status of nonwhites indicate that this generalization holds true for New York State, although there appear to
be some exceptions in some isolated suburban communities
that have large Negro populations. The conjunction of racial
and social class isolation in the schools appears to result from
a number of factors, of which the following are particularly
important: (1) disproportionate representation of ethnic minorities in lower income occupations or receiving public
assistance; (2) residential segregation and the corresponding
widespread application of the neighborhood school policy; and
(3) enrollment of large numbers of generally middle income
and upper income whites in private schools, especially in

the urban areas. This last factor tends to make available for public school attendance a white student population that is less well-off economically than the total white student population (RIPS report, 1967a).

Nonpublic Schools

Data from the RIPS report (1967a) show that, nation-wide, about 17 percent of the 1960 school enrollment was in private schools, the proportion being even higher in the central cities. Furthermore, the nonpublic school enrollment was nearly all white, 94 percent white in the cities and 97 percent white in the suburbs (p. 39). Analysis of the school enrollment figures for New York State for the 1968-69 school year shows that nonpublic school enrollment (elementary and secondary) constituted 20.4 percent of total school enrollment (NYSED, 1969). In the seven largest city school districts of the state (1966-67), nonpublic enrollment generally constituted larger proportions, ranging from 21.0 percent in Niagara Falls to 27.9 percent in New York City to 50.1 percent in Albany (BEDS, 1969; NYSED, 1969). An ethnic breakdown of non-public school enrollment figures for the State is not yet available for publication, but it is assumed on the basis of the RIPS report that the enrollment situation in New York State is basically comparable.

Economic Status of Minority Group Pupils

Negroes and Puerto Ricans have traditionally been dis-proportionately represented among lower income groups, al-though in recent years the number and proportion of Negroes in middle income and upper income groups has grown. In 1966, for example, 28 percent of Negro families in the Nation had incomes of more than $7,000, nearly double the propor-tion having similar incomes in 1960. At about the same time, 55 percent of white families in the Nation had incomes of more than $7,000. Although the data showed an increase in the pro-portion of Negroes attaining middle income status, the fact re-mained that 32 percent of all Negro families still earned less than $3,000 in 1966, as compared with 13 percent of all white families.

Other data indicate that the economic status of Negroes and other minority groups is more aggravated in the urban areas of the Nation than elsewhere. In 1966, the proportion of non-whites below the poverty level was about four times as great in the central cities as in the regions outside the central cities (42 percent as against 11 percent). New York City, with the largest number of minority pupils in the state public school system and the most extensive ethnic isolation, has a wide range of family incomes. A recent study of economic conditions in New York City (Gordon, 1969) estimated that 28.4 percent of Negro and Puerto Rican families and 3.7 percent of white families had incomes below the poverty level of $3,500 for a family of four. An additional 31.1 percent of Negro and Puerto Rican families earned between $3,500 and $6,000, versus 13.6 percent of white families. At the other end of the scale, 4.2 percent of the Negro families could be considered affluent (income in excess of $14,500), versus 26 percent of the white families. Altogether 36.5 of the New York City population of whites, Negroes, and Puerto Ricans were members of "poverty" or low income" families, and 17 percent were members of affluent families. Data on family size and income further indicate that low income families have greater numbers of children.

Figures on "poverty eligible" children used in determining district aid under Title I of ESEA for 1968 showed that more than 257,000 New York City children aged five to seventeen, were in families receiving AFDC support, and an additional 10,000 were being supported in foster homes. These numbers were equivalent to nearly 24 percent of the New York City school enrollment. Assuming that the great majority of AFDC children attend public schools, it can be inferred that at least 25 percent of New York City public school pupils are AFDC recipients.

AFDC figures are a rough guide to community socio-economic status, resulting only in an estimate of the number of children in the lowest economic groups, there being no estimate of the proportions affected within different ethnic groups. There is, however, a certain degree of consistency between the proportional representation in the schools of the two largest minority groups, Negroes and Puerto Ricans, and the proportions of AFDC children in the larger districts of the state. For example, in Buffalo in 1968, the equivalent of 20 percent of the school enrollment was receiving AFDC; in Rochester, 15.6 percent; in Syracuse, 19.9 percent; in Yonkers, 11.5 percent; in Albany and Utica, 16.6 percent each; in Mount Vernon, 15.3 percent; in Niagara Falls, 12 percent; and in Newburgh, 12.3 percent. The proportion of minority group pupils in these districts ranged from 13.2 percent in Utica to 38.5 percent in Buffalo.

Outside these city districts, there appears to be less correspondence between the proportion of minority group pupils in the district and the proportion of children receiving AFDC. In Wyandanch, having 93.6 percent minority group pupils, the equivalent of 37.6 percent of its enrollment was receiving AFDC. In Hempstead, having 73.2 percent minority group pupils, the equivalent of 19.1 percent was receiving AFDC. In Malverne and Amityville, having 47.6 and 41.4 minority group pupils, the equivalents of 6.7 and 8.8 percent were receiving AFDC. In New Rochelle, having 21.5 percent minority group pupils, practically the same minority proportion as Syracuse, the equivalent of only 5.1 percent was receiving AFDC.

Altogether, this attempt at translation of data on racial isolation into its socio-economic implications suggests several tentative generalizations:

1.   Racially isolated schools in New York State are likely to be predominantly lower status schools.

2.   The extent to which racially isolated schools contain predominantly lower status children is likely to be greater in the larger cities of the State.

3.   Schools having substantial numbers of white pupils in the larger cities may also tend toward a lower status composition because of the tendency for upper income whites to attend private schools and the greater proportions of minority group pupils in lower status families.

These generalizations must be viewed with caution because there is evidence of considerable variation in the economic status levels of isolated minority groups in different areas of the state. Socio-economic diversity in communities in which integration has been a concern was touched upon in a study by Dodson (1968) in ten New York State school districts; nine of the districts for which socio-economic data were available were among the forty-two districts analyzed in this study. Without specifying the basis for his designations, Dodson noted that Albany had both white collar Negroes and Negroes of low socio-economic status, the upper status Negroes being scattered residentially. Greenburgh's nonwhite population was described as running the gamut from middle class to low socio-economic status. Malverne's Negro population was noted to have a higher proportion of professional and high status occupations than its white population. New Rochelle was described as having a wide range of nonwhite residents, there being many upper middle class and middle class Negroes and a concentration of Negro professionals. It was said that, in Roosevelt, the minority group population had once been a low status group but that white persons withdrawing from the community were being replaced by high status Negro residents. Schenectady's minority group population, according to Dodson, consisted of professionals and government employees scattered throughout the city and a concentration of lower class Negroes who were more skilled occupationally than most.

The correspondence between racial and social class isolation in the schools of the State and Nation indicates that substantial numbers of children are deprived of one of the most important elements of quality education: the opportunity to interact socially and cognitively with children from more advantaged backgrounds. The possible damaging effects of the maintenance of schools along ethnic class lines is probably underestimated by statistics on racial isolation in the schools, since, the prevalent practice of ability grouping also appears to represent the creation of unequal educational conditions for different children.

Implications for Desegregation

The results of major studies reviewed in Chapter 4 showed that the social class composition of the school was a major factor in the generally lower achievement levels of students in segregated schools. It is apparent, however, that this rather stable finding has not had any noticable impact on the formulation of plans relating to school desegregation. Without major changes in the instructional process, certain types of desegregation programs could have been expected to be educationally harmful to whites and harmful or nonfacilitating to Negro and other minority group students. Such might be the case in the following instances, assuming roughly equal numbers of students:

1. A largely (75 percent) middle class predominantly (90 percent) white school is paired with a predominantly (90 percent) Negro school in which the students are largely (75 percent or more) from lower income families.

2. A marginally (50-60 percent) middle class predominantly (90 percent) white school is paired with a mixed school (50 percent Negro) in which the Negro population is predominantly (75 percent) lower status and the white population is marginally (50 percent) middle class.

In both situations described above, the exchange of students between schools would result in a social class composition that could, in effect, create educationally disadvantaged schools all around. Such could be the result in urban areas in which the social status composition of "white" schools varies from area to area within the city, the Negro student population is generally lower status, and policy dictates that integrated schools reflect the area distribution of Negroes and whites in the public schools.

In such areas as New York City, where a predominantly lower status Negro and Puerto Rican population constitutes more than 55 percent of public school enrollment, social class considerations in the implementation of plans for school desegregation might appear impractical. However, if private school facilities were made available and if minority group students in peripheral areas of the city could be transferred to suburban areas surrounding the city, large numbers of disadvantaged minority group students in New York City could find themselves in educationally more desirable situations.*

These brief considerations relating to the achievement of optimal levels of social class balance in integrated schools are intended only as explanatory examples. Much more detailed information on family status and other student variables relating to school success is required before systematic plans can be formulated. For example, the results of the analyses of ethnic composition within school districts in Chapter 2 suggests that certain districts could achieve "successful integration" within district confines, whereas others, such as New York City, might require solutions that would, in part, involve schools outside the city. Some segregated suburban districts appear to be more or less ideally placed to achieve integration by cooperation with surrounding districts, probably with a minor effect on the over-all social class composition of all schools involved. However, a careful examination of the educationally relevant backgrounds of the white and minority group student populations in individual schools may suggest plans for integration that differ considerably from those based on considerations of ethnic balance alone.

---

*In 1968, New York City's nonpublic school enrollment, elementary and secondary, amounted to 448,778 students. Assuming this enrollment to be predominantly white, it constitutes a large student population that could be made available for integration.

These considerations suggest that district personnel and the educational leadership at higher levels develop a systematic information base for sound decision-making relating to the elimination of the disadvantaged (segregated) school. Recognition of both ethnic and social class considerations in developing plans for successful integration may be facilitated through an identification and study procedure which would be conducted on a statewide, regional, or district basis. Appropriate procedures would first identify the disadvantaged school in relation to both ethnic and social class composition. Plans for initiating desegregation might then be further developed on the basis of a more detailed study of the disadvantaged school and its regional context. Very briefly illustrated, such procedures might be as follows:

1. Identification: The identification procedure should be based on at least three considerations that would require reporting on an over-all school basis: racial composition, social class composition, and relative achievement level. A range of perhaps from 10 to 30 percent Negro, Puerto Rican, and other minority groups combined, with the remainder consisting of white students, may be considered a generally appropriate criterion for ethnic balance in individual schools and classrooms. However, depending upon such factors as school social class, ability and achievement levels, and school and community morale, different proportions of the major ethnic groups in the schools in a particular area may be considered appropriate from educational and social points of view. With all other considerations aside, decisions relating to ethnic composition in a particular school or district should proceed largely from the question: Do the students in different ethnic groups have adequate opportunity to learn from, understand, and become friendly with each other? With the ethnic balance criterion remaining a flexible one, identification would further proceed to determination of the social class composition of the school. The appropriate criterion in the typical school setting seems to be a social class composition that approaches or exceeds a range of roughly from 30 to 40 percent economically and socially disadvantaged students. If the school meets this and the ethnic balance criterion and if over-all achievement approaches or exceeds perhaps one standard deviation below national (or other) norms, it appears that a clear-cut determination has been made.

2. Further Planning: The identification procedure completed, a sufficient basis has been created for the development of preliminary plans for achieving improved educational and

social opportunities in the schools under study. In some instances, it may be appropriate to initiate desegregation primarily on the basis of considerations of ethnic imbalance. For
example, in some suburban areas of New York State, it appears that a careful survey would indicate that social class
and related considerations would not represent a particular
problem and that integration could proceed without any serious
danger to the educational opportunities of the students involved.
Schools "flagged" on all three criteria outlined above would be
subject to further study, including an analysis of the educational and social characteristics of the flagged school and its regional educational, economic, ethnic, and cultural context.
Relevant information gathered might include the following:

    a. Information on individual student family background,
including such factors as economic status, family stability,
nutritional and health status, academic achievement and ability levels, and educationally relevant attitudes (within "flagged"
schools).

    b. Information relating to educational inequities re-
sulting from such factors as staff turnover; inadequate materials, facilities, and teaching procedures; level of community
participation; and low morale (within "flagged" schools).

    c. Information defining the local economic and social
resources that could be brought to bear on the problem.

    d. Information specifying the ethnic and economic com-
position of the schools in the region of the "flagged" school,
which might serve as facilities for transfer of disadvantaged
students--including both public and private facilities.

With the disadvantaged school identified in terms of relevant student, school, and contextual characteristics, a reasonably detailed basis would exist for the formulation of a variety
of different plans designed to achieve equality of educational
opportunity. As indicated earlier, some plans for school desegregation might be accomplished without extensive changes
in the school setting, as in suburban districts where the segregated minority group student population may tend toward
middle class. In other districts or schools, effective plans
may require radical departures from previous efforts to integrate and up-grade the schools. For example, special aid
might be required for transportation, compensatory education,
school reorganization, nutritional and health services, and
family service programs of both a psychological and economic
nature. The extent to which the plan for desegregation would
involve additional changes in the educational and social context of the school could be largely illuminated through identification and study procedures of the type illustrated here.

It should be noted that this brief plan is not intended as
a comprehensive formulation of the kinds of relevant information that might be gathered as a basis for systematic planning
of desegregation in the schools. The main point is the need for
explicit recognition of social class and related considerations
in formulating school integration programs. Current influen-
tial sources of guidelines for desegregation policy appear to
have failed to recognize the relevance of family background
factors and, instead, have focused largely on racial balance.
The result has been ambiguous criteria for school desegregation, which vary as a function of the over-all racial balance in
a particular district or group of districts being considered.
Extensive data reviewed in this report indicate that desegregation plans based primarily on considerations of racial balance
could have undesirable consequences for the schools, depending
upon the socio-economic composition of the schools in the
area affected.

Official policy statements and guidelines relating to
school desegregation may well require reexamination in light
of foregoing considerations. Examination of the many reports
and policy statements reviewed in preparation for this study
failed to turn up evidence of explicit recognition of findings
that show that social class mix makes a substantial difference
in the achievement levels of Negro and Puerto Rican students.
These and other findings have a number of implications for the
formulation of policy relating to school desegregation, as is
shown even more clearly in later sections of this chapter. A
further cause for reexamination of offical policy, and of the adequacy of programs that represent the translation of policy into
action, results from serious consideration of the evidence showing that the extent of racial isolation in many Northern states
(including New York) is increasing year by year and will undoubtedly continue to increase during the next five or ten years.

INFLUENCE OF GROUP PROCESSES IN INTEGRATED
AND DISADVANTAGED SCHOOL SETTINGS

One of the eminent failures of research on variations
in racial isolation in the schools is in the lack of any systematic examination of the effect of group processes on the learning
process in the classroom. There is also good reason to believe that the review of research on social interaction in the
interracial school and classroom reviewed in Chapter 5 is now

somewhat out of date, although many of these studies are but
a few years old.   The circular process in which Negro and
other lower status students are--by implication from research
largely in white classrooms--affected by the negative reactions
of white students and teachers, academic incapacities, and
other factors must now be placed within a context of increased
interracial hostility in the schools.   To be sure, fundamental
patterns of social interaction in the typical American classroom
may still generally apply in the interracial setting, but they may
be overlaid and even circumvented by extraordinary levels of
interracial hostility resulting from increasing racial cleavage
now present in the secondary schools.

In the typical highly segregated school, interracial ag
gression will obviously be a minor or nonexistent problem. Because of the nature of the typical instructional process, it is
here that the effects of school social class are allowed to have
their greatest impact on the learning process.   The data presented in Chapters 4 and 5 further indicate that classroom
social class composition has a negative effect on the outcomes
of instruction when the more advantaged student population constitutes less than a substantial majority.   Because of problems
in determining in correspondence between measures of social
class, from study to study, no highly exact statements about
educationally desirable proportions of students in different
social class levels may be made.   What is required in future
studies on this question is a breakdown of the student population into several levels of economic status, together with information on the education context in the home and other student characteristics, such as ability level.   The influence of
school social class composition on the outcomes of instruction
may be further illuminated by direct observation of the process
of classroom interaction.

Learning Through the Classroom Group

Even granting the coarseness of the available data, it
is yet possible to offer more than speculation into the whys and
wherefores of the effect of classroom social class composition
on achievement.   Casual observation in the American school
indicates a typical pattern in which the teacher plays the role
of information dispenser and behavior modifier, largely in relation to that amorphous concept the classroom group.   Those
familiar with the process know that the teacher typically attempts to gear the complexity of the information dispensed to

the comprehension of the average student in the classroom or some smaller portion thereof. It is a generally anachronistic procedure in which learning may be greatly influenced by group contagion. The teacher's effectiveness is heavily dependent upon the cooperation of group members, and upon such individual factors as level of conceptual development and attentiveness.

Reviews of the process of classroom interaction reveal that the teacher does most of the talking, composed mainly of lecturing, presenting instructions, and disciplining students (Baldwin, 1965; Amidon and Simon, 1965; Baldwin, 1965). This process appears to be subjected to gross interference in the lower class Negro school in which from 50 to 80 percent of classroom time may be given over to discipline and other irrelevant activities (Deutsch, 1960). Other studies have also demonstrated that the disruptive and destructive behaviors of individuals in the peer group are highly contagious (Polansky, Lippitt and Redl, 1954; Bandura and Walters, 1963), and may occur irrespective of competing values in the family. Individuals from middle class backgrounds conducive to learning may thus contribute to a general disintegration of the process of group learning in the classroom, or their positive influences on the learning process may not be felt because of the prevailing climate of interference contributed by the behaviors of their less advantaged peers. The conditions under which such influences constitute a substantial and continuing source of "noise" in the learning process have not generally been the subject of systematic investigation--for example, the proportion of lower status students needed to tip the balance in favor of disorder or inattentiveness, teacher factors, the influence of particular student characteristics, and the like--but the symptons of the deteriorated learning environment are widely recognized among educators.

Other factors contributing to interference with learning in the typical classroom include teacher expectations and resultant feelings about inferiority that are communicated to the student. In some measures, it appears that such expectations and feelings may be held in relation to an entire school in which educational deficits and ability differences relative to whites and other upper status students are made abundantly clear (Pettigrew, 1964). Green (1969) reports a further effect in the tendency of teachers in the "inferior" school to reduce the quality and quantity of information made available in instruction. It seems that interference with learning resulting from teacher expectations relates to school and classroom morale and is reflected in such factors as self-esteem, sense of control, and intellectual and occupational aspirations--which may in turn be reflected in more directly relevant factors, such as attentiveness in class and doing homework.

The learning-interference factors described in relation to the "inferior" school should also be relevant in schools with grouping policies that result in either social class isolation within school or combinations of different levels of racial and social class isolation, depending on the class status of the white student population and the proportion of "integrated" Negroes in the school. Green (1969) reports that intraschool segregation in multiracial schools results in white students' regarding minority group students as "different", minority group students come to regard themselves as "different" because of their attendance in special classes. Both groups relate the notion of "being different" to intellectual superiority and inferiority. An extensive empirical study of ability grouping reported by Borg (1966) generally supports Green's conclusion about the potentially harmful effects of grouping on students' personality characteristics. Randomly grouped students were found to differ significantly from students grouped by ability in the areas of self-concept, acceptance of self, and feelings of belonging, the differences favoring randomly grouped students.

Intraschool segregation appears likely to be an outcome of school desegregation plans that are initiated within the grouping structures found within typical secondary schools and middle schools and even within some elementary schools. The results of McPartland's analysis, reviewed in Chapter 4, suggest that the facilitating effects of integration on Negro achievement will be minor if Negro students are isolated within a school, having a majority of white students. On the other hand, an appropriate balance of Negro and white students on a classroom basis appears to be substantially facilitating, encompassing social class effects in both the classroom and total student body. Strangely, the results of integration programs reported by Hansen (1960) and Sullivan and Stewart (1969) both appear to involve isolation of Negro students through broad tracking programs, and both programs appear to indicate over-all facilitating effects on Negro achievement. In both cases, the extent of intraschool segregation is unknown, but the outcomes of this policy in both situations were substantial protest from the Negro community and eventual moves to eliminate tracking.

A further outcome of intraschool segregation within the biracial school is the attendant reduction of opportunities for increasing interracial understanding, which may occur through the close contact and interaction that can be made available in the interracial classroom. Segregated classrooms, on the other hand, can become a major source of interracial friction within the school (Sullivan and Stewart, 1969). Evidence discussed in Chapter 4 tends to indicate that the development of interracial friendships in the integrated school may be one of the major factors responsible for the successful adaptation of the disadvantaged Negro student in the white middle class school setting. Desegregation programs that result in the isolation of Negro students through tracking or other forms of grouping thus defeat the very purpose of integration and may in turn arouse serious conflict and disorder. The latter result may seriously delay the potentially positive impact of integration on both white and Negro students.

Conflict in the Interracial School

Turning now to some brief considerations of the problem of interracial conflict, reference is made to a report "Conflict in the Nation's High Schools" (Urban Crisis Monitor, May 1969), which documents recent evidence of student protest and active conflict in the nation's high schools.[*] This report begins by describing a racial explosion in a junior high school in the Watts area in Los Angeles in March 1969 and continues: "The pattern of confrontation in Los Angeles is typical of high school racial disorders across the nation" (p. 3). In January of 1969, in fact, 67 percent of all city and suburban high schools and 56 percent of all junior high schools were experiencing some kind of active student protest. Racial conflict was the most common single issue in these protests and was at the heart of the ugliest and most violent of the protests. In the January survey, about 10 percent of the secondary schools studied reported some race-related protest under way. In its detailed analysis of racial disruptions in American high schools during the first four months of 1969, The Urban Research Corporation identified five major characteristics common to high school racial protests as follows:

1. Conflict is usually triggered by a minor incident involving two students--one white, one Negro--which then explodes into a free-for-all.

---

*This account of conflict in the schools is taken from a communication prepared by John Harding, Department of Human Development and Family Studies, Cornell University, who graciously reviewed this study and suggested the inclusion of this information.

2.   The extent of violence experienced seems related
to the racial composition of the school.   Schools close to 50-50
in white-Negro proportions tend to direct violence in mass battles of Negro and white pupils against each other.   In schools
in which Negroes constitute a clear minority (20 percent or
less), protest is limited to peaceful disruptions.

3.   Negro students' demands focus on changes in curriculum, faculty, and administrative personnel and on disciplinary policies.   There are demands for black studies, including Afro-American history, African languages, and black
culture.   (Demands for more Negro teachers and administrators were made in almost every case; not uncommonly, demands were also made for the resignation of particular teachers or administrators.)

4.   The school boycott is the tool universally used to
gain acceptance of demands, usually with the support of concerned parents' groups and community organizations.

5.   Police and security guards have been unable to
do more than maintain an uneasy peace.   Police patrols are
now common in urban schools; in New York City, security
guards are stationed in every junior and senior high school
and Newark's schools now maintain a security force larger
than the police forces of many New Jersey communities.

6.   Schools appear to calm slowly, if at all.   Tensions
generally remain, (Assaults on teachers rose 30 percent during the first six months of 1969 over the same period in 1968.)
Many teachers carry guns.   Unrest in the schools appears to
be a general and long-term phenomenon resulting from the
search for excitement, educational grievances, and rising an-
tagonism between Negro and white students.

Obviously such disruptions are a relatively new dimension that must be considered in plans for school desegregation.   And the work of Chesler (1969) is one of the current
sources that provides some understanding of the underlying elements involved in interracial conflict in the schools, pinpointing the problem as partly historical:

> Centuries of cultural rejection and isolation
> prepare most young Negroes to be fearful and
> hostile of interaction with whites.   Centuries
> of isolation and a sense of cultural superior-
> ity prepare most young whites to be both
> cautious and arrogant about interaction with
> Negroes.   Contemporary cultural commit-
> ments and feelings of attraction and concern,

fear and guilt, work together to produce
tremendous ambivalence and hesitance
about personal or societal relationships
that are interracial. This societal ambivalence is reflected in the relative inability of youngsters to accept differences
as legitimate, in the fear of interracial
chaos and conflict inflamed by the press,
in their inability to understand our society's racial history and contemporary
confusion, in the pressure of parents to
protect and segregate their children, and
in the students' inability to probe surely
into the roots and symptoms of their own
feelings about race (pp. 97-98).

Chesler's research on intergroup contact in desegregated
schools led him to conclude that the feelings underlying
potential interracial conflict in the biracial school are by no
means idiosyncratic or unusual. His data and that of the Urban
Research Corporation underline the need for carefully planned
intervention in initiating desegregation in the schools.

Manipulating the Group Learning
Situation in the Racially Isolated School

When one examines past progress on school desegregation, it is evident that extensive segregation will probably
exist in the inner-city schools of the nation for some time to
come. In lieu of rapid change in the extent of racial isolation
in the schools, it appears that much effort should be expended
in reducing sources of learning interference presumed to be
generally present in the racially isolated school as a function
of social class homogeneity. The present interpretation of the
findings of Coleman et al. and other studies on the influence of
social class factors on the outcomes of instruction suggest the
following implications for educational practice in the racially
isolated school:
    1. That typical group processes in the learning situa-
tion be generally circumvented through replacement by individualized modes of instruction or small group learning in which
students are appropriately matched to avoid sources of interference with learning.
    2. That systematic group experiences be developed

in which students may gradually learn to participate effectively in group activities, particularly activities that may lead to increased socialization.

3.   That teachers be trained to communicate effectively their expectations that recognize the child's basic willingness to learn and discover and not the disabling conditions of his background.

4.   That the child's learning experiences at the outset involve extensive structuring or control, through various techniques and facilities, until self-maintenance of desirable learning behaviors become strongly evident.

5.   That the child receive systematic training in attending to relevant stimulation in the learning situation and responding appropriately.

The procedures outlined may also be relevant for instruction of disadvantaged Negro students in interracial schools. However, exclusive emphasis on individualized instruction or the use of tracking or ability grouping in interracial schools may defeat the very purposes of integration.

The findings of such studies as those of Coleman et al. and Wilson appear to extend beyond effects associated with intraschool segregation.   These findings should instigate serious examination of the entire question of the educational and psychological efficacy of ability grouping and tracking, which by implication result in the introduction of social class isolation in the schools, irrespective of racial composition.   The planning of school integration programs should explicitly avoid tracking and ability grouping in favor of other procedures that maximize positive social and cognitive interaction in an interracial setting.   Moreover, high level educational policy should give explicit recognition to the potential damage to all students represented by the widespread application of tracking and ability grouping at all educational levels.   Though this change is highly desirable, it should be recognized that if most teachers are to work within it, it will necessarily involve the commitment of substantial resources to both the development of materials and appropriate teacher behaviors that will make widespread individualized instruction a learning mode that teachers can confidently employ and establish as a reality in the schools throughout the Nation.

Arranging Appropriate Conditions of Social
Interaction in the Integrated School

The review of studies on social interaction in the classroom in Chapter 5 and the foregoing considerations of the increasing prevalence of racial cleavage in interracial schools suggest the following with regard to the establishment of a facilitating classroom climate in the newly integrated school:

1. Since the student's social status in the classroom seems to affect his level of academic success, and the contrary--it being a circular process--a major effort should be mounted to insure early and continuing success in the academic area. The application of certain approaches and programs designed to make up for learning difficulties may thus be necessary to the academic success of the desegregated Negro student.

2. Academic efforts by themselves do not take full advantage of the potential of the integrated school for positive educational and social change and may even fail in an atmosphere of potential interracial conflict. Specific attention must therefore be paid to the minority group student's own capabilities and tendencies in social interaction with whites, as well as to the typical social responses and tendencies of whites in the interracial situation.

3. Studies indicate that the classroom teacher typically exerts a major influence on the social status of students. Such influence is frequently exerted in relation to conforming, class-linked behaviors and other behaviors indicative of achievement, the sex of the student, and the students' racial status (Chesler, 1969). These forms of influence are rapidly communicated to the peer group, which, in turn, rejects the "offender." This pattern of teacher-peer group rejection is more likely to be experienced by the typical Negro child, and thus specific steps must be taken to train teachers to respond appropriately in the classroom.

4. Research shows that parents exert a powerful and continuing effect on their children's manifestations of racial attitudes in the classroom. Special efforts to create racial harmony in the school setting may thus fail or prove only partially effective if steps are not also taken to develop substantial community support for, and participation in, the school program. Special efforts should therefore be made to expand the integrated school into the role of community center and involve parents of both racial groups in the process of integration.

5. The introduction of black history, culture, and special studies into the curriculum appears to be an important

basis for improving interracial understanding. Careful and
fair attention should be given to minority group contributions
at all levels of the curriculum, and special courses relating
to the issue of cultural pluralism might be appropriately included in the school program.

Appropriate teacher training programs may include the
following experiences, further designed and specified in relation to appropriateness for different student groups:

1. Experiences designed to sensitize the teacher toward
typical patterns of interaction that reflect negative class - and
caste-linked attitudes. (These experiences would further incorporate direct practice in social responses that imply positive recognition of behavioral differences associated with variations in socio-cultural background.)

2. Experiences leading to knowledge of Negro history, social problems, individual and group differences relating to success in American society, and an understanding of current
forces of social unrest.

3. Practice in managing patterns of interracial interaction
that will focus on historical, cultural, economic, and attitudinal differences associated with race and class status.

4. Practice in the utilization of principles based on social
psychological research that relate to changing intergroup attitudes. (One of the prime examples proceeds from the work of
Sherif (1958), which showed that intergroup attitudes may be
changed when alienated groups pursue activities that involve
the achievement of a common goal.)

5. Practice in the application of techniques to allay the
stress of certain elements of the learning situation, such as
test-taking, verbal participation in classroom activities, and
the experience of difficulty with traditional learning materials
and approaches.

Teacher training programs that include the aforementioned
and other relevant experiences may provide an important basis
for the creation of harmonious and constructive racial relations in the classroom. Applications of relevant teacher training may then be used for constructive teaching of the elements
of cultural pluralism, as well as the implementation of intergroup experiences directly facing the implications of racial
prejudice and discrimination (See Chesler, 1969, for examples
of relevant teaching strategies). The teacher's role in promoting harmonious interracial relations in the classroom may
be further aided by explicit recognition of the history and culture of American minority groups in all relevant areas and
phases of the curriculum. A variety of such techniques are

given in Sullivan and Stewart's (1969) report on the Berkeley experience.

The introduction of black history and culture into the curriculum and sensitive classroom discussion of issues centering on cultural pluralism may assist both white and Negro students in understanding their differences and making successful adaptations in their patterns of social interaction. Such efforts would probably be most effective at the junior and senior high school levels, but only experience and carefully controlled study will offer definitive guidelines for optimum choice of procedures in relation to grade level and differential student background. Helpful though such efforts may be for the creation of harmonious interracial relations, they may yet fail or prove only partially effective if steps are not also taken to develop substantial community support for, and participation in, the academic program. The work of Chesler, Wittes, and Radin (1968) and a review of relevant studies by Proshansky (1966) indicate that parents exert a powerful and continuing effect upon the manifestations of their children's racial attitudes in the school.

The Berkeley integration program provides one of the outstanding examples of successful administrative efforts to obtain community involvement in all stages of the process of school integration. One of the efforts previously mentioned involved the introduction of some 500 volunteers, Negro and white, who engaged directly in the process of instruction. Other useful guidelines relating to community participation in the process of school integration include the following paraphrased from Sullivan and Stewart (1969, pp. 199-201):

1. Encouraging minority groups, particularly the poor, to take the initiative, speak out, and become leaders

2. Involving all civic, university, church, business, service groups, and minority organizations, including the Black Power leaders

3. Involving parents at all steps of the process, and particularly minority group parents

4. Continually informing the public of progress made and of plans for the future

5. Providing intergroup education in in-service units and seminars for the public

6. Scheduling social events, picnics, and week-end retreats, for both Negro and white parents

7. Involving students, parents, and teachers in interracial workshops, meetings, and neighborhood discussions

8. Integrating after-school recreational programs.

The approach used at Berkeley contains the important element of involvement of minority group parents in educational decision-making and change. And opportunities thus created for increased contact with whites should also assist in eliminating the parent-child conflict that can arise when the Negro child begins to acquire new attitudes and values in the integrated school (Bronfenbrenner, 1967). A similar effect could be expected among white parents. Although not entirely systematic, the approaches used at Berkeley seem to have generally applied Sherif's principle of working toward a common goal. To the extent that application of this principle can be implemented to involve teachers, students, the educational leadership, and parents and community leaders of both races, the potential for racial cleavage and conflict in the school and community can be replaced by a gradual development of harmonious interracial relations in all important areas of social and intellectual interaction.

The Need for Flexible Organization
in the Integrated School

The suggestions made in the chapter on compensatory education indicate a need for extensive and flexible change in the disadvantaged school and imply that the effective "integrated" school will necessarily depart from traditional organizational patterns and approaches to instruction. Social science literature may assist the educational planner in designing relevant approaches to instruction in the integrated school. Bronfenbrenner (1967), for example, has suggested some approaches to the education of the Negro student in the integrated school setting, based on a careful analysis of the psychological, intellectual, and cultural legacy of Negroes in America. These approaches include the use of male Negro figures as teachers and aides and after-school programs involving parents and adolescents (both white and Negro), modeled after procedures used in Soviet schools and in Head Start.

The flexibility required by the inclusion of a variety of new programs, activities, and personnel in the effective integrated school appear to necessitate basic changes in organizational structure. For example, one approach that has considerable potential for accommodating the great need for structural flexibility in the integrated school is the Continuous Learning Year, allowing the adoption of educational practices geared to the learning needs of the disadvantaged child and, of

greater practical significance, the introduction of compensatory education in the integrated school setting without remov-
ing the child from participation in the regular school program.
Some of the advantages of the Continuous Learning Year, in
this respect, can be outlined as follows:*

1.   A restructuring of the school year calendar provides
multiple vacations during the school year, as is shown in
Figure 13.   The new learning cycles of eight or nine weeks
followed by a two week vacation provide a continuity of learning that does not exist with the regular school year calendar.
The absence of a serious break in the learning process means
that teachers no longer have to spend weeks in the fall reviewing or reteaching in hope of bringing the students back to the
learning levels they had reached just prior to the close of
school in June.

2.   Another advantage of the Continuous Learning Year
calendar lies in the possibility of providing the children with
approximately 10 percent more education without necessarily
increasing school costs.   One variation of the Continuous
Learning Year cycling plan provides 200 days of instruction.
During the school year all students are provided recess periods of two weeks after eight or nine weeks of study.   The
periods of intermittent vacation made available, as shown in
Figure 13, provide up to 10 weeks of additional instructional
time that can be used for compensatory education as well as
other educational efforts deemed desirable in the interracial
school.   Such an arrangement may not necessarily entail large
increases in instructional costs if the school can avail itself
of low-cost instructional aides and volunteers as was done in
the Berkeley integration program.

3.   Implementation of the Continuous Learning Year cycling program calls for a new look at the curriculum and the
teaching process.   For example, teachers should be prepared
to take students where they find them.   This calls for the development of a curriculum that has been broken into short
learning units, or contracts.   If such a curriculum is set up,
teachers can work toward the individualization of the learning
process.

4.   The Continuous Learning Year cycling plan should enable a school system to operate without the gradual shutting
down in June and the arduous task of reopening in September.
Since learning is considered a continuous process, the time

---

*George Thomas, Coordinator for Rescheduling the School
Year, NYSED, provided the material for this section.

FIGURE 13

Student Vacation Patterns in the Continuous Learning Program:
The Eight- to Nine-Week Cycle

CALENDAR	GROUP I	GROUP II	GROUP III	GROUP IV	GROUP V	CALENDAR
1970 Sept 7 14 21 28	H 2 WEEKS 9 DAYS VAC. 2 WEEKS	H 4 WEEKS 19 DAYS	H 6 WEEKS 28 DAYS	H 8 WEEKS 38 DAYS	VAC. 2 WEEKS H 8 WEEKS 37 DAYS	**1970** Sept 7 14 21 28
Oct 5 12 19 26	H 9 WEEKS 40 DAYS	VAC. 2 WKS. H	VAC. 2 WEEKS	H	H	Oct 5 12 19 26
Nov 2 9 16 23 30	H H H H	H H 9 WEEKS 41 DAYS H H	H H H 9 WEEKS 39 DAYS	H 2 WKS VAC. H H H	H H VAC. 3 WKS. H H	Nov 2 9 16 23 30
Dec 7 14 21 28	VAC. 2 WEEKS H H VAC. 2 WKS H H			9 WEEKS 41 DAYS H H	9 WEEKS 42 DAYS H H	Dec 7 14 21 28
1971 Jan 4 11 18 25	9 WEEKS 41 DAYS	9 WEEKS 43 DAYS	VAC. 2 WEEKS	VAC. 3 WEEKS		**1971** Jan 4 11 18 25
Feb 1 8 15 22	H H VAC. 2 WEEKS	H H	H H 9 WEEKS 43 DAYS	H H 8 WEEKS 39 DAYS	H VAC. 2 WEEKS H	Feb 1 8 15 22
Mar 1 8 15 22 29	8 WEEKS 39 DAYS	VAC. 2 WEEKS	VAC. 2 WEEKS		8 WEEKS 39 DAYS	Mar 1 8 15 22 29
Apr 5 12 19 26	H	H 8 WEEKS 39 DAYS	H VAC. 2 WKS. H 8 WEEKS 39 DAYS		H VAC. 2 WEEKS	Apr 5 12 19 26
May 3 10 17 24 31	VAC. 2 WEEKS H	VAC. 2 WEEKS H		8 WEEKS 39 DAYS	8 WEEKS 39 DAYS	May 3 10 17 24 31
June 7 14 21 28	8 WEEKS 38 DAYS	8 WEEKS 38 DAYS	H VAC. 2 WKS.	VAC. 2 WEEKS	VAC. 2 WKS.	June 7 14 21 28
July 5 12 19 26	H VAC. 2 WEEKS	H	H 8 WEEKS 39 DAYS	H 8 WEEKS 39 DAYS	H VAC. 2 WKS. 8 WEEKS 40 DAYS	July 5 12 19 26
Aug 2 9 16 23 30	6 WEEKS 30 DAYS	VAC. 2 WEEKS 4 WEEKS 20 DAYS	VAC. 2 WEEKS 2 WEEKS 10 DAYS	VAC. 2 WEEKS		Aug 2 9 16 23 30
No. of School Days	197	200	198	196	197	
No. of Vac. Days	63	60	62	64	63	

normally wasted on closing and opening activities becomes available for the enrichment of the curriculum or lives of the students.

5. Dollar savings in the regular school program are possible with the adoption of cycling plans that can help change the setting for learning.

Besides incorporating the basic feature of making more time available for instruction, through a variety of plans, the lengthened school year may also make available large blocks of free time (referred to as "E" time) for independent study; special programs, such as Black studies, vocational and technical education programs; and experimentation with special programs designed for the disadvantaged child. The flexibility thus introduced merits serious consideration in plans involving school desegregation, but the basic features of the lengthened school year are no less desirable in the disadvantaged school.

COMPENSATORY EDUCATION:
IMPLICATIONS FOR RESEARCH AND PRACTICE

The analysis of the school population in Chapter 2 makes it abundantly clear that the educational and social problems represented by the disadvantaged school are growing rather than decreasing. When viewing the past record of progress in accomplishing desegregation in the schools in New York State, and generally in the nation, it appears unrealistic to expect that great numbers of minority group students will suddenly experience the educationally and socially facilitating effects of the integrated school setting. The only way out of this impasse in such areas as New York City is to provoke massive and radical change in the education process, while at the same time making all possible efforts to increase the pace of school desegregation. The notion of "compensation for educational inadequacies," which usually reflects something added to the educational process (which in itself is likely to prove ineffective), should now reflect the need to work basic changes in the schools as well as the need to "intervene" at appropriate stages in the child's development.

The discussion in this section outlines some suggested changes and considerations for improving upon current efforts to effect educational change among disadvantaged children. This is not a comprehensive set of suggestions; rather it treats a few key areas relating to research, program development, and staff training.

Changes Needed in Research
Relating to the Disadvantaged School [*]

It is obvious from what has been done so far that very little is known about why minority groups--and especially Negroes--do not seem to benefit from standard educational treatments. A large part of this ignorance is simply the result of poor research and the absence of a sustained research effort. Consequently, there is a need to establish a research center (or several centers) for the express purpose of conducting good research directed toward furthering understanding of and ability to successfully educate minority groups. The potentialities of such a center are almost unlimited and could range from operating a research and demonstration center in ghetto areas to furnishing specific school systems with advice and personnel for carrying out successful evaluations of their own educational efforts. Such a center might even be part of a minority studies program and provide graduate training for students interested in carrying out research in this area. It could also train service personnel. It could be a multidisciplinary center including medical and nutritional experts (an area needing much more study) and psychologists, educators and so on. Its establishment could overcome one of the major problems of the research in this area, the many uncoordinated, shotgun approaches employed by many independent researchers, which simply have not led to appropriate answers. It appears that the ability to find answers that really make a difference lies in sustained, well-planned efforts that have enough long-term support to prevent early failures (such as Head Start has experienced) from bringing about threats of financial abandonment or loss of confidence.

Specific Research Recommendations

The available evidence suggests that the major problems encountered in most intervention studies (procedures designed to intervene in the intellectual development of the disadvantaged child) conducted so far stem from deficiencies in

[*]Parts of the discussion and recommendations in this section were taken from material provided by Dr. Vernon C. Hall, Syracuse University.

the following interrelated areas: (1) evaluation procedures typically used; (2) degree of treatment specificity and monitoring of treatments; (3) provisions for longitudinal follow-up; and (4) specific knowledge about the environment or characteristics of the sample experiencing the intervention.

Nearly all intervention studies use a limited number of standardized tests (typically the Stanford-Binet, the Illinois Test of Psycholinguistic Abilities, and the Peabody Picture Vocabulary Test) for indications of success. Most of them are standardized and validated using either a representative group of the total population or only white subjects. Therefore no predictive validity coefficients are available that use lower class subjects without intervention or that are computed on scores raised through intervention. It is also strange that available intervention studies fail to report the specific skills that the children were taught <u>and</u> the percentage of children who successfully mastered these skills. Much of the effort seems to have been directed toward raising intelligence test scores and thus, by interference, increasing capacity. A more appropriate approach would include measures both of specific gain and of generalized of effects of specific gain. For instance, the Lesser, Fifer, and Clark (1965) measures could be used in measuring the effects of a program designed to increase verbal skills, along with a specific vocabulary test measuring the words taught. One could also see the effect of increased verbal skill on reasoning ability could then also be measured. Another approach is suggested by Jensen, who hypothesizes two levels of learning ability, essentially abstract and associative. A very specific test of skills taught could be applied in combination with the Raven Matrices, demanding abstract thinking and the digit span test, hypothesized to be associative in nature. In addition, it would be interesting and useful to compare the results of interventions designed to improve the strong areas of particular populations--such as i.e., vocabulary in the case of Negroes--and the results of interventions designed to improve weak areas--such as abstract thinking.

Major efforts are also needed in developing new testing approaches for evaluating intervention efforts in every area. It would also be valuable to establish predictive validity coefficients using minority groups on present tests. The most important need, however, is to demand that intervention researchers be required to assess specific skills being taught. In a perfect intervention project, every child would learn everything taught regardless of initial and subsequent IQ scores, and this would mean that the correlation of gain with IQ scores before and after would be zero. Such a procedure would also demand careful specification of instructional goals, which makes the construction of criterion tests relatively easy.

Some interventionists emphasize curriculum while others stress strategy, and it is possible that interesting interactions would be discovered if more studies would manipulate both curriculum and strategy at the same time. It is not enough, however, simply to describe treatments used in such research. Researchers must make provision for actually observing the teachers and empirically establishing the fact that the treatments which were supposed to be used were actually used.

Longitudinal follow-up of initially successful intervention projects should always be provided for, but in itself this is not enough; replications are also needed. A good model would be a three-year project providing for a replication (using hypothesized improvements learned from previous years) in the second and third years. Weikart (1967) uses such an approach.

The final weakness of intervention research derives from an incredible ignorance about the culture from which "culturally deprived" children come. The literature is filled with speculations about the critical differences between lower class and middle class homes, without any empirical basis. It includes statements that the lower class homes provides less stimulation, less organization, lower aspirations, more restricted codes of communication, and so forth. This study has shown, however, that lower class parents do indeed have middle class aspirations for their children but speculates that they do not do the things that are necessary to enable their children to reach the goals the parents have in mind. With regard to restricted codes of communication, Bernstein (1964) is careful to point out that his ideas apply to only English subjects.

The findings reviewed in this study have not focused in any substantial way on the sources of minority group inadequacy in settings other than the school. The findings of major studies reviewed, however, substantiate the idea that the socio-economic standing of the family is one of the most important factors contributing to the educational success of the child. Reviews of research on factors relating to family socio-economic status suggest that probable factors contributing to inadequacies among Negroes include inadequate prenatal nutrition and care, inadequate nutrition and health care in later stages of development, deteriorated family structure, inadequate intellectual stimulation, patterns of child rearing that appear to affect such educationally relevant factors as initiative and creativity, and the effects of discrimination and alienation from the broader society (Bronfenbrenner, 1967; Dreger and Miller, 1968; Ricciuti, 1969).

Although these and other factors relating to socio-economic and ethnic status have some relation to developmental status among Negroes, relatively little is known of the details of operation of their influences and of their specific effects on intellectual and educational development. Indeed, research on the contributions of particular class-linked factors to educational development is strangely indecisive. Bronfenbrenner (1967), for example, has presented a clear-cut case for a strong influence of father-absence on the educational development of the Negro child, based on evidence from generally small scale studies. Two larger-scale studies of this factor (Coleman et al., 1966; Wilson, 1967) failed to show any influence of the structural integrity of the home on achievement among Negro students, when the influences of other correlated factors had been accounted for. The findings of these latter studies are not necessarily interpretable as indicating that father-absence has no effect on educational development among Negroes, but only that the evidence is inconsistent with the hypothesis that father-absence has a direct effect. One is placed in similarly equivocal circumstances when examining the results of studies of the intellectual and educational consequences of such factors as bilingualism, child-rearing practices, family composition, maternal employment, family mobility, and nutritional status (NYSED, 1968; Ricciuti, 1969), all of which seem to have different and generally negative effects among lower status families.

The generally equivocal nature of research on individual family background factors, which theoretically contribute to success or failure in the educational setting, should not be taken to mean that research is a fruitless enterprise from a decision-making point of view. Rather, the strong contribution of gross indexes of socio-economic status to educational success should provide the basis for more extensive and new kinds of research and programatic efforts to discover what it is about the family lives of children that contributes to their intellectual and psychological development. Research directed toward the discovery of the sequences in which individual family background factors operate and then are operated upon can constitute a rational basis for action in working

directly with the family.   Various means of preschool intervention, along with appropriate interventions in the family,
may turn out to be what is needed to obtain more far-reaching
and longer-lasting effects on the progress of an individual's
development than appears to be possible with present techniques.

Compensatory Education and Integration

A final area of consideration that remains virtually un-
touched by experimentation is the nature of compensatory education programs that might prove effective with the disadvantaged minority group student who suddenly finds himself transferred to an integrated school setting.   At various points in
this volume, it has been stated or implied that the major focus
of compensatory efforts might well be in the preschool phase,
where intervention would be simpler to accomplish and might
generally prove more efficient and effective in the long run.
However, if integration in the schools is to become a reality,
educators, who are generally used to traditional approaches
to teaching as applied in a relatively ideal climate, will be
faced with groups of youngsters with special educational needs.
Current studies fail to indicate that teachers accomplish any
basic changes in instruction as a result of integration.   Rather,
the available evidence suggests that teachers make minor adjustments in the instructional program--by discussing black
history, for example--and that the facilitating effect of integration on Negro achievement is primarily a function of the
social milieu.
The educational gap remaining between Negroes and
whites in the integrated school setting thus becomes an important focus of intervention research.   Other sections of
this chapter have focused on the need to create an appropriate
social environment in the integrated school as an important
condition of the Negro student's academic success.   However,
academic success is also determined by the extent to which
the student's capabilities, attitudes, and learning styles match
the requirements of available instructional approaches and
materials.   The greater variance of Negro achievement in
integrated schools noted in Coleman et al. and other studies
reviewed in this volume indicate that many Negro students
fail to adapt to the learning requirements of the typical
middle class white school.

Program Formulation and Development

In the recommendations for research on compensatory education, it was proposed that the problem might be better handled through the development of centers that would focus on research, implementation, and the training of specialized personnel capable of conducting effective programs in the schools. The basis for this recommendation finds further cause from consideration of the larger-scale approaches to compensatory education in the schools that are generally dependent on educational practitioners as a primary source of ideas. Such is the case when programs are funded on the basis of competitive (or noncompetitive) proposal submissions. Generally, it appears that school district personnel react with proposals that reflect the training and experiences of teachers, administrators, and other supporting staff. Such training may be appropriate for running the typical school, but it appears to have been largely inappropriate for the development of the types of research and program development activities that may effect significant and needed change in the disadvantaged schools of the nation.

Where compensatory programs are formulated and directed by capable nonpublic school personnel, the results have frequently included wasteful duplication, lack of comparability because of dissimilarities in measurement approaches in other-wise similar programs, and faulty implementation because of a scarcity of adequately trained personnel. Moreover, many of the results of the more systematic efforts never reach school personnel in usable form. Chesler (1969) has correctly concluded that books, lectures, and films on new approaches to education seem to engender little change in the schools. It thus seems clear that certain organizational changes are required in the ways in which new educational programs for disadvantaged children are conceived, tested, selected, and finally implemented in the school.

An alternate procedure, recommended here, would involve the establishment of special centers focused on the special educational requirements of newly integrated schools and schools properly categorized as "disadvantaged." These institutions would serve the State educational agency, the community, and the public schools in a designated area. Operating and development costs would be derived from a pooling of portions of State and Federal funds normally devoted to such activities as compensatory education and innovation (perhaps 10 or 15 percent). Such centers would operate primarily within and around the urban centers of a single state or region in a fashion similar to the federally supported regional educational laboratories but would be further centralized to ensure comparability among certain elements of program activity, such as evaluation techniques.

The bulk of State and Federal funds intended for compensatory education and related efforts and normally apportioned to the schools would still be received by the public schools. However, the expenditures of these funds would be controlled or chanelled in such a way that a significant portion would be used to support specific programs generated by the intervention center for implementation in the schools (excluding any program funds intended to render additional <u>general aid to</u> urban and other districts.)

The centers' program activities would be founded on the basis of a careful analysis of the available information from prior research and development activities and would further reflect the knowledge and leadership of the State educational agency, the schools, and the broad social and educational needs of the communities served by the center. The plan, in its bare outlines, would begin with the determination of general priorities or broad program objectives formulated by the educational leadership. Initial stages of the centers' activities would focus on broad technical reviews of the scientific literature (allocated among centers), which would be further translated for consumption at different levels of the educational structure by teachers, guidance counselors, and others responsible for direct implementation of educational programs.

These broad technical reviews, called "state of the art reports, " would be designed to present an up-to-date analysis of the current state of research and program development in a particular field of study relevant to the educational process and/or broad social problems that impinge on the effectiveness of the schools. Such reports would also specify the form in which the information was to be transmitted, the target populations to which the information was to be transmitted, the procedures for dissemination, and when warranted, the procedures for implementation and demonstration. Some possible results of such state of the art reports include the following:

1. The creation of a basis for educational policy-making at high levels

2. When the findings of research and development activities in the problem area have been positive and systematic, relatively immediate packaging and dissemination of

instructional materials, procedures, and guides for program development

3. Specific direction for leadership efforts oriented toward the solution of major educational problems deriving from current social-psychological conditions and requiring extensive reorientation of the educational enterprise

4. Sorely needed direction for school districts for locally supported instructional and organizational changes required by their particular social contexts

5. Finally, an efficient basis for the formulation of new research and development efforts, which would constitute one of the major activities of the intervention center. (What had been done so far through research would be known. What remained to be done might be determined through an examination of priorities. The method of doing it might proceed more efficiently and effectively when relevant knowledge of the problem area was systematically surveyed and interpreted.)

To ensure that state of the art reports, resultant program packages, and the results of the intervention centers' own developments would have an intensive impact on educational practice, a major effort of center activities would involve direct assistance in implementing and researching programs in the schools. Some examples of possible service functions of the centers follow:

1. To interpret further the findings of significant state of the art reports and other relevant research efforts to local school staff

2. To plan, with school district staffs, the implementation of research findings in the local setting

3. To assist local school district staffs in the implementation process itself by bringing to bear the specialized knowledge of the social and behavioral sciences on a continuing basis

4. To provide more adequate validation of promising new programs through cooperative efforts with several school districts, thereby establishing an adequate basis for generalization of findings to other educational settings

5. To provide the leadership and resources for broad dissemination and demonstration of relevant research findings and successful program developments

6. To develop, for implementation by other agencies, guidelines and other resources presenting detailed plans and requirements for new staff training programs, for teaching specialists and teacher aides, for example

7. To provide a fertile field for the systematic training of school personnel in realistic situations, in cooperation with institutions of higher education

8.   To provide the resources for continuing supervision and adjustment of new programs inplemented in the schools

9.   To provide the independent leadership necessary to involve other relevant agencies such as social welfare agencies, foundations, and other Federal programs--in a concerted and experimental attack on social problems that grossly affect the lives of disadvantaged children, some of which cannot be easily or effectively circumvented by efforts in the school context alone.

The basic assumptions of the aforementioned plan for gaining more systematic control over funds allocated for intervention research and educational change in the disadvantaged school are clear: (1) Local control over program formulation and implementation has proven inefficient and largely ineffective, (2) The efforts and contributions of programs initiated by investigators independently of public school leadership have also had relatively little impact on school practice for a variety of reasons, (3) The present informal structure for getting into the hands of public school personnel the results of significant new research and development activities is totally inadequate to the task at hand, (4) And the entire process of decision-making relating to the allocation of funds for research and development activities relevant to effective changes in the disadvantaged school generally fails to relate to the available body of systematic knowledge of the educational process. If these assumptions are valid, it is difficult to imagine that any significant changes will occur in the context of the urban school as long as the present decision-making structure remains intact. The alternatives for changing this structure contained in the proposals outlined above are only one set of alternatives and may be appropriate only in a limited range of circumstances. Serious consideration of such alternatives appears to be required if the pace of positive change in the education of disadvantaged children is to achieve even a low correspondence with the need for such change.

The Teacher and the Disadvantaged School

Much of the discussion surrounding teaching requirements for the disadvantaged school indicates a strong need to recognize individual differences in formulating relevant instructional strategies. However, systematic matching of instructional strategies with individual learning requirements does not yet appear possible on any but an experimental basis. Recent research Lesser, Fifer, and Clark, 1965; Jensen, 1969 appears to suggest consideration of a wide variety of student characteristics and patterns among characteristics as relevant to the design of instructional environments but, at the same time, expand the complexity of the problem. Research on compensatory education programs, reviewed in Chapter 6, also suggests a number of approaches and principles that may have general applicability in the disadvantaged school and, to some extent, in education in general.

It is thus evident that strategies for teaching disadvantaged children are still essentially experimental. And strategies for teacher preparation and in-service training should reflect what is "known" about disadvantaged children, as well as the tentative nature of its possible applications. Consequently, an efficient approach to teacher training in this area might well focus on the development of basic capabilities that are likely to form the essential components of a broad variety of instructional and psychological techniques coordinated with varieties of cultural and economic disadvantagement. Based primarily on the findings reviewed in Chapters 3 and 6, some relevant capabilities might consist of the following:

1. Ability to assess and interpret measures of fundamental abilities and skills relevant to learning (for example, specific learning abilities and basic learning abilities)

2. Ability to select and apply basic teaching strategies that are coordinated with strategies for the measurement of abilities (for example, associative learning and concept learning at various levels)

3. Ability to apply systematically a variety of reinforcement strategies, utilizing different kinds of schedules and different types of reinforcers (concrete, abstract) under appropriate conditions

4. Ability to apply specific training techniques in a variety of areas where intellectual and educational deficits are most severe among the disadvantaged (for example, language training and reasoning)

5. Ability to manipulate affective tone in intergroup processes to create desired results

6. Ability to create instructional materials to meet the specific learning requirements of individual children

7. Ability to train children in certain specific behaviors, such as "attending to the task."

8. Ability to apply quasi-therapeutic procedures designed to circumvent or replace maladaptive defensive and other responses that interfere with efficient learning.

One could list other abilities or behaviors that seem relevant to the experimental tasks of the teacher of disadvantaged
children and that can be derived from research on ethnic and
social class differences in intellectual, educational, and psychological development.   But it is evident that few trainees
might live so long as to gain the experiences that would enable
them to carry out the variety of functions that seem to be required.   The requirements then suggest a team approach, in
which team members would receive further training in disadvantaged school settings in order to learn the procedures by
which different approaches and skills are combined to solve
instructional and related problems.

When one views the literature on current approaches to
training teachers of the disadvantaged in relation to the foregoing propositions, there is little evidence of a focus on the
development of basic teaching capabilities or on the combination of capabilities implied in the team approach.   The analysis by Haubrich (1969) of teacher preparation programs indicates that teacher training institutions are generally focusing
on one or more of the following approaches: (1) dispensing
information about the disadvantaged through the adoption of
new courses; (2) providing the trainee with first-hand experiences with community agencies serving disadvantaged youth;
and (3) providing direct teaching experience in disadvantaged
schools.   In general, teacher preparation programs appear to
place heavy emphasis on experiences designed to bring about
"understanding" of disadvantaged youth, while some place
heavier emphasis on the direct experience component, (such as
the Teacher Corps).   Haubrich's generalizations about the nature of in-service education indicate a similar heavy emphasis
on "understanding" the disadvantaged and apparently little emphasis on the learning of potentially relevant capabilities.

These generalizations about the nature of procedures for
training teachers of the disadvantaged reflect at least two assumptions that may well be called into question: (1) that the
development of "understanding" will necessarily be reflected
in appropriate strategies for instruction and (2) that experience in the disadvantaged school will likewise be reflected
in appropriate teaching strategies, attitudes, and so on.   With
respect to the latter assumption, it is not unlikely that the
wrong or ineffective strategies could be learned frequently;
but, in any event, there is no substantial proof that either of
these assumptions is valid.

These brief considerations suggest a somewhat extensive
rethinking and examination of the basic assumptions underlying
present programs for training teachers of the disadvantaged--

pointing out that though understanding and unsystematic "experience" may form useful components of an effective training program, they provide little guarantee that the teacher so trained will be capable of behaving in an effective manner in the classroom. What appears to be a prime requirement of an effective training program is a focus on specific but broadly applicable skills that can be flexibly translated to match a wide variety of competencies and developmental levels among children, as well as the procedural requirements of a variety of programs.

SUMMARY

The national commitment to integration in the schools and recent legislative programs designed to aid the poor have raised the hopes and expectations of Negroes and other disadvantaged minority groups. While lack of any general progress in realizing these expectations has created some degree of disaffection among Negroes, the majority remain committed to achieving the goal of equality of educational opportunity through a partnership with the more advantaged members of society.

The disaffected, though not a large segment of the poor, have nevertheless made their feelings and demands felt in the schools and in other major institutions in the social system. Current studies show that the demands and actions of Negroes for equality are firmly grounded in a level of economic and educational degredation that has shown little improvement relative to the status of whites over the past twenty years. Efforts to mitigate the economic and social disadvantagement of Negroes and other minority groups appear to have made hardly a dent. In fact, the problem of the poor appears to have intensified, and its social consequences have grown more serious, as reflected in the steady increase in racial isolation in the schools and the sudden swelling of interracial hostility in the Nation's high schools.

Indeed, the social consequences of racial isolation have become increasingly evident in the public educational context, as shown by a report (Urban Crisis Monitor, May, 1969) that documents recent evidence of student protest and active conflict in the Nation's high schools. This report begins by describing a racial explosion in a junior high school in the Watts area in Los Angeles in March of 1969, and continues: "The pattern of confrontation in Los Angeles is typical of high school racial disorders across the nation." In January, 1969, in fact, 67 percent of all city and suburban high schools and 56 percent of all junior high schools were experiencing some form of active student protest. Racial conflict was the most common single issue in these protests and was at the heart of the ugliest and most violent of the protests. In the January survey, about 10 percent of the secondary schools studied reported some race-related protest under way.

Current evidence indicates that a variety of forms of planned social contact may assist greatly in reducing the feelings of ambivalence and hostility generally existing between Negroes and whites. A few recent successful integration programs further show that the school setting provides a natural and effective focus for the development of positive feelings and contact between Negroes and whites. Of equal importance, the findings of research indicate that school integration appears to be the most effective approach known for generally reducing the educational disadvantagement exhibited by Negro children and other minority groups and that the interracial experiences gained in the integrated school potentially represent a long-term solution to the destructive social problems associated with racial cleavage.

Unfortunately, though there is considerable potential for eliminating racial isolation in the schools in many regions of New York State and the Nation, current population trends indicate that racial isolation in the schools is increasing and will continue to increase in the near future. Analysis of the economic status of Negroes and Puerto Ricans in New York State and in the Nation clearly shows that the racially isolated school is also isolated on the basis of social class level. The possible damaging effects of the maintenance of schools along social class lines are undoubtedly underestimated by statistics on racial isolation alone, since the prevalent practices of ability grouping and tracking also appear to represent the creation of unequal educational conditions for different children.

Even granting the coarseness of the available data, it is yet possible to offer more than speculation into the whys and wherefores of the effect of classroom social class composition on achievement. Casual observation in the American school indicates a typical pattern in which the teacher plays the role of information dispenser and behavior modifier, largely in relation to that amorphous concept the classroom group. Those familiar with the process know that the teacher typically

attempts to gear the complexity of the information dispensed
to the comprehension of the average student in the classroom
or some smaller portion thereof. It is a generally anachronistic procedure in which learning may be greatly influenced
by group contagion. The teacher's effectiveness is heavily
dependent upon the cooperation of group members, and upon
such individual factors as level of conceptual development and
attentiveness.

Reviews of the process of classroom interaction reveal
that the teacher does most of the talking, composed mainly
of lecturing, presenting instructions, and disciplining students. This procedure appears to be subject to gross interference in the lower class Negro school in which from 50 to
80 percent of classroom time may be given over to discipline
and other irrelevant activities. The disruptive and destructive
behaviors of individuals in the peer group are highly contagious
and may occur irrespective of competing values in the family.
Individuals from middle class backgrounds conducive to learning may thus contribute to a general disintegration of the process of group learning in the classroom, or their potentially
positive influences on the learning process may not be felt because of the prevailing climate of interference contributed by
the behaviors of their less advantaged peers.

Other factors contributing to interference with learning
in the typical classroom include teacher expectations and resultant feelings about inferiority communicated to the student.
In some measure, it appears that such expectations and feelings may be held in relation to an entire school in which educational deficits and ability differences relative to whites and
other upper status students are made abundantly clear. It
is also reported that teachers in the "inferior" school tend to
reduce the quality and quantity of information made available
in instruction. It seems that interference with learning resulting from teacher expectations relates to school and classroom morale and is reflected in such factors as self-esteem
sense of control, and intellectual and occupational aspirations
--which may in turn be reflected in more directly relevant
factors, such as attentiveness in class and doing homework.

The learning-interference factors described in relation
to the "inferior" school should also be relevant in schools
with grouping policies that result in either social class isolation within schools or combinations of different levels of
racial and social class isolation, depending on the class status
of the white student population and the proportion of "integrated" Negroes in the school. Intraschool de facto segregation

in multiracial schools results in white students' regarding minority group students as "different." Minority group students come to regard themselves as "different," because of their attendance in special classes. Both groups relate the notion of "being different" to intellectual superiority and inferiority.

The above considerations and realistic evaluations of the progress of integration in the schools indicate that major new efforts are needed to increase the pace of integration, while at the same time radical departures are needed to affect the educational opportunities of large numbers of students who are likely to remain in segregated schools in the immediate future. Accordingly, the recommendations made earlier in this chapter on the basis of the research review are summarized separately in relation to the integrated school and the disadvantaged school.

Toward the Effective Integrated School

Examination of the many reports and policy statements reviewed in preparation for this study failed to turn up evidence of explicit recognition of findings showing that the social class mix makes a substantial difference in the achievement levels of Negro students and other minority group children. Further than this, research findings indicate that the facilitating effects of integration are virtually absent unless integration is implemented at the classroom level. Current guidelines, however, generally focus on the concept of racial balance within individual schools, with resultant ambiguous criteria for the planning of school integration programs that may vary as a function of the over-all racial balance in the particular district or group of districts being considered.

When the details of the research findings on racial and social class isolation in the schools are examined, it is apparent that much care must be taken in planning for the integrated school if it is to have a positive effect on educational development among minority group students. The research findings relating to the social class composition of the school and classroom and other considerations enlarged upon in this study should receive explicit recognition in the development of plans for integrating the schools. Recognition of ethnic, social class, and other factors of importance for the development of systematic integration plans might be best accomplished through comprehensive identification and study procedures that could be conducted on a statewide, regional, or district basis. For example, appropriate procedures might first identify the disadvantaged school in relation to such factors as ethnic and social class compositions and achievement status. Plans for integration might then be further developed on the basis of a more detailed study of the disadvantaged school and its regional context.

Once the disadvantaged school is identified in relation to relevant student, school, and contextual characteristics, a reasonably detailed basis then exists for the formulation of a variety of preliminary plans designed to achieve equality of educational opportunity for all students. Some plans for integration may conceivably leave the basic structure of the school program intact, focusing primarily on interracial relations, as in suburban districts where the minority group student population may tend toward middle class. In other districts or schools, effective plans may require much more extensive efforts, in addition to mixing students from different ethnic groups and different social class levels. These more extensive efforts may include a radical reorganization of the school program, new approaches to compensatory education applied in an integrated context, and the "integration" of nutritional, health, and family service programs with the educational offerings of the school. The extent to which the plan for desegregating the school would involve additional changes in the educational and social context of the school and community could be largely illuminated through the types of identification and study procedures referred to in this volume.

Over and above consideration of such factors as ethnic and social class status in formulating plans for school desegregation, a preliminary analysis of other important conditions potentially affecting such plans is essential. As has been pointed out earlier in this chapter, a facilitating classroom climate is called for in various respects--the early experience of academic success by disadvantaged students, social interaction within the peer group, teacher responses, parental involvement, and curriculum content. Clearly, for such a climate to be achieved, teacher training procedures must be modified to provide relevant experience, as suggested in detail above. And to achieve the flexibility necessary for effective integration, school structure and organization must be altered, perhaps as outlined in the earlier discussion in this chapter of The Continuous Learning Year--a plan that allows the adoption of educational practices that are theoretically relevant to the learning needs of the disadvantaged child and, at the same time, supportive in practice of true integration.

Toward More Effective
Education in the Disadvantaged School

The analysis of school population in Chapter 2 makes it abundantly clear that the educational and social problems represented by the disadvantaged school are growing rather than decreasing. When viewing the past record of progress in accomplishing desegregation in the schools in New York State, and generally in the Nation, it appears unrealistic to expect that great numbers of minority students will <u>suddenly</u> experience the educationally facilitating effects of the integrated school setting. The only way out of this impasse, in such areas as New York City, is to provoke massive and radical change in the educational process, while at the same time making all possible efforts to increase the pace of school desegregation. The notion of "compensation for educational inadequacies, " which usually implies something added to the educational process, should imply the need to work basic changes in the schools as well as the need to intervene at appropriate stages in the child's development.

Evaluations of compensatory programs for the disadvantaged have shown that, in general, they are not succeeding in raising the achievement levels of the deprived. Similarly, while integration has had a beneficial effect, it has not succeeded in bringing the performance of minority group pupils up to national norms. It is apparent that many basic questions relating to the causes of inadequate educational development remain unanswered, and that programs that will produce academic change in the public schools have yet to be devised. It is also apparent that in those instances in which promising techniques for working with the disadvantaged have been discovered, they have not found their way into practice in the schools.

The current inadequacies in compensatory education stem from a number of sources. In the area of research there has been inadequate attention to defining the characteristics that differentiate the lower class and the middle class child and children from different ethnic backgrounds. Furthermore, intervention research has lacked continuity and comprehensiveness. It has been handicapped by questionable evaluative measures that do not tap the specific skills being taught, by a lack of specificity in treatment description, and by inadequate replication and follow-up.

Program effectiveness has been hampered by the present procedure of leaving much of program formulation and implementation up to the local school district and therefore to school practitioners, who, because of their experience and training, are unable to come up with the innovative approaches needed for the disadvantaged. Two additional conditions that appear to relate to the inadequacy of program formulation and development in the school setting are these: (1) The present informal structure for getting into the hands of public school personnel the results of significant new research and development activities is generally inadequate to the task at hand. (2) The entire process of decision-making relating to the allocation of funds for research and development activities, relevant to effective change in the disadvantaged school, generally fails to relate to the available body of systematic knowledge of the educational process.

All this suggests the need for a new approach to the conduct of research, development, and implementation activities in the education of the disadvantaged--an approach that will afford more systematic control over funds allocated for intervention research and educational change in the disadvantaged school. In this connection it is proposed that research and program efforts designed to up-grade the disadvantaged school be assigned to special centers to serve the State educational agency, the schools, and the community in a designated area. An initial activity of the centers would be the preparation of broad technical reviews, or "state of the art" reports, that would provide a basis for policy-making, lead to the packaging and distribution of instructional materials of proven value, give direction to leadership and efforts to solve problems stemming from social-psychological conditions and requiring a reorganization of the educational enterprise, give direction to school districts instituting locally supported instructional and organizational changes to meet the needs of their social contexts, and provide an efficient basis for the formulation of new research and development efforts. The centers would also undertake a variety of service activities to assure an intensive impact on the schools.

This proposal, outlined in detail earlier, constitutes only one set of alternatives for organizational change designed to improve the ways in which intervention research is conceived and conducted and in the ways in which it is implemented in the schools. Serious consideration of such alternatives appears to be required if the pace of positive change in the education of disadvantaged children is to achieve even a low correspondence with the need for such change.

With regard to the teaching requirements of the disadvantaged school, a strong need to recognize individual differences in formulating relevant instructional strategies is indicated. However, systematic matching of instructional strategies with individual learning requirements does not yet appear possible on any but an experimental basis. At the same time, certain changes can nevertheless be made to reduce the potentially deteriorating effects of the group learning situation on instruction in the disadvantaged school.

Reflecting the conditional nature of what is "known" about learning among disadvantaged children, as well as the tentative nature of its possible applications, strategies for training teachers of the disadvantaged may efficiently focus on the development of basic capabilities outlined earlier. These are likely to form the essential components of a broad variety of instructional and psychological techniques that can be positively coordinated with varieties of cultural and economic disadvantagement.

BIBLIOGRAPHY

REFERENCES CITED

General References

Amidon, E., and Simon, A. "Teacher-Pupil Interaction." Review of Educational Research 35: 130-39 (1965).

Atkinson, J. W. An Introduction to Motivation. Princeton, New Jersey: D. Van Nostrand, 1965.

Baker, R. L., Schutz, R. E., and Hines, R. H. "The Influence of Mental Ability on Achievement When Socio-economic Status Is Controlled." Journal of Experimental Education 30: 225-58 (1961).

Baldwin, C. P. "Naturalistic Studies of Classroom Learning." Review of Educational Research 35: 107-13 (1965).

Bandura, A., and Huston, A. C. "Identification as a Process of Incidental Learning." Journal of Abnormal and Social Psychology 63: 311-18 (1961).

Bandura, A., Ross, D., and Ross, S. "Transmission of Aggression Through Imitation of Aggressive Models." Journal of Abnormal and Social Psychology 63: 575-82 (1961).

Bandura, A., and Walters, R. H. Social Learning and Personality Development. New York: Holt, Rinehart and Winston, 1963.

Banks, R., and DiPasquale, M. E. A Study of the Educational Effectiveness of Integration: a Comparison of Pupil Achievement Before and One Year After Integration and a Survey of Principals, Teachers, Parents, and Pupils Involved in the Program. Buffalo, New York: Division of Curriculum Evaluation and Development, Buffalo Public Schools, January, 1969.

Barabasz, A. F. "An Investigation of the Relationship Between Intelligence and Temporal Orientation." Child Study Center Bulletin 4: 80-81 (1968).

_____. "Temporal Orientation and Academic Achievement in College." Journal of Social Psychology (1969a). (In press)

_____. "Time Constriction in Delinquent and Non-delinquent Girls." Adolescence, 3: 435-40 (1968-69).

_____. "Time Estimation in Delinquents: a Re-examination." Journal of General Psychology (1969b). (In press)

Bayley, N., and Jones, H. E. "Environmental Correlates of Mental and Motor Development: a Cumulative Study from Infancy to Six Years." Child Development 8: 329-41 (1937).

Bereiter, C., and Engelmann, S. Teaching Disadvantaged Children in the Preschool. Englewood Cliffs, New Jersey: Prentice-Hall, Inc., 1966.

Bernstein, B. "Elaborated and Restricted Codes: Their Social Origins and Some Consequences." American Anthropologist 66: 55-69 (1964).

Bienvenu, M. J. "Effects of School Integration on the Self Concept and Anxiety of Lower-Class Negro Adolescent Males." Doctor's dissertation, The Florida State University, 1968. Dissertation Abstracts 29: 692A (1968).

Birnbaum, L. "A Comparative Study of the Relation of Broken Homes to the Social Class and School Success of Secondary School Boys." Dissertation Abstracts 27: 928 (1966).

Blalock, H. M. Causal Inferences in Nonexperimental Research. Chapel Hill, North Carolina: The University of North Carolina Press, 1961.

Borg, W. R. Ability Grouping in the Public Schools. Madison, Wisconsin: Dembar Educational Research Services, Inc., 1966.

Bowles, S. "Towards Equality of Educational Opportunity." Harvard Educational Review 38: 89-99 (1968).

Brandt, R. J., and Johnson, D. M. "Time Orientation in Delinquents." Journal of Abnormal and Social Psychology 51: 343-45 (1955).

Brock, T. C., and Del Giudice, C. "Stealing and Temporal
Orientation." Journal of Abnormal and Social Psychology
66: 91-94 (1963).

Bronfenbrenner, U. "The Psychological Costs of Quality and
Equality in Education." Child Development 38: 909-25 (1967).

Campbell, W. J. "The Influence of Sociocultural Environment
on the Progress of Children at the Secondary-School Level."
Australian Journal of Psychology 7: 140-46 (1955).

Cattell, R. B. "Are I. Q. Tests Intelligent?" Psychology
Today, 1: 56-62 (1968).

Chesler, M. A. (Ed.). "How Do You Negroes Feel about
Whites and How Do You Whites Feel about Negroes?" Ann
Arbor, Michigan: Institute for Social Research, 1966.

_____. "Interaction and Teaching Alternatives in De-
segregated Classrooms," in R. L. Green, ed., Racial Crisis
in American Education. Chicago, Illinois: Follett Educational Corporation, 1969. Pp. 90-125.

Chesler, M. A., and Barakat, H. The Innovation and Sharing
of Teaching Practices I: a Study of Professional Roles and
Social Structures in Schools. U. S. Office of Education
Cooperative Research Project. Ann Arbor, Michigan: Institute for Social Research, 1967.

Chesler, M. A., and Fox, R. Role Playing in the Classroom.
Chicago, Illinois: Science Research Associates, 1966.

_____. "Teacher Peer Relations and Educational
Change." NEA Journal 56: 25-26 (1967).

Chesler, M. A., Wittes, S., and Radin, N. "What Happens
When Northern Schools Desegregate." American Education,
4: 2-4 (1968).

Clark, K. B., and Clark, M. P. "Racial Identification and
Preference in Negro Children," in T. M. Newcomb and E.
L. Hartley, eds., Readings in Social Psychology. New York:
Holt, Rinehart and Winston, 1947. Pp. 169-178.

Clausen, J. A., and Williams, J. R. "Sociological Correlates of Child Behavior," in H. W. Stevenson, J. Kagen and C. Spiker, eds., Child Psychology: the Sixty-second Yearbook of the National Society for the Study of Education. Chicago, Illinois: The National Society for the Study of Education, 1963. Pp. 62-107.

Cleveland, G. A., and Bosworth, D. L. "Study of Certain Psychological and Sociological Characteristics as Related to Arithmetic Achievement." Arithmetic Teacher, 14: 383-87 (1967).

Coleman, J. S. "The Concept of Equality of Educational Opportunity." Harvard Educational Review, 38: 7-22 (1968).

_____. "The Relationship of Socio-economic Status to the Performance of Junior High School Students." Journal of Experimental Education 9: 61-63 (1940).

_____. Equality of Educational Opportunity. Office of Education, U.S. Department of Health, Education, and Welfare. Washington: U.S. Government Printing Office, 1966.

Coles, R. "Northern Children under Desegregation." Psychiatry 3: 1-15 (1968).

Costello, C. G. "Ego-Involvement, Success, and Failure: a Review of the Literature," in H. J. Eysenck, ed., Experiments in Motivation. New York: Macmillan, 1964. Pp. 161-208.

Crain, R. L. The Politics of School Desegregation. With the assistance of M. Inger, G. A. McWorter and J. J. Vanecko. (Anchor Books Edition). Garden City, New York: Doubleday & Company, Inc., 1969.

Crandall, V. J. "Achievement," in H. W. Stevenson, J. Kagen, and C. Spiker, eds., Child Psychology: the Sixty-second Yearbook of the National Society for the Study of Education. Chicago, Illinois: The National Society for the Study of Education, 1963. Pp. 416-459.

Crescimbeni, J. "Broken Homes Affect Academic Achievement." Education, 84: 437-441 (1964).

Cronbach, L. Essentials of Psychological Testing. New York: Harper and Row Publishers, 1960.

Curry, R. L. "The Effects of Socio-economic Class Status on the Scholastic Achievement of Sixth Grade Children." British Journal of Educational Psychology 32: 46-49 (1962).

Davidson, H. H., and Lang, G. "Children's Perceptions of Their Teachers' Feelings Towards Them, Related to Self Perception, School Achievement and Behavior. Journal of Experimental Education 29: 107-18 (1960).

Denny, J. P. "The Effects of Anxiety and Intelligence on Concept Formation." Unpublished doctor's dissertation, Duke University, 1962.

Dentler, R. A. "Barriers to Northern School Desegregation." Daedalus 95: 45-63 (1966).

Desmond, J. Nelson Rockefeller. New York: The Macmillan Company, 1964.

Deutsch, C. P. "Learning in the Disadvantaged," in H. J. Klausmeier and C. W. Harris, eds., Analyses of Concept Learning. New York: Academic Press, Inc., 1966. Pp. 189-204.

Deutsch, M. "Minority Group and Class Status as Related to Social and Personality factors in Scholastic Achievement." Monograph of the Society for Applied Anthropology 2: 1-32 (1960).

Diamond, L. "The Effects of Anxiety and Stress on Children's Performance." Unpublished doctor's dissertation, Catholic University of America, 1965.

Di Lorenzo, L. T., Salter, R., and Brady, J. J. Prekindergarten Programs for the Disadvantaged: a Third-Year Report on an Evaluative Study. Albany, New York: Research Training and Special Studies, New York State Education Department, December, 1968.

Dimitz, S., Kay, B., and Reckless, W. C. "Group Gradients in Delinquency Potential and Achievement Scores of Sixth Graders." American Journal of Orthopsychiatry 28: 598-605 (1958).

Dodson, D. W. Citizen Response to School Desegregation.
Albany, New York: Bureau of Educational Integration, New
York State Education Department, 1968.

Dreger, R. M., and Miller, K. S. "Comparative Psychological Studies of Negroes and Whites in the United States: 1959-
1965." Psychological Bulletin, 1968 (Monograph Supplement
70, No. 3, Part 2).

Dressler, F. J. Study of Achievement in Reading of Pupils
Transferred from Schools 15 and 37 to Peripheral Schools
to Eliminate Overcrowding, to Abandon an Obsolete School,
and to Achieve a More Desirable Racial Balance in City
Schools. Buffalo, New York: Division of Curriculum Evaluation and Development, Buffalo Public Schools, 1967.

Education Law. Book 16 (McKinney's Consolidated Laws of
New York). Brooklyn, New York: Edward Thompson Company, 1953.

Ellis, L. M. et al. "Time Orientation and Social Class: an
Experimental Supplement." Journal of Abnormal and Social
Psychology 51: 146 (1955).

Engle, T. L. "Home Environments and School Records."
School Review, 42: 590-98 (1934).

Ervin-Tripp, S. "Language Development," in L. W. Hoffman
and M. L. Hoffman, eds., Review of Child Development Research, Volume II. New York: Russell Sage Foundation,
1966. Pp. 55-105.

Eysenck, H. J. Experiments in Motivation. New York:
Macmillan, 1964.

Feldhusen, J. H., and Klausmeier, H. J. "Anxiety, Intelligence and Achievement in Children of Low, Average, and
High Intelligence." Child Development 33: 402-9 (1962).

Fort, J. G., Watts, J. C., and Lesser, G. S. "Cultural
Background and Learning in Young Children." Phi Delta
Kappan 50: 386-88 (1969).

Franklin, J. From Slavery to Freedom. New York: Vintage
Books, 1969.

Frazier, E. F. Black Bourgeoisie. New York: The Free-press, 1957.

Furfey, P. H. "The Relation Between Socio-economic Status and Intelligence of Young Infants as Measured by the Linfert-Hierholzer Scale." Journal of Genetic Psychology 35: 478-80 (1928).

Gifford, E. M. "Test Anxiety, Reading Rate, and Task Experience." Unpublished manuscript. University of Wisconsin, 1964.

Gist, N., and Bennett, W. "Aspirations of Negro and White Students." Social Forces 42: 40-48 (1963).

Glidewell, J. C., et al. "Socialization and Social Structure in the Classroom," in L. W. Hoffman and M. L. Hoffman, eds., Review of Child Development Research, Volume II. New York: Russell Sage Foundation, 1966. Pp. 221-56.

Goodman, M. E. Race Awareness in Young Children. Reading, Massachusetts: Addison-Wesley, 1952; New York: Collier, 1964.

Gordon, E. W., and Jablonsky, A. "Compensatory Education in the Equalization of Educational Opportunity, I." The Journal of Negro Education, 37: 267-79 (1968a).

_____. "Compensatory Education in the Equalization of Educational Opportunity, II: an Organizational Model for Compensatory Education." The Journal of Negro Education 37: 280-90 (1968b).

Gordon, E. W., and Wilkerson, D. A. Compensatory Education for the Disadvantaged: Programs and Practices: Preschool through College. New York: College Entrance Examination Board, 1966.

Granick, S. "Intellectual Performance as Related to Emotional Instability in Children." Journal of Abnormal and Social Psychology 51: 653-56 (1955).

Granzow, K. R. "A Comparative Study of Underachievers, Normal Achievers, and Overachievers in Reading." Dissertation Abstracts 14: 631-32 (1954).

Green, R. L. "The Urban School Child," in R. L. Green, ed., Racial Crisis in American Education. Chicago, Illinois: Follett Educational Corporation, 1969. Pp. 72-89.

Gregor, A. J., and McPherson, D. A. "Racial Attitudes among White and Negro Children in a Deep-South Standard Metropolitan Area." Journal of Social Psychology 68: 95-106 (1966).

Grimes, J. W., and Allinsmith, W. "Compulsivity, Anxiety, and School Achievement." Merrill-Palmer Quarterly, 7: 247-69 (1961).

Guilford, J. P. The Nature of Human Intelligence. New York: McGraw-Hill Book Company, 1967.

Hall, V. C., and Mery, M. "Language Intervention Research: a Review." Unpublished. Albany, New York: New York State Education Department, 1969.

Hansen, C. F. "Six Years of Integration in the District of Columbia." Teachers College Record 62: 27-35 (1960).

Hanson, E., and Robinson, H. A. "Reading Readiness and Achievement of Primary Grade Children of Different Socioeconomic Strata." Reading Teacher 21: 52-56 (1967).

Haubrich, V. F. "Preparing Teachers for Disadvantaged Youth." in R. L. Green, ed., Racial Crisis in American Education. Chicago, Illinois: Follett Educational Corporation, 1969. Pp. 126-46.

Hess, R. D., and Shipman, V. C., and Jackson, D. "Early Experience and the Socialization of Cognitive Modes in Children." Child Development 36: 869-86 (1965)

Hill, K. T., and Sarason, S. B. "The Relation of Test Anxiety and Defensiveness to Test and School Performance over the Elementary-School Years." Monographs of the Society for Research in Child Development 31: 1-75 (1966).

Hillson, H. T., and Myers, F. C. The Demonstration Guidance Project, 1957-1962: Pilot Program for Higher Horizons. New York City: George Washington High School, Board of Education of the City of New York, May, 1963.

Hoehn, A. J. "The Study of Social Status Differentiation in the Classroom Behavior of 19 Third Grade Teachers." Journal of Social Psychology 39: 269-92 (1954).

Irwin, O. C. "Infant Speech: the Effect of Family Occupational Status and of Age on the Use of Sound Types." Journal of Speech and Hearing Disorders, 13: 224-26, 320-23 (1948).

Jahoda, G. "Social Class Differentials in Vocabulary Expansion." British Journal of Educational Psychology 34: 321-23 (1964).

Jaquith, D. H. School Integration in Syracuse, New York. A report prepared for the National Conference on Equal Educational Opportunity in America's Cities sponsored by the U.S. Commission on Civil Rights, Washington, D.C., November 16-18, 1967. ERIC ED 016 716. November, 1967.

Jencks, C. "A Reappraisal of the Most Controversial Educational Document of Our Time." The New York Times Magazine, August 10, 1969.

Jenkins, M. D., and Randall, C. M. "Differential Characteristics of Superior and Unselected Negro College Students." Journal of Social Psychology 27: 187-202 (1948).

Jensen, A. R. "How Much Can We Boost IQ and Scholastic Achievement?" Harvard Educational Review 39: 1-123 (1969).

_____. "Meaningfulness and Concepts; Concepts and Meaningfulness," in H. J. Klausmeier and C. W. Harris, eds., Analyses of Concept Learning. New York: Academic Press, Inc., 1966. Pp. 65-80.

_____. "Social Class and Verbal Learning." in M. Deutsch, I. Katz, and A. R. Jensen, eds., Social Class, Race, and Psychological Development. New York: Holt, Rinehart and Winston, Inc., 1968a. Pp. 115-174.

_____. "Social Class, Race and Genetics: Implications for Education." American Educational Research Journal 5: 1-42 (1968b).

John, V. P. "The Intellectual Development of Slum Children: Some Preliminary Findings. American Journal of Orthopsychiatry 33: 813-22 (1963).

Johnson, C. "Racial Balance: a Case study." New York State Education, 55: 16-19ff (1967).

Kasdon, L. M. "Some Characteristics of highly competent readers among college freshmen." Dissertation Abstracts 15: 1785-91 (1955).

Katz, I. "Review of Evidence Relating to Effects of Desegregation on the Intellectual Performance of Negroes." American Psychologist, 19: 381-99 (1964).

_____. "Academic Motivation and Equal Educational Opportunity." Harvard Educational Review 30: 57-65 (1968a).

_____. "Factors Influencing Negro Performance in the Desegregated School," in M. Deutsch, I. Katz and A. R. Jensen, eds., Social Class, Race, and Psychological Development. New York: Holt, Rinehart and Winston, Inc., 1968b. Pp. 254-89.

Katz, W. L. Eye Witness: the Negro in American History. New York: Pitman Publishing Corporation, 1967.

Kelly, F. J., North, J., and Zingle, H. "The Relation of the Broken Homes to Subsequent School Behaviors." Alberta Journal of Educational Research 11: 215-19 (1965).

Kerrick, J. "The Effects of Manifest Anxiety and I.Q. on Discrimination." Journal of Abnormal and Social Psychology 52: 136-38 (1956).

Klaus, R. A., and Gray, S. W. The Early Training Project for Disadvantaged Children: a Report After Five Years. Nashville, Tennessee: George Peabody College for Teachers, September, 1967.

Knief, L. M., and Stroud, J. B. "Intercorrelations among Various Intelligence, Achievement, and Social Class Scores." Journal of Educational Psychology 50: 117-20 (1950).

Knoblock, H., and Pasamanick, B. "Environmental Factors Affecting Human Development, Before and After Birth." Pediatrics 26: 210-18 (1960).

Krech, D. "The Chemistry of Learning." Saturday Review 51: 48-50ff (1968).

Kruger, D. H. "The Education and Employment Status of Blacks and Whites Since 1946: the Growing Disparity." in R. L. Green, ed., Racial Crisis in American Education. Chicago, Illinois: Follett Educational Corporation, 1969. Pp. 20-44.

LeShan, L. L. "Time Orientation and Social Class." Journal of Abnormal and Social Psychology 47: 589-92 (1952).

Lesser, G., Fifer, G., and Clark, D. "Mental Abilities of Children from Different Social-Class and Cultural Groups." Monographs of the Society for Research in Child Development, Serial No. 102, 30 (4). Chicago: The University of Chicago Press, 1965.

Lewis, J. Research Unit, Project Head Start, Washington, D. C. Personal communication, March, 1969.

Lighthall, F. F., et al. "Change in Mental Ability as a Function of Test Anxiety and Type of Mental Test." Journal of Consulting Psychology 23: 34-38 (1959).

Loban, W. "Language proficiency and school learning." In J. P. Krumboltz, ed., Learning and the Educational Process. Chicago, Illinois: Rand McNally and Company, 1965. Pp. 113-31.

Lomax, I. E. The Negro Revolt. New York: The New American Library, 1962.

Long, D. "Educational Performance in Integrated and Segregated Elementary Schools." Doctor's dissertation, Yeshiva University, 1968. Dissertation Abstracts 29: 412 (1968).

Lott, A. J., and Lott, B. E. Negro and White Youth: a Psychological Study in a Border-State Community. New York: Holt, Rinehart and Winston, 1963.

Lovell, K., and Woolsey, M. E. "Reading Disability, Non-Verbal Reasoning, and Social Class." Educational Research 6: 226-29 (1964).

Mack, R. W. (ed.). Our Children's Burden: Studies of Deseg-regation in Nine American Communities. New York: Random House, 1968.

Mahan, T. "The Busing of Students for Equal Opportunities." The Journal of Negro Education 37: 291-300 (1968).

McCandless, B. R. Children: Behavior and Development. New York: Holt, Rinehart and Winston, Inc., 1967.

McClelland, D. C. "Issues in the Identification of Talent." in D. C. McClelland, et al., eds., Talent and Society. Princeton, New Jersey: D. Van Nostrand Company, Inc., 1958.

McPartland, J. The Relative Influence of School Desegregation and of Classroom Desegregation on the Academic Achievement of Ninth Grade Negro Students: Interim Report. Project No. 6-1610. Baltimore, Maryland: The Johns Hopkins University, September, 1967. ERIC ED 014 341.

Meisels, M. "Test Anxiety, Stress, and Verbal Behavior." Journal of Consulting Psychology 31: 577-82 (1967).

Metropolitan Council for Educational Opportunity. A Report to the Carnegie Corporation. Dorchester, Massachusetts: METCO, December 18, 1968.

Miner, B. "Sociological Background Variables Affecting School Achievement." Journal of Educational Research 61: 372-81 (1968).

Morland, J. K. "A Comparison of Race Awareness in Northern and Southern Children." American Journal of Orthopsychiatry 36: 22-31 (1966).

_____. "Racial Acceptance and Preferences of Nursery School Children in a Southern City." Merrill-Palmer Quarterly 8: 271-80 (1962).

The National Advisory Council on the Education of Disadvan-taged Children. Title I - ESEA: a Review and a Forward Look - 1969: Fourth Annual Report. Washington: U.S. Gov-ernment Printing Office, 1969.

Neville, D., Pfost, P., and Dobbs, V. "The Relationship Between Anxiety and Silent Reading Gain." American Education
Research Journal 4: 45-50 (1967).

Newcomb, T. M., Turner, R. H., and Converse, P. E.
Social Psychology. New York: Holt, Rinehart and Winston,
1965.

Newsweek. Report from Black America: a Newsweek Poll,
June 30, 1969.

New York State Assembly. Resolution 58, 1964.

New York State Commission for Human Rights. Non-White
Populations in New York State: 1960-1967. The Commission,
270 Broadway, New York, New York, 1967. (Mimeo)

_____. Non-White Populations in Rockland County:
1960-1966. The Commission, 270 Broadway, New York,
New York, 1966. (Mimeo)

_____. Non-White Population Trends in Westchester
County: 1960-1965. The Commission, 270 Broadway, New
York, New York, 1965a. (Mimeo)

_____. Non-Whites in Suburbia: an Analysis of
Population Changes in Nassau County, 1960-1965. The Com-
mission, 270 Broadway, New York, New York, 1965b.
(Mimeo)

New York State Division of Human Rights. Population and Race
in Suffolk County: 1960-1968. The Division, 270 Broadway,
New York, New York, 1968.

_____. Puerto Ricans in New York State: 1960-
1969. The Division, 270 Broadway, New York, New York,
1969.

New York State Division of the Budget. New York State statistical yearbook: 1968-1969. Office of Statistical Coordination,
March, 1969.

New York State Education Department. Bulletin to the Schools.
Albany, New York: The Department, September 1, 1963a.

_____. Closing the Gap: a Report of the First Two Years of Experience with ESEA, Title I in New York State. Albany, New York: The Department, August, 1968a.

_____. Correcting Racial Imbalance: a Report on the Projects Funded under State Aid for Correcting Racial Imbalance, 1966-1968. Albany, New York: Bureau of Department Programs Evaluation, The Department, October, 1968b.

_____. Desegregating the Public Schools of New York City. A report prepared for the Board of Education of the City of New York with the assistance of the Institute of Urban Studies, Teachers College, Columbia University. Albany, New York: Commissioner's Advisory Committee on Human Relations and Community Tensions, May 12, 1964.

_____. Guiding Principles for Dealing with De Facto Segregation in Public Schools. A report prepared by the State Education Commissioner's Advisory Committee on Human Relations and Community Tensions. Albany, New York: Office of the President of the University and Commissioner of Education, The Department, June 17, 1963b.

_____. Integration and the Schools. Albany, New York: The Department, 1968c.

_____. Non-School Factors Related to School Achievement. Albany, New York: Division of Research, The Department, 1968d.

_____. Problems of Urban Education: Buffalo. (New York State Studies) Albany, New York: The Department, 1966.

_____. Racial Imbalance in Schools. Letter of June 14, 1963c to all chief local school administrators and presidents of boards of education.

_____. Regents Statement on Intercultural Relations in Education. Albany, New York: The Department, 1960.

_____. Survey of Nonpublic Schools: New York State, 1968-69. Albany, New York: Information Center on Education, The Department, 1969.

_____. Urban Education. A statement of policy and proposed action by the New York State Board of Regents. (A position paper; No. 1 of a series). Albany, New York: The Department, November, 1967.

New York State Senate. Resolution 178, 1965a.

_____. Resolution 215, 1965b.

The New York Times. "Excerpts from report by the Commission on the Causes and Prevention of Violence," November 24, 1969.

_____. "Panel sees crime turning the cities into armed camps;" by J. Herbers, November 24, 1969.

_____. "South moves slowly;" by C. Sitton, January 16, 1964.

Office of Economic Opportunity. Upward Bound Guidelines. Washington: U. S. Government Printing Office, 1965.

O'Reilly, R. P. "Conceptulizing Questionnaire Research on Anxiety in the School Culture: a Theoretical and Methodological Viewpoint." Unpublished master's thesis, Cornell University, 1966.

_____. "The Relationship of Anxiety, Creativity, Intelligence, and Prior Knowledge of Program Content to Children's Performance with Programmed Instructional Materials." Unpublished doctor's dissertation, Cornell University, 1969.

Pettigrew, T. F. A Profile of the Negro American. Princeton, New Jersey: Van Nostrand, 1964.

_____. "Race and Equal Educational Opportunity." Harvard Educational Review 38: 66-76 (1968).

_____. "Racially Separate or Together?" Integrated Education 7: 32-52 (1969).

Pettigrew, T. F., and Pajonas, P. J. Social-Psychological Considerations of Racially Balanced Schools. A paper presented at the New York State Education Department Conference on Racial Issues in Education at Greystone Conference Center, New York City, March 31-April 1, 1964. In New York State Education Department, State of Knowledge Conference. Albany, New York: Division of Intercultural Relations, The Department.

Phillips, B. N. An Analysis of Causes of Anxiety Among Children in School. Cooperative Research Project No. OE-5-10-012, Office of Education, U.S. Department of Health, Education, and Welfare. Washington: U.S. Government Printing Office, 1966.

Phillips, B. N., and McNeil, K. "Differences between Anglo and Non-Anglo Children on Factorial Dimensions of School Anxiety and Coping Style." A paper presented at a meeting of the American Educational Research Association at Chicago, Illinois, 1968.

Polansky, N., Lippitt, R., and Redl, F. "An Investigation of Behavioral Contagion in Groups," in W. E. Martin and C. B. Stendler, eds., Readings in Child Development. New York: Harcourt Brace, 1954. Pp. 493-513.

Poling, J. (Ed.). The Rockefeller Record. New York: Thomas Y. Crowell Company, 1960.

Proshansky, H. M. "The Development of Intergroup Attitudes," in L. W. Hoffman and M. L. Hoffman, eds., Review of Child Development Research, Volume II. New York: Russell Sage Foundation, 1966. Pp. 311-71.

Proshansky, H. M., and Newton, P. "The Nature and Meaning of Negro Self-identity," in M. Deutsch, I. Katz, and A. R. Jensen, eds., Social Class, Race, and Psychological Development. New York: Holt, Rinehart and Winston, 1968. Pp. 178-218.

Purl, M. C. "Social Acceptance and Academic Behavior of Desegregated Minority Children." Claremont Reading Conference Yearbook 32: 147-54 (1968).

Reiss, A. J., and Rhodes, A. L. "Are Educational Norms and Goals of Conforming, Truant and Delinquent Adolescents Influenced by Group Position in American Society?" The Journal of Negro Education. 28: 252-67 (1959)

Rentsch, G. J. Open Enrollment: an Appraisal. Rochester, New York: City School District, Rochester Public Schools, October, 1966.

Ricciuti, H. N. "Malnutrition, Learning and Intellectual Development: Research and Remediation." Paper presented at the Division of School Psychologists, American Psychological Association Annual Meeting, Washington, D.C., September 2, 1969.

Riessman, F. "Ebb and Flow in the School Integration Movement." Integrated Education 4: 8-18 (1966).

Rock, W. C., Goldberg, H. R., Knapp, T., and Lang, J. E. An Interim Report on a Fifteen Point Plan to Reduce Racial Isolation and Provide Quality Integrated Education. Rochester, New York: City School District, Rochester Public Schools, June 21, 1968.

Rock, W. C., Goldberg, H. R., Lang, J. E., and Heinrich, L. W. An Interim Report on a Cooperative Program Between a City School and a Suburban School District. Rochester, New York: City School District, Rochester Public Schools, July 25, 1967.

Rockefeller, N. A. Let Freedom Ring: a Centennial Memorandum for the 1960 Republican Party Platform. July 19, 1960.

Ruebush, B. E. "Anxiety," in H. W. Stevenson, J. Kagan and C. Spiker, eds., Child Psychology: the Sixty-second Yearbook of the National Society for the Study of Education. Chicago, Illinois: The University of Chicago Press, 1963.

Samuels, I. G. "Desegregated Education and Differences in Academic Achievement." Doctor's dissertation, Indiana University, 1958. Dissertation Abstracts 19: 1294 (1958).

_____. "Empirical Findings and Theoretical Problems in the Use of Anxiety Scales." Psychological Bulletin 57: 403-15 (1960).

_____ . Anxiety in Elementary School Children.
New York: John Wiley and Sons, 1960.

Sarason, S. B. , Hill, K. T. , and Zimbardo, P. G. "A Longitudinal Study of the Relation of Test Anxiety to Performance
on Intelligence and Achievement Tests." Monographs of the
Society for Research in Child Development 98: 29, Whole
No. 7 (1964).

Saye, A. B. , Pound, M. B. , and Allums, J. F. Principles of
American Government. Englewood Cliffs, New Jersey:
Prentice Hall, 1964.

Schmalzried, B. L. "The Relationship of Anxiety to the Educational and Vocational Aspirations of Lower-Class Adolescent
Males." Doctor's dissertation, The Florida State University,
1967.

Scrimshaw, N. S. "Infant Malnutrition and Adult Learning."
Saturday Review, 51: 64-66ff (1968).

Sheldon, W. D. , and Carillo, L. "Relation of Parents, Home,
and Certain Developmental Characteristics to Children's
Reading Ability." Elementary School Journal 52: 262-70
(1952).

Sherif, M. "Superordinate Goals in the Reduction of Intergroup
Tensions." American Journal of Sociology 53: 349-56 (1958).

Sibley, E. "Some Demographic Clues to Stratification."
American Sociological Record 7: 322-30 (1942).

Simpson, G. E. , and Yinger, J. M. Racial and Cultural
Minorities. Third edition. New York: Harper and Row, 1965.

Sizemore, B. A. "Separatism: a Reality Approach to Inclusion." in R. L. Green, ed. , Racial Crisis in American Education. Chicago, Illinois: Follett Educational Corporation,
1969. Pp. 249-79.

Smock, C. "The Relationship between Intolerance of Ambiguity,
Generalization and Speed of Perceptual Closure." Child Development 28: 27-36 (1957).

Speilberger, C. D. "The Effects of Manifest Anxiety on the Academic Achievement of College Students." Mental Hygiene 46: 420-26 (1962).

Sprey, J. "Sex Differences in Occupational Choice Patterns among Negro Adolescents." Social Problems 10: 11-12 (1962).

Stallings, F. H. "A Study of the Immediate Effects of Integration on Scholastic Achievement in the Louisville Public Schools." The Journal of Negro Education 28: 439-534 (1959).

Stevenson, H. W., and Odom, R. D. "The Relation of Anxiety to Children's Performance on Learning and Problem-Solving Tasks." Child Development 36: 1003-12 (1965).

Stevenson, H. W., and Stevenson, N. G. "Social Interaction in an Inter-racial nursery school." Genetic Psychology Monographs 61: 37-75 (1960).

Stoff, S. The Two-Way Street: Guideposts to Peaceful School Desegregation. Indianapolis, Indiana: David-Stewart Publishing Company, 1967.

Strodtbeck, F. L. "Family Interaction, Values and Achievement." In D. C. McClelland, et al., eds., Talent and Society. Princeton, New Jersey: D. Van Nostrand Company, Inc., 1958. Pp. 259-66.

_____. "The Hidden Curriculum in the Middle-Class Home." In J. D. Krumboltz, ed., Learning and the Educational Process. Chicago, Illinois: Rand McNally and Company, 1965. Pp. 91-112.

Sullivan, N. V. "The Berkeley Unified School District." Harvard Educational Review 38: 148-55 (1968).

_____. "Educational Leadership at the Crossroads," in R. L. Green ed., Racial Crisis in American Education. Chicago, Illinois: Follett Educational Corporation, 1969. Pp. 280-98.

Sullivan, N. V., and Stewart, E. S. Now is the Time: Integration in the Berkeley Schools. Bloomington, Indiana: Indiana University Press, 1969.

Teahan, J. E. "Future Time Perspective, Optimism, and Academic Achievement." Journal of Abnormal and Social Psychology 57: 379-80 (1958).

Tyler, L. E. The Psychology of Human Differences. New York: Appleton-Century-Crofts, 1965.

U.S. Bureau of the Census. Statistical Abstract of the United States. (88th edition) Washington: U.S. Government Printing Office, 1967.

U.S. Commission on Civil Rights. Hearing before the United States Commission on Civil Rights. Rochester, New York: September 16-17, 1966. Washington: U.S. Government Printing Office, 1966.

_____. Racial Isolation in the Public Schools, Part 1. Washington: U.S. Government Printing Office, 1967a.

_____. Racial Isolation in the Public Schools, Part 2. Washington: U.S. Government Printing Office, 1967b.

U.S. National Advisory Commission on Civil Disorders. Report of the National Advisory Commission on Civil Disorders. Washington: U.S. Government Printing Office, 1968.

Urban Crisis Monitor. "Conflict in the Nation's High Schools." Chicago, Illinois: Urban Research Corporation, May 16, 1969.

Vaughn, G. M. "Concept Formation and the Development of Ethnic Awareness." Journal of Genetic Psychology 103: 93-103 (1963).

Vogel, W., Raymond, S., and Lazarus, R. S. "Intrinsic Motivation and Psychological Stress." Journal of Abnormal and Social Psychology 58: 225-33 (1959).

Waite, W. H. "The Relationship between Performances on Examinations and Emotional Responses." The Journal of Experimental Education 11: 88-96 (1942).

Watson, C. G. "Cross-Validation of Certain Background Variables as Predictors of Academic Achievement." Journal of Educational Research 59: 147-48 (1965).

Webster, S. W., and Kroger, M. N. "A Comparative Study of Selected Perceptions and Feelings of Negro Adolescents with and without White Friends in Integrated Urban High Schools." The Journal of Negro Education 35: 55-61 (1966).

Weikart, D. P. "Preliminary Results from a Longitudinal Study of Disadvantaged Preschool Children." A paper presented at the 1967 convention of the Council for Exceptional Children, St. Louis, Missouri. Ypsilanti, Michigan: Ypsilanti Public Schools, 1967.

Weikart, D. P., Kamii, C. K., and Radin, N. L. Perry Preschool Project: Progress Report. Ypsilanti, Michigan: Ypsilanti Public Schools, June, 1964.

Weinberg, M. Research on School Desegregation: Review and Prospect. Chicago, Illinois: Integrated Education Associates, 1965.

Weltz, N., and Wilkinson, N. J. "The Relationship between Certain Non-Intellective Factors and Academic Success in College." Journal of Counseling Psychology 4: 54-60 (1957).

West, E. H. "Progress toward Equality of Opportunity in Elementary and Secondary Education." The Journal of Negro Education 37: 212-19 (1968).

Westinghouse Learning Corporation and Ohio University. The Impact of Head Start: an Evaluation of the Effects of Head Start Experience on Children's Cognitive and Affective Development. Preliminary draft. Bladensburg, Maryland: Westinghouse Corporation, April, 1969.

Westley, C. H. The History of Alpha Phi Alpha. Washington: Foundation Publisher, 1953.

Wey, H. W. "Desegregation - It Works." Phi Delta Kappan 45: 382-87 (1964).

Wilcox, P. "The Thrust toward Community Control of the School in Black Communities," in R. L. Green ed., Racial Crisis in American Education. Chicago, Illinois: Follett Educational Corporation, 1969. Pp. 299-318.

Wilkerson, D. A. "Programs and Practices in Compensatory Education for Disadvantaged Children." Review of Educational Research 35: 426-40 (1965).

Wilson, A. B. "Educational Consequences of Segregation in a California Community," in U.S. Commission on Civil Rights, Racial Isolation in the Public Schools, Part 2. Washington: U.S. Government Printing Office, 1967. Pp. 165-206.

Winkel, G. H., and Sarason, I. G. "Subject, Experimenter, and Situational Variables in Research on Anxiety." Journal of Abnormal and Social Psychology, 68: 601-8 (1964).

Wirt, R. D., and Broen, E. "The Relation of the Children's Manifest Anxiety Scale to the Concept of Anxiety as Used in the Clinic." Journal of Consulting Psychology 20: 482 (1956).

Wogaman, T. D. "Desegregation in Berkeley: Some Applicable Lessons." The Urban Review 3: 13-16 (1969).

Wolman, T. G. "Learning Effects of Integration in New Rochelle." Integrated Education 2: 30-31 (1964-65).

Wrightstone, J. W. "Demonstration Guidance Project in New York City." Harvard Educational Review 30: 237-51 (1960).

Wrightstone, J. W., et al. Evaluation of the Higher Horizons Program for Underprivileged Children. Cooperative Research Project No. 1124. New York City: Bureau of Educational Research, Board of Education of the City of New York, 1964.

Wrightstone, J. W., McClelland, S. D., and Forlano, G. Evaluation of the Community Zoning Program. New York City: Bureau of Educational Research, Board of Education of the City of New York, 1966.

Young, W. N., Jr. To Be Equal. New York: McGraw-Hill, 1966.

Zweibelson, I. "Test Anxiety and Intelligence Test Performance." Journal of Consulting Psychology 20: 479-81 (1956).

Legal References

Addabo v. Donovan, 43 Misc. 2d 621; 22 AD 2d 383; 16 NY 2d 619; cert. den. 382 U.S. 905.

Barksdale v. Springfield School Committee, (Massachusetts) 237 F. Supp. 543.

Bell v. School City of Gary, Indiana, 324 F. 2d 209.

Blocker v. Board of Education, 226 F. Supp. 208.

Branch v. Board of Education, 204 F. Supp. 150.

Brown v. Board of Education, 347 U.S. 483.

Di Sano v. Storandt, 43 Misc. 2d 272; revd. 22 AD 2d 6.

Etter v. Littwitz, 47 Misc. 2d 473.

Fuller v. Volk et al., (New Jersey) 230 F. Supp. 25.

Gaines, State of Missouri ex rel v. Canada, 305 U.S. 337.

Henry v. Godsell, 163 F. Supp. 87.

Hobson v. Hansen, 269 F. Supp. 401.

Jackson v. Pasadena City School District, 382 Pac. 2d 878, 59 Cal. 2d 876.

Johnson v. Board of Trustees of the University of Kentucky, et al. 83 F. Supp. 707.

Katalinic v. Syracuse Board of Education, 44 Misc. 2d 734.

MaLaurin v. Oklahoma State Regents for Higher Education et al. 339 U.S. 637.

Matter of Balahan v. Rubin, 40 Misc. 2d 249, revd. 20 AD 438, affd. 14 N.Y. 2d 193, cert. den. 379 U.S. 881.

Matter of Mitchell, 2 Ed. Dept. Rep. 501.

Matter of Vetere v. Allen, 41 Misc. 2d 200, revd. 21 AD 2d 561, affd. 15 N.Y. 2d 259, cert. den. 382 U.S. 825.

Morean v. Montclair Board of Education, (New Jersey) 42 N.J. 237.

Offerman v. Nitkowski, 248 F. Supp. 129, affd. 378 F. 2d 22.

Olsen v. Allen, 250 F. Supp. 1000, 367 F. 2d 22.

Plessey v. Ferguson, 163 U.S. 537.

Schnepp v. Donovan, 42 Misc. 2d 917.

Steinberg v. Donovan, 45 Misc. 2d 432.

Strippoli v. Bickal, 42 Misc. ad. 475, revd. 21 AD 2d 365, affd. 16 N.Y. 2d 652.

Sweatt v. Painter, 339 U.S. 629.

Taylor v. Board of Education, 191 F. Supp. 181, 195 F. Supp. 231, 288 F. 2d 600, affd. 294 F. 2d 36, cert. den. 368 U.S. 940.

United States v. School District 151 of Cook County, Illinois, 286 F. Supp. 786.

Van Blerkom v. Board of Education, 44 Misc. 2d 356, 22 AD 2d 71, 15 N.Y. 2d 399.

ADDITIONAL REFERENCES

Auld, U. "Lansing Busing Meets Road Block." Michigan Education Journal, 44: 12-17 (1966).

Ayers, W. "The Children's Community." Harvard Educational Review 38: 142-48 (1968).

Barritt, L. S., Semmel, M. I., and Weener, P. The Changes in Psycholinguistic Functions of Children After One Year in an "Integrated" School. ERIC ED 015 217. September, 1967.

Berkowitz, M. I. Studies of School Desegregation and Achievement: a Summary. Pittsburgh, Pennsylvania: Pittsburgh
Commission on Human Relations, May, 1967.

Bloom, B., Davis, A., and Hess, R. Compensatory Educa-
tion for Cultural Deprivation. Based on working papers con-
tributed by participants in the Research Conference on
Education and Cultural Deprivation, June 8-12, 1965.
Chicago, Illinois: Department of Education, University of
Chicago, July, 1964.

Board of Education of the City of New York. Evaluation of the
Community Zoning Program: Summary Report. New York:
Office of Educational Research. P. N. 22-362. September,
1966.

Boger, R., Hervey, S., and Hamachek, J. Heterogeneous vs.
Homogeneous Social Class Grouping of Preschool Children
in Head Start Classrooms. Michigan State University: Head
Start Evaluation and Research Center and the Lansing Public
Schools, 1967-68.

Brickner, C. A. An Experimental Program Designed to Increase Auditory Discrimination with Head Start Children.
Huntington, New York: Educational Developmental Laboratories.

"Bridgeport: Upgrading a School System." The Center Forum
3: 3 (1968).

Brophy, J. E. Mothers as Teachers of Their Own Preschool
Children: the Influence of Socio-economic Status and Task
Structure on Teaching Specificity. Austin, Texas: The
University of Texas at Austin, February, 1969.

Buskin, M. "City-to-Suburb Busing." School Management
11: 67-76 (1967).

_____. "City-to-Suburb Busing: What Next for
Great Neck?" School Management, 1969 (April), 58-65.

Calhoun, L. S. "New York: Schools and Power--Whose?"
Integrated Education 7: 11-35 (1969).

Cameron, H. "Nonintellectual Correlates of Academic Achievement." The Journal of Negro Education 37: 252-57 (1968).

Campbell, J. D. "Peer Relations in Childhood," in M. L. Hoffman and L. W. Hoffman, eds., Review of Child Development Research, Volume I. New York: Russell Sage Foundation, 1964. Pp. 289-322.

Carter, R. L. "The Law and Racial Equality in Education." The Journal of Negro Education 37: 204-11 (1968).

The Center for Urban Education. New York City and the Politics of School Desegregation. Edited from a study by D. Rogers with F. Kortheuer and R. Manzel. New York City: The Center, July, 1968.

The Center Forum. Entire issue on desegregation/integration, 1968, 3(4).

Clausen, J. A. "Family Structure, Socialization, and Personality," in L. W. Hoffman and M. L. Hoffman, eds., Review of Child Development Research, Volume II. New York: Russell Sage Foundation, 1966. Pp. 1-54.

Cleaver, E. "The white race and its heroes." Psychology Today 2: 33ff (1968).

Coles, R. The Desegregation of Southern Schools: a Psychiatric Study. New York, New York and Atlanta, Georgia: Anti-Defamation League of B'nai B'rith and Southern Regional Council, July, 1963.

"Confrontation in White Plains." Inside Education 55: 4-5ff (1969).

Cooke, P. P. "Equal Educational Opportunity: Some Findings and Conclusions." The Journal of Negro Education 37: 330-39 (1968).

Cullen, R. J. "The Relationship between Ethnic Prejudice and Student Teaching Behavior." Paper presented at the Annual Meeting of the American Educational Research Association, Los Angeles, California, February, 1969.

Day, N. A. "Organization for Social and Technical Innovation." Harvard Educational Review 38: 138-42 (1968).

"De Facto Segregation." NEA Research Bulletin 43: 35-37 (1965).

Delaney, L. T. "The Other Bodies in the River." Psychology Today 2: 26-31ff (1968).

Denmark, F. L., Guttentag, M., and Riley, R. Communication Patterns in Integrated Classrooms and Pre-Integration Subject Variables as They Affect the Academic Achievement and Self-Concept of Previously Segregated Children. ERIC ED 016 721. August, 1967.

Dentler, R. A. "Community Behavior and Northern School Desegregation." The Journal of Negro Education 34: 258-67 (1965).

Deutsch, C. P. "Environment and Perception." In M. Deutsch, I. Katz, and A. R. Jensen, eds., Social Class, Race, and Psychological Development. New York: Holt, Rinehart and Winston, Inc., 1968. Pp. 58-85.

Deutsch, M., et al. The Disadvantaged Child: Selected Papers of Martin Deutsch and Associates. New York: Basic Books, Inc., 1967.

Dreger, R. M., and Miller, K. S. "Comparative Psychological Studies of Negroes and Whites in the United States." Psychological Bulletin 57: 361-402 (1960).

Dunn, C. "The Characteristics and the Measured Language Arts Abilities of Deprived Youth in the School Desegregation Institute." Elementary English 46: 266-72 (1969).

Dworkin, R. J. "Segregation and Suburbia," in R. W. Mack, ed., Our Children's Burden: Studies of Desegregation in Nine American Communities. New York: Random House, 1968. Pp. 190-234.

Dyer, H. S. "School Factors and Equal Educational Opportunity." Harvard Educational Review 38: 38-56 (1968).

Edwards, T. B., and Wirt, F. M., eds., School Desegregation in the North: the Challenge and the Experience. San Francisco, California: Chandler Publishing Company, 1967.

Elsbery, J. W. "Educational Reform: Changing the Premise." The Urban Review 3: 4ff (1969).

Ervin-Tripp, S., and Miller, W. R. "Language Development," in H. W. Stevenson, J. Kagen and C. Spiker, eds., Child Psychology: the Sixty-second Yearbook of the National Society for the Study of Education. Chicago, Illinois: The National Society for the Study of Education, 1963. Pp. 108-43.

Fantini, M. D. "The Ford Foundation." Harvard Educational Review 38: 160-75 (1968).

Finch, R. H. "Establishing a Nationwide School Desegregation Program under Title VI of the Civil Rights Act of 1964." A report to the Congress from Robert H. Finch, Secretary of Health, Education, and Welfare, March 1, 1969. Integrated Education 7: 56-62 (1969).

Fischer, J. H. "Desegregating City Schools." Integrated Education 1966-67, 4 (6).

Fox, D. J. Expansion of the More Effective School Program: Evaluation of New York City Title I Educational Projects 1966-67. New York: The Center for Urban Education, September, 1967.

Friedenberg, E. Z. "Requiem for the Urban School." Saturday Review, 1967 (November 18), 77-79ff.

Goldblatt, H., and Tyson, C. Likes and Dislikes of Pupils in an Integrated School (P.S. 198M): Interim Report. Research Report No. 5. New York City: Commission on Intergroup Relations, New York City Commission on Human Rights, February, 1964.

Gordon, E. W. "Equalizing Educational Opportunity in the Public School." IRCD Bulletin, 1967, 3 (5).

Granville, T., Obinani, F., and Wilson, C. "Bedford-Stuyvesant: Departure from Conventional Procedure." The Center Forum 2: 7-9 (1968).

Greer, C. "Immigrants, Negroes, and the Public Schools." The Urban Review 3: 9-12 (1969).

Harootunian, B. "Achievement Motivation of Segregated Negroes, Desegregated Negroes, and Whites." Paper presented at the Annual Meeting of the American Educational
Research Association at Los Angeles, February 8, 1969.
Syracuse, New York: Syracuse University.

Hauser, P. M. Report to the Board of Education, City of
Chicago, by The Advisory Panel on Integration of the Public
Schools. Chicago: The Advisory Panel, March 31, 1964.

Hawkes, T. H., and Koff, R. H. "Social Class Differences
in Anxiety of Elementary School Children." Paper presented
at the Annual Meeting of the American Educational Research
Association, Los Angeles, California, February, 1969.

Helms, L. Preliminary Report on the Survey of Penfield
School District Residents' Reactions to the Penfield-Roches-
ter Transfer Program. Brockport, New York: Department
of Political Science, State University College at Brockport,
April 1, 1969.

Herson, P. S. "Changes in Achievement Motivation Among
Upward Bound Participants at the University of Maryland."
The Journal of Negro Education 37: 383-91 (1968).

Hickrod, G. A., and Sabulao, C. M. "Social and Economic
Inequality among Suburban School Districts: a Longitudinal
Study." A paper presented at the Annual Meeting of the
American Educational Research Association at Los Angeles,
California, February 8, 1969. Normal, Illinois: Department
of Educational Administration, Illinois State University, 1969.

Hicks, L. D. "To Bus--or Not to Bus." Massachusetts
Teacher 46: 11ff (1966).

Inger, M., and Stout, R. T. "School Desegregation: the
Need to Govern." The Urban Review 3: 35-38 (1968).

Jacoby, S. L. "Big City Schools IV--Washington: National
Monument to Failure." Saturday Review, 1967 (November 18),
71-73ff.

Johnson, T. A. A Report on the Status of Desegregation in
New York State. Albany, New York: Division of Intercultural
Relations, New York State Education Department, January 31,
1966.

Jones, R. L. School Morale in the Metropolis: Pupil Race, Teacher Race, Teacher Satisfaction, and Other Correlates. The Ohio State University.

Justman, J. "Children's Reaction to Open Enrollment." The Urban Review 3: 32-34 (1968).

Kapel, D. E. "Environmental Factors, Student Variables, Post-High-School Employment Adjustment, and Post-High-School Education of Male Negroes from the Project TALENT Sample." Paper read at the 1969 American Educational Research Association Meeting, Los Angeles, California, February, 1969.

Kaplan, J. New Rochelle, New York. Crisis in the Public Schools. Based on reports by D. W. Dodson. New York: Council for American Unity, 1965. Pp. 7-13.

Katz, I. "Desegregation or Integration in Public Schools?" The policy implications of research. Integrated Education 5: 15-28 (1968).

——————————. "Research on Public School Desegregation." Integrated Education 4: 14-25 (1966).

Katzenmeyer, W. G. "Social Interaction and Differences in Intelligence Test Performance of Negro and White Elementary School Pupils." Doctor's dissertation, Duke University, 1962. Dissertation Abstracts 24: 1905 (1963).

Kohl, H. "Teachers and Writers Collaborative." Harvard Educational Review 38: 155-60 (1968).

Koslin, S., et al. Effects of School Balance on Racial Attitudes. A report prepared by the Riverside Research Institute and Princeton University, 1969.

Kvaraceus, W. C., Scruggs, A. W., and Scruggs, C. E. "Self-Concept and Education of Negro Children: a Research Summary and Bibliography." Unpublished paper resulting from a Conference on the Relationship of the Self-Concept of Negro Youth to Education and Citizenship at Tufts University, September 16-19, 1963.

Lang, G. E., and Brodbeck, A. J. A Plan for Accelerating
Quality Integrated Education in the Buffalo Public School
System. A report prepared by the Center for Urban Education. Albany, New York: New York State Education Department, August 19, 1966.

Lansman, M. "The Relation of Self-Image to Negro Achieve-
ment and Attendance in a Racially Integrated Elementary
School." Doctor's dissertation, New York University, 1968.
Dissertation Abstracts, 29: 442-43 (1968).

Larson, R. G., and Olson, J. L. "Compensatory education:
how much is enough?" The Journal of Negro Education 37:
164-67 (1968).

Lesser, G. S., et al. "Some Effects of Segregation and Desegregation in the Schools." Integrated Education 2: 20-26
(1964).

Lesser, K., and Fox, R. E. "An Evaluation of a Head Start
Program in a Low Population Area." The Journal of Negro
Education 38: 46-54 (1969).

Levy, R. L. "This Business of Busing." Massachusetts
Teacher 46: 8-9 (1966).

Lewin, K. Dynamic Theory of Personality. New York: Mc-
Graw-Hill, 1935.

_____. Field Theory in Social Science. New York:
Harper, 1951.

Meyer, W. J., and Hall, V. Contingency Management In-
service Training Program. Syracuse, New York: College
of Education, Syracuse University.

New York City Department of Labor. An Economic Profile of
the Negro in New York City. New York City: Division of
Labor Research, June 24, 1963.

New York State Education Department. Forty-fifth Annual
Report of the Education Department: for the School Year
Ending June 30, 1948. Albany, New York: The Department,
1950.

_____. Forty-sixth Annual Report of the Education Department: for the School Year Ending June 30, 1949. Albany, New York: The Department, 1952.

_____. Proposal to Evaluate the Effects of Racial Imbalance Programs upon Student Development. A report prepared by the Riverside Research Institute, 632 West 125th Street, New York, New York. Albany, New York: Division of Evaluation, The Department, January 31, 1969.

_____. Reaching the Disadvantaged: Programs for Progress. Albany, New York: Office of Title I, ESEA, The Department, February, 1969.

_____. Study of Buffalo Schools: a Report on Educational Program, Facilities and Finance in the City School District, Buffalo, New York. Albany, New York: The Department, 1967.

_____. "Summary of State Education Department's Position with Respect to the Elimination of De Facto Segregation in the Schools." Unpublished report. Albany, New York: The Department, March 6, 1964.

The New York Times. Text of Civil Rights Commission statement on school desegregation. September 13, 1969.

O'Reilly, R. P. Empirical Studies of the Effects of Racial and Social Class Integration on Student's School Performance and Related Behaviors. Albany, New York: Bureau of School and Cultural Research, Division of Research, New York State Education Department, June 10, 1969. (Mimeo)

Pettigrew, T. F. "School integration in current perspective." The Urban Review 3: 4-7 (1969).

Poussant, A., and Atkinson, C. "Negro Youth and Psychological Motivation." The Journal of Negro Education 37: 241-51 (1968).

Powledge, F. "Segregation, Northern Style." American Education, 3: 1-5 (1966-67).

"Report of the Committee on Education of the Syracuse Area Council of the State Commission for Human Rights." Unpublished report. Syracuse, New York: The Committee, July 11, 1963.

Risley, T. "Learning and Lollipops." Psychology Today 1: 28-31ff (1968).

Rochester Public Schools. Increasing Intercultural Understanding through Pupil Transfer Plans: Profile of Title I Project. Rochester, New York: City School District, 1967.

Roy, L., and Heath, R. Interviews with Four Black Parents. Research and Development Memorandum No. 37. Stanford, California: Stanford Center for Research and Development in Teaching, School of Education, Stanford University, September, 1968.

Sacramento City Unified School District. Evaluation of the Effectiveness of Project Aspiration during 1967-68. Research Report No. 2. (Series 1968-69) Sacramento, California: Planning and Research Services, 1969.

St. John, N. H. "Minority Group Performance under Various Conditions of School, Ethnic and Economic Integration." IRCD Bulletin, 1968, 4 (3).

Shagaloff, J. "Progress Report on Northern Desegregation." Integrated Education 4: 44-46 (1966).

Sizer, T., and Whitten, P. "A Proposal for a Poor Children's Bill of Rights." Psychology Today 1968 (August), 59-63.

Spergel, H. "Boston's METCO Program Provides Answers-- and Questions--about the Value of Busing Kids to the Suburbs." American Education, April, 1967.

Stember, C. H. "Evaluating Effects of the Integrated Classroom." The Urban Review 2: 3-4ff (1968).

Swanson, B., and Montgomery, C. "White citizen response to the 'Open Enrollment Program.'" Integrated Education 2: 44-49 (1964).

Thompson, C. "Race and Equality of Educational Opportunity: Defining the Problem. " The Journal of Negro Education 37: 191-203 (1968).

Tyson, H. S. , and Tyson, C. Some Self-Perceptions and Teacher Evaluations of Puerto Rican, Negro and White Pupils in Fourth, Fifth, and Sixth Grades (P. S. 198M). Research Report No. 12. New York City: New York City Commission on Human Rights, 1962.

United States Commission on Civil Rights. Process of Change: the Story of School Desegregation in Syracuse, New York. Clearinghouse Publication No. 12. Washington: U. S. Government Printing Office, June, 1968.

Williams, R. M. , Jr. "Factors Affecting Reactions to Public School Desegregation in American Communities. " Paper prepared for the New York State Education Department Conference on Racial Issues in Education at Greystone Conference Center, New York City, March 31-April 1, 1964. In New York State Education Department, State of Knowledge Conference. Albany, New York: Division of Intercultural Relations, The Department.

Willie, C. "New Perspectives in School-Community Relations. " The Journal of Negro Education 37: 220-26 (1968).

Willie, C. V. , and Baker, J. "A Study of School Integration. " Integrated Education, June-July 1965. Reprinted in M. Weinberg, ed. , Integrated Education: a Reader. Beverly Hills, California: The Glencoe Press, 1968. Pp. 281-83.

APPENDIX

Population Statistics: New York State
and Selected School Districts

TABLE 41

Total and Nonwhite Populations in New York State: 1940-67[1]

Year	Total	Nonwhite	% Nonwhite	% Increase in Nonwhite
1940	13,479,142	599,596	4.4	--
1950	14,830,192	958,097	6.5	59.8
1960	16,782,304	1,495,233	8.9	56.1
1967[a]	18,072,089	1,834,026	10.1	22.7

[1]Based on data from the New York State Commission for Human Rights (1967)

[a]Estimated

TABLE 42

Comparison of Minority Proportions in 42 Selected
School Districts with Minority Proportions in Counties
of Location and All Other Districts in Those Counties: 1968[1]
(Counties Arranged by Standard Statistical Metropolitan
Areas; Districts Ranked within Counties by Size)

Area	Total School Population	Percent Negro	Percent Puerto Rican	Percent[a] Minority
NEW YORK CITY SMSA				
New York City	1,118,676	31.9	23.3	55.2
Westchester County	169,093	12.6	1.8	14.4
Yonkers	30,794	12.0	4.3	16.3
Mount Vernon	12,332	51.4	1.4	52.8
New Rochelle	12,331	20.8	.7	21.5
White Plains	8,964	18.3	2.5	20.8
Ossining	5,473	15.4	1.6	17.0
Peekskill	3,340	29.0	4.6	33.6
Greenburgh	4,174	32.6	.5	33.1
Rest of County	91,685	4.3	1.0	5.3
Rockland County	53,056	5.0	1.9	6.9
Spring Valley	15,283	8.3	.7	9.0
Suffern	5,104	1.4	.4	1.8
Nyack	3,651	23.2	.3	23.5
Rest of County	29,018	1.6	3.0	4.6
Nassau County	333,166	5.4	.8	6.2
Freeport	7,429	28.5	2.2	30.7
Long Beach	6,279	9.8	2.7	12.5
Hempstead	5,828	71.4	1.8	73.2
Glen Cove	5,364	11.2	5.5	16.7
Westbury	5,040	39.8	1.4	41.2
Rockville Centre	4,373	5.7	1.6	7.3
Roosevelt	3,906	70.4	1.1	71.5
Malverne	2,905	47.4	.2	47.6
Rest of County	292,042	1.4	.6	2.0
Suffolk County	284,120	5.7	1.9	7.6
Amityville	4,531	40.9	.5	41.4
Bellport	4,377	18.2	2.3	20.5
Riverhead	4,240	29.7	.9	30.6
Middle Island	2,925	23.7	.9	24.5
Wyandanch	2,304	91.6	2.0	93.6
Southampton	1,860	23.8	0	23.8
Bridgehampton	378	55.6	0	55.6
Peconic	27	22.2	0	22.2
Rest of County	263,478	3.3	1.9	5.3
BUFFALO SMSA				
Erie County	214,045	12.9	.8	13.7
Buffalo	71,665	36.8	1.8	38.6
Lackawanna	5,865	16.2	2.6	18.8
Rest of County	136,515	.2	.2	.4
Niagara County	57,056	6.4	.3	6.7
Niagara Falls	18,426	16.2	.1	16.3
Rest of County	38,630	1.8	.4	2.1

390

Area	Total School Population	Percent Negro	Percent Puerto Rican	Percent[a] Minority
ROCHESTER SMSA				
Monroe County	139,398	10.3	1.2	11.5
Rochester	47,372	28.9	3.3	32.2
Rest of County	92,026	.8	.1	.9
SYRACUSE SMSA				
Onondaga County	101,804	6.5	.1	6.6
Syracuse	30,428	20.9	.2	21.1
Rest of County	71,376	.4	b	.4
ALBANY-SCHENECTADY-TROY SMSA				
Albany County	46,921	8.7	.2	8.8
Albany	12,010	30.7	.2	30.9
Rest of County	34,911	1.1	.1	1.2
Schenectady County	31,515	3.3	.2	3.5
Schenectady	12,928	7.3	.3	7.6
Rest of County	18,550	.4	.1	.5
Rensselaer County	28,231	4.0	.1	4.1
Troy	7,292	12.3	.1	12.4
Rest of County	20,939	1.1	.1	1.2
UTICA-ROME SMSA				
Oneida County	58,668	3.9	.4	4.3
Utica	14,581	11.8	1.1	12.9
Rest of County	44,087	1.3	.2	1.5
OUTSIDE SMSAs				
Orange County	49,487	8.8	1.8	10.6
Newburgh	12,720	23.0	2.9	25.9
Rest of County	36,797	3.9	1.4	5.3
Dutchess County	45,889	7.5	.7	8.2
Poughkeepsie	5,937	32.7	.2	32.9
Beacon	3,393	17.6	4.8	22.4
Rest of County	36,559	2.5	.4	2.9
Ulster County	30,880	4.4	1.7	6.1
Kingston	10,926	5.3	.6	5.9
Rest of County	19,954	4.0	2.3	6.3
Chemung County	23,858	4.0	b	4.0
Elmira	14,126	6.4	b	6.4
Rest of County	9,732	.5	b	.5
Ontario County	18,932	2.2	.7	2.9
Geneva	3,383	9.4	1.3	10.7
Rest of County	15,549	.6	.5	1.1

[1]Data from BEDS, NYSED, 1969.

[a]Negro and Puerto Rican combined.

[b]Less than 0.1 percent.

391

TABLE 43

Changes in Total Enrollment in 42 Selected School Districts: 1966-68[1]
(Districts Ranked by Percent Negro and Puerto Rican in 1968)

| District | Number | | | Percent Change |
	1966	1967	1968	1966 - 1968
Wyandanch	2,255	2,253	2,304	+ 2.2
Hempstead	5,306	5,497	5,828	+ 9.8
Roosevelt	3,676	3,846	3,906	+ 6.3
Bridgehampton	404	389	378	- 6.4
New York City	1,084,818	1,105,549	1,118,676	+ 3.1
Mount Vernon	12,059	12,964	12,332	+ 2.3
Malverne	2,999	2,911	2,905	- 3.1
Amityville	4,496	4,499	4,531	+ 0.8
Westbury	5,044	5,078	5,040	a
Buffalo	72,762	72,692	71,665	- 1.5
Peekskill	3,244	3,322	3,340	+ 3.0
Greenburgh	2,989	3,073	4,174	+39.6
Poughkeepsie	5,811	5,809	5,937	+ 2.2
Rochester	45,365	46,570	47,372	+ 4.4
Albany	12,991	12,674	12,010	- 7.6
Freeport	7,262	7,334	7,429	+ 2.3
Riverhead	3,898	4,211	4,240	+ 8.8
Newburgh	11,531	12,204	12,720	+10.3
Middle Island	2,854	2,868	2,925	+ 2.5
Southampton	1,784	1,710	1,860	+ 4.3
Nyack	3,584	3,589	3,651	+ 1.9
Beacon	3,173	3,227	3,393	+ 6.9
Peconic	24	30	27	+12.5
New Rochelle	12,273	12,581	12,331	+ 0.5
Syracuse	30,650	30,862	30,428	- 0.7
White Plains	8,831	8,867	8,964	+ 1.5
Bellport	3,849	4,023	4,377	+13.7
Lackawanna	5,644	5,742	5,865	+ 3.9
Ossining	5,183	5,525	5,473	+ 5.6
Glen Cove	5,025	5,234	5,364	+ 6.7
Niagara Falls	19,043	18,860	18,426	- 3.2
Yonkers	29,475	30,296	30,794	+ 4.5
Utica	15,120	14,869	14,581	- 3.6
Long Beach	6,089	6,195	6,279	+ 3.1
Troy	6,827	6,865	7,292	+ 6.8
Geneva	3,195	3,325	3,383	+ 5.9
Spring Valley	12,366	14,327	15,283	+23.6
Schenectady	12,409	12,624	12,928	+ 4.2
Rockville Centre	4,201	4,314	4,373	+ 4.1
Elmira	13,870	14,151	14,126	+ 1.8
Kingston	10,089	10,495	10,926	+ 8.3
Suffern	4,286	4,908	5,104	+19.1

[1]Data from BEDS, NYSED, 1969.

[a]Less than 0.1 percent.

TABLE 44

Changes in Numbers and Percents of "Other" Pupils in 42
Selected School Districts: 1966-68[1]
(Districts Ranked by Percent Negro and Puerto Rican in 1968)

District	Number			Percent of Total Enrollment			Percent Change
	1966	1967	1968	1966	1967	1968	1966-1968
Wyandanch	355	273	145	15.7	12.1	6.3	- 59.2
Hempstead	1,628	1,561	1,564	30.7	28.4	26.5	- 5.0
Roosevelt	1,709	1,494	1,108	46.5	38.8	28.4	- 35.2
Bridgehampton	200	192	168	49.5	49.4	44.4	- 16.0
New York City	540,591[a]	529,930[a]	501,321[a]	49.8	47.9	44.8	- 7.3
Mount Vernon	6,468	6,594	5,770	53.6	50.9	46.8	- 10.8
Malverne	1,641	1,537	1,515	54.7	52.8	52.2	- 7.7
Amityville	2,859	2,807	2,650	63.6	62.4	58.5	- 7.3
Westbury	3,272	3,182	2,944	64.9	62.7	58.4	- 10.0
Buffalo	45,922	45,430	43,538	63.1	62.5	60.8	- 5.2
Peekskill	2,295	2,328	2,216	70.7	70.1	66.3	- 3.4
Greenburgh	1,886	1,886	2,773	63.1	61.4	66.4	+ 47.0
Poughkeepsie	4,205	4,132	3,973	72.4	71.1	66.9	- 5.5
Rochester	32,350	32,370	32,016	71.3	69.5	67.6	- 1.0
Albany	9,300	8,959	8,272	71.6	70.7	68.9	- 11.1
Freeport	5,574	5,359	5,142	76.8	73.1	69.2	- 7.8
Riverhead	2,755	2,926	2,921	70.7	69.5	68.9	+ 6.0
Newburgh	8,836	9,229	9,348	76.6	75.6	73.5	+ 5.8
Middle Island	2,017	2,075	2,207	70.7	72.4	75.5	+ 9.4
Southampton	1,301	1,218	1,320	72.9	71.2	71.0	+ 1.5
Nyack	2,750	2,718	2,787	76.7	75.7	76.3	+ 1.3
Beacon	2,439	2,463	2,624	76.9	76.3	77.3	+ 7.6
Peconic	14	18	21	58.3	60.0	77.8	+ 50.0
New Rochelle	9,992	9,961	9,580	81.4	79.2	77.7	- 4.1
Syracuse	25,223	24,779	23,873	82.3	80.3	78.5	- 5.4
White Plains	7,322	7,289	7,063	82.9	82.2	78.8	- 3.5
Bellport	3,107	3,167	3,472	80.7	78.7	79.3	+ 11.7
Lackawanna	4,596	4,625	4,754	81.4	80.5	81.1	+ 3.4
Ossining	4,424	4,682	4,536	85.4	84.7	82.9	+ 2.5
Glen Cove	4,286	4,478	4,426	85.3	85.6	82.5	+ 3.3
Niagara Falls	16,027	15,760	15,312	84.2	83.6	83.1	- 4.5
Yonkers	25,192	25,617	25,599	85.5	84.6	83.1	+ 1.6
Utica	13,467	13,151	12,697	89.1	88.4	89.1	- 5.7
Long Beach	5,463	5,468	5,476	89.7	88.3	87.2	+ 0.2
Troy	6,014	6,035	6,369	88.1	87.9	87.3	+ 5.9
Geneva	2,835	2,968	3,010	88.7	89.3	89.0	+ 6.2
Spring Valley	11,442	13,072	13,886	92.5	91.2	90.9	+ 21.4
Schenectady	11,530	11,687	11,924	92.9	92.6	92.2	+ 3.4
Rockville Centre	3,976	4,012	4,035	94.6	93.0	92.3	+ 1.5
Elmira	13,082	13,244	13,213	94.3	93.6	93.5	+ 1.0
Kingston	9,542	9,880	10,248	94.6	94.1	93.8	+ 7.4
Suffern	4,093	4,713	5,008	95.5	96.0	98.1	+ 22.4

[1]Data from BEDS, NYSED, 1969.

[a]Includes all N.Y.C. public school pupils who are neither Puerto Rican
nor Negro.

TABLE 45

Changes in Numbers and Percents of Negro Pupils in
42 Selected School Districts: 1966-68[1]
(Districts Ranked by Percent Negro and Puerto Rican in 1968)

District	Number			Percent of total enrollment			Percent change
	1966	1967	1968	1966	1967	1968	1966-1968
Wyandanch	1,840	1,918	2,110	81.6	85.1	91.6	+ 14.7
Hempstead	3,575	3,833	4,159	67.4	69.7	71.4	+ 16.3
Roosevelt	1,920	2,278	2,751	52.2	59.2	70.4	+ 43.3
Bridgehampton	204	197	210	50.5	50.6	55.6	+ 2.9
New York City	317,613	332,192	356,392	29.3	30.0	31.9	+ 12.2
Mount Vernon	5,476	6,244	6,336	45.4	48.2	51.4	+ 15.7
Malverne	1,332	1,363	1,378	44.4	46.8	47.4	+ 3.5
Amityville	1,618	1,688	1,855	36.0	37.5	40.9	+ 14.6
Westbury	1,707	1,850	2,008	33.8	36.4	39.8	+ 17.6
Buffalo	25,314	25,641	26,356	34.8	35.3	36.8	+ 4.1
Peekskill	826	863	967	25.5	26.0	29.0	+ 17.1
Greenburgh	1,094	1,173	1,359	36.6	38.2	32.6	+ 24.2
Poughkeepsie	1,588	1,648	1,940	27.3	28.4	32.7	+ 22.2
Rochester	11,956	12,781	13,679	26.4	27.4	28.9	+ 14.4
Albany	3,691	3,684	3,685	28.4	29.1	30.7	- 0.2
Freeport	1,577	1,841	2,117	21.7	25.1	28.5	+ 34.2
Riverhead	1,105	1,245	1,260	28.3	29.6	29.7	+ 14.0
Newburgh	2,457	2,647	2,925	21.3	21.7	23.0	+ 19.0
Middle Island	836	722	693	29.3	25.2	23.7	- 17.1
Southampton	387	408	442	21.7	23.9	23.8	+ 14.2
Nyack	796	854	846	22.2	23.8	23.2	+ 6.3
Beacon	607	619	598	19.1	19.2	17.6	- 1.5
Peconic	10	12	6	41.7	40.0	22.2	- 40.0
New Rochelle	2,174	2,429	2,569	17.7	19.3	20.8	+ 18.2
Syracuse	5,399	5,946	6,365	17.6	19.3	20.9	+ 17.9
White Plains	1,509	1,499	1,637	17.1	16.9	18.3	+ 8.5
Bellport	661	761	796	17.2	18.9	18.2	+ 20.4
Lackawanna	917	963	951	16.2	16.8	16.2	+ 3.7
Ossining	733	809	845	14.1	14.6	15.4	+ 15.3
Glen Cove	485	502	600	9.7	9.6	11.2	+ 23.7
Niagara Falls	2,855	2,973	2,986	15.0	15.8	16.2	+ 4.6
Yonkers	3,297	3,486	3,698	11.2	11.5	12.0	+ 12.2
Utica	1,491	1,573	1,715	9.9	10.6	11.8	+ 15.0
Long Beach	445	543	617	7.3	8.8	9.8	+ 38.7
Troy	787	809	899	11.5	11.8	12.3	+ 14.2
Geneva	310	297	319	9.7	8.9	9.4	+ 2.9
Spring Valley	841	1,165	1,264	6.8	8.1	8.3	+ 50.3
Schenectady	840	896	950	6.8	7.1	7.3	+ 13.1
Rockville Centre	197	242	250	4.7	5.6	5.7	+ 26.9
Elmira	772	891	902	5.6	6.3	6.4	+ 16.8
Kingston	505	559	583	5.0	5.3	5.3	+ 15.4
Suffern	113	136	73	2.6	2.8	1.4	- 35.4

[1] Data from BEDS, NYSED, 1969.

TABLE 46

Changes in Numbers and Percents of Puerto Rican Pupils
in 42 Selected School Districts: 1966-68[1]
(Districts Ranked by Percent Negro and Puerto Rican in 1968)

District	Number			Percent of Total Enrollment			Percent Change
	1966	1967	1968	1966	1967	1968	1966-1968
Wyandanch	48	52	46	2.1	2.3	2.0	− 4.2
Hempstead	65	76	102	1.1	1.4	1.8	+ 56.9
Roosevelt	42	30	43	1.1	.8	1.1	+ 2.4
Bridgehampton	0	0	0	0	0	0	b
New York City	226,614	243,427	260,963	20.9	20.9	23.3	+ 15.2
Mount Vernon	71	71	173	.6	.5	1.4	+ 143.7
Malverne	7	4	6	.2	.1	.2	− 14.3
Amityville	19	2	22	.4	a	.5	+ 15.8
Westbury	26	25	73	.5	.5	1.4	+ 180.8
Buffalo	1,055	1,136	1,276	1.4	1.6	1.8	+ 20.9
Peekskill	118	129	153	3.6	3.9	4.6	+ 29.7
Greenburgh	2	1	21	a	a	.5	+ 950.0
Poughkeepsie	3	4	11	a	a	.2	+ 266.7
Rochester	938	1,280	1,553	2.1	2.7	3.3	+ 65.6
Albany	0	10	30	0	a	.2	c
Freeport	89	68	163	1.2	.9	2.2	+ 83.1
Riverhead	17	17	37	.4	.4	.9	+ 117.6
Newburgh	238	301	374	2.1	2.5	2.9	+ 57.1
Middle Island	1	37	25	a	1.3	.9	+ 2400.0
Southampton	1	0	0	a	0	0	− 100.0
Nyack	13	3	12	.4	a	.3	− 7.7
Beacon	121	137	162	3.8	4.2	4.8	+ 33.9
Peconic	0	0	0	0	0	0	b
New Rochelle	24	48	85	.2	.4	.7	+ 254.2
Syracuse	4	41	62	a	.1	.2	+ 1450.0
White Plains	0	62	224	0	.7	2.5	d
Bellport	71	89	101	1.8	2.2	2.3	+ 42.3
Lackawanna	93	123	155	1.6	2.1	2.6	+ 66.7
Ossining	7	24	85	.1	.4	1.6	+ 1114.3
Glen Cove	187	206	295	3.7	3.9	5.5	+ 57.8
Niagara Falls	28	11	24	.1	a	.1	− 14.3
Yonkers	745	935	1,323	2.5	3.1	4.3	+ 77.6
Utica	152	133	155	1.0	.9	1.1	+ 2.0
Long Beach	154	161	171	2.5	2.6	2.7	+ 11.0
Troy	10	5	9	.1	a	.1	− 10.0
Geneva	39	50	45	1.2	1.5	1.3	+ 15.4
Spring Valley	47	43	101	.4	.3	.7	+ 114.9
Schenectady	30	26	44	.2	.2	.3	+ 46.7
Rockville Centre	7	34	69	.2	.8	1.6	+ 885.7
Elmira	6	3	5	a	a	a	− 16.7
Kingston	23	32	62	.2	.3	.6	+ 169.6
Suffern	23	12	21	.5	.2	.4	− 8.7

[1]Data from BEDS, NYSED, 1969.

aLess than 0.1 percent.

bNo Puerto Rican pupils in district.

cChange from 0 to 30 pupils.

dChange from 0 to 224 pupils.

TABLE 47

Distribution of Minority Pupils in 42 Selected School Districts in Schools with Varying Percent of "Other": 1968 and 1967[1]

Number of Negro and Puerto Rican Pupils in Schools Categorized by Percent "Other"

District	Year	% Negro & P.R.	I 0-10.9	II 11.0-20.9	III 21.0-30.9	IV 31.0-40.9	V 41.0-50.9	I-V 0-50.9	VI 51.0-60.9	VII 61.0-70.9	VIII 71.0-80.9	IX 81.0-90.9	X 91.0-100	I-X 0-100
Wyandanch	1968	93.6	2,156					2,156						2,156
	1967	87.4	709	1,261				1,970						1,970
Hempstead	1968	73.2	2,619			1,046	278	3,943		318				4,261
	1967	71.1	2,481			933	275	3,689		283				3,972
Roosevelt	1968	71.5		1,227	585	967		2,779				15		2,794
	1967	60.0		70	873	590	761	2,294				14		2,308
Bridge-hampton	1968	55.6					210	210						210
	1967	50.6					197	197						197
New York City	1968	55.2	337,902	68,176	37,135	46,353	33,579	523,145	18,391	26,180	27,283	18,986	3,370	617,355
	1967	52.0	270,313	79,985	42,660	39,988	28,331	461,277	29,829	28,861	23,979	25,779	5,894	575,619
Mount Vernon	1968	52.8	1,751	1,560	398	209		3,918	803	1,218	500	70		6,509
	1967	48.7	1,256	1,973	333	164		3,726	624	1,412	243	310		6,315
Malverne	1968	47.6				730		730	257	397				1,384
	1967	46.9				222	232	454	651	262				1,367
Amity-ville	1968	41.4					371	371	1,203	303				1,877
	1967	37.5					0	0	938	503	249			1,690
Westbury	1968	41.2					774	774	584	415	308			2,081
	1967	36.9					326	326	927	357	265			1,875
Buffalo	1968	38.6	16,614	660	550	1,075	912	19,811	1,565	1,811	1,335	2,565	545	27,632
	1967	36.9	16,832	328	1,175		1,485	19,820	1,116	1,925	926	2,161	829	26,777
Peekskill	1968	33.6				74	294	368	146	193	413			1,120
	1967	29.9					169	169	250	140	387	46		992
Greenburgh	1968	33.1			81			81		1,028	228	43		1,380
	1967	38.2				77		77	439	658				1,174
Pough-keepsie	1968	32.9			467	595		1,062	175	184	305	214	11	1,951
	1967	28.4			436	204		640	167	385	251	201	8	1,652
Rochester	1968	32.2	4,005	937	2,556		503	8,001	2,232	663	2,215	1,557	564	15,232
	1967	30.1	3,581	1,598	1,515	1,061		7,755	1,437	925	1,276	1,892	776	14,061

Number of Negro and Puerto Rican Pupils in Schools Categorized by Percent "Other"

District	Year	% Negro & P.R.	I 0-10.9	II 11.0-20.9	III 21.0-30.9	IV 31.0-40.9	V 41.0-50.9	I-V 0-50.9	VI 51.0-60.9	VII 61.0-70.9	VIII 71.0-80.9	IX 81.0-90.9	X 91.0-100	I-X 0-100
Albany	1968	30.9	80	1,482				1,562	1,004	420	405	234	90	3,715
	1967	29.1	95	1,482			393	1,970	687	124	559	279	75	3,694
Freeport	1968	30.7						0	1,160		1,120			2,280
	1967	26.0						0	512	276	775	346		1,909
Riverhead	1968	30.6						0		1,044	248		5	1,297
	1967	30.0						0		907	340	15		1,262
Newburgh	1968	25.9	1,013		509	311		1,833		430	199	711	126	3,299
	1967	24.2	878			740		1,618		280	299	667	84	2,948
Middle Island	1968	24.5						0		149	569			718
	1967	26.5						0		178	513	68		759
Southampton	1968	23.8						0		356		86		442
	1967	23.9						0		342		66		408
Nyack	1968	23.5						0			858			858
	1967	23.8					274	274	215		356		12	857
Beacon	1968	22.4						0		237	323	169	31	760
	1967	23.4						0	243		334	149	30	756
Peconic	1968	22.2						0			6			6
	1967	40.0						0	12					12
New Rochelle	1968	21.5					260	260	186	676	304	1,177	51	2,654
	1967	19.7				264		264	505	226	100	1,328	54	2,477
Syracuse	1968	21.1			1,203	498	359	2,060	680	429	1,429	1,273	556	6,427
	1967	19.4			951	1,226		2,177	390	459	1,079	1,208	674	5,987
White Plains	1968	20.8						0		590	406	865		1,861
	1967	17.6						0			689	872		1,561
Bellport	1968	20.5						0			442	455		897
	1967	21.1						0		205	322	323		850
Lackawanna	1968	18.8		200	449	218		867			53	136	50	1,106
	1967	18.9		220	440	209		869			56	133	28	1,086

(Continued)

397

Table 47 (Continued)

Number of Negro and Puerto Rican Pupils in Schools Categorized by Percent "Other"

District	Year	% Negro & P.R.	I 0-10.9	II 11.0-20.9	III 21.0-30.9	IV 31.0-40.9	V 41.0-50.9	I-V 0-50.9	VI 51.0-60.9	VII 61.0-70.9	VIII 71.0-80.9	IX 81.0-90.9	X 91.0-100	I-X 0-100
Ossining	1968	17.0						0	235	223	72	369	31	930
	1967	15.0					35	35		420		369	9	833
Glen Cove	1968	16.7			115			115			102	678		895
	1967	13.5			96			96			182	307	123	708
Niagara Falls	1968	16.3		324				324		99	1,245	1,163	179	3,010
	1967	15.8	431		139			570		424	722	1,071	197	2,984
Yonkers	1968	16.3			976	390		1,366	1,298	212	1,368	333	444	5,021
	1967	14.6			878	341		1,219	889	467	806	690	350	4,421
Utica	1968	12.9	221					221	258	231	406	419	335	1,870
	1967	11.5		201				201	256	193	357	157	542	1,706
Long Beach	1968	12.5						0	346			329	113	788
	1967	11.4						0		292		174	238	704
Troy	1968	12.4						0	241	112	89	402	64	908
	1967	11.8				41	236	277			153	97	287	814
Geneva	1968	10.7						0				311	53	364
	1967	10.4				138		138					209	347
Spring Valley	1968	9.0						0			256	735	374	1,365
	1967	8.4						0				796	412	1,208
Schnectady	1968	7.6						0	141		180	337	336	994
	1967	7.3						0	171	99	57	103	492	922
Rockville Centre	1968	7.3						0		77		76	166	319
	1967	6.4						0		71			205	276
Elmira	1968	6.4						0		189	59	348	311	907
	1967	6.3				206		206	256			133	299	894
Kingston	1968	5.9						0			213	49	383	645
	1967	5.6						0		162	46	158	225	591
Suffern	1968	1.8						0					94	94
	1967	3.0					88	88					60	148
TOTAL	1968		366,361	74,566	45,024	51,736	38,270	575,957	30,905	38,184	42,939	34,105	8,282	730,372
	1967		296,576	87,118	49,4 %	46,404	32,802	512,396	40,514	40,836	35,321	39,898	12,126	681,091

[1]Data from BEDS, NYSED, 1969

398

TABLE 48

Percent Distribution of Minority Pupils in 42 Selected School Districts in Schools with Varying Percent of "Other": 1968 and 1967[1]

District	Year	% Negro & P.R.	Percent of Negro and Puerto Rican Pupils in Schools Categorized by Percent "Other"										
			I 0-10.9	II 11.0-20.9	III 21.0-30.9	IV 31.0-40.9	V 41.0-50.9	I-V 0-50.9	VI 51.0-60.9	VII 61.0-70.9	VIII 71.0-80.9	IX 81.0-90.9	X 91.0-100
Wyandanch	1968	93.6	100.0					100.0					
	1967	87.4	36.0	64.0				100.0					
Hempstead	1968	73.2	61.5			24.5	6.5	92.5		7.5			
	1967	71.1	62.5			23.5	6.9	92.9		7.1			
Roosevelt	1968	71.5		43.9	20.9	34.6		99.5				.5	
	1967	60.0		3.0	37.8	25.6	33.0	99.4					.6
Bridgehampton	1968	55.6					100.0	100.0					
	1967	50.6					100.0	100.0					
New York City	1968	55.2	54.7	11.0	6.0	7.5	5.4	84.7	3.0	4.2	4.4	3.1	0.5
	1967	52.0	47.0	13.9	7.4	6.9	4.9	80.1	5.2	5.0	4.2	4.5	1.0
Mount Vernon	1968	52.8	26.9	24.0	6.1	3.2		60.2	12.3	18.7	7.7	1.1	
	1967	48.7	19.9	31.2	5.3	2.6		59.0	9.9	22.4	3.8	4.9	
Malverne	1968	47.6					52.7	52.7	18.6	28.7			
	1967	46.9				16.2	17.0	33.2	47.6	19.2			
Amityville	1968	41.4					19.8	19.8	64.1	16.1			
	1967	37.5							55.5	29.8	14.7		
Westbury	1968	41.2					37.2	37.2	28.1	19.9	14.8		
	1967	36.9					17.4	17.4	49.4	19.0	14.1		
Buffalo	1968	38.6	60.1	2.4	2.0	3.9	3.3	71.7	5.7	6.6	4.8	9.3	2.0
	1967	36.9	62.9	1.2	4.4		5.5	74.0	4.2	7.2	3.5	8.1	3.1
Peekskill	1968	33.6				6.6	26.3	32.9	13.0	17.2	36.9		
	1967	29.9					17.0	17.0	25.2	14.1	39.0	4.6	
Greenburgh	1968	33.1			5.9			5.9		74.5	16.5	3.1	
	1967	38.2				6.6		6.6	37.4	56.0			
Poughkeepsie	1968	32.9			23.9	30.5		54.4	9.0	9.4	15.6	11.0	.6
	1967	28.4			26.4	12.3		38.7	10.1	23.3	15.2	12.2	.5
Rochester	1968	32.2	26.3	6.2	16.8		3.3	52.5	14.7	4.4	14.5	10.2	3.7
	1967	30.1	25.5	11.4	10.8	7.5		55.2	10.2	6.6	9.1	13.5	5.5

(Continued)

Table 48 (Continued)

Percent of Negro and Puerto Rican Pupils in Schools Categorized by Percent "Other"

District		% Negro & P.R.	I 0-10.9	II 11.0-20.9	III 21.0-30.9	IV 31.0-40.9	V 41.0-50.9	I-V 0-50.9	VI 51.0-60.9	VII 61.0-70.9	VIII 71.0-80.9	IX 81.0-90.9	X 91.0-100
Albany	1968	30.9	2.2	39.9				42.1	27.0	11.3	10.9	6.3	2.4
	1967	29.1	2.6	40.1			10.6	53.3	18.6	3.4	15.1	7.6	2.0
Freeport	1968	30.7							50.9		49.1		
	1967	26.0							26.8	14.5	40.6	18.1	.4
Riverhead	1968	30.6								80.4	19.1		
	1967	30.0								71.9	26.9	1.2	
Newburgh	1968	25.9	30.7		15.4	9.4		55.5		13.0	6.0	21.6	3.8
	1967	24.2	29.9			25.1		55.0		9.5	10.1	22.6	2.8
Middle Island	1968	24.5								20.8	79.2		
	1967	26.5								23.5	67.6	9.0	
Southampton	1968	23.8								80.5		19.5	
	1967	23.9								83.8		16.2	
Nyack	1968	23.5									100.0		1.4
	1967	23.8					32.0	32.0	25.1		41.5		
Beacon	1968	22.4								31.2	42.5	22.2	4.1
	1967	23.4							32.1		44.2	19.7	4.0
Peconic	1968	22.2									100.0		
	1967	40.0							100.0				
New Rochelle	1968	21.5					9.8	9.8	7.0	25.5	11.5	44.3	1.9
	1967	19.7				10.7		10.7	20.4	9.1	4.0	53.6	2.2
Syracuse	1968	21.1			18.7	7.7		32.0	10.6	6.7	22.2	19.8	8.7
	1967	19.4			15.9	20.5	5.6	36.4	6.5	7.7	18.0	20.2	11.3
White Plains	1968	20.8								31.7	21.8	46.5	
	1967	17.6									44.1	55.9	
Bellport	1968	20.5									49.3	50.7	
	1967	21.1									37.9	38.0	
Lackawanna	1968	18.8		18.1	40.6	19.7		79.4		24.1	4.8	12.3	4.5
	1967	18.9		20.3	40.5	19.3		80.1			5.2	12.2	2.6
Ossining	1968	17.0			12.8		4.2	4.2		24.0	7.7	39.7	3.3
	1967	15.0			13.6			12.8	25.3	50.4		44.3	1.1
Glen Cove	1968	16.7						13.6			11.4	75.8	17.4
	1967	13.5						10.8			25.7	43.4	
Niagara Falls	1968	16.3	14.4	10.8	4.7					3.3	41.4	38.6	5.9
	1967	15.8						19.1		14.2	24.2	35.9	6.6

400

Percent of Negro and Puerto Rican Pupils in Schools Categorized by Percent "Other"[1]

District		% Negro & P.R.	I 0-10.9	II 11.0-20.9	III 21.0-30.9	IV 31.0-40.9	V 41.0-50.9	I-V 0-50.9	VI 51.0-60.9	VII 61.0-70.9	VIII 71.0-80.9	IX 81.0-90.9	X 91.0-100
Yonkers	1968	16.3			19.4	7.8		27.2	25.9	4.2	27.2	6.6	8.8
	1967	14.6			19.9	7.7		27.6	20.1	10.6	18.2	15.6	7.9
Utica	1968	12.9	11.8					11.8	13.8	12.4	21.7	22.4	17.9
	1967	11.5		11.8				11.8	15.0	11.3	20.9	9.2	31.8
Long Beach	1968	12.5							43.9			41.8	14.3
	1967	11.4								41.5		24.7	33.8
Troy	1968	12.4							26.5	12.3	9.8	44.3	7.0
	1967	11.8				5.0	29.0	34.0			18.8	11.9	35.3
Geneva	1968	10.7										85.4	14.6
	1967	10.4				39.8		39.8					60.2
Spring Valley	1968	9.0									18.8	53.8	27.4
	1967	8.4										65.9	34.1
Schenectady	1968	7.6							14.2		18.1	33.9	33.8
	1967	7.3							18.5	10.7	6.2	11.2	53.4
Rockville	1968	7.3								24.1		23.8	52.0
Centre	1967	6.4								25.7			74.3
Elmira	1968	6.4							28.6			38.4	34.3
	1967	6.3				23.0		23.0		20.8		19.9	33.4
Kingston	1968	5.9									33.0	7.6	59.4
	1967	5.6								27.4	7.8	26.7	38.1
Suffern	1968	1.8											100.0
	1967	3.0					59.5	59.5					40.5

[1]Data from BEDS, NYSED, 1969.

ABOUT THE CONTRIBUTORS

ROBERT P. O'REILLY is Chief, Bureau of School and
Cultural Research, New York State Education Department.
He has had extensive experience as an educational researcher,
most recently with the problems represented by segregated
education in New York State and the Nation. He has given
testimony as an expert witness in Keyes et al. v. the Denver
Public Schools, which resulted in a Federal ruling that the
Denver Public Schools must desegregate.

Dr. O'Reilly's experience includes teaching in a black
school and in the Sierra Leone Peace Corps training program
and membership in the Distinguished Visitors Program at the
University of Massachusetts. His work has been published
widely in educational journals, and a number of his reports
on school integration have been published in connection with
state and national conferences.

Dr. O'Reilly received his Ph. D. and master's degree in
educational psychology from Cornell University.

HOWARD D. BERKUN is Associate in Education Research,
Bureau of School and Cultural Research, New York State Education Department, and co-ordinator of Experimental Programs
for the Department. Mr. Berkun has taught in the Albany
public schools and at the State University of New York at
Albany. He has also helped organize and has headed several
community action groups in the Albany area.

Mr. Berkun received his undergraduate degree in social
studies from the State University of New York at Albany. He
has continued his study there as an NDEA Fellow and has completed his course work toward a doctoral degree in curriculum
and instruction.

KATHERINE S. BLUEGRASS is Education Aide, Bureau of School and Cultural Research, New York State Education Department. Miss Bluegrass spent two summers as the primary research assistant to Sherwood Fox, Chairman of the Department of Sociology and Anthropology at Union College, conducting a research study on the employment patterns, experiences, and aspirations of the Negro population in the local community. Before joining the Department in the fall of 1968, she worked at the Mental Health Research Unit of Columbia Presbyterian Hospital in New York City.

Miss Bluegrass attended Mount Holyoke College and Union College, from which she received her bachelor of arts degree in sociology.

ESTHER SMITH PATTI is Assistant in Education Research, Bureau of School and Cultural Research, New York State Education Department. She has twenty-eight years of experience in all phases of educational research in the New York State Education Department. She has recently completed a study of the education of disadvantaged children and a history of the New York State Education Department.

Mrs. Patti received her bachelor of arts degree from the New York State College for Teachers at Albany where she majored in mathematics and social studies. She is also a graduate of the State College for Teachers at Oneonta in the area of elementary education, and has done graduate work at the Graduate School of Public Administration at Albany.

RUTH SALTER is Associate in Education Research, Bureau of School and Cultural Research, New York State Education Department. Miss Salter has been on the staff of the Department for twelve years, having had previous experience in the fields of personnel and social work. She has published research articles dealing with innovative programs and has written several New York State Education Department publications.

Miss Salter was graduated cum laude from Mount Holyoke College and is a member of Phi Beta Kappa. She received her master's degree in vocational guidance from Teachers College of Columbia University and has done additional postgraduate study at Yale University, Trinity College, the State University of New York at Albany, and St. Rose College. She holds permanent teaching certificates for nursery, kindergarten, and elementary and secondary English.

WILLIAM A. SHAPIRO was Assistant Attorney on the staff of the New York State Education Department at the time this study was made.

He received his bachelor's degree from Harvard University and his LL.B. from Harvard Law School.